Professional Hibernate

Professional Hibernate

Eric Pugh
Joseph D. Gradecki

WILEY

Professional Hibernate

Published by
Wiley Publishing, Inc.
10475 Crosspoint Boulevard
Indianapolis, IN 46256
www.wiley.com

ISBN: 0-7645-7677-1

Manufactured in the United States of America

10 9 8 7 6 5 4 3 2

Credits

Authors
Eric Pugh
Joseph D. Gradecki

Executive Editor
Robert Elliott

Production Editor
Felicia Robinson

Book Producer
Ryan Publishing Group, Inc.

Copy Editors
Linda Recktenwald
Tiffany Taylor

Compositor
Gina Rexrode

Vice President & Executive Group Publisher
Richard Swadley

Vice President and Publisher
Joseph B. Wikert

Executive Editorial Director
Mary Bednarek

About the Authors

Eric Pugh is a member of the Maven development team and an experienced Java enterprise developer specializing in database application design and development, and open source tool integration. He has contributed Hibernate-related code to many projects, including XDoclet and OSWorkflow, and is currently leading development of the Hibernate plugin for Maven. Eric has built several Hibernate applications for clients (including a Web-based lab automation application) and regularly uses Hibernate with Eclipse and Maven. In addition to writing documentation and specifications, Eric has written for OnJava.

Joseph D. Gradecki is a software engineer at Comprehensive Software Solutions, where he works on their SABIL product, an enterprise-level securities processing system. He has built numerous dynamic, enterprise application using Java, Hibernate, MySQL, XML, AspectJ, servlets, JSPs, Resin, BroadVision, and other technologies. He is the author of *Mastering JXTA* and the co-author of *MySQL and Java Developers Guide* and *Professional Java Tools for Extreme Programming*. Joe holds Bachelors and Masters degrees in Computer Science and is currently pursuing a Ph.D.

Introduction

Application development is hard work. Handling requirements, building a design, and coding the application usually take the majority of a team's time. In the meantime, they need to be concerned with the data that will be used throughout the application. In many cases, the data is stored in a relational database. Over the years, we've advanced our development techniques to include OOP and aspects, yet the database side of the equation has remained fairly static.

Developers have often used brute-force techniques to store and retrieve data from a database and populate their objects. Usually this means building a proprietary persistence layer to act as the conduit between the application and the database. If the objects change or the database is altered, the persistence layer must be changed as well.

Thankfully, there are now more elegant and effective options for the Java developer. Hibernate is an object/relational mapping (ORM) tool that also provides data querying and retrieval functions in a Java environment. Whether you're using simple objects or collections, Hibernate reduces your development time by handling most of the common data persistence tasks. It's designed for performance with a comprehensive caching layer as well as its own query language to take advantage of its persisted objects. Hibernate is a SourceForge.net project and a mature technology with widespread support within the Java community.

Who Should Read This Book?

This book is written for professional Java developers who already understand how to build sophisticated applications. We assume thorough knowledge of Java, general familiarity with databases, and familiarity with Java application and Web development. The book assumes no previous experience with Hibernate.

Professional application development requires more than mastering a single tool such as Hibernate. You will need to integrate Hibernate into your development process, using it with other tools and technologies. We have written this book to help you accomplish just that: by not only explaining how Hibernate works, but also demonstrating how to use Hibernate with a suite of tools and technologies, we hope to set you on the fast track to using Hibernate for professional application development.

Versions Used in This Book

Hibernate is designed to be used with an assortment of development tools, databases, and technologies; it's intended to be dropped into an active application development process. For this reason, our book spends a considerable amount of time demonstrating how to use Hibernate with other popular tools you may be using (including Eclipse, Tomcat, Maven, Struts, and XDoclet). We use the following software versions in this book:

- ❑ **Hibernate:** 2.1.6
- ❑ **Java:** Java SDK 1.4.2_03 and SDK 1.5 Beta
- ❑ **Maven:** 1.0
- ❑ **MySQL:** 4.0.17
- ❑ **Tomcat:** 5.0.24
- ❑ **XDoclet:** 1.2.1
- ❑ **Microsoft SQL Server:** 2000

Where to Get the Code

This book takes a real-world, hands-on approach to Hibernate and includes many working code examples, as well as two more sophisticated sample applications. The book also contains example code for using Hibernate with XDoclet, Maven, AspectJ, and other tools and technologies. All the code examples, sample applications, and supporting files can be downloaded from www.wrox.com.

Organization of This Book

This book is split into three parts. Chapters 1–13 walks you through Hibernate's major components and how to use them. Chapters 14–19 discusses how to use Hibernate is your current development practices and toolsets. The Appendixes provide additional information that will help you get the most out of Hibernate.

Contents

Contents

Contents

Contents

Contents

Contents

Contents

Contents

Contents

Contents

Introduction to Mapping Objects to Relational Databases

In the computer industry, we commonly have discussions, disagreements, and even shouting matches over which of the latest languages are the best and where they should be used. Discussions turn to the best platform currently available and who's suing whom. However, each of us is also thinking about the latest project we've been given and its strict deadline. Overall, the project isn't complex, but we have to support numerous database backend systems. This means we need to incorporate a persistence layer to handle the database differences. That part isn't too difficult, but what about the data itself? Do we just store it in some proprietary database and deal with the details later? No, we need to have a strategy that works with our application and the language the application is written in.

Today's programming languages take advantage of the latest in object-oriented techniques. As you know, an *object* is a construct to enforce encapsulation. The problem is how to store an object for use by the same application at a later time or by another application. Some of the common solutions to this problem are:

❑ Serialization

❑ XML

❑ Object-oriented database systems mapping

Let's consider these possible solutions and determine their advantages and disadvantage before looking at the solution around which this book is written.

Serialization

You can save data stored in an object by creating a flat-file representation of the object. In the Java language, this process is called *serialization*. An object that is serialized has all its attributes and their class types saved into a file or a buffer. The resulting information string can be saved to a file, placed in a column in a traditional relational database, or sent to another machine. An example is the CD class:

```java
public class CD implements Serializable {
String title;
String artist;
public CD(String title, String artist) {
this.title = title;
this.artist = artist;
    }
}
```

The CD class has two attributes that need to be saved when the object is serialized. In Java, all primitive types as well as many of the foundational classes are defined such that they implement the Serializable interface. The system automatically recurses into each of the attributes as needed.

The serialization of the CD class results in a binary representation of the data currently contained in the represented object. The binary representation could be placed in a BLOB column type of a relational database; this process would allow other applications to access the data. However, if a legacy application has been tweaked to access the column where the object is held, it won't be able to make sense of the data unless the legacy application can deserialize Java objects. Even worse, the serialization process doesn't migrate well from Java application to Java application.

Further, the serialization process isn't fast, and a large object can take a considerable amount of time to be put into its binary representation. Thus, serialization as a practice has a specific place in the development process; but as a mechanism for persisting data, it should be avoided.

XML

In the past few years, XML has been one of the hottest technologies. With this popularity comes the issue of using XML in both objects and mapping to a database. First, consider an XML document like the following:

```xml
<cd>
    <title>
        Grace Under Pressure
    </title>

    <artist>
        Rush
    </artist>
</cd>
```

A database to handle the XML document can be created with the following schema:

```
create table cd (
   title varchar,
   artist varchar
);
```

From the XML, we can easily build a class like this:

```
public class cd {
   String title;
  String artist;
 }
```

Having the XML representation creates an additional level of complexity and processing required to go from an object to the database. This processing can be extensive, given the complexity of the objects in an application.

Object-Oriented Database Systems

When object-oriented programming first began to be used, the issue of storing objects for later use was an important topic. The most widely used component for storage is a database, so several companies started down the path of developing a new database technology used specifically to store objects. The object-oriented database system handles the storing and loading of objects in a transparent manner. The complexity in the system comes from querying the database. For example, we might have a query like this:

```
select x from user x where x.name = \"John Doe\"");
```

The database will access all the user objects in the database and return those whose name attribute is equal to "John Doe". The database needs to be designed in a manner that automatically allows the query to access the attributes of the stored objects.

Although these new database systems can transparently store and load objects to Java or other object-oriented languages, there is typically an issue when a legacy system or a quick RAD application needs to access the same information. In addition, the OO databases haven't made a large impact in the database market; they're still coming of age when compared to those offered by Oracle, Microsoft, and others.

Mapping

The three solutions we've just covered can work, but they present issue when put into the mix of legacy applications and traditional relational database systems. If you're working with an application that uses a database, you'll most likely need to use databases having names like Oracle, MySQL, Sybase, Microsoft SQL Server, and others. These databases are based on the traditional relational model; somehow we need to use them along with our Java objects.

An object can be placed in a relational database through the process of *mapping*. Mapping is a technique that places an object's attributes in one or more fields of a database table. For example, the earlier CD class has two attributes that would need to be mapped to a relational database table for permanent storage. The title and artist fields can be mapped to a schema like the following:

```
create table CD (
ID int not null primary key auto_increment,
title varchar(256),
artist varchar(256)
);
```

The ID field is used to create unique rows in the database. Each title and artist field holds the appropriate value from the CD object. This is an example of a *one-to-one mapping* between the class and the database. Figure 1.1 shows the appropriate UML diagram to accompany the class and the resulting database table.

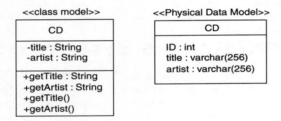

Figure 1.1

From a database standpoint, consider a CD object instantiated using the following constructor:

```
new CD("Grace Under Pressure", "Rush");
```

When the object is mapped to the database table defined earlier, the values in the database might look like this:

```
+----+--------------------------+-------+
| ID | Title                    | Artist|
+----+--------------------------+-------+
| 1  | Grace Under Pressure     | Rush  |
+----+--------------------------+-------+
```

For any additional CD objects that are instantiated, new rows are created in the database; the ID column maintains their uniqueness.

Typically, the classes you're dealing with in a production application will include more than just simple attributes. Consider the following CD class:

```
public class CD implements Serializable {
String title;
String artist;
```

```
ArrayList tracks;

public CD(String title, String artist) {
this.title = title;
this.artist = artist;

tracks = new ArrayListO;
 }

public void addTrack(String track) {
tracks. add(track);
 }
}
```

In this new CD class, we've added an ArrayList to hold the name of each title on the CD. As you might expect, this additional attribute introduces a hidden complexity to the mapping between the objects instantiated from the CD class and the permanent storage: The ArrayList attribute can contain no values or hundreds of values. There might be 8 to 10 tracks on a CD; an MP3 CD could include hundreds of songs. In either case, we need to be able to map the ArrayList attribute into a database structure so it can be permanently recorded when the entire CD is committed.

A common solution is to create a second database table just for the attribute. For example, we might create a table like this:

```
create table CD_tracks (
ID int not null primary key.
track varchar(256)
);
```

Using the Rush CD object created earlier, we can make a couple of calls to the addTrack() method and fill the tracks ArrayList:

```
rush.addTrack("Distant Early Warning");
rush.addTrack("Afterimage");
rush.addTrack("Red Sector A");
```

When the CD object is saved to the database, information is placed in two different tables: a CD table

```
+----+-------------------------+-------+
| ID | Title                   | Artist|
+----+-------------------------+-------+
| 1  | Grace Under Pressure    | Rush  |
+----+-------------------------+-------+
```

and a CD_tracks table

```
+----+-----------------------------+
| ID | Track                       |
+----+-----------------------------+
| 1  | Distant Early Warning       |
+----+-----------------------------+
| 2  | Afterimage                  |
+----+-----------------------------+
| 3  | Red Sector A                |
+----+-----------------------------+
```

If we have another CD to store, should another track table be added to the system, or should the tracks be added to the existing CD_tracks table? If we add a track to the CD_tracks table, how do we keep track of the fact that some of the tracks relate to specific CDs in the CD table?

We need to add a *foreign key* to the CD_tracks table; it will relate to the primary key in the CD table. Here's what the new CD_tracks table looks like:

```
create table CD_tracks (
ID int not null primary key auto_increment,
cd_id int,
track varchar(256)
);
```

Using this schema, the Rush CD's tracks appear as follows:

```
+----+------+----------------------------+
| ID | cd_id| Track                      |
+----+------+----------------------------+
| 1  |   1  | Distant Early Warning      |
+----+------+----------------------------+
| 2  |   2  | Afterimage                 |
+----+------+----------------------------+
| 3  |   3  |   Red Sector A             |
+----+------+----------------------------+
```

With the addition of the cd_id column, we can relate the two tables needed to fully map the CD object to permanent storage. The addition of the new CD_tracks table expands our UML diagram, as shown in Figure 1.2.

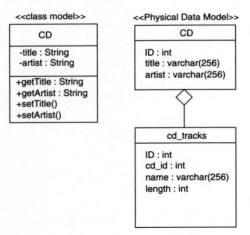

Figure 1.2

Our CD class can be further complicated by adding an attribute based on another class type. For example:

```java
public class CD implements Serializable {
String title;
String artist;
ArrayList tracks;

public CD(String title, String artist) {
this.title = title;
this.artist = artist;

tracks = new ArrayList();
}

public void addTrack(Track track) {
tracks.add(track);
 }

private class Track {
String name;
int length;

public track(String name, int length) {
this.name = name;
this.length = length;
        }
 }
}
```

We've added another class called Track, which is added to the track ArrayList instead of a single string. With the Track class added to the class model, we have a new situation that needs to be handled through an appropriate mapping. The most obvious choice is to add another database table for mapping between the class and the permanent storage. For example:

```sql
create table tracks (
   ID int not null primary key auto_increment,
   name varchar(256),
   length int
);
```

The new database table looks similar to the CD_tracks database created in the previous example but includes a little more information. (We could have used the CD_tracks schema and added the length column.)

After these examples, it should be clear that saving a set of objects to permanent storage isn't a simple task. In order to correctly put an object's attributes in a database, you must have a clear plan in place with the proper databases and mappings. As you can see, though, once a class has been defined, the database tables and mappings become clear. Thus, in most design situations, the database modeling should occur after the classes have been defined.

Primary Keys, Timestamps, and Version Numbers

In the examples presented so far, all the database tables have included a primary key that isn't part of the original object being mapped. The primary key is needed in order for the database server to uniquely distinguish and manage the objects stored in the database. Without the primary key, the database might have duplicate rows in a table because two objects in the system have identical attribute values. The primary key also gives us the ability to determine whether or not an object has actually been added to the database and if the object needs to be updated.

Depending on the system used to handle the mapping from objects to permanent storage, there are different ways to determine whether an object is up to date. One way is to use a timestamp in the database table. When the persistence layer needs to determine whether an object should be persisted to the database, it can check the timestamp in the table row for the object. If the timestamp is less than a timestamp kept in the object itself, the persistence layer knows the object should be persisted. If the timestamps are the same, the object hasn't been changed and doesn't need to be saved.

Another technique involves a version number stored in the database. When the object is pulled from the database, it has an associated version number. If the application changes the object in any way, the persistence layer updates the version number by a single digit. The layer can then use the version number to determine whether the object needs to be persisted.

Handling Inheritance

Obtaining efficiencies in the software development process means using all of a methodology's features. This is especially true when you're developing the classes for an application. During the development of the class structure, a clear hierarchy can sometimes be created through inheritance. For example, for our CD class, we might have another class called SpecialEditionCD that inherits its foundational attributes from the CD class:

```
public class SpecialEditionCD extends CD {
String newFeatures;
int cdCount;

public SpecialEditionCD(
String title,
String artist,
String newFeatures,
int cdCount) {
this.title = title;
this.artist = artist;
this.newFeatures = newFeatures;
this.cdCount = cdCount;
    }
}
```

The SpecialEditionCD class adds two more attributes that need to be persistent to our permanent storage in addition to the attributes from the CD parent class. We can't easily store the SpecialEditionCD information in the CD database table because of these new attributes. How do we perform the mapping? There are several solutions:

- ❑ Create a single table using the attributes from the lowest child.
- ❑ Create a table per class.
- ❑ Create a table per concrete class.

Let's consider each of these inheritance mappings using the CD and SpecialEditionCD classes as examples.

Lowest-Child Inheritance Mapping

If we have a hierarchy of classes, our mapping needs to be able to handle both the CD and SpecialEditionCD classes using a single table. We can accomplish this by taking all the attributes for the *lowest child* in the inheritance chain, mapping them, and then moving up the chain until we've mapped the topmost parent. The result is a table with attributes from all classes. Using our two classes, this process produces a table like the one in Figure 1.3.

```
create table cd (
ID  int not null primary key auto_increment,
type varchar(256),
title varchar(256),
artist varchar(256),
newFeatures varchar(256),
count int
);
```

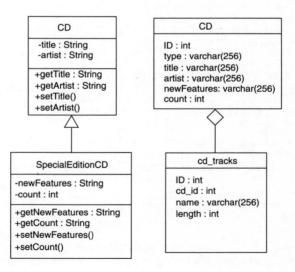

Figure 1.3

If we have an object of type SpecialEditionCD, all the necessary columns are available to persist it to the database. If we have a CD object, all the necessary columns are still available; however, both the newFeatures and count columns need to be populated with a value such as null. But will this work? Can't we have a SpecialEditionCD object where both the count and newFeatures attributes are null? In that case, how can we tell which object has been stored? We add to the database schema an addition field called type that the mapping software uses to keep track of the class type to which a particular row belongs.

As you can see from this example, adding new classes to the class model as well as the database is as simple as adding columns to the single hierarchy table. There is complete support for polymorphism because of the type column. Changing the type value from one class to another changes the object class type. We don't need to keep track of additional tables since all the information for the class hierarchy can be found in the single table.

If you have a large hierarchy, the single-table option isn't ideal because of the potential for wasted space from row to row. If an object is higher in the hierarchy, there will be quite a few nulled column values. Further, the database may potentially have a large number of columns. This isn't usually a problem for database-management software, but the database can be difficult to read and maintain.

Table-Per-Class Inheritance Mapping

If you want to eliminate some of the issues with the single-table approach to mapping an inheritance hierarchy, consider creating a single table for each of the classes. Figure 1.4 shows an example of the object-to-table mapping.

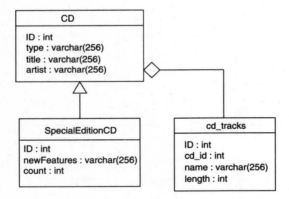

Figure 1.4

In Figure 1.4, we've created three tables to handle the CD inheritance hierarchy. The CD and cd_tracks tables monitor the attribute needed for a CD object. For the SpecialEditionCD class, we create another table to hold the information new to this class. If the object we're mapping to the database is a CD class, then we just need to access the two base tables. However, if we have a SpecialEditionCD, we need to access three tables to pull out all the information needed to save or load the object from the database. If the persistence layer is intelligent, we won't necessarily hit all three tables for a SpecialEditionCD—only the tables needed at a particular moment.

If we add more classes to the hierarchy, we need to build the appropriate database table to fulfill the necessary mappings. Various relationship must be maintained between the rows for each subchild object created. Maintaining these relationships can be complex, depending on the hierarchy being mapped. We aren't wasting database space if we have a CD object instead of a SpecialEditionCD since we won't need a row for the child object.

Table-Per-Concrete-Class Inheritance Mapping

In our example CD class hierarchy, it's clear that we'll be creating objects of type CD and SpecialEditionCD. Thus both of these classes are concrete. However, you might have a hierarchy in which one or more classes aren't concrete. In this type of situation, mapping all the classes to database tables isn't necessary; instead, you can make the concrete classes only. This technique will save you time and database space. The real advantage comes in the time needed to access the database for attributes from the nonconcrete classes when an object needs to be saved or loaded.

Working With Relationships

In almost all applications, numerous objects relate to one another in some fashion. For example, we might have an account object that holds information about a specific account in an accounting application. Each account might be associated with a single owner object; this association is a *one-to-one* relationship. Each account might have numerous addresses where account information could be sent; this association is a *one-to-many* relationship. Finally, each account can be assigned to numerous securities, and securities can be assigned to numerous accounts; this association creates a *many-to-many* relationship.

These three different relationships are called *multiplicity*; however, there is another relationship type called *directionality*. To illustrate, consider the account/securities many-to-many relationship just discussed. If you have an account, you can determine which securities it's associated with; and if you have a security, you can determine which accounts it's associated with. This is an example of a *bidirectional* relationship. For the account-to-address association, an account knows about the addresses it needs, but the addresses don't know which account they're bound to; this is an example of a *unidirectional* relationship.

Mapping a One-to-One Relationship

In our one-to-one relationship example, we'll consider a situation where we have a single account and a single owner. Figure 1.5 shows an example of the classes we'll map.

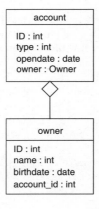

Figure 1.5.

To map the relationship shown in Figure 1.5 to a relational database, we need to use a foreign key that associates the owner with the account. Since there will be a single owner for each account, we know there will be a single row in the database table that holds the owner information. The following table schemas can be used to map the relationship in Figure 1.5:

```
create table account (
    ID int not null primary key auto_increment,
    type int,
    opendate
);

create table owner (
    ID int not null primary key auto_increment,
    account_id int,
    name varchar(256),
    birthdate date
);
```

The one-to-one mapping is created between the account and owner tables through the account_id field in the owner table. When a new row is added to the account table, a new ID is created. This ID uniquely identifies the account to the accounting system. No matter how many accounts are added to the system, no other one will have the same ID value. Therefore, this value can be used to associate the account and its database row with any other necessary data. Some of that data is found in the owner table. Just after the account is added to the database, the owner row is inserted. Part of the owner information to be stored is the ID of the account. The ID is stored in the account_id field, which is a foreign key to the primary key (ID) of the account table.

When the application needs to pull the account, it accesses the account through the primary key or, potentially, through a query that pulls the ID as well. The application can then pull the owner row using the ID value.

Mapping a One-to-Many Relationship

In the previous example, we also have a one-to-many relationship when the account object relates to one or more addresses. Figure 1.6 shows an example of the objects we need to map.

A single account in our application can have one or more addresses. Thus, each account needs an array of address objects that hold the full address where information can be sent and associated with the account. The following schemas show how the information is kept in the database:

```
create table account (
    ID int not null primary key auto_increment,
    type int,
    opendate date
);

create table address (
    ID int not null primary key auto_increment,
    account_id int,
    address varchar(256),
    city varchar(256),
    state varchar(256),
    zip varchar(256)
);
```

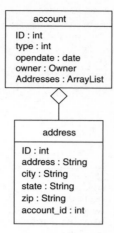

Figure 1.6

As you can see, the foreign key, `account_id`, is used in the mapping just as it is in the one-to-one relationship map. When an account is added to the database, its ID is obtained and used to store one or more addresses in the address table. The ID is stored in the `account_id` foreign key column. The application can perform a query against the address table using the ID as a search value.

Mapping a Many-to-Many Relationship

In the final type of relationship, an account relates to securities and at the same time securities relate to accounts. Figure 1.7 shows the classes in the relationship.

As you might expect, doing the mapping for a many-to-many relationship isn't as easy as it is for the one-to-one and one-to-many cases. For every account and security in the system, we need to be able to relate one or more of the other classes. For example, if we have an account with an ID of 3425, it might be associated with the securities 4355, 3245, 3950, and 3954. How can we associate these securities with the single account? We could have four columns in the account table called sec1, sec2, sec3, and sec4. But what if we added two more securities to the account? We wouldn't have enough columns in the account table.

The solution is to use an association table between the account table and the security table. Here are the table schemas:

```
create table account (
  ID int not null primary key auto_increment,
  type int,
  opendate date,
  securities int
);

create table security (
  ID int not null primary key auto_increment,
  name varchar(256),
```

```
      cost int,
      accounts int
);

create table account_security (
    ID int not null primary key auto_increment,
    account_id int,
    security_id int,
);
```

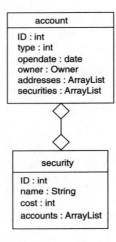

Figure 1.7

For every relationship between an account and a security, there will be a unique row in the
`account_security` association table. If we have an account ID, we can query the `account_`
`security` table to find all the securities associated with the account. We can also go the other direction
and use a security ID to query for all the accounts using that security.

Summary

When you're writing applications using the object-oriented methodology, real-world information is
stored in classes where the information can be encapsulated and controlled. At some point during the
execution of the application, the information in each of the objects will need to be persisted. The goal of
this chapter has been to provide you with an overview of the issues and techniques involved in object
mapping from the application to permanent storage. By far the most popular technique is mapping a
class to one or more database tables. We've covered many of the issues involved in object/relational
mapping; now we'll push forward and discuss Hibernate as a tool for providing the necessary mapping.

2

Introduction to Hibernate

Most production-level applications need to be able to store data in one form or another. The question is, should you store that data in its natural container—the object—or pull it out? With Hibernate, you can handle the data in the object and not worry about the details of extracting, storing, and loading individual data components. In this chapter, we'll explain what Hibernate is and how it works.

Hibernate

Hibernate is Java-based middleware designed to complete the Object Relational (O/R) mapping model. For the most part, you'll see little disruption to your classes and code as a result of using Hibernate. In fact, one of the most complex parts of many O/R mapping mechanisms—writing SQL code—can be simplified significantly with Hibernate. Figure 2.1 shows a high-level illustration of where Hibernate fits into the development picture.

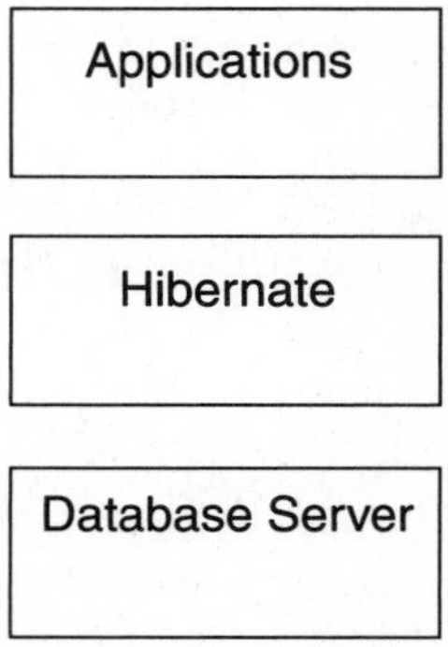

```
┌───────────────────────┐
│     Applications       │
│                        │
└───────────────────────┘

┌───────────────────────┐
│     Hibernate          │
│                        │
└───────────────────────┘

┌───────────────────────┐
│   Database Server      │
│                        │
└───────────────────────┘
```

Figure 2.1

In the figure, you can see that Hibernate sits between traditional Java objects and handles all the work in persisting those objects based on the appropriate O/R mechanisms and patterns. Your goal is to accurately map how Hibernate will persist objects to the database tables of the underlying database server; in most cases, the mapping exercise is straightforward. As you'll see in later chapters, Hibernate can persist even the most complex classes, including those using composition, inheritance, and collections. As we move through this chapter, we'll begin to point out Hibernate's key issues and features.

Hibernate Architecture

In order to help you fully understand what Hibernate brings to you, let's start drilling into the system's architecture based on the initial view in Figure 2.1. Figure 2.2 expands the architecture to show the individual classes that make up a typical Java application.

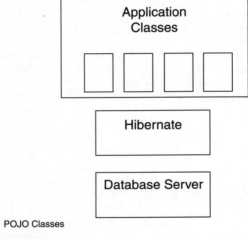

POJO Classes

Figure 2.2

When you're using Hibernate to provide the O/R mapping, it's your responsibility to determine which classes need to be persisted and which can be reconstructed without storing or loading data from the database. Clearly, you don't want to take the time and expense of persisting transient objects that are routinely created and destroyed in the application. The most important objects in the application are those that provide information about a product or a user. As a developer, you don't have to do much work when an object is designated to be stored by Hibernate: The most important task is determining how the object will be persisted.

If a class exists on its own and generally isn't part of a composition relationship with another object, the class needs to expose an identifier. The identifier is designed to provide uniqueness to the object when it's stored in the database. Hibernate allows for several different identifier types, including string and int. Further, Hibernate lets you use various generators to build the identifier; these generators range from using the native functionality of the database server to building a unique identifier using components of the operating system including the clock and network address.

In addition to the identifier, all Java objects that will be persisted must follow the JavaBean specification and include the appropriate mutator and accessor functions. Depending on your implementation, the function may be public or private; in either case, Hibernate can access the functions as long as they're JavaBean-like. Further, all persisted classes need to include a default constructor so Hibernate can instantiate the object when it's requested from the database.

As you'll see in later chapters, Hibernate supports complex class structures: Inheritance hierarchies can be successfully persisted and the polymorphic behavior behind the inheritance structure utilized. Just about all Java applications use collections. Hibernate can persist collections when they're part of an object's attribute structure. The collection can be automatically stored when the parent object is persisted, or the application can choose to store the collection independently. If you incorporate the design concept of composition in a Java class, Hibernate will be able to honor the implementation when the object is stored.

Vital to the functionality of Hibernate is a database server and the connection between itself and the server. Fortunately, Hibernate is rich in this area: It supports a variety of the most popular open-source and commercial servers. However, Hibernate isn't limited to these servers; you can use just about any server, assuming an appropriate JDBC driver is available. As you'll see in Chapter 3, Hibernate supports basic SQL and allows individual dialect changes to be made as appropriate for the database being used in the application. Thus even if you're using a database that includes some quirky syntax, Hibernate can support it using a specific dialect class.

Figure 2.3 shows that JDBC isn't the only additional technology used between Hibernate and the database server. Hibernate can be used with applications that rely on an application server to handle servlets and Enterprise JavaBeans. In these situations, it's normal to use Java Naming and Directory Interface (JNDI) to handle the database resource associated with the environment. Once a JNDI resource has been created, Hibernate can access the resource with just a few changes to its configuration file. Further, transaction support is available through both the JDBC connection and the Java Transaction API (JTA) specification and its implementation classes. When you're using JTA, options are available to use either an open-source implementation or one provided by the application server; it's a matter of setting up the configuration file correctly.

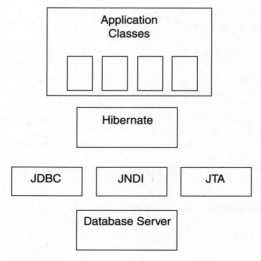

Figure 2.3

Hibernate Configuration

Figure 2.4 shows the Configuration class, which is critical to launching Hibernate. The Configuration class's operation has two keys components: the database connection and the class-mapping setup.

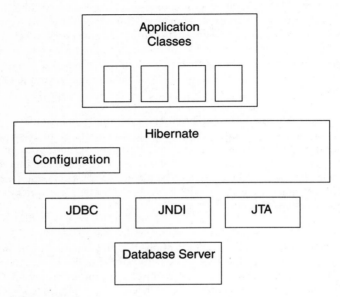

Figure 2.4

The first component is handled through one or more configuration files supported by Hibernate. These files are hibernate.properties and hibernate.cfg.xml, as shown in Listing 2.1.

```xml
<?xml version="1.0" encoding="utf-8"?>
<!DOCTYPE hibernate-configuration PUBLIC
"-//Hibernate/Hibernate Configuration DTD//EN"
"http://hibernate.sourceforge.net/hibernate-configuration-2.0.dtd">

<hibernate-configuration>

 <session-factory>
    <property name="connection.driver">com.mysql.jdbc.Driver</property>
    <property name="connection.url"
            jdbc:mysql://localhost/products</property>
    <property name="dialect">
            net.sf.hibernate.dialect.MySQLDialect</property>
 </session-factory>

</hibernate-configuration>
```

```
hibernate.dialect net.sf.hibernate.dialect.MySQLDialect
hibernate.connection.driver_class com.mysql.jdbc.Driver
hibernate.connection.url jdbc:mysql://localhost/products
hibernate.connection.username
hibernate.connection.password
hibernate.show_sql true
hibernate.cglib.use_reflection_optimizer false
```

Listing 2.1

One of the files handles setting up Hibernate using XML, and another doesn't. For the most part, we'll use the hibernate.cfg.xml file throughout this book. You can set up both JDBC and JNDI connections through these files as well as a host of other options.

The second component makes the connection between the Java classes and database tables. Listing 2.2 shows an example of a mapping for a simple Java class.

```xml
<?xml version="1.0" encoding="UTF-8"?>
<!DOCTYPE hibernate-mapping
 PUBLIC "-//Hibernate/Hibernate Mapping DTD//EN"
 "http://hibernate.sourceforge.net/hibernate-mapping-2.0.dtd">

<hibernate-mapping>

<class name="Notes"
       table="notes">
  <id name="id" unsaved-value="0">
    <generator class="native"/>
  </id>

  <property name="info" type="string"/>
  <property name="count" type="integer" not-null="true"/>
  <property name="zipcode" type="string"/>
  <property name="fullname" type="string"/>
</class>

</hibernate-mapping>
```

Listing 2.2

As you can see in Listing 2.2, the mapping document is XML based and includes elements for specifying an identifier as well as the attributes of the mapped object. Once a mapping document has been created, the appropriate database table can be added to the database server, thus completing an O/R mapping from a Java class to the database.

19

Hibernate Sessions

When you begin using Hibernate, a singleton class called `SessionFactory` is instantiated. As shown in Figure 2.5, the `SessionFactory` configures Hibernate for the application using the supplied config-uration file (as described in the previous section) and allows for a `Session` object to be instantiated. As you might expect, the `SessionFactory` object is heavyweight; you should take care to create only one `SessionFactory` per application. (This is true for both traditional applications and those that execute in an application server.)

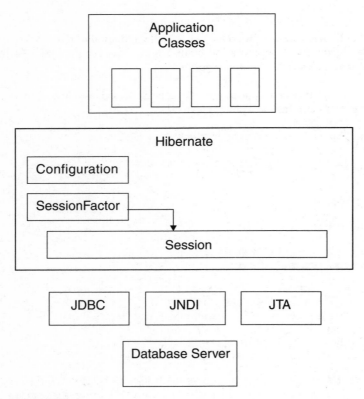

Figure 2.5

When you begin persisting or loading objects to/from the database, a `Session` object is instantiated. The `Session` object is lightweight and designed to be instantiated each time an interaction is needed with the database. Thus, the `Session` object is created, an object or two is persisted or loaded from the database, and the `Session` object is closed. When a `Session` object is instantiated, a connection is made to the database; thus the interactions should be fairly quick to ensure the application doesn't keep database connections open needlessly.

In the process of working with persisted objects, two additional interfaces are commonly used, as shown in Figure 2.6. The Transaction interface lets you make sure that all the operations on persisted objects occur in a transaction supported by either JDBC or JTA. When you're using a transaction, any error that occurs between the start and end of the transaction will cause all the operations to fail; this is important when the persisted objects rely on each other to maintain integrity in the database. The `Query` interface lets you query the database for objects instead of having to rely solely on an object's identifier.

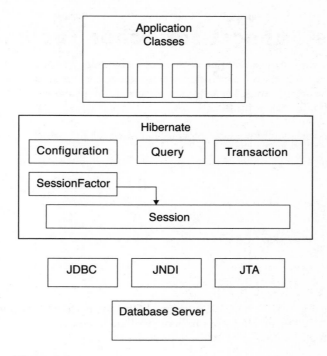

Figure 2.6

Hibernate Callbacks

When Hibernate is in the process of persisting or loading an object, it provides support for you to be warned of certain events so you can respond appropriately. The process is implemented through callbacks. The available events are as follows:

```
public Boolean onSave(Session s); - called before the object is saved to the
database

public Boolean onUpdate(Session s); - called before the object is updated

public boolean onDelete(Session s); - called before the object is deleted

public Boolean onLoad(Session s); - called after the object is loaded from
the database
```

Hibernate also implements a `Validatable` interface that you can use to verify the state of an object before it's persisted to the database. The goal of the interface isn't to change the state of the object but to make sure the object is in a state appropriate to be stored; otherwise an exception is thrown.

Hibernate's Support for Other Technologies

Hibernate supports a variety of external processes and methodologies to help with the execution and setup of the system. Some of the tools include a schema generator that automatically creates the necessary schema for a host of mappings. The mapping-file generator generates a skeleton file for Java classes, using reflection to find the class's attributes.

Hibernate supports a variety of other technologies, including the following:

❑ XDoclet Spring

❑ J2EE

❑ Eclipse plug-ins

❑ Maven

Summary

In this quick introduction to Hibernate, we've shown how easy it is to provide persistence to ordinary Java objects. Throughout the remainder of this book, we'll build on the concepts discussed here and show numerous examples to fully explore the Hibernate product.

Hibernate Development Environment

After the background information you've learned in the previous two chapters, it should be clear that Hibernate presents a comprehensive solution to the problem of persisting Java objects to permanent storage. Hibernate works with all the major database-management systems and, as you'll see, is easy to use. In this chapter, we'll explain how to install Hibernate, configure it, and develop a "Hello World"-type application both in a standalone setting and in a J2EE container using Tomcat.

Obtaining Hibernate

To use Hibernate, you first need to obtain it from the Hibernate home page. Follow these steps:

1. Browse to www.hibernate.org.

2. Locate the Download link in the left navigational bar. Click it to bring up the download page.

3. Part way down the new page is a Download from Sourceforge link. Click it to display a list of available downloads.

4. The first two files in the list are the most recent ZIP and GZ distributions. Download the appropriate version for your platform.

Once you've downloaded the file, open it to reveal a directory structure similar to that shown in Figure 3.1.

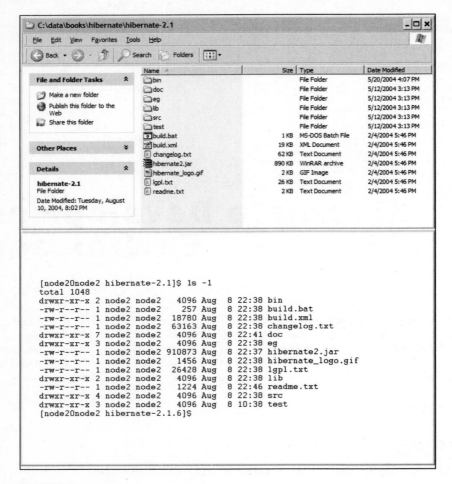

Figure 3.1

Hibernate Prerequisites and Requirements

As you might expect, the developers of Hibernate wanted to concentrate on the mechanics of persisting objects instead of writing logging packages. So, Hibernate uses a few additional libraries that are common in the Java development community. You'll find the libraries used in the development and execution of Hibernate in the /lib directory of the Hibernate installation.

The current packages required by Hibernate handle the following tasks:

- **dom4j:** XML parsing (www.dom4j.org/)
- **Xalan:** XSLT processing (http://xml.apache.org/xalan-j/)
- **Xerces:** XML parsing, specifically SAX in this case (http://xml.apache.org/xerces-j/)
- **CGLIB:** Appropriate changes to Java classes at runtime (http://cglib.sourceforge.net/)
- **log4j:** Logging in the application (http://logging.apache.org/log4j/docs/index.html)
- **Commons:** Logging, collections, and so on (http://jakarta.apache.org/commons

Copy the following library files from /lib into your `classpath`, and change your `classpath` variable to include the JARs:

- cglib2.jar
- commons-collections.jar
- commons-Logging.jar
- dom4j.jar
- ehcache.jar
- jdbc2.0-stdext.jar
- jta.jar
- log4j.jar
  - odmg.jar
  - xalan.jar
- xerces.jar
- xml-apis.jar

[handwritten margin note:]

Hibernate 3

jta.jar
xml-apis.jar
Commons-logging
asm-attrs.jar
dom4j.jar
cglib.jar
asm.jar
Jdbc20.jar
Commons Collection.jar

For the moment, assume you're writing a standalone application. When you develop code for an application server environment, you place the libraries in a specific location in the application server's /webapps directory.

If you browse to the /lib directory, you'll find numerous other JARs. They're used in building Hibernate, connection pooling, and caches. We'll discuss these topics later in the book.

Installing Hibernate

One of the JARs in the Hibernate distribution is called hibernate2.jar; it's in the root directory of the installation. This is the primary JAR that Hibernate needs to do its work. Place this file in your classpath just as you did the required JARs in the previous section. For a standalone application, this is all the installation needed for Hibernate.

Hibernate Configuration File

The database is one of Hibernate's key components. You configure the database using a file called hibernate.properties, which is usually saved in the root directory of your application. The following are examples of some of the properties and property values found in the file:

```
hibernate.dialect net.sf.hibernate.dialect.MySQLDialect
hibernate.connection.driver_class com.mysql.jdbc.Driver
hibernate.connection.url jdbc:mysql://<host>/<table>
hibernate.connection.username <username>
hibernate.connection.password <password>
```

You can set all the database options and various other options in the hibernate.properties file. We'll discuss all the properties and configuration options available in Chapter 4. For our purposes in this chapter, you only need to know about the five options shown here.

Hooking Up a Database Server

Before you begin to work with Hibernate, you need to install a database so that Hibernate has a place to store the persisted Java classes. Hibernate can be used on different platforms and with a variety of databases; we've chosen two databases to discuss here: MySQL and Microsoft SQL Server. If you're interested in using another database supported by Hibernate, please see Appendix A, which provides installation instructions and Hibernate configurations for each of the supported databases. In this section, we'll show you the configuration needed for the three databases.

As we mentioned, the Hibernate configuration file holds various properties. For databases in a standalone situation, the properties available are as follows:

❑   **hibernate.dialect:** Relates to the SQL generated by Hibernate. Including this property makes Hibernate generate the appropriate SQL for the chosen database.

❑   **hibernate.connection.driver_class:** Relates to the JDBC driver class used to communicate between Java and the database server.

❑   **hibernate.connection.url:** Relates to the URL used to specify the location of the database server, the optional port to use, and (potentially) a database and table to access upon connection.

❑   **hibernate.connection.username:** The username to use when connecting to the database server.

❑   **hibernate.connection.password:** The password for the supplied username.

❑   **hibernate.connection.pool_size:** The total number of pooled connections for Hibernate to manage. Hibernate includes a simple connection pool for testing and development purposes; you'll see how to use more advanced pooling in Chapter 4.

If you're using a database in an application server situation, you'll use the following configuration element:

❑   **hibernate.connection.datasource:** The JNDI name defined in the application server context you're using for the application.

Depending on the definition of the JNDI source, the following properties can also be defined:

- ❑ **hibernate.jndi.class:** The JNDI `InitialContextFactory` class.
- ❑ **hibernate.jndi.url:** The JNDI provider URL.
- ❑ **hibernate.connection.username:** The username to use when connecting to the database server.
- ❑ **hibernate.connection.password:** The password for the supplied username.

As we define the configuration for each of the databases, we'll touch on these properties in more detail.

Setting Up Hibernate to Use MySQL

MySQL is one of the most popular open-source database systems available today. The home page for the database is www.mysql.com; this Web site provides downloads of the current database system for most platforms. Pull the database for your platform, and install it based on the instructions provided. Basically, if you're running Windows, you'll perform a standard wizard "Click-Next" install. On a Unix-based platform, you'll do the familiar source install of ./configure, make, make install; an RPM install; or a create-directory-and-copy install for a binary.

Once you've installed MySQL, you're halfway to using the database with Hibernate. You need a second component—a JDBC driver—which is also available at www.mysql.com. For MySQL, the JDBC driver of choice is Connector/J. You can find it in the downloads area (www.mysql.com/downloads/api-jdbc-stable.html); select the download appropriate for your platform. After you've completed the download, extract the compressed file and find the file with a name like mysql-connector-java-3.0.11-stable-bin.jar. Place this file in your classpath so our example application will be able to find it.

Now you need to build an appropriate hibernate.properties file. Here's an example:

```
hibernate.dialect net.sf.hibernate.dialect.MySQLDialect
hibernate.connection.driver_class com.mysql.jdbc.Driver
hibernate.connection.url jdbc:mysql://localhost/products
hibernate.connection.username test
hibernate.connection.password test
```

You should only need to change the last three lines of the properties file. In this example, we've used the server location `localhost` and the database name `products`. Our example application creates a table called `CD` in the products database. You should also set up a username/password on this system and place those values appropriately in the file.

Setting Up Hibernate to Use Microsoft SQL Server

As you might expect, installing Microsoft SQL Server is a point-and-click wizard process. For our purposes, we've used a developer's version of Microsoft SQL Server 2000 with Service Pack 3a installed.

After you've installed SQL Server on the target database machine, you need to obtain a JDBC driver so the Java application can access the database. You can get such a driver directly from Microsoft at www.microsoft.com/sql/downloads. Click the JDBC for SQL Server link, and scroll to the bottom of the page. Two downloads are available: setup.exe for Windows and mssqlserver.tar for Unix. Also in the list is a file called InstallationGuide_SP2.txt: Open it for Unix instructions. In Windows, launch setup.exe and walk through the screens.

Next, you need to add the JDBC driver to your global `classpath`. For example, using the base installation directory, the `classpath` needs to contain the following :

```
c:\Microsoft SQL Server 2000 Driver for JDBC\lib\msbase.jar
c:\Microsoft SQL Server 2000 Driver for JDBC\lib\msutil.jar
c:\Microsoft SQL Server 2000 Driver for JDBC\lib\mssqlserver.jar
```

(You may want to pull the JARs from the installation directory and place them in a directory with a shorter name.) Once you've added the JARs to the classpath, you can set up the hibernate.hbm.xml or hibernate.properties file. Let's say you've installed SQL Server on a box with the IP address 192.168.1.55, and a user is defined in the server with the username "readwrite" and the password "secret". The Hibernate configuration file will appear as follows:

```
hibernate.dialect net.sf.hibernate.dialect.SQLServerDialect
hibernate.connection.driver_class
        com.microsoft.jdbc.sqlserver.SQLServerDriver
hibernate.connection.url jdbc:Microsoft:sqlserver://localhost:1433/products
hibernate.connection.username sa
hibernate.connection.password sa
```

You'll need to specify the location of your database server; we've used localhost in this case. Also add the appropriate username and password to the file.

A Standalone Hibernate Application

With some of the preliminaries out of the way, let's dive into an example of using Hibernate to provide Java persistence in a standalone application. For this example, we'll use the CD class designed in Chapter 1 and create a simple application that displays a list of CDs. The user can select one CD and change or add information about it.

Creating the Java Class

The first step in creating an application is to build the Java class or classes, depending on the application that will be persisted to the database. As you might expect, a typical application has many objects; but only a few key objects hold information that should be kept permanently.

The primary data in our application describes a CD, so we need an appropriate class. Listing 3.1 shows an example CD class.

```
import java.io.*;
import java.util.*;
```

```
public class CD {
  int id;
  String title;
  String artist;
  Date purchaseDate;
  double cost;

  public CD() {
  }

  public CD(String title,
            String artist,
            Date purchaseDate,
            double cost) {
    this.title = title;
    this.artist = artist;
    this.purchaseDate = purchaseDate;
    this.cost = cost;
  }

  public void setId(int id) {
    this.id = id;
  }

  public int getId(){
    return id;
  }

  public void setTitle(String title) {
    this.title = title;
  }

  public String getTitle() {
    return title;
  }

  public void setArtist(String artist) {
    this.artist = artist;
  }

  public String getArtist() {
    return artist;
  }

  public void setPurchasedate(Date purchaseDate) {
    this.purchaseDate = purchaseDate;
  }

  public Date getPurchasedate() {
    return purchaseDate;
  }

  public void setCost(double cost) {
```

```
      this.cost = cost;
    }

    public double getCost() {
      return cost;
    }
  }
```

Listing 3.1

The CD class in Listing 3.1 isn't fancy—it's a JavaBeans-compliant class that holds the necessary information for CDs. When you're writing classes to be persisted by Hibernate, it's important to provide JavaBeans-compliant code as well as an index attribute like the id attribute in the CD class. Hibernate uses the id attribute to determine uniqueness among the objects persisted to the database. Notice that we haven't inherited or implemented any type of class or interface. Thus, Hibernate will use reflection based on the JavaBean setter/getter methods to persist the object.

Creating a Database Table

As you learned in Chapter 1, once the object or objects to be persisted have been created, you create the database table. The hardest part of this process is matching the database column types to the defined class. The following command creates the necessary table for a MySQL database:

```
create database products;
use products;

create table CD(
ID int not null primary key,
title text,
artist text,
purchasedate datetime,
cost double
);

create table hibernate_unique_key (
next_hi int
);

insert into hibernate_unique_key values(1);
```

Use the appropriate interface for the database you've chosen to create the database tables in a database called products. Hibernate uses the second table, hibernate_unique_key, to keep values it will need when generating unique IDs for the objects it will be persisting to the database. We need to seed the table, as well; that's the purpose of the insert command executed after the table is created.

Building a Mapping Document for Database Tables

At this point, we've defined a class to hold information about a CD as well as a database table where the CD information will be permanently kept. The next step is to build a mapping document that tells

Hibernate how to map the CD class to the database. Listing 3.2 shows the mapping document needed for our CD class.

```xml
<?xml version=" 1.0" encoding="utf-8"?>
<!DOCTYPE hibernate-mapping PUBLIC
 "-//Hibernate/Hibernate Mapping DTD//EN"
 http://www.sourceforae.net/hibernate-mapping-2.0.dtd>

<hibernate-mapping>
        <class name="CD"
        table="cd">
                <id name="id"
                    type="int"
                    unsaved-value="null">
                     <column name="ID"
                             sql-type="int"
                             not-null="true"/>
                  <generator class="hilo"/>
                </id>

        <property name="title"/>
        <property name="artist"/>
        <property name="purchasedate" type="date"/>
        <property name="cost" type="double"/>
        </class>
</hibernate-mapping>
```

Listing 3.2

In Listing 3.2, we've created a mapping document for Hibernate that relates the CD class to the underlying cd database table. As you'll see in Chapter 15, tools are available to help you with the process of mapping Java class that need to be persisted. Also, in Chapter 5, we'll provide a comprehensive review of the mapping document; for now, let's discuss the document in Listing 3.2.

The mapping document is an XML document, and it includes the necessary tags to indicate its status. The root element is `<hibernate-mapping>`; it contains all the `<class>` elements used to define specific mappings from a Java class to the database. The `<hibernate-mapping>` element in our example doesn't include any attributes; but if the class to be persisted was part of a package, we'd have an attribute called `package`. The full package declaration can be used to provide a package prefix for all the classes in this mapping file. If you don't include a package attribute in the `<hibernate-mapping>` element, you must provide a fully qualified class name in the `<class>` element.

The `<class>` element in our example includes two attributes:

❑ **name:** Identifies the fully qualified class name for the class or interface being mapped; if the package prefix is used in the `<hibernate-mapping>` element, the class name can be the unqualified name.

❑ **table:** Specifies the name of the table in the database where the mapped class will be persisted.

The `<class>` element includes numerous elements to fully map the Java class. In our example, we use two subelements: `<id>` and `<property>`. The `<id>` element maps the unique ID attribute added to our CD class to the primary key of the database. In our example, the `<id>` element includes both attributes and subelements. The attributes include the following:

❑   **name:** The attribute name found in the CD.

❑   **type:** The class type given to the ID attribute.

❑   **unsaved-value:** Specifies whether Hibernate should persist an object. The identifier attribute of our CD class is called id; it holds a value of null for a new object and an integer value for an object pulled from storage. Hibernate obtains the value of the identifier and compares it to the value specified in the unsaved-value attribute to determine whether Hibernate should persist the object. If the default value of the identifier used in your application isn't null, you need to place the default value in the unsaved-value attribute.

The `<id>` element also includes a couple of subelements: `<column>` and `<generator>`. The `<column>` element tells Hibernate what specific column in the mapped database table relates to the identifier for the class. In our case, we use a `<column>` element with the name, sql-type, and not-null attributes set to the values used in the definition of the cd database table.

When Hibernate places an object in the database, it must be sure that each row is unique, because the rows represent specific objects. It's possible for two objects in the system to have the same attribute values. If this occurs, the system needs to be able to distinguish the objects in the database. To do this, we specified the identifier with our Java class and added the ID column to the database table. Hibernate uses the identifier to assign a unique value, which is created using a generator. The `<generator>` element specifies the generator to be used when creating the unique identifier. The generator class is specified in the name attribute of the `<generator>` element. Hibernate includes quite a few generators; we'll discuss them in Chapter 4. For our example, we've chosen the hilo generator; it generates an int, short, or long value that is unique for a given database table.

After the `<id>` element has been specified, we need to let Hibernate know about the attributes to be persisted from our CD class. The specification comes from the `<property>` element.

You can build objects in an application and not persist all the attributes. When Hibernate pulls an object from the database, those attributes that aren't part of the persisted attributes are given their Java default value. In our example, we've persisted four attributes using the following elements:

```
<property name="title"/>
<property name="artist"/>
<property name="purchasedate" type="date"/>
<property name="cost" type="double"/>
```

The only required attribute in the `<property>` element is name, which is the name of the attributes in our CD class. Hibernate uses reflection to locate the setter/getter methods for each attribute specified. Any attributes that we don't want to be persisted aren't listed. In the purchasedate and cost elements, we've included the type to be used for the attribute: If the type attribute isn't included in an element, Hibernate uses reflection to try to guess the attribute type; and for these two elements, we want to make sure Hibernate gets the type right. For title and artist, the String type will be easily obtained through the reflection mechanism.

You should save the mapping document in a file with the format *<classname>*.hbm.xml. We saved our mapping document in the file CD.hbm.xml.

As you might expect, much more can appear in a Hibernate mapping document. We'll cover the additional attributes and elements throughout the book as we discuss more advanced topics.

Application Skeleton Code

Because we don't just want to present a "Hello World" application, we've come up with a small application that stores a list of CDs. The full code for the application appears in Listing 3.3. We'll refer to this code throughout this section of the chapter.

```java
import java.io.*;
import java.awt.*;
import javax.swing.*;
import java.util.*;
import javax.swing.table.*;
import javax.swing.event.*;
import java.awt.event.*;

import net.sf.hibernate.*;
import net.sf.hibernate.cfg.*;

public class CDTest extends JFrame implements ListDataListener {

    JList list;
    CDList listModel;
    JTextField artistField;
    JTextField titleField;
    JTextField costField;
    JTextField IDField;
    JLabel IDLabel;
    int selectedListIndex;

    SessionFactory sessionFactory;


    public CDTest(){
        try {
            Configuration cfg = new Configuration().addClass(CD.class);
            sessionFactory = cfg.buildSessionFactory();
        } catch (Exception e) {
            e.printStackTrace();
        }

        buildGUI();
    }

    private void buildGUI() {
        Container container = getContentPane();
        listModel = new CDList();
//      listModel.addCD("Grace Under Pressure", "Rush", new Date(), 9.99);
```

```java
        list = new JList();
        list.setModel(listModel);
        list.setCellRenderer(new CDRenderer());
        container.add(list, BorderLayout.NORTH);

        list.addListSelectionListener(new ListSelectionListener() {
          public void valueChanged(ListSelectionEvent ae) {
            JList list = (JList)ae.getSource () ;
            CDList model = (CDList)list.getModel();

            selectedListIndex = ((JList)ae.getSource()).getSelectedIndex();

            CD cd = (CD)model.getElementAt(selectedListIndex);
            IDLabel.setText(""+cd.getId());
            titleField.setText(cd.getTitle());
            artistField.setText(cd.getArtist());
            costField.setText(""+cd.getCost());
          }
        });

        JPanel panel = new JPanel(new GridLayout(7,2));
        artistField = new JTextField(25);
        titleField = new JTextField(25);
        costField = new JTextField(25);
        IDLabel = new JLabel();

        panel.add(new JLabel("ID"));
        panel.add(IDLabel);
        panel.add(new JLabel("Title"));
        panel.add (titleField);
        panel.add(new JLabel("Artist"));
        panel.add (artistField);
        panel.add(new JLabel("Cost"));
        panel.add(costField);

        JButton button = new JButton("Update");
        button.addActionListener(new ActionListener() {
          public void actionPerformed(ActionEvent ae) {
            CD cd = (CD)listModel.getElementAt(selectedListIndex);

            cd.setTitle(titleField.getText());
            cd.setArtist(artistField.getText());
            cd.setCost((double)Double.parseDouble(costField.getText()));

try {
            Session session = sessionFactory.openSession();
            session.update(cd);
    session.flush();
            session.close();
          } catch (Exception e) {}

        IDLabel.setText("");
        titleField.setText("");
```

```
          artistField.setText("");
          costField.setText("");
            }
        });
        panel.add (button);

        button = new JButton("Add");
        button.addActionListener(new ActionListener() {
           public void actionPerformed(ActionEvent ae) {
              CD cd = new CD(artistField.getText(),
                       titleField.getText(),
                       new Date(),
                       Double.parseDouble(costField.getText()));
              listModel.addCD(cd);

              try {
Session session = sessionFactory.openSession();
                 session.save(cd);
session.flush();
                 session.close();
              } catch (Exception e) {
                 e.printStackTrace();
              }

         IDLabel.setText("");
         titleField.setText("");
         artistField.setText("");
         costField.setText("");
            }
        });
        panel.add (button);
        button = new JButton("Delete");
        button.addActionListener(new ActionListener() {
           public void actionPerformed(ActionEvent ae) {
              CD cd = (CD)listModel.getElementAt(selectedListIndex);

              try {
Session session = sessionFactory.openSession();
                 session.delete(cd);
session.flush();
session.close();
              } catch (Exception e) {}

              listModel.removeElement(selectedListIndex);

            }
        });
        panel.add (button);

        button = new JButton("Pull All");
        button.addActionListener(new ActionListener() {
           public void actionPerformed(ActionEvent ae) {
              try {
                 Session session = sessionFactory.openSession();
```

```
            java.util.List cds = session.find("from CD");
    session.close();

        listModel.addCDs(cds);
      } catch (Exception e) {
        JOptionPane.showMessageDialog(null,
          "No CD", "problem pulling cds", 0);
      }
    }
  });
  panel.add(button);

  IDField = new JTextField(25);
  panel.add(IDField);

  button = new JButton("Pull Single");
  button.addActionListener(new ActionListener() {
    public void actionPerformed(ActionEvent ae) {
      int index = Integer.parseInt(IDField.getText());
      try {
        Session session = sessionFactory.openSession();
        CD cd = new CD();
        session.load(cd, new Integer(index));
        session.close();

        listModel.addCD(cd);
      } catch (Exception e) {
        JOptionPane.showMessageDialog(null,
              "No CD", "No CD with that ID", 0);
      }
    }
  });
  panel.add (button);

  container.add(panel, BorderLayout.SOUTH);

  setSize(300,250);
  setVisible(true);
}

public void intervalAdded(ListDataEvent e) {
  list.invalidate();
}

public void contentsChanged(ListDataEvent e) {
  list.invalidate();
}

public void intervalRemoved(ListDataEvent e) {
  list.invalidate();
}


public static void main(String [] args) {
    CDTest t = new CDTest() ;
```

```
      }

   private class CDList extends AbstractListModel {
     Vector v = new Vector();

     public void addCD(String title,
                       String artist,
                       Date pdate, double cost) {
       CD cd = new CD(title, artist, pdate, cost);
       v.add(cd);
       fireContentsChanged(this, 0, 0);
     }

     public void addCD(CD cd) {
       v.add(cd) ;
       fireContentsChanged(this, 0, 0);
     }

     public void addCDs(java.util.List cds) {
       v.addAll(cds);
       fireContentsChanged(this, 0, 0);
     }

     public int getSize() {
       return v.size();
     }

     public void removeElement(int index) {
       v.removeElementAt(index);
       fireContentsChanged(this, 0, 0);
     }

     public Object getElementAt(int index) {
       return v.elementAt(index);
     }
   }

   private class CDRenderer extends JLabel implements ListCellRenderer {
     private Color HIGHLIGHT = new Color(0,0,128);

     public CDRenderer() {
       setOpaque(true);
     }

     public Component getListCellRendererComponent(JList list,
                                        Object value,
int index,
boolean isSelected,
boolean cellHasFocus) {

       CD cd = (CD)value; setText(cd.getTitle());
       if (isSelected) {
         setBackground(HIGHLIGHT);
         setForeground(Color.white);
       } else {
```

```
            setBackground(Color.white);
            setForeground(Color.black);
        }
        return this;
    }
  }
}
```

Listing 3.3

The code in Listing 3.3 creates the GUI shown in Figure 3.2. This application lists all the CDs it knows about by title and lets you enter, delete, and update CDs. Unfortunately, once you enter a CD, it's lost when the application exits; therefore, we need to add persistence to the CD objects. That is the goal of the remainder of this section.

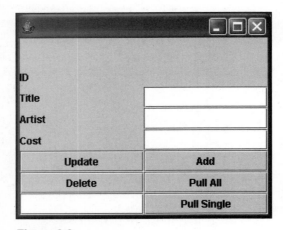

Figure 3.2

Loading the Mapping into an Application

With our example application ready and the mapping established between the CD class and the database, we can begin to incorporate Hibernate into our application. The first step is to build a Configuration object. The Configuration object is responsible for pulling, parsing, and compiling the mapping documents into a format that Hibernate uses internally. We'll create the configuration file in the constructor of the example code. Here's the new code:

```
public CDTest() {
    Configuration cfg = new Configuration().addClass(CD.class);
    buildGU();
}
```

This code creates a new `Configuration` object and then tries to load the mapping documents for the class specified in the `addClass()` method. By default, the code attempts to find a file named CD.hbm.xml. As you look at other Hibernate code, you'll also see an `.addFile(String)` method used to load the mapping component file. The `.addFile(String)` method takes the name of the mapping component filename as its parameter.

It's also possible to load a specific properties file when instantiating the `Configuration` object. For example, instead of loading the default hibernate.properties file, we could load our own with the following code:

```
Properties props = new Properties();
Configuration cfg = new Configuration().
                        addClass(CD.class).setProperties(props);
```

This technique of instantiating the `Configuration` object lets an application load specific properties based on a determination like a runtime flag, which determines the database type being used. Different property files can be set up with the appropriate properties for each database to be used.

Obtaining the SessionFactory

The `Configuration` object handles all the parsing and internal processing of mapping documents. Most of the real work done by Hibernate occurs in a `Session` object. To build a `Session` object, a `SessionFactory` object needs to be instantiated from the `Configuration` object. We further expand the CD class's constructor:

```
public CDTest() {
   Configuration cfg = new Configuration().addClass(CD.class);
   sessionFactory = cfg.buildSessionFactory();

   buildGUI();
}
```

The constructor assumes there is a class attribute defined as follows:

```
sessionFactory = null;
```

The `buildSessionFactory()` method builds a factory based on the specifics of the mapping documents processed by the `Configuration` object. Once the `SessionFactory` object has been created, the `Configuration` object can be discarded.

Creating Persistent Classes

Now that we have a `SessionFactory`, we need to do two things: create a new CD object and create a session for when we want to save the object to storage. Creating the CD object is easy. If you look back at our skeleton code, you'll see that we create a new CD object when the Add button is clicked. As far as Hibernate is concerned, this is all we need to do to create a new object. However, once the object has been created, we should save it to permanent storage. We do this by obtaining a `Session` object and using the `save()` method:

```
button.addActionListener(new ActionListener() {
   public void actionPerformed(ActionEvent ae) {
```

```
            CD cd = new CD(artistField.getText(),
                   titleField.getText(),
                   new Date(),
                Double.parseDouble(costField.getText()));
            listModel.addCD(cd);

            try {
        Session session = sessionFactory.openSession();
            session.save(cd);
        session.flush();
            session.close();
            } catch (Exception e) {
              e.printStackTrace();
            }

    IDLabel.setText("");
    titleField.setText("");
    artistField.setText("");
    costField.setText("");
        }
    });
```

The code for the Add button includes both application code and statements for the heart of Hibernate. First we instantiate a new CD object. Note that if you glanced at the value of the id attribute just after the CD object was created, it would have a default value of null. Remember when we created the mapping document, we told the system the unsaved value for our object was null. Hibernate will know that this object hasn't been persisted.

After the new CD object is added to the internal vector, we begin the Hibernate processing. The first step in persisting our CD object is to create a Session object. The Session object handles all the work involved in saving, updating, and loading objects from permanent storage. A Session should be invoked for a short time, to save or load an object. Generally, a Session object isn't created when the application is started and closed when the application exits; instead, it's created when needed and closed when a persistence operation has completed.

With this in mind, we create a Session object using the SessionFactory that was created when the application's constructor was called. One of the most important actions performed by the Session object is creating a connection to the database. The Session object includes a few methods to use when you're persisting an object to the database, including save(), saveOrUpdate(), and update(). The methods are differentiated based on the following criteria:

❏ **save():** An object hasn't been persisted before.

❏ **update():** An object has been persisted before.

❏ **saveOrUpdate():** The object might have been persisted before, but we don't know.

Since we just created a new CD object, clearly we want to use the save() method. To persist the new object, we call the save() method of the Session object, passing in the object that needs to be persisted. Hibernate checks the identifier in the new object and compares it against the unsaved value defined in the mapping component. We expect the value to be null, so the system will save the object to the database. Just before closing the session, we perform a flush on the session; the flush causes the system to automatically perform the Hibernate operation on the database instead of caching it. Finally, the session is closed, which ultimately closes the connection to the database.

We don't need to do anything else at this point in the code. We've created a new CD, added it to the list model for our GUI, and persisted the object to permanent storage. The last line in the addCD() method displays the ID assigned to the object by Hibernate. For our example code, the ID created is:

```
131073
```

As you add more CDs to the application, the identifier will change based on the generator specified in the mapping document:

```
mysql> select * from cd;
+--------+------------+----------------------+---------------------+-------+
| ID     | title      | artist               | purchasedate        | cost  |
+--------+------------+----------------------+---------------------+-------+
| 131073 | Rush       | Grace Under Pressure | 2004-04-03 00:00:00 |  9.99 |
| 131074 | Evanescence| Fallen               | 2004-04-03 00:00:00 | 13.84 |
| 163841 | Nickelback | The Long Road        | 2004-04-03 00:00:00 | 11.99 |
+--------+------------+----------------------+---------------------+-------+
3 rows in set (0.01 sec)
```

Updating Objects

The applications you'll build will do more than just create an object and be done with it. Sometimes the object will be updated with new information from either external processes or the user. You can change the information found in a CD object through our example application. If you click one of the CDs listed, the information for that CD appears in the text fields at the bottom of the application window. Figure 3.3 shows an example of this action.

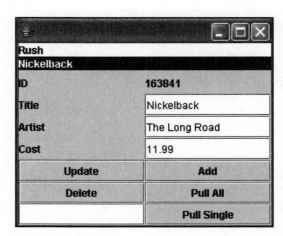

Figure 3.3

You can change each of the values displayed and then click the Update button. For the Update button, we've added an ActionListener through an anonymous inner class:

```
        button.addActionListener(new ActionListener() {
          public void actionPerformed(ActionEvent ae) {
            CD cd = (CD)listModel.getElementAt(selectedListIndex);

            cd.setTitle(titleField.getText());
            cd.setArtist(artistField.getText());
            cd.setCost((double)Double.parseDouble(costField.getText()));

        try {
            Session session = sessionFactory.openSession();
            session.update(cd);
            session.flush();
            session.close();
        } catch (Exception e) {}

        IDLabel.setText("");
        titleField.setText("");
        artistField.setText("");
        costField.setText("");
          }
        });
```

The first few lines of code obtain a reference to the CD object selected from the list and edited in the application text fields. Each attribute in the CD object is updated with the new value edited by the user. (This code would be the same with or without Hibernate.)

After the object has been updated in the application, we obtain a Session object from the SessionFactory and make a call to the update() method, passing in the CD object. We're using the update() method because we know the object has already been stored in the database (the save() method is used when the CD object is first created). If you need to verify this, you can include a couple of println() calls and output the identifier for the object before and after the update() call. The identifier is defined, and it doesn't change after the update.

The result of the update() method is an UPDATE SQL statement issued to the database using the identifier as an index to the table. After the object has been updated, the session is closed. The following information from our database shows that the price for the Nickelback CD has been updated:

```
mysql> select * from cd;
+--------+------------+---------------------+---------------------+-------+
| ID     | title      | artist              | purchasedate        | cost  |
+--------+------------+---------------------+---------------------+-------+
| 131073 | Rush       | Grace Under Pressure | 2004-04-03 00:00:00 |  9.99 |
| 163841 | Nickelback | The Long Road       | 2004-04-03 00:00:00 | 11.99 |
+--------+------------+---------------------+---------------------+-------+
2 rows in set (0.00 sec)

mysql> select * from cd;
+--------+------------+---------------------+---------------------+-------+
| ID     | title      | artist              | purchasedate        | cost  |
+--------+------------+---------------------+---------------------+-------+
| 131073 | Rush       | Grace Under Pressure | 2004-04-03 00:00:00 |  9.99 |
| 163841 | Nickelback | The Long Road       | 2004-04-03 00:00:00 | 11.5  |
+--------+------------+---------------------+---------------------+-------+
2 rows in set (0.00 sec)
```

Deleting Objects

When you delete an object, you normally remove the application's reference to the object; this eventually lets the Java garbage collector recover the memory space. However, with persisted objects, the idea of performing a delete has more meaning. We're no longer just talking about using the object but about removing the data from permanent storage.

In our example application, we can remove an object from our list of CDs. The code is as follows:

```
button.addActionListener(new ActionListener() {
    public void actionPerformed(ActionEvent ae) {
        CD cd = (CD)listModel.getElementAt(selectedListIndex);

        try {
Session session = sessionFactory.openSession();
            session.delete(cd);
    session.flush();
    session.close();
        } catch (Exception e) {}

        listModel.removeElement(selectedListIndex);

    }
});
```

The first part of this code should look familiar: We obtain a reference to the currently selected CD object from the list model. Once we have the reference, we obtain a session and call the delete() method, passing in the object we want to remove from permanent storage. As you'd expect, the Session object creates a connection to the database and issues a DELETE SQL command. As a result, the object is permanently removed from the database.

We also need to add a new method to our CDList model class. The method is

```
public void removeElement(int index) {
    v.removeElementAt(index);
}
```

This method handles removing the CD object from the list model and updating the list.

Loading Persistent Classes

In developing our example application, we've added code that lets us create a new CD record and put it in permanent storage. The object can be updated both in the application and in the database. If necessary, the object can be removed from the list of available CDs and permanently removed from the database. So, what's missing?

At this point, when we restart the application, it won't have any CDs to display. All the CDs are in the database but not in the application. To access the CDs in the database, we need to load them. There are two basic ways to load a persisted object from the database, and they differ based on whether you know the value of the identifier for each object. In this section, we'll explain how to load an object if you know the identifier; we'll discuss loading without the identifier in the next section.

We obtain an object from the database using the object's unique identifier with code like the following:

```
Session session = sessionFactory.openSessionO;
CD cd = new CDO;
session. load(cd, 45);
session.close();
```

Hibernate issues a SELECT to the appropriate database table to obtain the object corresponding to the provided identifier. In this case, the system attempts to pull a row where ID equals 45. If the database contains such a row, the fields of the provided CD object are filled, and the object can be used in the application as needed. If the object row can't be found, an exception is thrown.

If there is a chance the object row won't be found in the database, you can use an alternative method: get (). Here's some example code:

```
Session session = session Factory.openSession();
CD cd = session. get(CD.class. 45);
if (cd ==null) {
   cd = new CD("","" );


   session.save(cd, 45);
}
session.close();
```

In this code snippet, we attempt to get the object where the identifier is 45. If the row is found, the CD object is populated. If the row isn't found, the CD object is null. In this case, we create a new CD object, populate it with the appropriate values, and immediately save the object to permanent storage using the identifier value 45. Notice that in this code we use the save() method without specifying an identifier. For most applications, you'll allow the Hibernate system to generate the identifier. This is what occurs when you use the save(Object) method. In the previous snippet, we knew there was no object row with an ID value of 45, so we could safely save the object with a specific identifier.

Our example lets the user instantiate a specific CD object by entering the ID into the ID field and clicking the Pull Single button (Figure 3.4 shows an example).

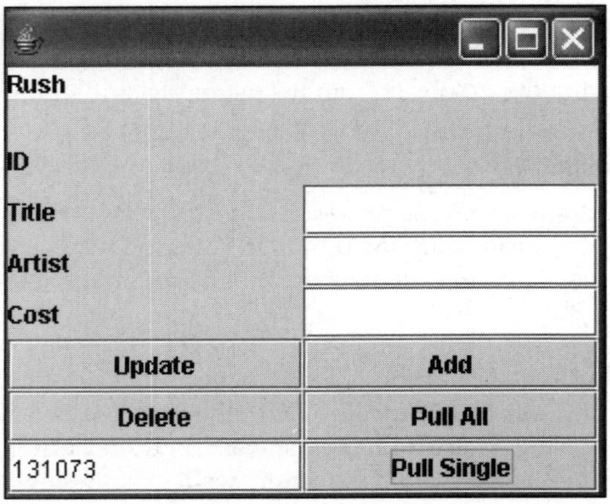

Figure 3.4

The code for the Pull Single button is as follows:

```
button.addActionListener(new ActionListener() {
  public void actionPerformed(ActionEvent ae) {
    int index = Integer.parseInt(IDField.getText());
    try {
      Session session = sessionFactory.openSession();
      CD cd = new CD();
      session.load(cd, new Integer(index));
      session.close();

      listModel.addCD(cd);
    } catch (Exception e) {
      JOptionPane.showMessageDialog(null,
              "No CD", "No CD with that ID", 0);
    }
  }
});
```

For the new button code, we obtain the value of the CD index for the user, convert it to an integer, and then attempt to load the object. If the load is successful, the object is added to the listModel for the list component and displayed to the user. Otherwise the user sees an error message.

Finding Data Objects

Our example application GUI also has a Pull All button that pulls all the objects from the cd database. Based on the code we've already written, pulling the objects from the database one at a time won't be efficient. In fact, how would we know when to stop pulling objects? Do we know that the identifier values will start at 1 and increment by 1?

Fortunately, Hibernate has a solution: We can do a query against the object table using Hibernate's query language or traditional SQL. We'll explore both of these options in more detail in Chapter 8, but we'll use them a little now. To find objects in the object table, Hibernate includes a method called find() in the Session object. The find() method accepts Hibernate Query Language (HQL).

Here's the code in the Pull All button:

```
button.addActionListener(new ActionListener() {
  public void actionPerformed(ActionEvent ae) {
    try {
      Session session = sessionFactory.openSession();
      java.util.List cds = session.find("from CD");
session.close();

      listModel.addCDs(cds);
    } catch (Exception e) {
      JOptionPane.showMessageDialog(null,
              "No CD", "problem pulling cds", 0);
    }
  }
});
```

We begin by obtaining the Session object. Next, we have the Session object execute the find() method using an HQL expression. The "from CD" tells Hibernate to pull all the object rows from the table CD. You can see the similarity to SQL, where the query would read SELECT * FROM CD. Since we don't pull individual columns from the object rows but instead pull the entire object, the SELECT * is redundant; it isn't used when formulating a query string with HQL.

The result of the find() method call is a list of CD objects. We pass this list to the list model object, and the CDs are displayed to the user. The find() method is a great way to obtain all the objects (or just a few) from a table, depending on the query. We'll look at additional queries in Chapter 8.

Exercising the Application

At this point, we've covered all the pieces of our example application. You can add new CDs, update them, and load them as needed, and all the information is kept permanently in the database. This example shows how to use Hibernate in a standalone application. We'll now turn our attention to the Web and create a Web form that lets the user view the same CD information remotely.

A Servlet-Based Hibernate Application

Imagine that the standalone application we created is being used in an office situation. Some employees need access when they're on the road, but the VPN isn't reliable. The solution is to build a Web application that can access the persisted CD objects. In this section, we'll show how to set up Tomcat and develop a servlet that interacts with Hibernate to provide full access.

Installing and Configuring Tomcat

The first step toward the remote application is to obtain and install Tomcat. We'll leave the particulars of this task to you; you can find Tomcat at http://jakarta.apache.org/tomcat/.

Once you've installed Tomcat, you need to set up the JARs. First, if you previously set up the classpath to use the standalone application, you should remove the JAR from the global classpath to prevent Java from choosing the wrong JAR files. Now take the JDBC driver for your database and place in the global classpath so Tomcat can find it.

Next, let's create a directory structure for our new application so we'll have a place to put the other Hibernate JARs. In the /webapps directory of the Tomcat installation, add the following structure:

```
/cdviewer/WEB-INF/lib
/cdviewer/WEB-INF/classes
```

Place all the JARs from the /lib directory of the Hibernate installation into the /webapps/cdviewer/ WEB-INF/lib directory. With all the libraries installed, you can set up Tomcat to access the database.

Setting Up Tomcat Database Access

When you're using an application server like Tomcat, it's customary to build a resource declaration for JDBC database connections in Tomcat's configuration file: /conf/server.xml. Add the following XML to the server.xml file:

```
<Context path="/cdviewer" docBase="/cdviewer">
  <Resource name="jdbc/pullcd"
scope="Shareable"
type="javax.sgl.DataSource"/>
<ResourceParams name="jdbc/pullcd">
<parameter>
<name>factory</name>
<value>
      org.apache.commons.dbcp.BasicDataSourceFactory
</value>
</parameter>

<parameter>
<name>url</name>
<value>jdbc:mysgl://localhost/CD</value>
</parameter>
<parameter>
<name>driverClassName</name>
<value>com.mysql.jdbc.Driver</value>
</parameter>
<parameter>
<name>username</name>
<value></value>
</parameter>
<parameter>
<name>password</name>
<value></value>
</parameter>
<parameter>
<name>maxWait</name>
<value>2000</value>
</parameter>
<parameter>
<name>maxIdle</name>
<value>250</value>
</parameter>
<parameter>
<name>maxActive</name>
<value>5</value>
</parameter>
</ResourceParams>
</Context>
```

This <Context> element was pulled directly from one of the test machines for this application. You'll need to make the appropriate changes for the url and driverClassName entries based on the database you're using. Be sure to update the username and password values and set to the appropriate values. From the entries in this XML file, you can see that Tomcat handles connection pooling for the application through the Jakarta Commons DBCP connection pool class.

With Tomcat's database JNDI information configured, you can move to the hibernate.cfg.xml or hibernate.properties file, depending on which one you chose to use for configuration. If you're using a MySQL database, the configuration file might appear as follows:

```xml
<?xml version="1.0" encoding="utf-8"?>
<!DOCTYPE hibernate-configuration PUBLIC
"-//Hibernate/Hibernate Configuration DTD//EN"
 http://hibernate.sourceforge.net/hibernate-configuration-2.0.dtd>

<hibernate-configuration>
<session-factory>
<property name="connection.datasource">
java:comp/env/jdbc/pullcd
</property>

<property name="show_sql">false</property>
<property name="dialect">
net.sf.hibernate.dialect.MySQLDialect
</property>

<mapping resource="CD.hbm.xml"/>
</session-factory>
</hibernate-configuration>
```

You'll notice that instead of specifying the URL, driver, and other database information in the configuration file, we reference the JNDI parameter java:comp/env/jdbc/pullcd.

We've also added an appropriate web.xml file to the /cdviewer directory. The web.xml file looks like this:

```xml
<?xml version="1.0" encoding="ISO-8859-1"?>
<!DOCTYPE web-app    PUBLIC
"-//Sun Microsystems, Inc.//DTD Web Application 2.3//EN"
"http://java.sun.com/dtd/web-app_2_3.dtd">
<web-app>
  <servlet>
    <servlet-name>viewer</servlet-name>
    <servlet-class>CDViewer</servlet-class>
  </servlet>

  <servlet-mapping>
    <url-pattern>/viewer</url-pattern>
    <servlet-name>viewer</servlet-name>
  </servlet-mapping>
</web-app>
```

Adding Hibernate to the Web Application

To build our Web application, the first step is to copy the CD class created earlier into the /classes directory. Since we'll be accessing the same CD objects in our Web application, we need the CD class to save the objects.

Next, we need to write the servlet. You might decide to dive right in, but you need to know a few key things before writing the servlet code.

There should only be a single `SessionFactory` for your application. This means you won't be able to put the `SessionFactory` instantiation code in your servlet and instantiate it every time the servlet executes. When a `Session` object is created from the `SessionFactory`, it's designed to handle the work at hand and then be closed. Thus, it isn't thread-safe. In fact, when you're working with servlets, you should have a specific session for each threaded instance of the servlet. You can handle this situation a few different ways.

You can create a static class to hold the `SessionFactory` and use a `ThreadLocal` attribute for the session variable; this is the option provided in the Hibernate reference manual. Alternatively, you can use the `init()` method in a servlet. For example, consider Listing 3.4, which contains the traditional skeleton code for a servlet.

```
import java.io.*;
import javax.servlet.*;
import javax.servlet.http.*;
import javax.naming.*;

public class CD Viewer extends HttpServlet {
  private SessionFactory sessionFactory;

  public void init(ServletConfig config) throws ServletException {
    super.init(config);

    sessionFactory = new Configuration().
                        addClass(CD.class).buildSessionFactoryO;
  }

  public void doGet(HttpServletRequest request,
                            HttpServletResponse response)
        throws IOException, ServletException {

    response.setContentType("text/html");
    PrintWriter out = response. getWriter();
  }

  public void doGet(HttpServletRequest request,
                            HttpServletREsponse response)
        throws IOException, ServletException {
    doGet(request, response);
  }
}
```

Listing 3.4

We've added an `init()` method to the servlet code to handle the creation of the `SessionFactory` object. The application server calls the `init()` method when the servlet is first prepared to handle incoming requests. For the execution lifecycle of the servlet, we're assured the `init()` method will be called once. We'll instantiate specific `Session` objects in the servlet code, since a session isn't thread-safe; thus we should obtain the session, use it, and close it like any other database connection. Using this methodology, we can be sure the session is closed before the response is returned to the user.

Interface Page

To let outside employees access the CD objects in permanent storage, we need to have an appropriate Web page. Figure 3.5 shows an example of the page presented to users.

Figure 3.5

Figure 3.6 shows an example of the output when the user clicks Pull All CDs.

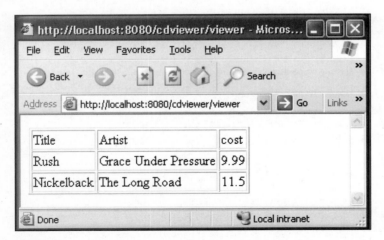

Figure 3.6

The initial Web page is created using HTML; it's shown in Listing 3.5.

```html
<HTML>
<HEAD>
<TITLE>CD VIEWER</TITLE>

<BODY>

<form action="/cdviewer/viewer" method="post">

<input type="submit" name="submit" value="Pull All CDs">

</form>
</BODY>

</BODY>
</HTML>
```

Listing 3.5

The most important aspect of the HTML code is found in the <form> tag, where the action specifies the /cdviewer/viewer servlet. When the use clicks the Submit button, the servlet we'll build next is executed.

Writing a Servlet to Use Hibernate

To produce the output shown in Figures 3.5 and 3.6, we need to begin writing the code in our servlet. Listing 3.6 shows the servlet code.

```java
import java.io.*;
import javax.servlet.*;
import javax.servlet.http.*;
import javax.naming.*;
import java.util.*;

import net.sf.hibernate.*;
import net.sf.hibernate.cfg.*;

public class CDViewer extends HttpServlet {
  private SessionFactory sessionFactory;

  public void init(ServletConfig config) throws ServletException {
    super.init(config);

    try {
      sessionFactory = new Configuration().
                 addClass(CD.class).buildSessionFactory();
    } catch(Exception e) {
      e.printStackTrace();
    }
  }
```

```java
private void displayAll(PrintWriter out, Session session) {
  try {
    out.println("<html>");
    out.println("<table border='1'>");
    out.println("<tr><td>Title</td><td>Artist</td><td>cost</td></tr>");
    List cds = session.find("from CD");

    Iterator iter = cds.iterator();
    while (iter.hasNext()) {
      CD cd = (CD)iter.next();
      out.println("<tr><td>");
      out.println(cd.getTitle());
      out.println("</td><td>");
      out.println(cd.getArtist());
      out.println("</td><td>");
      out.println(cd.getCost());
      out.println("</td></tr>");
    }
  } catch(Exception e) {}

  out.println("</table>");
  out.println("</html>");
}

public void doGet(HttpServletRequest request,
                  HttpServletResponse response)
                    throws IOException, ServletException {

  response.setContentType("text/html");
  PrintWriter out = response. getWriter();

    Session session = null;

    try {
      session = sessionFactory.openSession();

      String action = request.getParameter("submit");
      if (action.equals("Pull All CDs")) {
        displayAll(out, session);
      } else {
        out.println("Bad Input");
      }

      session.flush();
      session.close();

    } catch (Exception e) {
      e.printStackTrace();
    }
}

public void doPost(HttpServletRequest request,
                  HttpServletResponse response)
```

```
                              throws IOException, ServletException {
        doGet(request, response);
    }
}
```

Listing 3.6

When the servlet is first executed, the application server executes the init() method that instantiates the SessionFactory object. Since the init() method is executed only once, we get a single SessionFactory object.

Next, the code in the doGet() method executes. This code begins by setting up for HTML output. Next, the tags for an HTML table are output along with the values for the table heading. Finally, we begin to access the data needed for the rows of the table. All the CD objects are obtained through the find() method of the Session object that was instantiated before we began to output the HTML.

We haven't done anything special to access the CD objects; we've obtained a Session object, pulled the objects, and displayed their attributes for the user. Note that we close the Session object before exiting the servlet. It's important to close the Session object before the servlet is finished; otherwise a database connection could be left in a precarious position.

Summary

When you're using Java to develop either standalone applications or Web servlets, persisting the object to permanent storage should be as easy as using Java itself. As you saw from the two applications in this chapter, adding persistence to Java with Hibernate is a simple process. We've touched on how you can use Hibernate in Java applications; we'll expand on these topics in the coming chapters.

Database Connecting and Schema Generation

The most fundamental component of Hibernate is the database: The system must have a place to persist Java objects. For the most part, setting up the database is a simple process as long as it's supported by Hibernate and a JDBC driver is available. The current list of supported databases is as follows:

- ❏ DB2
- ❏ FrontBase
- ❏ HypersonicSQL
- ❏ Informix
- ❏ Ingres
- ❏ InterBase
- ❏ Mckoi SQL
- ❏ Microsoft SQL Server
- ❏ MySQL
- ❏ Oracle
- ❏ Oracle 9
- ❏ PointBase
- ❏ PostgreSQL
- ❏ Progress
- ❏ SAP DB
- ❏ Sybase
- ❏ Sybase Anywhere

Hibernate supports these databases because a specific Dialect class implemented for the database provides a listing of the available column types as well as SQL replacement strings. The SQL replacement strings are used when the database doesn't support or deviates from generic SQL. A common situation, as you'll see in Chapter 5, involves Identity columns: Some databases support them, and some don't. The databases that do support Identity columns obtain the identity value in different ways, so there's a specific dialect for each.

In addition to the dialect, a database must have a JDBC driver so Hibernate (written in Java) can access the system. JDBC drivers are available for most major databases either from the database developers or from a third party.

Because the database is so important to Hibernate, we'll devote this chapter to discussing the finer points of using databases in Hibernate. Topics include Hibernate versus user-supplied connections, connection pooling, using multiple databases, and working with database schemas and the mapping document.

Overview of Hibernate JDBC Properties

As we touched on in Chapter 3, configuring Hibernate consists of two parts: database setup and mappings. You configure the system using one of two files: hibernate.properties or hibernate.cfg.xml. Both of these files can be used to configure the database to be used in persisting Java objects. However, only hibernate.cfg.xml can be used to specify the mappings in the current application. For this reason, most people use the hibernate.cfg.xml file for the entire Hibernate configuration. (It wouldn't be surprising to see the hibernate.properties file deprecated in the future.)

Regardless of how you configure the database, you can use a couple dozen properties to set up the system properly. In this section, we'll list and describe the available properties; they affect either the database connection or the JDBC driver.

hibernate.connection.driverclass

All JDBC drivers are implemented in a Java class, and you must specify that class with this property. You should provide the fully qualified class. For example, the MySQL JDBC driver provided by MySQL is com.mysgl.jdbc.Driver. The JAR file containing the JDBC driver needs to be in the application's global classpath.

You can find a listing of available JDBC drivers at http://servlet.java.sun.com/products/jdbc/drivers/index.html. Figure 4.1 shows an example of what you'll see at that page.

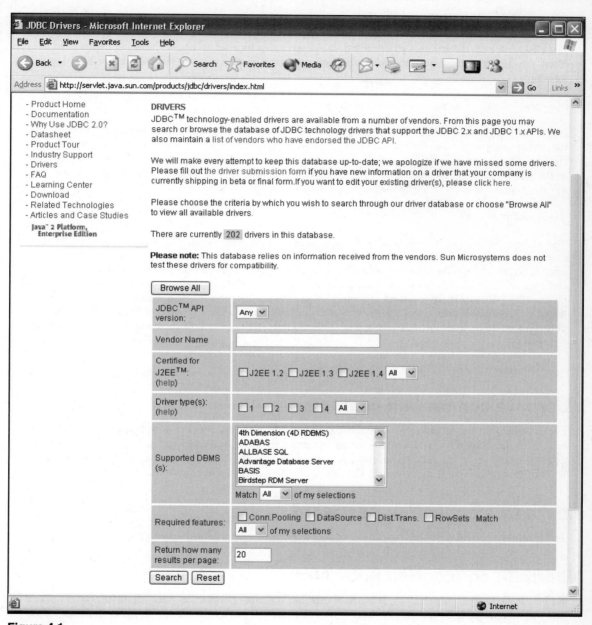

Figure 4.1

hibernate.connection.url

The URL property determines where the database server is located and how to connect with it. In many cases, you'll also supply the database to be accessed once a connection is established. The URL has this format:

```
<protocol>:<subprotocol>:<subname>
```

Just as with any other URL, a protocol is involved in the transfer of information between the client and the server associated with the URL. In this case, the `<protocol>` is jdbc. The `<subprotocol>` is associated with the driver to be used for the connection; this value depends on the JDBC driver being used. In the case of MySQL, the `<subprotocol>` is mysql. Finally, the `<subname>` is a string of connection information for the source of the database. The format of the `<subname>` is:

```
//<host>[: <port>] [/<database>]
```

The `<host>` part of the subname is an IP address or domain name of the database server where a connection should be attempted. In addition to the IP address of the server, the port to use must also be known. When the database server software is installed, it has a default port value. If you haven't changed the port on which the database software listens for connections, you don't need to specify a port on the URL string. If you have changed the port value, append it along with a colon to the end of the IP address or domain name specified. Finally, if you want to use a particular database on the server, you can specify by appending it along with a slash character (/) to the URL string. Here's an example string:

```
jdbc:mysgl:// 192.168.1.21/products
```

hibernate.connection.username

Each application that attaches to a database should have a unique username and password associated with it. You can specify the username using this property. A unique username is important because in most database systems, you can specify the permissions available to that username; doing so adds a level of protection when you're running multiple databases on a single system.

hibernate.connection.password

This property specifies the password to be used with the corresponding username.

hibernate.connection.pool_size

As you'll see later in this chapter, Hibernate includes a simple connection pool for development use. You can use this property to specify the total number of connections to initially establish with the database server.

hibernate.connection.datasource

If you're working with a JNDI connection, the datasource string is specified in this property.

hibernate.jndi.url

The URL, as defined earlier, is specified in this property when a JNDI source is being used and a URL isn't specified with the datasource. This property is optional.

hibernate.jndi.class

This property specifies the name of the JNDI class that implements `InitialContextFactory`. This property is optional.

hibernate.dialect

This property specifies the name of the dialect to use for the database connection. We outline the dialect functionality in detail shortly.

hibernate.default_schema

In SQL query strings, you provide the table or tables from which information should be pulled without specifying schema or tablespaces. If you want your table to be fully qualified, use the `default_schema` property to specify the schema or tablespace Hibernate can generate with its SQL calls to the database server.

hibernate.Session_factory_name

If you're using JNDI and wish to provide a binding between the `SessionFactory` class and a JNDI namespace, use the session `factory_name` property. Provide the name, and Hibernate uses the values specified in hibernate.jndi and hibernate.jndi.class to create the initial context.

hibernate.use_outer_join

As you may have noticed in your SQL experience, an outer join can provide a performance increase because fewer database accesses are needed. By default, the `use_outer_join` property is true. If you don't want to allow outer joins, set the property to `false`. For each relationship in an application's set of tables, the outer join attribute determines the correct action.

hibernate.max_fetch_depth

The database server can create an outer join using a graph, where the nodes in the graph are tables and the edge and relationships are join conditions. Using the graph, a depth-first search can be performed to determine which tables will be part of the outer join. You can limit the depth of the search using this property. Note that outer joins may reduce the communication with the database, but a lot of work goes into building the outer join SQL string correctly.

hibernate.jdbc.fetch_size

When JDBC performs a query against the database, some rows are returned based on the fetch size for the JDBC driver being used. You can use this property to set the total number of rows retrieved by each JDBC fetch from the database. If you have a SELECT query, and JDBC returns one row at a time to populate a ResultSet object, the performance will be bad. Much of the literature on this subject suggests that an appropriate number of rows for JDBC to pull is 10.

hibernate.jdbc.batch_size

If you're using a JDBC driver that supports JDBC 2.x, you may be able to use batch updates. In a batch update, the JDBC driver groups some number of INSERT, UPDATE, DELETE commands together and sends them as a batch to the server, thus reducing the communication time between the client and the database. If the batch_size property is set to a nonzero value, Hibernate attempts to use batch updates. The value used in the batch_size property dictates the total number of updates to use per batch.

hibernate.jdbc.use_scrollable_resultset

Another update to JDBC is the concept of a scrollable resultset. If you're using a user-supplied connection and wish to have Hibernate use scrollable resultsets, set this property to true. If you're using a Hibernate-created connection to the database server, this property has no effect.

hibernate.jdbc.use_streams_for_binary

Although there is debate about how much binary data should be stored in a database, many times you'll need to put large quantities into a row. Instead of directly copying the binary data to the query string, JDBC lets you use a stream. To make JDBC use streams for binary data, set this property to true.

hibernate.cglib.use_reflection_optimizer

By default, Hibernate uses CGLIB; but you can defeat this behavior by setting this property to false. If the property has a false value, Hibernate uses runtime reflection instead.

hibernate.jndi.<property>

You can provide extraneous properties for JNDI's InitialContextFactory class using this property. The property and its value are passed to the JNDI factory.

hibernate.connection.isolation

It can be argued that data integrity is the most important topic when discussing databases. When a database is confronted with multiple clients making updates and queries (a situation called *database concurrency*), data may be changed and returned to clients with wrong values. There are three primary concurrency issues:

- ❑ **Dirty reads:** One transaction changes a value in the database. But before the first transaction is committed (or possibly before it's even rolled back), another transaction reads the new data. If the first transaction performs a rollback of the transaction, the second transaction will have a bad value.

- ❑ **Nonrepeatable reads:** One transaction performs a read on a row in the database. A second transaction updates the row and commits the transaction. The first transaction performs a reread on the row and gets modified data (or no data, if the first transaction deleted the row).

- ❑ **Phantom inserts:** One transaction performs a read on a number of rows with a specific query. Another transaction inserts new rows that match the specific query. If the first transaction performs another read with the query, it will receive a different resultset.

You can solve all three of these situations using the isolation levels associated with a database and ANSI SQL; the following table shows the isolation level needed. Note that not all databases support all four isolation levels. And, as the level increases, so does the time needed by the database to handle the issues.

Level	Name	Dirty Read	Nonrepeatable Read	Phantom Insert
1	Read Uncommitted	May occur	May occur	May occur
2	Read Committed	Can't occur	May occur	May occur
4	Repeatable Read	Can't occur	Can't occur	May occur
8	Serializable	Can't occur	Can't occur	Can't occur

hibernate.connection.provider_class

If you're using a JDBC driver that includes a custom `ConnectionProvider` class, you need to specify that class in this property.

hibernate.transaction.factory_class

This property names a specific `TransactionFactory` class to be used with Hibernate. We discuss transactions in more detail in Chapter 10.

jta.UserTransaction

This property specifies the JNDI name for the `JTATransactionFactory`.

hibernate.show_sql

If you want a log of the SQL commands generated by Hibernate to the underlying database, set the show_sql property to true. The result will be the SQL query strings output to the console window. For example, here's some of the output from our example application in Chapter 3:

```
Hibernate: select cd0_.ID as ID, cd0_.title as title,
    cd0_.artist as artist, cd0_.purchasedate as purchase4_,
    cd0_.cost as cost from cd cd0_
```

```
Hibernate: insert into cd (title, artist, purchasedate, cost, ID)
       values (?, ?, ?, ?, ?)

Hibernate: update cd set title=?, artist=?, purchasedate=?,
       cost=? where ID=?

Hibernate: delete from cd where ID=?
```

Query Substitutions

When you're using the Hibernate Query Language (HQL), Hibernate formulates appropriate SQL statements according to the dialect specified for the database. If you need to help Hibernate with a query, you can specify substitutions in the Hibernate configuration file. The property for the substitutions is hibernate.query.substitutions. For example:

```
hibernate.query.substitutions true "Y" false "N"
```

SQL Dialect Determination

When you're defining a database connection, you can add the `hibernate.dialect` property to the properties or configuration file. This property tells Hibernate the type of database the current connection is associated with. Although it isn't a required property, hibernate.dialect allows Hibernate to customize itself and the SQL queries for a specific database.

Some of the information Hibernate customizes is based on the `Dialect` parent class. The `Dialect` class and subsequent child classes include methods like `public String getIdentitySelectString()`; this function specifies the SQL needed to obtain an `Identity` value from the database. If you look at the code for `MySQLDialect` and `SybaseDialect` (used for both Sybase and Microsoft SQL Server), found in the Hibernate installation at \src\net\sf\hibernate\dialect, you'll see that it's different. In `MySQLDialect`, the `String` returned for this method is:

```
return "SELECT LAST_INSERT_ID()";
```

For Sybase/Microsoft SQL Server, the String returned is:

```
return "select @@identity";
```

Another important part of the `Dialect` class and its child classes is a method called `registerColumnType()`. In each of the `Dialect` classes, this method tells Hibernate the column types available as well as the names appropriate in Hibernate. For example, here is the constructor for the `MySQLDialect` class:

```
public MySQLDialect() {
super();
registerColumnType( Types.BIT, "BIT" );
registerColumnType( Types.BIGINT, "BIGINT" );
registerColumnType( Types.SMALLINT, "SMALLINT" );
```

```
registerColumnType( Types.TINYINT, "TINYINT" );
registerColumnType( Types.INTEGER, "INTEGER" );
registerColumnType( Types.CHAR, "CHAR(1)" );
registerColumnType( Types.VARCHAR, "LONGTEXT" );
registerColumnType( Types.VARCHAR, 16777215, "MEDIUMTEXT" );
registerColumnType( Types.VARCHAR, 65535, "TEXT" );
registerColumnType( Types.VARCHAR, 255, "VARCHAR($1)" );
registerColumnType( Types.FLOAT, "FLOAT" );
registerColumnType( Types.DOUBLE, "DOUBLE PRECISION" );
registerColumnType( Types.DATE, "DATE" );
registerColumnType( Types.TIME, "TIME" );
registerColumnType( Types.TIMESTAMP, "DATETIME" );
registerColumnType( Types.VARBINARY, "LONGBLOB" );
registerColumnType( Types.VARBINARY, 16777215, "MEDIUMBLOB" );
registerColumnType( Types.VARBINARY, 65535, "BLOB" );
registerColumnType( Types.VARBINARY, 255, "VARCHAR($1) BINARY" );
registerColumnType( Types.NUMERIC, "NUMERIC(19, $1)" );
registerColumnType( Types.BLOB, "LONGBLOB" );
registerColumnType( Types.BLOB, 16777215, "MEDIUMBLOB" );
registerColumnType( Types.BLOB, 65535, "BLOB" );
registerColumnType( Types.CLOB, "LONGTEXT" );
registerColumnType( Types.CLOB, 16777215, "MEDIUMTEXT" );
registerColumnType( Types.CLOB, 65535, "TEXT" );

getDefaultProperties().
            setProperty(Environment.USE_OUTER_JOIN, "true");
getDefaultProperties().
            setProperty(Environment.STATEMENT_BATCH_SIZE,
DEFAULT_BATCH_SIZE);
}
```

This list includes each of the MySQL column types Hibernate can deal with during the mapping of a Java object to the database. If any problems occur during the configuration of a mapping between an object and a specific database, you can consult the specific dialect and see if you've specified the column correctly; you can also check the constraints for the column.

Another important issue for the dialect and its use is the <generator> element. Some of the ID generator functions can only be used with specific databases. For example, the identity generator can be used with DB2, MySQL, Microsoft SQL Sever, Sybase, and HypersonicSQL. It's a good idea to specify the database dialect, because Hibernate will be able to determine if the generator is valid.

The following dialects are available in the current version of Hibernate:

- ❑ net.sf.hibernate.dialect.DB2Dialect
- ❑ net.sf.hibernate.dialect.FirebirdDialect
- ❑ net.sf.hibernate.dialect.FrontBaseDialect
- ❑ net.sf.hibernate.dialect.HSQLDialect
- ❑ net.sf.hibernate.dialect.InformixDialect
- ❑ net.sf.hibernate.dialect.Informix9Dialect

- ❏   net.sf.hibernate.dialect.IngresDialect

- ❏   net.sf.hibernate.dialect.InterbaseDialect

- ❏   net.sf.hibernate.dialect.MckoiDialect

- ❏   net.sf.hibernate.dialect.MySQLDialect

- ❏   net.sf.hibernate.dialect.Oracle9Dialect

- ❏   net.sf.hibernate.dialect.OracleDialect

- ❏   net.sf.hibernate.dialect.PointbaseDialect

- ❏   net.sf.hibernate.dialect.PostreSQLDialect

- ❏   net.sf.hibernate.dialect.ProgressDialect

- ❏   net.sf.hibernate.dialect.SQPDBDialect

- ❏   net.sf.hibernate.dialect.SQLServerDialect

- ❏   net.sf.hibernate.dialect.Sybase11_9_2Dialect

- ❏   net.sf.hibernate.dialect.SybaseAnywhereDialect

- ❏   net.sf.hibernate.dialect.SybaseDialect

If your database isn't listed here, then it isn't directly supported by Hibernate. If you want to experiment with your own database, you can use the net.sf.hibernate.dialect.GenericDialect class, which defines several column types and no specific SQL statements.

Using Connection Pooling

When Hibernate needs to persist a Java object, it must have access to the database. There are two ways to provide access to the database from a connection standpoint: Either the connection has been previously opened and the current connection can be used, or a new connection can be created.

First, let's consider opening a single connection for every database interaction. If you need to open a single connection, the system must locate the server's IP address by resolving the domain for the server (although the IP address may have been given already in the database URL). The system contacts the database server and does some handshaking between the server and the client, including exchanging username and password information. After the handshake communication is finished, the client (Hibernate, in this case) can begin using the database system. When Hibernate is finished, it closes the connection. On average, using a database server on the local LAN running MySQL, a connection can be made in 2.5 to 3.0 seconds. That's quite a bit of time—especially if you need to handle many transactions.

Now, consider a situation where a connection was made when the application started. In this scenario, the application doesn't need to go through the entire handshake process; it can just use the connection. Of course, in a multithreaded or Web situation, there must be a monitor on the connection so that only one thread uses the connection at a time. With synchronization out of the picture, you can quickly obtain and use the previously established connection.

We need an easy-to-use mechanism between these two scenarios that can handle multiple threads and provide fast access to a database connection. The solution is called a *connection pool*: a mechanism that establishes an optimum number of connections to the database when the application is first executed. These connections are maintained in a data structure like a queue, commonly called a *pool*. When the application needs to communicate with the database, it contacts the mechanism and asks for a connection. If a connection is available in the pool, the mechanism returns it to the application. If the application is multithreaded, each thread can ask for a connection; the mechanism returns a unique connection to the database. Since the connections were established with the database server at application start, there is no need to spend time handshaking with the server: The application can immediately begin using the connection. When the application or thread is finished with the connection, the connection is returned to the pool and queued up for use at another time. The connection pool optimizes the number of connections available in the pool by closing some when they've been inactive for a long time and reestablishing connections as needed.

The ability to quickly access a database connection increases Hibernate's performance. Providing a connection pool for an application that uses Hibernate requires very little work; Hibernate includes a simple connection pool that you can use in a development setting. If you need performance- or production-level connection pooling, Hibernate provides three options: C3P0, Apache DBCP, and Proxool. Each of these packages provides a seamless connection pool with a JDBC driver and can be used in a standalone or JNDI situation. In the rest of this section, we'll describe the connection pools, discuss their strengths and weaknesses, and explain how to configure them for use with Hibernate.

Using Hibernate's Built-in Pooling

The first connection pool we'll discuss is the one that comes with Hibernate. This connection pool provides *N* number of connections to the database and uses them as needed. The number of initial connections to the database is specified by the following property:

```
hibernate.connection.pool_size
```

For development purposes, you'll probably use a number like 5 or 10 for this value, since little performance testing should occur with the application and the database during development.

When you move to the end of your development phase (and especially in your test phase), you should use a production-level connection pool package.

Using C3P0

C3P0 is an open-source project available at http://sourceforge.net/projects/c3p0/. A library for it is supplied with Hibernate in the /lib directory. As of this writing, version 0.8.3 of C3P0 is supplied with Hibernate, and version 0.8.4.5 is on the sourceforge.net Web site. For our purposes, we'll use the version supplied with Hibernate.

The first step in using C3P0 is to put its JAR file (c3p0-0.8.3.jar) in the classpath of the client machine where the application and Hibernate are executing. Next you need to tell Hibernate that you want to use the C3P0 connection pool. You do so by using one or more of the C3P0 properties in the configuration file. The available properties are as follows:

❑ **hibernate.c3p0.acquire_increment:** The total number of connections C3P0 will create when all connections in the pool have been used. The default value for this property is 3.

❏ **hibernate.c3p0.idle_test_period:** The time before a connection in the pool is validated against the database. The default value for this property is 0. A value greater than 0 causes C3P0 to test all unused connections every *X* seconds; where *X* is the value for this property.

❏ **hibernate.c3p0.max_size:** The maximum number of connections in the pool. The default value is 15.

❏ **hibernate.c3p0.max_statements:** The maximum size of the C3P0 statement cache. The default value is 0, meaning the cache is turned off.

❏ **hibernate.c3p0.min_size:** The minimum number of connections in the pool. The default value is 3.

❏ **hibernate.c3p0.timeout:** The maximum time a connection will be kept in the pool without being used. The default value is 0, meaning that all connections in the pool won't expire.

Once you put a property in the configuration file, Hibernate will begin using the C3P0 connection pool.

Using Apache DBCP

One of the projects in Apache's Jakarta Commons package is DBCP; this open-source package supports connection pooling for JDBC connections to a database. You can obtain it at http://jakarta.apache.org/commons/dbcp/. Downloads for the package are available in both zip and tar format. Once you've downloaded the package, uncompress it; a single JAR file called commons-dbcp-1.1jar will be added to the root directory. Place this file in your classpath so Hibernate will be able to locate it.

Again, if you want Hibernate to use DBCP for database connection pooling, you must set one of the following properties:

❏ **hibernate.dbcp.maxActive:** The total number of connections that can be used from the pool at any given time. The default is 8.

❏ **hibernate.dbcp.maxIdle:** The maximum number of connections that can remain in the pool at any given time. The default is 8.

❏ **hibernate.dbcp.maxWait:** The number of milliseconds a connection can be used from the pool. The default value of -1 means indefinitely.

❏ **hibernate.dbcp.testOnBorrow:** Specifies whether a connection is validated before being taken out of the pool. The default is true.

❏ **hibernate.dbcp.testOnReturn:** Determines whether a connection is validated upon return from the application. The default is false.

❏ **hibernate.dbcp.validationQuery:** The query string used to validate the connection.

Using Proxool

The final connection pool package available for Hibernate is called Proxool. You can obtain it from http://proxool.sourceforge.net/ in both zip and tar formats. Once you've downloaded it, locate the /lib directory, which contains a single JAR called proxool-0.8.3.jar; place this file in your classpath. To activate Proxool in Hibernate, set one of the following properties.

❏ **hibernate.proxool.existing_pool:** Determines whether the current pool should be configured from an existing pool. Possible values are true and false.

❏ **hibernate.proxool.pool_alias:** An alias to use with the Proxool pool. You need to use this value, because it will be referenced in the existing pool, properties, or XML file.

❏ **hibernate.proxool.properties:** The path to the proxool.properties property file.

❏ **hibernate.proxool.xml:** The path to the proxool.xml property file.

JDBC Database Connection

As an experiment in how Hibernate uses a database connection, remove or rename the file hibernate .properties, or remove the database elements in hibernate.cfg.xml (if you're using it), in either the stand-alone or servlet application written in the previous chapter. When you've changed the file, execute the application and attempt an action that accesses the database, such as showing all the CDs. Since our error handling displays the stack trace, you should get a fairly large trace dump on the console window where you launched the application. If you're using the servlet example, you might need to open a log file to see the errors.

At the top of the stack trace, you should see a message like "user needs to supply connection". This error tells you that Hibernate was unable to obtain a connection to any database for more than just a wrong password. But, in fact, no hibernate.properties file or database elements are available to the application; as such, the application doesn't know how to connect to a database. This is obviously bad, because Hibernate accomplishes most of its work through a database.

The point is, the developers of Hibernate developed the system in a manner that lets you handle a variety of design situations. In this case, Hibernate can either create its own connection to the underlying database or use a connection that's already in place. The examples in Chapter 3 show you how to use Hibernate connections. If you're developing an application from scratch, you'll probably let Hibernate handle the connection; there aren't any glaring issues with this type of situation, and there are no performance problems. So, why does Hibernate allow user-based connections? Primarily to handle legacy issues.

Given the constant evolution of software systems, you won't always be able to rewrite your code. In some cases, you must refactor live systems. The application has already been written, and database connections are established and available, so why not use them? You need to consider a couple of issues. The first is connection pooling, which we discuss in detail later in this chapter. If you're using a previously established connection, you'll bypass any connection pooling defined in Hibernate. Second is the issue of transactions. When you're using a user-based connection, you can use Hibernate's transaction system (discussed in Chapter 10), or the application can handle transactions through the underlying database using JDBC transactions or through JTA.

Here's an example of the code for using a previously established connection:

```
try {
   Class.forName("com.mysql.jdbc.Driver").newInstance();
```

```
    Connection connection = DriverManager.
        getConnection("jdbc:mysql://localhost/accounts");

    SessionFactory sessionFactory = Configuration.buildSessionFactory();

    Session session = sessionFactory.openSession(connection);
} catch (Exception e) {}
```

Using More Than One Database Server

During the development of a complex application, you may need to connect to more than one database server. This requirement typically arises when you're developing a replacement application for a legacy system. The legacy applications has its own database servers, and you may have another one. The new application code must communicate effectively with all the servers. Of course, you want to keep everything working with Hibernate, so you must have a way to communicate with multiple database servers.

Fortunately, this isn't a big deal to Hibernate, because it's all in the configuration file(s). When you instantiate a Configuration object, the system will by default attempt to find either a hibernate.properties or a hibernate.cfg.xml file in the application's root directory. One of these files contains the database configuration information needed to contact a database server. To communicate with a second database server, you need another configuration file.

For example, let's say we have a MySQL database and a Microsoft SQL Server database that will be used in an application. We'll let the hibernate.cfg.xml file contain the connection and mapping information for the MySQL database. For the Microsoft SQL Server database, we'll build a configuration file called sqlserver.cfg.xml, which looks like this:

```
<?xml version="I.0" ?>
<!DOCTYPE hibernate-configuration PUBLIC
"-//Hibernate/Hibernate Configuration DTD 2.0//EN"
http://hibernate.sourceforge.net/hibernate-configuration-2.0.dtd>

<hibernate-configuration>

<session-factory>

<property name="connection.driver class">
com.microsoft.jdbc.Driver</property> <property name="connection.url">
  jdbc.Microsoft://localhost/products</property> <property
name="username">sa</property>
<property name="password">sa</property>

</session-factory>

</hibernate-configuration>
```

We now have two different configuration files for our databases. Next we create an application that uses the files. Here's an example piece of code:

```
Configuration configuration = new ConfigurationO.addClass(CD.class);
SessionFactory mysqlSession = configuration.buildSessionFactoryQ;
```

```
configuration = new Configuration().
configure("sglserver.cfg.xml").addClass(CD.class);
SessionFactory sqlserverSession = configuration.buildSessionFactoryO;
```

This code handles two different database servers. Remember, the key to using Hibernate is the `SessionFactory` built from a `Configuration` object. The first part of the code creates a `Configuration` object and a `SessionFactory` object using the technique from Chapter 3. This code uses the default hibernate.cfg.xml file for its connection and mapping information.

The trick to using multiple databases comes into play in the second part of the code. Here we build a new `Configuration` object, but we use a method called `configure()` to bring in the SQL Server configuration file. The `configure()` method accepts an XML document that adheres to the hibernate-configuration-2.0.dtd file. Our configuration file is designed to work with hibernate-configuration-2.0.dtd; as such, the `Configuration` object gladly accepts it as a valid configuration file. Subsequently, the object ignores the default configuration file.

Building the Mapping Document

As you learned in Chapter 3, Hibernate can't persist Java objects without a mapping document for each class that tells Hibernate how to store the information it finds in the objects. In this section, we'll lay out the full mapping document and all the elements available to you. Then, in Chapter 5, we'll show how to map from real Java classes to your database.

The format of the mapping document is:

```
<?xml version=" 1.0" ?>
<!DOCTYPE hibernate-mapping PUBLIC
"-//Hibernate/Hibernate Mapping DTD 2.0//EN"
http://hibernate.sourceforge.net/hibernate-mapping-2.0.dtd>

<hibernate-mapping>
</hibernate-mapping>
```

To give you a good handle on this document, we'll run through all the available elements and how they affect Hibernate when you're mapping Java objects to a database. Some of these mappings are complicated, such as relationships and collections. We'll touch on the elements here so you have a good idea how they work, and then we'll devote chapters to more detailed discussions of the topic.

<hibernate-mapping> Element

The `<hibernate-mapping>` element is the root element for the mapping document. Its format is:

```
<hibernate-mapping
schema="name" [optional]
default-cascade="none I save-update" [optional - default none]
auto-import="true | false" [optional - default true]
package="name" [optional]
/>
```

This element has four available attributes:

- **package:** Fully qualifies unqualified classes in the mapping document. As you'll see later, the `<class>` element includes a name attribute that relates to the name of the Java class being mapped. You can choose to use the `package` attribute and fully qualify the Java class. For example:

```
<hibernate-mapping package="com.company">
<class name="Account"/>
</hibernate-mapping>
```

  In this example, we're mapping the `class com.company.Account`. If we didn't add the `package` attribute to the element, the system would expect to map a class called `Account`.

- **schema:** Like the `package` attribute, fully qualifies the table used in this particular mapping. If you add the `schema` attribute, the supplied namespace is appended to the table. For example:

```
<hibernate-mapping schema="products">
<class table="CD"> </class>
</hibernate-mapping>
```

  In this example, the fully qualified database/table is `products.CD`. The `schema` attribute is optional.

- **default-cascade:** Specifies how actions that are performed on a parent are cascaded to a child. The parent/child relationship is created through one-to-one, many-to-many, or one-to-many mappings. (We'll discuss these mappings in detail in Chapter 5.) For each mapping, you can specify a `cascade` attribute; if you don't, the `default-cascade` attribute's value is used.

  There are four possible values for `default-cascade`: `all`, `none`, `save-update`, and `delete`. (The meanings are self-explanatory.) If you don't specify a `default-cascade` attribute, the default is none (no cascading of options occurs).

- **auto-import:** If set to `false`, doesn't allow unqualified class names in query strings. When you build queries using HQL, you specify the class name provided in the `<class name= "">` element. The default is `true`; this attribute is optional.

<class> Element

Since we're building a mapping file between a class and a database table, we need to specify the class this mapping document references. The `<class>` element is designed for this purpose:

```
<class
name="name"
table="table" discriminator-value="value" [optional]
mutable="true | false" [optional - defaults to true]
schema="name" [optional]
proxy="interface" [optional]
dynamic-update="true | false" [optional - defaults false]
dynamic-insert="true | false" [optional - defaults false]
select-before-update="true | false" [optional - defaults false]
polymorphism="implicit | explicit" [optional - defaults implicit]
where="string" [optional]
```

```
persister="class" [optional]
batch-size="#" [optional -defaults 1]
optimistic-lock=""none | version | dirty | all"
    [optional - defaults version]
lazy="true | false" [optional]
/ >
```

The element includes 15 attributes:

❑ **name:** Specifies the name of the Java class this mapping document is designed to represent. Hibernate expects a fully qualified class name in this attribute if you don't include the package attribute in the `<hibernate-mapping>` element.

❑ **table:** Specifies the name of the table to be used when persisting the Java object for this mapping.

❑ **discriminator-value:** Distinguishes between different classes in an inheritance hierarchy. The default is the class name.

❑ **mutable:** Signals whether an object persisted by Hibernate can be updated/deleted. If this attribute is set to `false`, then the object is essentially read-only. The object can be persisted by Hibernate but never updated or deleted from permanent storage.

❑ **schema:** Overrides the value for the schema attribute specified in the `<hibernate-mapping>` root element (if such a value has been set).

❑ **proxy:** Tells Hibernate whether to use lazy initialization for objects of this mapping type. Lazy initialization lets Hibernate stub out the data in an object. If you're using lazy initialization, you create objects and load them just in the example application in Chapter 3; but Hibernate won't populate (make a call to the database for data) until the object is used. The proxy attribute requires that you provide a class to be used for the lazy initialization; this should normally be the class name used in the name attribute.

❑ **dynamic-update:** If `true`, then when Hibernate updates a row in the database for a class attribute that has changed, it generates an `UPDATE SQL` statement at runtime during the `update()` method call on the session and only include the columns of the table that have been updated. This is an optional attribute; the default is `false`.

❑ **dynamic-insert:** The same as dynamic-update in principle; but Hibernate dynamically creates an `INSERT SQL` statement with only those columns that aren't null values. This is an optional attribute; the default is `false`.

❑ **select-before-update:** If `true`, Hibernate performs a select to determine if an update is needed (by default, Hibernate won't perform an update unless the object has been modified). This is an optional attribute; the default is `false`.

❑ **polymorphism:** Specifies whether to use implicit or explicit polymorphism. As you'll see later in this chapter and in Chapter 6, you can define mappings that specify a hierarchy of objects based on inheritance between Java classes. When a query, usually a `find()`, is executed, Hibernate returns instances of this class when the class name or superclass is named in the query; this is implicit polymorphism. In explicit polymorphism, Hibernate returns instances of the class and its mapped subclasses. This attribute is optional; the default is `implicit`.

❑ **where:** Specifies a global where clause for this class mapping.

❑   **persister:** Specifies the class that will be used to persist this particular class to the database.

❑   **batch-size:** Specifies the total number of instances to pull when Hibernate pulls instances from the database for this class. This attribute is optional; the default is 1.

❑   **optimistic-lock:** Specifies the type of locking used for the row, table, or database when updates need to occur in the database. The values available are:

   ❑   **none:** No optimistic locking.

   ❑   **version:** Checks the version or timestamp column.

   ❑   **dirty:** Checks those columns that have been changed.

   ❑   **all:** Checks all columns.

   This attribute is optional; the default is `version`.

❑   **lazy:** If true, assumes the proxy attribute is included and the proxy class name is the same as the mapped class name.

<id> Element

When you're mapping a Java class to a database table, an ID is required. The ID is the primary key column of the database table used to persist a specific Java object. In addition, you should define a setter/getter pair of methods, with the Java class for the ID following the JavaBean style. The <id> element specifies information about the ID column. The format of the <id> element is as follows:

```
<id
name="name"  [optional]
type="type"  [optional]
column="column"  [optional - defaults to name value]
unsaved-value="ant | none | null | value" [optional - defaults to null]
access="field | property | class" [optional - defaults to property]

<generator/>
/>

<generator class="class"
<param/>
/>
```

The <id> element has five elements and one subelement:

❑   **name:** Specifies the name of the ID. This is an optional attribute; it's included in many mappings with a value of `"id"`.

❑   **type:** Specifies the Hibernate type for the ID. If a type isn't provided, Hibernate uses reflection to try to determine the type. For a list of the Hibernate types, see the later description of the <property> element.

❑   **column:** Specifies the name of the database column. This is an optional attribute; if it isn't specified, the database column name is the value in the name attribute. You need to include either the name or the column attribute in the <id> element.

- ❏ **unsaved-value:** Determines whether a newly instantiated object needs to be persisted (as mentioned in Chapter 3). This is an optional attribute; the default is `null`.

- ❏ **access:** Specifies the way Hibernate accesses an object's attribute using traditional JavaBean style setter/getter methods. The values available for the access attribute are `field`, `property`, or a class name. If you want Hibernate to use reflection and access the Java object's attribute directly, use the value `"field"`. To build your own class for accessing the attribute of an object, use as a value a class that implements `net.sf.hibernate.property.PropertyAccessor`.

- ❏ **<generator> subelement:** Defined in the following section, "<generator> Element."

<generator> Element

When Hibernate needs to add a new row to the database for a Java object that has been instantiated, it must fill the ID column with a unique value in order to uniquely identify this persisted object. The `<generator>` subelement of `<id>` specifies how the unique identifier should be created. The element contains a single attribute called `class`, which specifies the class used to generate the ID. If parameters are passed to the class, you use the `<param name= "">value</param>` element. Hibernate includes a number of built-in generators that we'll discuss next.

Increment

The increment generator is probably the most familiar creator of IDs. Each time the generator needs to generate an ID, it performs a select on the current database, determines the current largest ID value, and increment to the next value. Note that if you're in a multithreaded environment this generator isn't safe, because two or more threads could obtain the same ID value and cause an exception on the database server.

This generator supports all databases. It has no parameters. The possible column types are short, int, and long. Here's some example output:

```
+---------+------------+---------------------+---------------------+------+
| ID      | title      | artist              | purchasedate        | cost |
+---------+------------+---------------------+---------------------+------+
| 1       | Rush       | Grace Under Pressure | 2004-04-03 00:00:00 | 9.99 |
| 2       | Nickelback | The Long Road       | 2004-04-03 00:00:00 | 11.5 |
+---------+------------+---------------------+---------------------+------+
2 rows in set (0.23 sec)
```

Identity

If the database has an identity column associated with it, Hibernate can take advantage of the column to indicate when an object hasn't been added to the database. Supported databases include DB2, MySQL, Microsoft SQL Server, Sybase, and HypersonicSQL. Be sure you use this generator with the correct database. It has no parameters. The possible column types are short, int, and long.

Sequence

If the database has a sequence column associated with it, Hibernate can take advantage of the column to determine if the object has been added to the database. Supported databases include DB2, PostgreSQL,

Oracle, SAP DB, McKoi, and InterBase. Be sure you use this generator with the correct database. It has no parameters. The possible column types are short, int, and long.

Hilo

The hilo generator generates unique IDs for a database table. The IDs won't necessarily be sequential. This generator must have access to a secondary table that Hibernate uses to determine a seed value for the generator. The default table is hibernate-unique-key, and the required column is next-value. You need to insert one row in the table, as you saw in Chapter 3. Here's a possible table-creation query:

```
create table hibernate-unique-key next-value int
);

insert into hibernate-unique-key values(100);
```

The hilo generator must be used with a Hibernate-generated connection. It shouldn't be used with JTA connections, according to the Hibernate reference manual.

You can provide three parameters to this generator to change the table name, column name, and maximum low value. For example:

```
<generator class="hilo">
<param name="table">hilo</param>
<param name="column">next</param>
<param name="max to">500</param>
</generator>
```

The possible column types are short, int, and long. Here's some example output:

```
mysql> select * from cd;
+--------+------------+----------------------+---------------------+------+
| ID     | title      | artist               | purchasedate        | cost |
+--------+------------+----------------------+---------------------+------+
| 131073 | Rush       | Grace Under Pressure | 2004-04-03 00:00:00 | 9.99 |
| 163841 | Nickelback | The Long Road        | 2004-04-03 00:00:00 | 11.5 |
+--------+------------+----------------------+---------------------+------+
2 rows in set (0.23 sec)
```

seqhilo

With the seqhilo generator, Hibernate combines the sequence and hilo generators. Supported databases include DB2, PostgreSQL, Oracle, SAP DB, McKoi, and InterBase. Be sure you use this generator with the correct database.

You can provide a sequence name with a value of hi_value or low_value depending on the sequence start. You can also provide a max_lo name with the starting value of the sequence. The possible column types are short, int, and long.

Uuid.hex

This generator creates a unique strings based on appending the following values: the machine's IP address, the startup time of the current JVM, the current time, and the counter value. It supports all databases and has no parameters. The possible column types are string, varchar, and text. Here's some example output:

```
mysql> select * from cd;
+-------------------+-------+-------------------+--------------------+----+
| ID                | title | artist            | purchasedate       |cost|
+-------------------+-------+-------------------+--------------------+----+
| 40288195fbd50bb...| Rush  | Grace Under Pressure| 2004-04-10 00:00:00 |9.99|
+-------------------+-------+-------------------+--------------------+----+
1 row in set (0.00 sec)
```

Uuid.string

This generator is like Uuid.hex, but the result is a string 16 characters long. It supports all databases except PostgreSQL, and it has no parameters. Possible column types are string, varchar, and text. In the following example output, the Marcus Roberts CD is using `uuid.string`:

```
mysql> select * from cd;
+--------------+---------------+---------------------+--------------------+------+
| ID           | title         | artist              | purchasedate       |cost  |
+--------------+---------------+---------------------+--------------------+------+
| 40288195f... | Rush          |Grace Under Pressure |2004-04-10 00:00:00 |9.99  |
| _¿_§{U?_?... |Marcus Roberts |the truth is spoken  |2004-04-10 00:00:00 |13.88 |
+--------------+---------------+---------------------+--------------------+------+
2 rows in set (0.00 sec)
```

Native

The native generator picks identity, sequence, or hilo, depending on the database.

Assigned

If you need to assign the identifier yourself in your application, then use the assigned generator. You set the identifier using the set<identifier> method of the Java class. The application assumes the responsibility of making sure the id value is unique; otherwise, you'll probably get a database insert exception.

This generator supports all databases. Some level of application validation may need to occur. It has no parameters. The column types are application dependent.

Foreign

When a class is part of a one-to-one relationship, it can be helpful to have a common ID between the objects. By specifying the foreign generator, you make the class use the ID of the other class. This generator supports all databases and has no parameters.

<composite-id> Element

You can use Hibernate in many different coding situations, including accessing legacy databases. One of the situations you'll encounter when using a legacy database is a composite ID. A composite ID is made up of numerous individual values to form a whole. Hibernate can handle the composite ID using the <composite-id> element. (Chapter 5 includes a complete example that uses this element.)

The format of the <composite-id> is as follows:

```
<composite-id
[name=-string"]
[class="string"]
[unsaved-value=" [any] [none]"]
access=" [field] [property] [component class name]"

<key-property/>
<key-many-to-one/>
</composite-id>
```

There are two versions of <composite-id>. The first doesn't include the name, class, and unsaved-value, but uses the <key-property> and <key-many-to-one> elements to map the ID. For example:

```
<composite-id>
<key-property name="ss"/>
<key-property name="account"/>
</composite-id>
```

In another situation, we'll use a component class to represent the composite ID (as demonstrated in Chapter 5).

The element's attributes are as follows:

❑   **name:** Attribute in the component class for the identifier class; the component class for the composite ID.

❑   **unsaved-value:** Default value for the attribute specifying whether the newly instantiated object should be persisted to the database.

❑   **access:** Possible values: field, property, or a class name. Hibernate accesses an object's attribute using traditional JavaBean style setter/getter methods. This form of access is specified using the property value for the access attribute. If you want Hibernate to use reflection and access the Java object's attribute directly, use the value "field". If you want to build your own class to access the attribute of an object, use as a value a class that implements net.sf.hibernate.property.PropertyAccessor.

<discriminator> Element

If you're mapping a hierarchy of objects with Hibernate, you have the option of using a mapping of a table-per-class-hierarchy scheme, as we discussed in Chapter 1. For the single table to work properly, a column is used to distinguish one class from another in the hierarchy. The <discriminator> element identifies the column in the table. The format of the element is:

```
<discriminator
column="column" [optional - defaults to class]
type="type" [optional - defaults to string]
force="true | false" [optional - defaults to false]
/>
```

The element has three attributes:

- ❑ **column:** Specifies the name of the column in the table to use as the discriminator column. This attribute is optional; the default is `class`.

- ❑ **type:** Specifies the type of the discriminator column. The default is `string` if the attribute isn't included. The valid types are string, character, integer, byte, short, Boolean, yes no, and true false. Some of these types will only handle two different classes.

- ❑ **force:** Determines whether Hibernate uses discriminator values when retrieving all instances of a root class. This attribute is optional; the default is `false`.

Notice that the element doesn't specify the value to place in the column. The value is determined with the `discriminator-value` attribute, which we discuss in the sections on the `<class>` element and the `<subclass>` element.

<version> Element

If data in your object needs to be versioned as opposed to having a unique ID, you can use the `<version>` or `<timestamp>` (discussed next) element to keep the data up to date. There is no generator for the version or timestamp. The application must handle populating the Java `class` attribute with the correct value. You'll see an example of using a version/timestamp column in Chapter 5.

The format of the element is

```
<version
column="column" [optional - defaults to name value]
name="name"
type="type" [optional - defaults to integer]
access="field | property | class" [optional - defaults to property]
unsaved-value="null | negative | undefined"
   [optional - defaults to undefined]
/>
```

The `<version>` element has five attributes:

- ❑ **column:** Specifies the name of the column to use for the identifier. This attribute is optional; the default is the value of the `name` attribute.

- ❑ **name:** Specifies the name of the Java class's `version` attribute.

- ❑ **type:** Specifies the type of the `version` attribute. This attribute is optional; the default is `int`.

- ❑ **access:** See the description in our discussion of the `<id>` element.

- ❑ **unsaved-value:** Indicates whether the object is newly instantiated. Hibernate uses the value to determine whether the object needs to be persisted. This is an optional attribute; the default is `undefined`.

<timestamp> Element

The `<timestamp>` element is used in much the same manner as the `<version>` element. It has five attributes:

- ❑ **column:** Specifies the name of the column to use for the identifier. This attribute is optional; the default is the value of the `name` attribute.

- ❑ **name:** Specifies the name of the Java class's `timestamp` attribute.

- ❑ **type:** Specifies the type of the `timestamp` attribute. This attribute is optional; the default is `int`.

- ❑ **access:** See the description in our discussion of the `<id>` element.

- ❑ **unsaved-value:** Indicates whether the object is newly instantiated. Hibernate uses the value to determine whether the object needs to be persisted. This is an optional attribute; the default is `undefined`.

<property> Element

For each of the attributes in your Java class that should be saved to the database when an object is persisted, you need to define a `<property>` element in the mapping document. The persisted attributes must be JavaBean compliant. The format of the element is as follows:

```
<property
name="name"
column="column" [optional - defaults to name value]
type="type" [optional]
update="true | false" [optional - defaults to true]
insert="true | false" [optional - defaults to true]
formula="sql string" [optional]
access="field | property | class" [optional - defaults to property]
/>
```

The `<property>` element has seven possible attributes:

- ❑ **name:** Specifies the name of the property. Note that the first character of the name must be lowercase.

- ❑ **column:** Specifies the name of the column in the database table where this attribute should be saved. This is an optional attribute; Hibernate uses a column name equal to the value of the name attribute if it's missing.

- ❑ **type:** Specifies the name of the Hibernate type for this mapped Java attribute. If the type isn't specified, Hibernate attempts to determine the type using reflection. The reflection process isn't as easy as you'd expect, but it's based on a set of rules. The Hibernate types available as well as the rules are as follows:

    - ❑ First attempt: to reflect to a basic type:

Java Class Attribute Type	Hibernate Type	Possible SQL Type— Vendor Specific
Integer, int, long short	integer, long, short	Appropriate SQL type
char	character	char
java.math.BigDecimal	big_decimal	NUMERIC, NUMBER
float, double	float, double	float, double
java.lang.Boolean, boolean	boolean, yes_no, true_false	boolean, int
java.lang.string	string	varchar, varchar2
Very long strings	text	CLOB, TEXT
java.util.Date	date, time, timestamp	DATE, TIME, TIMESTAMP
java.util.Calendar	calendar, calendar_date	TIMESTAMP, DATE
java.util.Locale	locale	varchar, varchar2
java.util.TimeZone	timezone	varchar, varchar2
java.util.Currency	Currency	varchar, varchar2
java.sql.Clob	clob	CLOB
java.sql.Blob	blob	BLOB
Java object	serializable	binary field
byte array	binary	binary field
java.lang.Class	class	varchar, varchar2

❑ Second attempt: a Java basic type of `int`, `float`, `char`, `java.lang.String`, `java.util.Date`, `java.lang.Integer`, or `java.sql.Clob`.

❑ Third attempt: an enum based on the class `PersistentEnum` (see Chapter 5 for an example of `PersistentEnum`).

❑ Fourth attempt: a serializable Java class.

❑ Fifth attempt: a custom type match.

❑ **update:** Determines whether this specific attribute should be used in an UPDATE SQL query. This is an optional attribute; the default is `true`.

❑ **insert:** Determines whether this specific attribute should be used in an INSERT SQL query. This is an optional attribute; the default is `true`. Note that if both the `update` and `insert` attributes are `false`, then you must assume this attribute will be filled by another attribute or possibly by a database trigger.

❑ **formula:** Contains a SQL query string that is executed to produce a value for this mapping value. (See Chapter 5 for an example.)

❑ **access:** See the description in our discussion of the `<id>` element.

As you begin mapping Java classes to the database, sometimes you'll need to quote the identifier being stored in the database. You can perform this quoting in the <property> element. For example:

```
<property name="value" column="' ValueColumnName"'/>
```

In this mapping, the value of the Java class attribute is mapped to the ValueColumnName of the database. The value is put inside the appropriate quotation characters, based on the current dialect being used.

Relationship Elements

One of Java's most widely used features is associating one class with another through composition or some other means. For example, you might have an employee object that contains a social security object. You need to be able to map these relationships in the database. In this section, we aren't talking about situations where you have a vector of another class as an attribute.

Hibernate's mapping document uses two relationship elements: <many-to-one> and <one-to-one>. In this section, we'll describe the mappings; we'll look at them in detail in Chapter 5.

<many-to-one> Element

In the course of object mapping, in some situations many objects associate to a single object. This is a many-to-one relationship; you use the <many-to-one> element for the mapping. The format of the element is as follows:

```
<many-to-one
name="string"
column="string"
class="string"
cascade=- [all] [none] [save-update] [delete]"
outer-join="[true] [false] [auto]"
update=" [true] [false]"
insert="[true] [false]"
property-ref="associated class"     [optional]
access=" [field] [property] [component class name]"
/>
```

This element has the following attributes:

❑   **name:** Specifies the name of the Java attribute associated with the relationship.

❑   **column:** Specifies the name of the database column for the mapping. This is an optional attribute; the default is the name attribute value.

❑   **class:** Specifies the name of the class that is part of the relationship. Hibernate uses reflection if this attribute isn't included.

❑   **cascade:** See the description in our discussion of the <hibernate-mapping> element.

❑ **outer-join:** Determines whether an outer join should be used when pulling this object from the database row. This attribute is optional; the default is `auto`. The possible values include `auto`, `true`, and `false`. If the value is `auto`, an outer join is used if the related class isn't using a proxy.

❑ **update:** Determines whether this specific attribute should be used in an `UPDATE SQL` query. This is an optional attribute; the default is `true`.

❑ **insert:** Determines whether this specific attribute should be used in an `INSERT SQL` query. This is an optional attribute; the default is `true`. Note that if both the `update` and `insert` attributes are `false`, then you must assume this attribute will be filled by another attribute or possibly by a database trigger.

❑ **property-ref:** In most relationships, the related class's primary key is stored in this mapped column. In some databases, the relationship from the primary class to the related class isn't based on the primary key but on some other column. Since Hibernate attempts to use the identifier of the related class, you need to specify the exact column to use. The `property-ref` attribute specifies the exact column. (You'll see an example in Chapter 5.)

❑ **access:** See the description in our discussion of the `<id>` element.

<one-to-one> Element

In the course of object mapping, in some situations one object is associated with a single object. This is a one-to-one relationship; you use the `<one-to-one>` element for the mapping. The format of the element is as follows:

```
<one-to-one
name="name"
class="class"
cascade=" [all] [none] [save-update] [delete]"
   [optional - default none] constrained=" [true] [false]"
outer-join=" [true] [false] [auto]"
property-ref="property other than primary key of mapped table"
   [optional] access=" [field] [property] [component class name]"
/>
```

This element has the following attributes:

❑ **name:** Specifies the name of the Java attribute associated with the relationship.

❑ **class:** Specifies the name of the class that is part of the relationship. Hibernate uses reflection if this attribute isn't included.

❑ **cascade:** See the description in our discussion of the `<hibernate-mapping>` element.

❑ **outer-join:** Determines whether an outer join should be used when pulling this object from the database row. This attribute is optional; the default is `auto`. The possible values include `auto`, `true`, and `false`. If the value is `auto`, an outer join is used if the related class isn't using a proxy.

❑ **constrained:** Determines that a foreign key constraint exists with the primary key of the mapped table.

❑ **property-ref:** In most relationships, the related class's primary key is stored in this mapped column. In some databases, the relationship from the primary class to the related class isn't based on the primary key but on some other column. Since Hibernate attempts to use the identifier of the related class, you need to specify the exact column to use. The `property-ref` attribute specifies the exact column. (You'll see an example in Chapter 5.)

❑   **access:** See the description in our discussion of the `<id>` element.

<component> Element

The `<component>` element is designed to allow a property to be saved in the current object's mapping from another class. The format of the element is:

```
<component
name="name"
class="class"
update="true | false" [optional - defaults to true]
insert="true | false" [optional - defaults to true]
access="field | property | class"   [optional - defaults to property]

<property/>
<many-to-one/>
/>
```

This element has the following attributes:

❑   **name:** Specifies the name of the property to map.

❑   **class:** Specifies the child class where the named property appears.

❑   **update:** Determines whether this specific attribute should be used in an UPDATE SQL query. This is an optional attribute; the default is `true`.

❑   **insert:** Determines whether this specific attribute should be used in an INSERT SQL query. This is an optional attribute; the default is `true`. Note that if both the update and insert attributes are `false`, then you must assume this attribute is filled by another attribute or possibly by a database trigger.

❑   **access:** See the description in our discussion of the `<id>` element.

For all the properties in the child class that need to be mapped, you need to include `<property>` elements. You can also add appropriate relationships to the `<component>` element.

<subclass> Element

When an inheritance relationship is defined for your Java classes, the hierarchy needs to be defined. Since Hibernate recommends the table-per-class-hierarchy mapping, you should define all subclasses with the `<subclass>` element. Subclass definitions include attributes as well as the properties that have been added to this specific subclass.

The format of the element is as follows:

```
<subclass
name="name"
```

```
discriminator-value="value" [optional - defaults to name value]
proxy="interface" [optional]
lazy="true ( false" [optional]
dynamic-update="true | false" [optional - defaults to false]
dynamic-insert="true | false" [optional - defaults to false]

<property/>
/>
```

This element has the following attributes:

❑ **name:** Specifies the name of the Java class this mapping document is designed to represent. Hibernate expects a fully qualified class name in this attribute if you don't have the package attribute in the `<hibernate-mapping>` element.

❑ **discriminator-value:** Specifies the value used to distinguish between different classes in an inheritance hierarchy. The default is the class name.

❑ **proxy:** Tells Hibernate whether to use lazy initialization for objects of this mapping type. Lazy initialization allows Hibernate to basically stub out the data in an object. If you're using lazy initialization, you create objects and load them just as in the example application in Chapter 3, but Hibernate won't populate or make a call to the database for data until the object is used. The proxy attribute requires you to provide a class that is used for the lazy initialization; this should normally be the class name used in the name attribute.

❑ **dynamic-update:** If `true`, then when Hibernate updates a row in the database for a class attribute that has changed, it generates an `UPDATE SQL` statement at runtime during the `update()` method call on the session and only include the columns of the table that have been updated. This is an optional attribute; the default is `false`.

❑ **dynamic-insert:** The same as dynamic-update in principle; but Hibernate dynamically creates an `INSERT SQL` statement with only those columns that aren't null values. This is an optional attribute; the default is `false`.

Once the attributes have been defined for the subclass, you need to define all the new attributes that should be persisted. Use the `<property>` element to define each attribute.

<joined-subclass> Element

If you don't want to use the recommended inheritance mapping, you can choose the `table-per-subclass` mapping. Each subclass must have its own `<joined-subclass>` element. You include all the usual elements like `<property>`, `<key>`, and so on for this subclass.

The format of the element is as follows:

```
<joined-subclass
name="name"
proxy="interface" [optional]
lazy="true | false" [optional]
dynamic-update="true | false" [optional - defaults to false]
dynamic-insert="true | false" [optional - defaults to false]
```

```
<key/>
<property/>
/>
```

This element has the following attributes:

- ❑ **name:** Specifies the name of the Java class this mapping document is designed to represent. Hibernate expects a fully qualified class name in this attribute if you don't have the package attribute in the `<hibernate-mapping>` element.

- ❑ **proxy:** Tells Hibernate whether to use lazy initialization for objects of this mapping type. Lazy initialization allows Hibernate to basically stub out the data in an object. If you're using lazy initialization, you create your objects and load them as you saw in the example application in Chapter 3, but Hibernate won't populate or make a call to the database for data until the object is used. The proxy attribute requires you to provide a class that is used for the lazy initialization; this should normally be the class name used in the name attribute.

- ❑ **dynamic-update:** If true, then when Hibernate updates a row in the database for a class attribute that has changed, it generates an UPDATE SQL statement at runtime during the update() method call on the session and only include the columns of the table that have been updated. This is an optional attribute; the default is false.

- ❑ **dynamic-insert:** The same as dynamic-update in principle; but Hibernate dynamically creates an INSERT SQL statement with only those columns that aren't null values. This is an optional attribute; the default is false.

Collection Elements

If you're using Java collections of the type Map, Set, SortedMap, SortedSet, List, Collection, and arrays, Hibernate can persist them for you like other Java objects. This is such an important topics that we devote Chapter 6 to it. We'll cover the elements needed to handle the collections here, and then we'll present numerous examples in Chapter 6. For all the collections that can be mapped, there are appropriate elements: `<map>`, `<set>`, `<list>`, `<array>`, and `<primitive-array>`.

The format of the elements is:

```
<map | list | bag
name="name"
table="table" [optional - defaults to name value]
schema="name" [optional]
lazy="true | false" [optional - defaults to false]
inverse="true | false" [optional - defaults to false]
cascade="all | none | save-update | delete | all-delete-orphan"
  [optional - defaults to none"
sort="unsorted I natural I class" [optional]
order-by="name asc | desc" [optional]
where="sql where string" [optional]
outer join="true ( false I auto" [optional]
batch-size=="#" [optional -defaults to 1]
access="field I property I class" [optional - defaults to property]
```

```
<key/>
<index/>
<element/>
/>
```

These elements have the following attributes available:

- ❑   **name:** Specifies the name of the property.

- ❑   **table:** Specifies the name of the table where the collection should be saved.

- ❑   **schema:** Specifies the schema to be used with this collection mapping. This value overrides the global schema value, if any.

- ❑   **lazy:** Determines whether lazy initialization should be used. Possible values include `true` or `false`. The default is `false` if the attribute doesn't appear in the element. Arrays can't use lazy initialization.

- ❑   **cascade:** See the description in our discussion of the `<hibernate-mapping>` element.

- ❑   **sort:** Specifies the sort attribute used to determine how a collection should be sorted. The values available are `unsorted`, `natural`, and a class name based on `ComparatorClass`.

- ❑   **inverse:** If `true`, specifies that a collection is part of a bidirectional relationship, as discussed in Chapter 7. This is an optional attribute; the default is `false`.

- ❑   **order-by:** If you're using JDK 1.4, specifies one or more columns that can be used to determine the iteration order of the collection. The `attribute` value is the name of the column followed by `[asc] [desc]`, depending on the required order. This is an optional attribute.

- ❑   **where:** Allows a `SQL WHERE` clause to be added to the Hibernate query when the collection is persisted or loaded.

- ❑   **outer-join:** Determines whether an outer join is used during the object loading. The possible values are `true`, `false`, and `auto`.

- ❑   **batch-size:** Specifies the total number of instances to pull when Hibernate pulls instances from the database for this class. This attribute is optional; the default is 1.

- ❑   **access:** See the description in our discussion of the `<id>` element.

<key> Element

Since a collection is owned by a class, you use the `<key>` element to indicate the property of the class. The format is:

```
<key
column="column"
/>
```

This element has a single attribute: `column`, which specifies the foreign key column.

<index> Element

If the collection is indexed like a list or map, you need to use the `<index>` subelement. The format of the element is:

```
<index
column="column"
type="class"    [optional]
/>
```

The attributes are as follows:

- ❑ **column:** The column for the index values of the collection. This is a required attribute.

- ❑ **type:** The type of the index. This is an optional attribute; the default is `integer`.

If a map is being used, the index might be a class. In this case, you use the `<index-many-to-many>` subelement with two attributes:

- ❑ **column:** The column for the index values of the collection. This is a required attribute.

- ❑ **class:** The class used as the index.

<element> Element

If the collection only includes values, you need to specify the `<element>` subelement. The format of the element is:

```
<element
column="column"
type="type"
/>
```

It has two attributes:

- ❑ **column:** The column for the element values.

- ❑ **type:** The type of the element values.

Summary

This chapter has been filled information about the mapping document. Our goal has been to provide a reference for all the details you may encounter when you're mapping a Java object to a database table. In the next chapter, we'll put this knowledge to good use as we begin the process of mapping example Java objects to our database system.

5

Creating Persistent Classes

In the previous chapter, we spent considerable time discussing the databases available for use with Hibernate as well as the makeup of the mapping document. The mapping document is where you'll spend the vast majority of your time during the development of the object persistence plan. In this chapter as well as the next two, we'll bridge the gap between the database and your Java classes: We'll illustrate how to create mapping documents and database tables for countless Java classes. We encourage you to read the next three chapters carefully so you have a solid understanding of how to map your Java classes in an efficient manner.

Creating Persistent Java Classes

The entire work of Hibernate is encapsulated in its ability to take the values from Java class attributes and persist them to a database table. As you saw in the Chapter 4, the mapping document is key in determining how Hibernate pulls the values from the classes. Unless Hibernate is changed from its default behavior, it uses reflection to determine how to access the attributes of the Java class. As a developer of the Java class, it's your responsibility to create the class in a consistent manner.

You need to follow some simple guidelines when developing Java classes:

❑ Hibernate will only persist attributes specified in the mapping document; therefore you can include in your class as many temporary attributes as needed. If the temporary attributes aren't persisted, their values will be lost when the object is loaded from permanent storage in the future.

❑ All attributes that will be persisted should be declared private and have setter/getting methods defined in the JavaBean style. For example:

```
private String firstname;
public String getFirstname() {
  return firstname;
```

```
  }

public void setFirstname(String s) {
  firstname = s;
}
```

Note that the setter/getter methods don't need to be declared public, because Hibernate can locate them using reflection even if they're protected or private. Further, you can use a method name like isFirstname() as well as set and get.

❏ Hibernate can handle mapping from just about any data type. If you're using Java primitives and JDK types, use the type, and refer to the Hibernate types described in the Chapter 4 when creating the mapping document.

❏ If an attribute type is a collection like a Map, List, or Set, you'll need to do additional work when creating the mapping. For collections, refer to Chapter 6 for a complete overview.

❏ Mapped classes can use the concept of composition, where an attribute's type is another class. The last half of Chapter 6 discusses composition mapping also called components in Hibernate in full detail.

❏ All classes should contain an ID in order to allow easy identification of your objects within Hibernate and the database. As you read in Chapter 4, IDs have values like int, long, or String. Be sure to use the right type when defining your ID, especially if you're using an ID generator.

❏ Interfaces, final classes, and some inner classes can be mapped to permanent storage using Hibernate. See later sections in this chapter for more information.

❏ All Java classes that will be persisted need a default constructor.

With these guidelines in place and all the information you learned in Chapter 4, let's map a few simple classes. You'll learn about mapping as follows over the next few chapters:

❏ In this chapter, we'll show you the basics of mapping, including inheritance.

❏ Collections are covered in Chapter 6.

❏ Composition is covered in Chapter 6.

❏ Relationships are discussed in Chapter 7.

Mapping a Basic Java Class

To get the mapping process moving, let's consider the simple but typical Java class shown in Listing 5.1. The Book class contains attributes that relate to a book as well as an ID attribute that is an int. We need to map this class so Hibernate can persist any objects instantiated from the class. Listing 5.2 shows the possible mapping.

```
package example.products;

public class Book{
  private int id;
  private String title;
  private String author;
```

```java
private String isbn;
private int pages;
private int copyright;
private float cost;

public Book() {
}

public void setId(int i) {
   id = i;
}

public int getId() {
   return id;
}

public void setTitle(String s) {
   title = s;
}

public String getTitle() {
   return title;
}

public void setAuthor(String s) {
   author = s;
}

public String getAuthor() {
   return author;
}

public void setIsbn(String s) {
   isbn = s;
}

public String getIsbn() {
   return isbn;
}

public void setPages(int i) {
   pages = i;
}

public int getPages() {
   return pages;
}

public void setCopyright(int i) {
   copyright = i;
}

public int getCopyright() {
   return copyright;
```

```
    }

    public void setCost(float f) {
      cost = f;
    }

    public float getCost() {
      return cost;
    }
  }
```

Listing 5.1

```xml
<?xml version="1.0" encoding="utf-8"?>
<!DOCTYPE hibernate-mapping PUBLIC
"-//Hibernate/Hibernate Mapping DTD//EN"
"http://hibernate.sourceforge.net/hibernate-mapping-2.0.dtd">

<hibernate-mapping>
  <class name="example.products.Book" table="books">
  <id name="id"
      type="int"
      unsaved-value="0">
    <generator class="hilo"/>
  </id>

    <property name="title"/>
    <property name="author"/>
    <property name="isbn"
              not-null="true"/>
    <property name="pages"
              type="integer"
              column="pagecount" />
    <property name="copyright"/>
    <property name="cost">
      <column name="cost"
              sql-type="NUMERIC(12,2)"/>
    </property>
  </class>
</hibernate-mapping>
```

Listing 5.2

The mapping in Listing 5.2 is contained in a file called book.hbm.xml so the Configuration object can locate it. Since the Book class is fairly simple, the mapping document isn't complex either. Throughout the examples in this chapter, we'll mix things up by changing how the mapping document handles the attributes in the class and explaining the differences. For the book mapping, we've included the required <class> element and fully qualified the class in the name attribute. Recall that we could have used the package attribute of the <hibernate-mapping> element to specify the package prefix of our mapped class. After the name attribute, the table attribute tells Hibernate the name of the database table where all Book objects should be persisted. If you look back at Chapter 4, you'll see that the <class> element has quite a few options for you to use in different situations. In most mappings, the default values for the <class> element attributes will suffice.

Once the <class> element has been filled out, it's a good idea to immediately handle the definition of the identifier for the class. We've designed our Book class to include an int identifier so the objects can be uniquely identified in the database. For the identifier, the name attribute specifies the name of the attribute in the class being mapped. In the Book class, the identifier is called id; that value is placed in the assignment part of the attribute. Next, we specify the type of the identifier. The type is an optional parameter to the <id> element because Hibernate will use reflection to determine the type of the identifier specified in the name attribute.

You should follow a standard for specifying the type of the identifier in your development process. There are advantages and disadvantages to specifying the type for the identifier as well as the attributes in the class. If you're using reflection, you can change the identifier type in the class without too much issue in the mapping document, although you may need to change the <generator>.

A very important attribute in the <id> element is unsaved-value. When a new object is instantiated, Hibernate needs to know whether the object needs to be persisted to the database through a save or update operation. Hibernate uses the value in the unsaved-value attribute to make the determination. When the value in the identifier is null, the default value for the unsaved-value attribute, or a value specified in the mapping document, Hibernate knows the object has been newly instantiated and thus that it needs to be saved or INSERTed into the database. If the identifier value isn't the same as the unsaved-value value, then the object has been previously INSERTed into the database; thus any changes to the object need to be UPDATEd to the database.

For every <id> element, there should be a corresponding <generator> element that populates the identifier with a value. The list of generators available in Hibernate was discussed in Chapter 4. For our Book mapping, we'll use the hilo generator. This generator requires a second table to keep track of row information for Hibernate. (You saw an example of using this generator in Chapter 3.)

Once we've completed the <id> element, we provide a mapping from the Book class attributes we want to be persisted. Remember that not all the attributes have to be saved when the object is persisted: just those that hold nongeneratable values. The class attributes to be persisted with the object are defined in the <property> element. This element tells Hibernate at a minimum the name of the attribute in the class and the name of the column in the database table where the attribute's value should be stored. In some of our <property> elements, we've just listed the name of the attribute: Hibernate will use reflection to determine the attribute type and use the name of the property as the column name in the table. In the case of the isbn attribute, we've used the not-null attribute to let Hibernate know that this attribute must have a value before being sent to the database.

For the pages attribute, we've taken the liberty of specifying the attribute type as well as the name of the database table column. Since the name of the attribute is pages and the column name is pagecount, we need to specify the actual value so Hibernate can properly populate the table.

Finally, the cost attribute uses the <column> element in the <property> element, because we need to let Hibernate know there is a restriction on the database table. The <column> element specifies the name of the table as well as the SQL type. For our example, we've specified that the type is NUMERIC(12,2).

Chapter 5

The database schema for this class is:

```
mysql> create table books(
id int,
title text,
author text,
isbn text not null,
pagecount int,
copyright int,
cost numeric(12,2)
);
```

Here's an example of an object persisted to the database:

```
mysql> select * from books;
+------+--------------------+---------+-----------+---------+---------+------+
| id   | title              |author   |isbn       |pagecount|copyright|cost  |
+------+--------------------+---------+-----------+---------+---------+------+
|229377|Professional Hibernate|Some Guys|003948490309|    300|       0 |29.99 |
+------+--------------------+---------+-----------+---------+---------+------+
1 row in set (0.01 sec)

mysql>
```

To put the data into the database, we've used the sample application in Listing 5.3. We'll use the same code for the remainder of the mappings to verify that they work.

```java
import java.io.*;
import net. sf.hibernate.*;
import net. sf.hibernate.cfg.*;

import example.products.Book;

public class BookTest {

  public static void main(String [] args) {

    try {
      Session session = HibernateSession.currentSession();

      Book book = new Book();
      book.setTitle("Professional Hibernate");
      book.setIsbn("003948490309");
      book.setAuthor("Some Guys");
      book.setPages(300);
      book.setCost(29.99f);

      session.save(book);
      session.flush();

      session.close();
```

```
    } catch (Exception e) {
      e.printStackTrace();
    }
  }
}
```

Listing 5.3

Mapping a Class with Binary Data

There has always been a debate about whether binary data should be stored in the database or whether you should just maintain a link to a binary file on the local filesystem. If you want to keep an application consistent, you need a way to map binary data stored in a Java class into a database row. Fortunately, Hibernate does all the hard work. Consider the encrypted image Java class in Listing 5.4.

```java
package example.encryption;

import java.sql.*;

public class EncryptedImage {
  private int id;
  private String filename;
  private Blob data;

  public EncryptedImage() {
  }

  public int getId() {
    return id;
  }

  public void setId(int id) {
    this.id = id;
  }

  public String getFilename( ) {
    return filename;
  }

  public void setFilename(String s) {
    this.filename = s;
  }

  public Blob getData() {
    return data;
  }

  public void setData(byte[] b) {
  this.data = b;
  }
}
```

Listing 5.4

The `EncryptedData` class in Listing 5.4 has an attribute called `data`, which is designed to hold an array of bytes. The bytes represent an arbitrary binary data; the actual type is `Blob`, because Hibernate doesn't automatically persist an array of byte to the database without a user-defined type. For this reason, we'll take advantage of the SQL types in our Java class.

In addition to the data, we have the filename attribute and an integer `ID`. Now we need to map the attributes to a database table. The question for the mapping surrounds the binary data: How do we represent it? As you'll see in Chapter 6, we could consider the data as an array of data; but typically we consider an array to be a collection of objects, and the bytes don't make the grade. If you look back at Chapter 3 and the available Hibernate types, you'll find that binary is a good choice. Listing 5.5 shows the Hibernate mapping document for the `EncryptedData` class.

```xml
<?xml version="1.0" encoding="UTF-8"?>
<!DOCTYPE hibernate-mapping PUBLIC
"-//Hibernate/Hibernate Mapping DTD//EN"
http://hibernate.sourceforge.net/hibarnte-mapping-2.0.dtd>

<hibernate-mapping>
  <class name="example.encryption.EncryptedData"
         table="encrypteddata">
    <id name="id"
        type="integer"
        unsaved-value="0">
      <column name="id"
              sql-type="int"
              not-null="true"/>
      <generator       class="native"/>
    </id>

    <property name="filename">
      <column name="filename"
              sql-type="varchar(255)"/>
    </property>
    <property name="data"
              type="binary">
      <column name="data"
          sql-type="blob"/>
    </property>
  </class>
</hibernate-mapping>
```

Listing 5.5

For the `EncryptedData` mapping, we've changed the generator from a hilo to a native type. This allows the database server to use the column as defined in the table.

Next, we create the `<property>` elements for each of the attributes in the class. The first element is for the `filename` attribute. We've specified the `name` attribute but not the `type`, thus allowing Hibernate to use reflection to determine its type. In addition, we include the `<column>` element to specify the column in the database for the class attribute and also define the SQL type being used in the database.

The most important mapping is for the class's `data` attribute. In the `<property>` element, we specify the name of the attribute in the class and then use a type of binary. Looking back at Chapter 4, a Hibernate type of binary maps an attribute to a Blob. We take the extra step and specify a `<column>` element with a SQL type of `BLOB` to make sure Hibernate does the proper mapping.

The database schema for this class is:

```
create table encryptedData(
ID int not null,
filename varchar(256),
data blob
);
```

Mapping a Serializable Class

In most cases, you persist a Java object by specifying attributes in the class that will be stored in the database. Hibernate loads the stored object by instantiating a new object and populating the attributes from the values stored in a row. An alternative mechanism takes advantage of the `Serializable` interface available to Java classes. Consider the Java class in Listing 5.6.

```java
package example.count;

public class Counter {
   private String id;
   private Integer ivalue;

   public Counter() {
   }

   public String getId() {
     return id;
   }

   public void setId(String id) {
     this.id = id;
   }

   public Integer getIvalue() {
     return ivalue;
   }

   public void setIvalue(Integer value) {
     ivalue = value;
   }
}
```

Listing 5.6

The `Counter` class shown in Listing 5.6 has two attributes: an identifier defined to be a `String` and an `Integer` attribute that represents an attribute we want to store as an object (not just its attributes). The Hibernate mapping document for the `Counter` class is found in Listing 5.7.

```
<?xml version="1.0" encoding="UTF-8"?>
<!DOCTYPE hibernate-mapping PUBLIC
"-//Hibernate/Hibernate Mapping DTD//EN"
 "http://hibernate.sourceforge.net/hibarnte-mapping-2.0.dtd">

<hibernate-mapping>
  <class name="example.count.Counter"
         table="counter">
    <id name="id"
       type="string"
       unsaved-value=" null">
      <generator        class="uuid.hex"/>
    </id>

    <property name="ivalue"
              type="serializable" >
      <column name="value"
              sql-type="blob"/>
    </property>
  </class>
</hibernate-mapping>
```

Listing 5.7

The mapping document looks similar to the others, but we've made a few changes. Instead of using an int for the identifier class type, we're using a `String`. Further, we've changed the generator from hilo to uuid.hex, to take advantage of the string type of the `id`.

The biggest change comes in the `<property>` element for our class's `ivalue` attribute. Notice that the type for the attribute is serializable instead of int or integer. The specified type tells Hibernate that we won't just access the attribute but instead will serialize it. For the database column, we tell the system to use the value column and specify the type to be BLOB so the `serialized` attribute can be stored properly.

The database row created from this class and mapping look like the following:

```
create table counter (
id text not null,
value blob
);
```

The following example shows the rows for a specific object:

```
mysql> select * from counter;
+--------------------------------+-----------+
| id                             | value     |
+--------------------------------+-----------+
| 40288195fbf116a800fbf116ab830001 | __      |
+--------------------------------+-----------+
1 row in set (0.01 sec)
```

The code to produce the table is shown in Listing 5.8.

```
import java.io.*;
import net. sf.hibernate.*;
import net. sf.hibernate.cfg.*;

import example.count.Counter;

public class CounterTest {

  public static void main(String [] args) {

    try {
      Session session = HibernateSession.currentSession();

      Counter counter = new Counter();

      Integer i = new Integer("34");
      counter.setIvalue(i);

      session.save(counter);
      session.flush();

      Counter counter2 = (Counter)session.load
          (Counter.class, counter.getId());

      System.out.println(counter.getId() +
          " : " + counter.getIvalue().intValue());
      System.out.println(counter2.getId() +
          " : " + counter2.getIvalue().intValue());

      session.close();
    } catch (Exception e) {
      e.printStackTrace();
    }
  }
}
```

Listing 5.8

Mapping a Class with Data/Calendar Attributes

With Hibernate and Java, you can map more than just strings and integers, as you just saw. Of course, if you serialize a class and store it in a BLOB column of the database, that data will only make sense to a Java application. Some other Java objects will translate into standard SQL types; some of those include the Date, Calendar, and Time classes. Consider the Account Java class in Listing 5.9.

```
package example.accounting;

public class Account {
  private String id;
  private String name;
  private String accountnumber;
  private Date setupdate;
  private double balance;
}
```

Listing 5.9

The `Account` class includes a new attribute called `setupdate`, which is populated with the date when the account is first opened. We don't want to serialize this attribute, because a report-generation application might want to perform a SQL query based on the `Date` and we need a real value in the column. The mapping that stores the `Account` class is shown in Listing 5.10.

```xml
<?xml version=- 1.0" encoding="UTF-8"?>
<!DOCTYPE hibernate-mapping PUBLIC
"-//Hibernate/Hibernate Mapping DTD//EN"
"http://hibernate.sourceforge.net/hibernate-mapping-2.0.dtd">

<hibernate-mapping>
  <class name="example.accounting.Account"
         table="account">
    <id name="id"
        type="string"
        unsaved-value="null">
      <generator class="uuid.hex"/>
    </id>

    <property name="name"/>
    <property name="accountnumber"/>
    <property name="setupdate">
      <column name="setup"
              sql-type="Date"/>
    </property>
    <property name="balance"
              type="double"/>
  </class>
</hibernate-mapping>
```

Listing 5.10

The mapping looks much the same as the other mappings. We've included an identifier based on a `String` type using a UUID generator. Next, each of the attributes in the class is mapped to appropriate columns in the database. For the `Date` attribute, we specify the Hibernate `Date` type using the `type` attribute of the `<property>` element. We use the `<column>` element to specify the column where the setup date should be stored as well as a hint to Hibernate that the SQL type for the column is `Date`.

The database schema for this mapping is:

```sql
create table account (
id text not null,
name text,
accountnumber text,
setup Date,
balance double
);
```

Here's an example row for an object:

```
mysql> select * from account;
+----------------------------------+------+--------------+------------+---------+
| id                               | name | accountnumber | setup      | balance |
+----------------------------------+------+--------------+------------+---------+
|40288195fbf1333000fbf13334280001  | Joe  | 39084        | 2004-04-15 |    4054 |
+----------------------------------+------+--------------+------------+---------+
1 row in set (0.04 sec)
```

The code that produced the table is as follows:

```java
import java.io.*;
import java.util.*;

import net. sf.hibernate.*;
import net. sf.hibernate.cfg.*;

import example.accounting.BasicAccount;

public class AccountTest {

   public static void main(String [] args) {

     try {
       Session session = HibernateSession.currentSession();

       BasicAccount account = new BasicAccount();

       account.setName("Joe");
       account.setAccountnumber("39084");
       account.setSetupdate(new Date());
       account.setBalance(4054.00);

       session.save(account);
       session.flush();

       BasicAccount account2 = (BasicAccount)session.load
             (BasicAccount.class, account.getId());

       System.out.println(account.getId() + " : " + account.getSetupdate());
       System.out.println(account2.getId() +
             " : " + account2.getSetupdate());

       session.close();
     } catch (Exception e) {
       e.printStackTrace();
     }
   }
}
```

Mapping a Read-Only Class

In many Java applications, objects are created that can be considered read-only. The application might create the objects during an initialization phase or during an event in the application's life cycle.

Hibernate gives you the ability to persist read-only or immutable objects. Consider the `Support` Java class in Listing 5.11.

```java
package example.util;

public class Support {
   private int id;
   private String name;
   private String support;

   public Support() {
   }

   public Support(String n, String s) {
      name = n;
      support = s;
   }

   public void setId(int i) {
      id = i;
   }

   public int getId() {
      return id;
   }

   public void setName(String s) {
      name = s;
   }

   public String getName() {
      return name;
   }

   public void setSupport(String s) {
      support = s;
   }

   public String getSupport() {
      return support;
   }
}
```

Listing 5.11

Not much is special in the `Support` class as far as Java is concerned, except the fact that all the class attributes (not including the identifier) are defined to be final. Using our mapping skills and another `<class>` element attribute, we can tell Hibernate that the object is immutable. The resulting mapping is shown in Listing 5.12.

```xml
<?xml version="1.0" encoding="UTF-8"?>
<!DOCTYPE hibernate-mapping
```

```
PUBLIC "-//Hibernate/Hibernate Mapping DTD//EN"
"http://hibernate.sourceforge.net/hibernate-mapping-2.0.dtd">

<hibernate-mapping>
  <class name="example.util.Support"
         table="support" mutable="false">
    <id name="id"
        type="integer"
        unsaved-value="0">
      <generator class="hilo"/>
    </id>

    <property name="name"/>
    <property name="support"/>
  </class>
</hibernate-mapping>
```

Listing 5.12

For the mapping in Listing 5.12, the class attribute `<property>` elements aren't anything out of the ordinary. The added functionality is found in the `<class>` element, where we've included the `mutable` attribute and set its value to `false`. The default value for `mutable` is `true`; with a `false` value, Hibernate allows only two operations on the `Support` objects. The first saves an object using an `INSERT` SQL command; Hibernate persists the object and assigns an identifier based on the specified generator. The second is the `SELECT` command, which Hibernate uses to load a persisted object from the database. Hibernate won't allow a `DELETE` or `UPDATE` SQL command to be executed against the object. Even if the Java class is defined to allow its attributes to be changed, Hibernate still won't let an update occur.

The database schema for the `Support` class is:

```
create table support(
id int,
name text,
support text
);
```

Here's an example output row:

```
mysql> select * from support;
+--------+-------+---------+
| id     | name  | support |
+--------+-------+---------+
| 262145 | First | Second  |
+--------+-------+---------+
1 row in set (0.00 sec)
```

Listing 5.13 contains an example application that exercises the `Support` class:

```
import java.io.*;
import java.util.*;

import net.sf.hibernate.*;
import net.sf.hibernate.cfg.*;
```

101

```
import example.util.Support;

public class SupportTest {

  public static void main(String [] args) {

    try {
      Session session = HibernateSession.currentSession();

      Support support = new Support("First", "Second");

      session.save(support);
      session.flush();

      support.setName("Name");
      session.update(support);
      session.flush();

      session.close();
    } catch (Exception e) {
      e.printStackTrace();
    }
  }
}
```

Listing 5.13

In this example, we've added an immutable object to the database and then tried to update it in the application. The row doesn't change, since Hibernate knew the object couldn't be updated.

Mapping Classes Using Versioning/Timestamps

When you're developing commercial applications, much of the data is time dependent or versioned. To keep track of the current version or time when data changed, you need to track an appropriate attribute in the class structure. Hibernate lets you use versioning and timestamping to keep track of the most recent version of an object. The version or timestamp is used as a replacement for the identifier that would typically be found in the class and corresponding database table. Since the version and timestamp change when an object is updated in the database, you don't need the identifier for uniqueness. Consider the Java class in Listing 5.14, which shows a class with a version attribute.

```
package example.code;

public class VModule {
  public int id;
  private String name;
  private String owner;
  private int version;

  public void setId(int i) {
    id = i;
```

```
    }

    public int getId() {
      return id;
    }

    public void setName(String s) {
      name = s;
    }

    public String getName() {
      return name;
    }

    public void setOwner(String s) {
      owner = s;
    }

    public String getOwner() {
      return owner;
    }

    public void setVersion(int i) {
      version = i;
    }

    public int getVersion() {
      return version;
    }

}
```

Listing 5.14

The VModule class holds information about a code module. The version attribute is an int type and is incremented each time the data in the class is updated. The Hibernate mapping required to use the version is shown in Listing 5.15.

```xml
<?xml version="1.0" encoding="UTF-8"?>
<!DOCTYPE hibernate-mapping PUBLIC "-//Hibernate/Hibernate Mapping DTD//EN"
"http://hibernate.sourceforge.net/hibernate-mapping-2.0.dtd">

<hibernate-mapping>
  <class name="example.code.VModule"
         table="vmodule">

    <id name="id"
        type="int"
        unsaved-value="0">
      <generator class="native"/>
    </id>
```

```
    <version name="version"
            column="version"
            type="integer"
             unsaved-value="undefined"/>

      <property name="name"/>
      <property name="owner"/>
    </class>

  </hibernate-mapping>
```

Listing 5.15

The most important part of the Hibernate mapping in Listing 5.15 is the introduction of the `<version>` element. This element includes many of the attributes typically found in the `<id>` element. We specify the name of the attribute in the mapped class that holds the version information. The column and type used to hold the version information are specified as well as the unsaved-value attribute. Just like the identifier `<id>` element, it's important for the unsaved-value to hold the value of a newly instantiated object. Hibernate uses the value to determine whether the object should be saved or updated.

The database schema for this version mapping is:

```
create table vmodule(
id int not null auto_increment primary key,
version int,
name text,
owner text
);
```

A possible row in the database for an insert of a new object into the database is as follows:

```
mysql> select * from vmodule;
+----+---------+----------+-----------+
| id | version | name     | owner     |
+----+---------+----------+-----------+
|  4 |       0 | Module 1 | James Doe |
+----+---------+----------+-----------+
1 row in set (0.00 sec)
```

When the object is updated and saved, the database row becomes:

```
mysql> select * from vmodule;
+----+---------+----------+-----------+
| id | version | name     | owner     |
+----+---------+----------+-----------+
|  4 |       1 | Module 1 | James Doe |
+----+---------+----------+-----------+
1 row in set (0.00 sec)
```

Listing 5.16 contains the code that created the two rows:

```
import java.io.*;
import java.util.*;

import net. sf.hibernate.*;
import net. sf.hibernate.cfg.*;

import example.code.VModule;

public class VModuleTest {

  public static void main(String [] args) {

    try {
      Session session = HibernateSession.currentSession();

      VModule mod = new VModule();

      mod.setOwner("John Smith");
      mod.setName("Module 1");

      session.save(mod);
      session.flush();
      System.out.println(mod.getVersion());

      mod.setOwner("James Doe");
      session.save(mod);
      session.flush();

      System.out.println(mod.getVersion());
      session.close();
    } catch (Exception e) {
      e.printStackTrace();
    }
  }
}
```

Listing 5.16

We use the code in Listing 5.17 when a timestamp should be used instead of just a version. The java.sql.Timestamp class holds the timestamp. The mapping document for the class is shown in Listing 5.18.

```
package example.code;

import java.sql.*;

public class Module {
  public int id;
  private String name;
  private String owner;
  private Timestamp timestamp;
```

```java
public void setId(int i) {
  id = i;
}

public int getId() {
  return id;
}

public void setName(String s) {
  name = s;
}

public String getName() {
  return name;
}

public void setOwner(String s) {
  owner = s;
}

public String getOwner() {
  return owner;
}

public void setTimestamp(Timestamp t) {
  timestamp = t;
}

public Timestamp getTimestamp() {
  return timestamp;
}

}
```

Listing 5.17

```xml
<?xml version="1.0" encoding="UTF-8"?>
<!DOCTYPE hibernate-mapping PUBLIC "-//Hibernate/Hibernate Mapping DTD//EN"
"http://hibernate.sourceforge.net/hibernate-mapping-2.0.dtd">

<hibernate-mapping>
  <class name="example.code.Module"
         table="module">

  <id name="id"
      type="int"
      unsaved-value="0">
    <generator class="native"/>
  </id>

  <timestamp  name="timestamp"
              column="stamp"
              unsaved-value="undefined"/>
```

```
      <property name="name"/>
      <property name="owner"/>
   </class>

</hibernate-mapping>
```

Listing 5.18

When you're using a timestamp instead of a version value, the `<timestamp>` element is used in the mapping. The same attributes are specified in the element as in the `<version>` element. Note that there is no `type` attribute in the `<timestamp>` element: This element is a shortcut for the `<version>` element using an attribute of type timestamp.

The database schema for the timestamp mapping is

```
create table module(
id int not null auto_increment primary key,
stamp timestamp,
name text,
owner text
);
```

Here's an initial row in the database:

```
mysql> select * from module;
+----+----------------+----------+-----------+
| id | stamp          | name     | owner     |
+----+----------------+----------+-----------+
|  1 | 20040416174130 | Module 1 | James Doe |
+----+----------------+----------+-----------+
```

1 row in set (0.02 sec)An updated row in the database is as follows:

```
mysql> select * from module;
+----+----------------+----------+-----------+
| id | stamp          | name     | owner     |
+----+----------------+----------+-----------+
|  1 | 20040416174310 | Module 1 | James Doe |
+----+----------------+----------+-----------+
2 rows in set (0.00 sec)
```

The code to produce the rows and objects for this example looks the same as the code for the `<version>` example.

Mapping Inheritance with Java Classes

In just about any application, some kind of inheritance hierarchy needs to be mapped to permanent storage. As you saw in Chapter 1, there are several ways to map the inherence hierarchy. In our mapping, we'll consider the following methods:

- ❏ Table-per-class hierarchy
- ❏ Table-per-subclass
- ❏ Table-per-concrete class

For our inheritance example, we'll use the CD class defined in Chapter 3 along with two subclasses called `SpecialEditionCD` and `InternationalCD`. The three classes are listed in Listing 5.19.

```java
package example.products;

import java.io.*;
import java.util.*;

  public class CD {
     int id;
     String title;
     String artist;
     DatepurchaseDate;
     double cost;

     public CD() {
     }

     public CD(String title,
               String artist,
               Date purchaseDate, double cost) {
       this.title = title;
       this.artist = artist;
       this.purchaseDate = purchaseDate;
       this.cost = cost;
     }

     public void setId(int id) {
       this.id = id;
     }

     public int getId(){
       return id;
     }

     public void setTitle(String title) {
       this.title = title;
     }

     public String getTitle() {
       return title;
     }

     public void setArtist(String artist) {
         this.artist = artist;
     }

     public String getArtist() {
```

```
        return artist;
    }

    public void setPurchasedate(Date purchaseDate) {
        this.purchaseDate = purchaseDate;
    }

    public Date getPurchasedate() {
        return purchaseDate;
    }

    public void setCost(double cost) {
        this.cost = cost;
    }

    public double getCost() {
        return cost;
    }
}


package example.products;

import java.util.*;

public class SpecialEditionCD extends CD {

    private String newfeatures;

    public SpecialEditionCD() {
    }

    public SpecialEditionCD(String title,
                            String artist,
                            Date purchaseDate,
                            double cost, String features) {
        super(title, artist, purchaseDate, cost);

        newfeatures = features;
    }

    public void setNewfeatures(String s) {
        newfeatures = s;
    }

    public String getNewfeatures() {
        return newfeatures;
    }
}


package example.products;
```

```
import java.util.*;

public class InternationalCD extends CD {

  private String languages;
  private int region;

  public InternationalCD() {
  }

public InternationalCD(String title, String artist,
      Date purchaseDate, double cost, String language, int region) {
    super(title, artist, purchaseDate, cost);

    languages = language;
    this.region = region;
  }

  public void setLanguages(String s) {
    languages = s;
  }

  public String getLanguages() {
    return languages;
  }

  public void setRegion(int i) {
    region = i;
  }

  public int getRegion() {
    return region;
  }
}
```

Listing 5.19

Table-Per-Class Hierarchy Mapping

In our first mapping example, we'll create a mapping document for the three classes that stores objects of the hierarchy in a single table structure. The mapping is shown in Listing 5.20.

```
<?xml version="1.0" encoding="utf-8" ?>
<!DOCTYPE hibernate-mapping
    PUBLIC "-//Hibernate/Hibernate Mapping DTD//EN"
    "http://hibernate.sourceforge.net/hibernate-mapping-2.0.dtd">

<hibernate-mapping package="example.products">
  <classname="CD"
        table="cd"
        discriminator-value="cd">
    <id name="id"
        type="integer"
```

```
                 unsaved-value="0">
        <generator          class="hilo"/>
      </id>

    <discriminator column="cd_type"
                   type= "string"/>

  <property name="title"/>
  <property name="artist"/>
  <property name="purchasedate" type="date"/>
  <property name="cost" type="double"/>

    <subclass name="SpecialEditionCD"
              discriminator-value="SpecialEditionCD">
      <property name="newfeatures" type="string"/>
    </subclass>

    <subclass name="InternationalCD"
              discriminator-value="InternationalCD">
      <property name="languages"/>
      <property name="region"/>
    </subclass>

    </class>

</hibernate-mapping>
```

Listing 5.20

The mapping in Listing 5.20 is more complex than the mappings you've seen so far. The first addition in the mapping is the `<discriminator>` element. To understand how the mapping works, consider what Hibernate will attempt to accomplish with the hierarchy objects: When the user instantiates and saves a CD object, it's saved to a table called CD with the appropriate attributes from the CD class mapped to the database columns. When the user instantiates and saves a `SpecialEditionCD` object, it's saved to the same CD table as the CD object. The difference is that additional attributes are mapped from the `SpecialEditionCD`. Those additional attributes are set to null for the CD object. To differentiate between the three classes in the hierarchy, we add a discriminator column to the table and enter a specific value in the column for each object type.

The `<discriminator>` element includes two attributes in our example. The first attribute, `column`, relates to the column in the database to be used for the discriminator value. The second attribute, `type`, determines the column type.

In the `<class>` element, an element called `<discriminator-value>` relates to the value to be placed in the discriminator column for an object instantiated from the CD class. Figure 5.1 shows all of the rows in the cd table.

```
mysql> select * from cd;
+---------+--------------------+--------+---------------------+------+-------------+-----------+--------+------------------+
|id       | title              | artist | purchasedate        | cost | newfeatures | languages | region | cd_type          |
+---------+--------------------+--------+---------------------+------+-------------+-----------+--------+------------------+
|360449   | Grace Under Pressure | Rush | 2004-04-16 00:00:00 | 9.99 | NULL        | NULL      | NULL   | cd               |
| 360450  | Grace Under Pressure | Rush | 2004-04-16 00:00:00 | 9.99 | Widescreen  | NULL      | NULL   | SpecialEditionCD |
| 360451  | Grace Under Pressure | Rush | 2004-04-16 00:00:00 | 9.99 | NULL        | Spanish   | 4      | InternationalCD  |
+---------+--------------------+--------+---------------------+------+-------------+-----------+--------+------------------+
3 rows in set (0.00 sec)
```

Figure 5.1

The database schema for this mapping is:

```
create table cd(
id int,
title text,
artist text,
purchasedate datetime,
cost double,
newfeatures text,
languages text,
region int,
cd_type text
);
```

Notice that the database schema consists of a single table and columns for all the possible attributes in the base CD class as well as the child SpecialEditionCD and InternationalCD classes. By using the table-per-class method, we need only one table for all object types in the mapped hierarchy. Hibernate can do this by using the discriminator column, defined as cd_type in the schema, to hold a string value indicating the class of object held in a particular row.

Here's the code for an example use of the CD hierarchy. We used this code to produce the database rows illustrated earlier:

```
import java.io.*;
import java.util.*;

import net. sf.hibernate.*;
import net. sf.hibernate.cfg.*;

import example.products.CD;
import example.products.SpecialEditionCD;
import example.products.InternationalCD;

public class CDTest {

  public static void main(String [] args) {

    try {
      Session session = HibernateSession.currentSession();

      CD cd = new CD("Grace Under Pressure", "Rush", new Date(), 9.99);
      SpecialEditionCD secd = new SpecialEditionCD
        ("Grace Under Pressure", "Rush", new Date(), 9.99, "Widescreen");
```

```
InternationalCD icd = new InternationalCD
   ("Grace Under Pressure", "Rush", new Date(), 9.99, "Spanish", 4);

session.save(cd);
session.save(secd);
session.save(icd);

session.flush();

session.close();
    } catch (Exception e) {
    e.printStackTrace();
    }
  }
}
```

We create three different objects, one for each class type, and persist them to permanent storage.
Hibernate puts the appropriate column values in the rows, depending on the class type.

Table-Per-Subclass Hierarchy Mapping

If you need to separate out the various classes into individual tables, one option is to use a table per subclass. Listing 5.21 shows the mapping needed to support this method.

```xml
<?xml version="1.0" encoding="utf-8" ?>
<!DOCTYPE hibernate-mapping
    PUBLIC "-//Hibernate/Hibernate Mapping DTD//EN"
    "http://hibernate.sourceforge.net/hibernate-mapping-2.0.dtd">

<hibernate-mapping package="example.products">
  <class name="CD"
        table="cd">
    <idname="id"
        type="integer"
        unsaved-value="0">
      <generator class="hilo"/>
    </id>

  <property name="title"/>
        <property name="artist"/>
        <property name="purchasedate" type="date"/>
        <property name="cost" type="double"/>

  <joined-subclass name="SpecialEditionCD"
                table="secd">
    <key column="id"/>
    <property name="newfeatures" type="string"/>
</joined-subclass>

  <joined-subclass name="InternationalCD"
                table="icd">
    <key column="id"/>
    <property name="languages"/>
    <property name="region"/>
```

```
    </joined-subclass>

  </class>

</hibernate-mapping>
```

Listing 5.21

In the mapping document, we've removed the discriminator element and attributes and replaced them with a `<key>` element and the names of database tables to be used when storing objects of a particular type. What's most interesting about the `table-per-subclass` method is the fact that the attribute inherited from the parent only appears in the parent database table. Hibernate uses the `<key>` element to determine which field in the parent database should be used to create a relationship between the parent and child. Our example program places rows in all three tables.

Since there will be three tables, we need three database schemas—they're shown in Listing 5.22.

```
create table cd(
id int,
title text,
artist text,
purchasedate datetime,
cost double,
);

create table secd(
id int,
newfeatures text,
);

create table icd(
id int,
languages text,
region int,
);
```

Listing 5.22

Using the same example program a in the previous `table-per-class` example, Hibernate creates rows in each of the tables as shown here:

```
mysql> select * from cd;
+--------+---------------------+--------+---------------------+------+
| id     | title               | artist | purchasedate        | cost |
+--------+---------------------+--------+---------------------+------+
| 425985 | Grace Under Pressure | Rush  | 2004-04-16 00:00:00 | 9.99 |
| 425986 | Grace Under Pressure | Rush  | 2004-04-16 00:00:00 | 9.99 |
| 425987 | Grace Under Pressure | Rush  | 2004-04-16 00:00:00 | 9.99 |
+--------+---------------------+--------+---------------------+------+
3 rows in set (0.00 sec)
```

```
mysql> select * from secd;
+--------+-------------+
| id     | newfeatures |
+--------+-------------+
| 425986 | Widescreen  |
+--------+-------------+
1 row in set (0.00 sec)

mysql> select * from icd;
+--------+-----------+--------+
| id     | languages | region |
+--------+-----------+--------+
| 425987 | Spanish   |      4 |
+--------+-----------+--------+
1 row in set (0.00 sec)
```

Recall that the example program creates three objects of types CD, SpecialEditionCD, and InternationalCD. All three objects share the attributes found in the CD table, since it's a parent to SpecialEditionCD and InternationalCD. When the CD object is persisted, Hibernate inserts a single row in the cd table. When a SpecialEditionCD is persisted, Hibernate writes a row into the cd table and then writes the additional fields for the object into the secd table. Notice that the id field values are matched between the second row in the cd table and the single row in the secd table. The same process is used when storing the InternationalCD.

Table-Per-Concrete-Class Hierarchy Mapping

Finally, you can use the table-per-concrete-class method, where Hibernate uses database tables containing all the fields for a particular class. In other words, the SpecialEditionCD and InternationalCD class have all the fields found in the CD class. All three approaches store the same type of information, but in different ways. Both this method and the previous one require either two selects to the database or a join.

The database schema used for this approach is shown in Listing 5.23.

```
create table cd(
id int,
title text,
artist text,
purchasedate datetime,
cost double
);

create table secd(
id int,
title text,
artist text,
purchasedate datetime,
cost double,
newfeatures text,
);

create table icd(
id int,
```

```
title text,
artist text,
purchasedate datetime,
cost double,
languages text,
region int,
);
```

Listing 5.23

The mapping required uses three `<class>` elements with no embedding of the various elements, as shown in Listing 5.24.

```
<?xml version="1.0" encoding="utf-8" ?>
<!DOCTYPE hibernate-mapping
    PUBLIC "-//Hibernate/Hibernate Mapping DTD//EN"
    "http://hibernate.sourceforge.net/hibernate-mapping-2.0.dtd">

<hibernate-mapping package="example.products">
  <classname="CD"
        table="cd"
        discriminator-value="cd">
    <id name="id"
        type="integer"
        unsaved-value="0">
      <generator      class="hilo"/>
    </id>

  <property name="title"/>
        <property name="artist"/>
        <property name="purchasedate" type="date"/>
        <property name="cost" type="double"/>
  </class>

  <class name="SpecialEditionCD"
                table="secd">

    <id name="id"
        type="integer"
        unsaved-value="0">
      <generator      class="hilo"/>
    </id>

  <property name="title"/>
        <property name="artist"/>
        <property name="purchasedate" type="date"/>
        <property name="cost" type="double"/>
  <property name="newfeatures" type="string"/>
  </class>

  <class name="InternationalCD"
                table="icd">
    <id name="id"
```

```
            type="integer"
            unsaved-value="0">
      <generator class="hilo"/>
    </id>


    <property name="title"/>
            <property name="artist"/>
            <property name="purchasedate" type="date"/>
            <property name="cost" type="double"/>
    <property name="languages"/>
    <property name="region"/>
  </class>



  </hibernate-mapping>
```

Listing 5.24

Using the same example program as in the last two sections, we obtain the following rows in the three databases:

```
mysql> select * from cd;
+--------+---------------------+--------+---------------------+------+
| id     | title               | artist | purchasedate        | cost |
+--------+---------------------+--------+---------------------+------+
| 458753 | Grace Under Pressure | Rush   | 2004-04-16 00:00:00 | 9.99 |
+--------+---------------------+--------+---------------------+------+
1 row in set (0.00 sec)

mysql> select * from secd;
+--------+---------------------+--------+---------------------+------+------------+
|id      | title               | artist | purchasedate        | cost |newfeatures |
+--------+---------------------+--------+---------------------+------+------------+
|491521  | Grace Under Pressure | Rush   | 2004-04-16 00:00:00| 9.99 | Widescreen |
+--------+---------------------+--------+---------------------+------+------------+
1 row in set (0.00 sec)

mysql> select * from icd;
+--------+-------------------+--------+---------------------+----+---------+--------+
|id      |title              |artist  |purchasedate         |cost|languages| region |
+--------+-------------------+--------+---------------------+----+---------+--------+
|524289  |Grace Under Pressure|Rush   |2004-04-16 00:00:00|9.99|Spanish  |      4 |
+--------+-------------------+--------+---------------------+----+---------+--------+
1 row in set (0.00 sec)
```

Persisting Interfaces

As you know, in many situations interfaces denote the information needed in an application. The interface is used to fully build a set of classes. Hibernate allows the interfaces to be persisted, but that doesn't make much sense since interfaces don't exist without an implementing class. Let's look at an example interface and a couple of classes that implement it.

We've defined an interface called AppAccount that represents a bank account. There are numerous bank accounts, so we chose an interface to represent the common functions but allow the implementation to develop. Two different implement the AppAccount interface: SavingsAccount and CheckingAccount.

Listing 5.25 contains an example mapping for the interface and classes—it looks just like the mapping for our inheritance example.

```xml
<?xml version="1.0" encoding="utf-8" ?>
<!DOCTYPE hibernate-mapping
    PUBLIC "-//Hibernate/Hibernate Mapping DTD//EN"
    "http://hibernate.sourceforge.net/hibernate-mapping-2.0.dtd">

<hibernate-mapping package="example.products">
<class name="AppAccount"
table="accounts">
<id name="id"
type="integer"
unsaved-value="0">
<generator class="hilo"/>
</id>

<discriminator column="type"
type= "string"/>

    <property name="title"/>
    <property name="artist"/>
    <property name="purchasedate" type="date"/>
    <property name="cost" type="double"/>

<subclass name="CheckingAccount"
  discriminator-value="CheckingAccount">
...
</subclass>

<subclass name="SavingsAccount"
  discriminator-value="SavingsAccount">
...
</subclass>

</class>
</hibernate-mapping>
```

Listing 5.25

Notice that the interface class doesn't include a discriminator-value attribute in the <class> element; thus Hibernate can't create an entry in the database for an object of type AppAccount. But that's good, because it's an interface, and we can't create an object of the AppAccount type. We can represent the interface and classes using any of the three inheritance mappings available.

Mapping Enums

One of the most common language constructs left out of the Java language is the Enum. An *enumeration* is typically a set of string values that have unique integer values but are considered a type in themselves. Until Java 1.5, developers had to devise ways to produce an Enum. The creators of Hibernate saw the need to be able to persist enumerations, so they developed an Enum design using the class net.sf .hibernate.PersistentEnum. To make Hibernate persist your enums, you must build them by implementing this class type. Consider the Java class in Listing 5.26.

```java
package example.enums;
import net.sf.hibernate.PersistentEnum;
public class Display implements PersistentEnum {
  private final int code;
  private Display(int code) {
    this.code = code;
  }

  public static final Display FULL = new Integer (0);
  public static final Display SEMI = new Integer(1);
  public static final Display NONE = new Integer(2);
  public int toInt() {
    return code;
  }

  public static Display fromInt(int code) {
    switch(code) {
      case 0: return FULL;
      case 1: return SEMI;
      case 2: return NONE;
      default: throw new RuntimeException("Unknown display code");
    }
  }
}
```

Listing 5.26

An example class to use the Display enumeration looks like Listing 5.27.

```java
package example.enum;

public class UseDisplay {

  private String id;
  private Display display;

  public UseDisplay() {
  }

  public void setId(String i) {
    id = i;
  }
```

```
  public String getId() {
    return id;
  }

  public void setDisplay(Display e) {
    display = e;
  }

  public Display getDisplay() {
    return display;
  }
}
```

Listing 5.27

This class includes a single enumeration attribute and an identifier. The mapping needed to handle the class is shown in Listing 5.28.

```xml
<?xml version="1.0" encoding="UTF-8"?>
<!DOCTYPE hibernate-mapping PUBLIC "-//Hibernate/Hibernate Mapping DTD//EN"
"http://hibernate.sourceforge.net/hibernate-mapping-2.0.dtd">

<hibernate-mapping>
  <class name="example.enum.UseDisplay"
         table="display">

    <id name="id"
        type="string"
        unsaved-value="null">
      <generator       class="uuid.hex"/>
    </id>

    <property name="display"
              type="example.enum.Display">
      <column name="display" sql-type="int"/>
    </property>
  </class>

</hibernate-mapping>
```

Listing 5.28

This mapping is a little different than the previous ones, because we include the class type for the enumeration in the type attribute of the <property> element. The type value is example.enum .Display; we place the entire name in the attribute. In the same <property> element, we include a <column> element to indicate the database field name as well as the database type. Hibernate handles converting the enumeration from its display name to an integer so it can be stored properly. The database schema for the mapping is:

```
create table display(
  id text,
  display int
  );
```

Here's an example row in the database for a persisted object:

```
mysql> select * from display;
+-----------------------------------+---------+
| id                                | display |
+-----------------------------------+---------+
| 40288195fbf8a14400fbf8a148710001  |       1 |
+-----------------------------------+---------+
1 row in set (0.04 sec)
```

This row has persisted an object with an enumeration value of SEMI; thus the value 1 is stored in the display column. The example application that uses both the class and the enumeration is shown in Listing 5.29.

```java
import java.io.*;
import java.util.*;

import net. sf.hibernate.*;
import net. sf.hibernate.cfg.*;

import example.enum.UseDisplay;
import example.enum.Display;

public class DisplayTest {

  public static void main(String [] args) {

    try {
      Session session = HibernateSession.currentSession();

      UseDisplay display = new UseDisplay();

      display.setDisplay(Display.SEMI);

      session.save(display);
      session.flush();

      session.close();
    } catch (Exception e) {
      e.printStackTrace();
    }
  }
}
```

Listing 5.29

Working with Column Formulas

In Chapter 4, you learned that the `<property>` element has an attribute called formula designed to let Hibernate pull information from the persisted object and place the result in the object being loaded. Basically, Hibernate takes the SQL query string placed in the attribute and puts it in the SELECT command used to pull the object from the database. The value from the SELECT is placed in a specified attribute of the class. You can place any SQL in the formula attribute that would be valid in a SELECT clause. Consider the following Account class:

```java
package example.accounting;

import java.io.*;

public class Account {
  private String id;
  private String accountnum;
  private double balance;
  private String firstname;
  private String lastname;
  private String fullname;

  public Account() {
  }

  public void setId(String s) {
    id = s;
  }

  public String getId() {
    return id;
  }

  public void setAccountnum(String s) {
    accountnum = s;
  }

  public String getAccountnum() {
    return accountnum;
  }

  public void setBalance(double b) {
    balance = b;
  }

  public double getBalance() {
    return balance;
  }

  public void setFirstname(String s) {
    firstname = s;
  }

  public String getFirstname() {
```

```
      return firstname;
   }

   public void setLastname(String s) {
      lastname = s;
   }

   public String getLastname() {
      return lastname;
   }

   public void setFullname(String s) {
      fullname = s;
   }

   public String getFullname() {
      return fullname;
   }
}
```

The Account class includes attributes for firstname, lastname, and fullname. Obviously the full-name attribute is a concatenation of the firstname and lastname values; we let Hibernate create the value. The mapping to produce the value is shown here:

```xml
<?xml version="1.0" encoding="UTF-8"?>
<!DOCTYPE hibernate-mapping PUBLIC "-//Hibernate/Hibernate Mapping DTD//EN"
"http://hibernate.sourceforge.net/hibernate-mapping-2.0.dtd">

<hibernate-mapping>
<class name="example.accounting.Account"
table="account2">

<id name="id"
type="string"
unsaved-value="null">
<generator class="uuid.hex"/>
</id>


<property    name="accountnum"/>
<property    name="firstname"/>
<property    name="lastname"/>
<property    name="balance"/>
<property    name="fullname" formula="concat(firstname, ' ', lastname)"/>
</class>

</hibernate-mapping>
```

All the work takes place in the <property> element with the name="fullname" attribute. Notice the formula that creates the value we're after for our class. Here's the database schema for the mapping:

```
create table account2(
id text,
accountnum text,
```

```
        firstname text,
        lastname text,
        balance double
        ) ;
```

To determine whether the mapping works, we use the following example code:

```
import java.io.*;
import java.util.*;

import net. sf.hibernate.*;
import net. sf.hibernate.cfg.*;

import example.accounting.Account;

public class AccountTest {

  public static void main(String [] args) {

    try {
       Session session = HibernateSession.currentSession();

       Account account = new Account();

       account.setFirstname("Joe");
       account.setLastname("Smith");
       account.setAccountnum("39084");
       account.setBalance(4054.00);

       session.save(account);
       session.flush();

       Account account2 = (Account)session.load(Account.class,
account.getId());
       System.out.println(account2.getFullname());

       session.close();
    } catch (Exception e) {
       e.printStackTrace();
    }
  }
}
```

When the object is loaded from the database, the `fullname` attribute is populated with the correct value based on a call to the database instead of the object having to create the value.

Using the Session Pattern

In Chapter 2, we provided an implementation of a servlet that takes advantage of the `init()` method to obtain a single `SessionFactory` object and a local `Session` object when the servlet is ready to save or load persistent classes. As we mentioned, it's important that your application instantiate only a single `SessionFactory` object, because Hibernate is designed to work with a single instance. Further, the

Session object created to allow an application to save() and load() persisted objects isn't thread-safe, and you must take care that a single session isn't shared or accessed across threads.

Fortunately, Java provides a couple of mechanisms that ensure these two rules are followed: static attributes and the ThreadLocal construct. The developers of Hibernate created a pattern that uses these two mechanisms to ensure safe SessionFactory and Session object instantiation and use. The pattern is shown in Listing 5.30.

```java
import net. sf.hibernate.*;
import net. sf.hibernate.cfg.*;

public class HibernateSession {
  private static final SessionFactory sessionFactory;

  static {
    try {
      sessionFactory = new Configuration().
        configure().buildSessionFactory();
    } catch (HibernateException e) {
      throw new RuntimeException
        ("SessionFactory Error - " + e.getMessage(), e);
    }
  }

  public static final ThreadLocal session = new ThreadLocal();

  public static Session currentSession() throws HibernateException {
    Session s = (Session) session.get();

    if (s == null) {
      s = sessionFactory.openSession();
      session.set(s);
    }

    return s;
  }

  public static void closeSession() throws HibernateException {
    Session s = (Session) session.get();
    session. set(null);
    if (s != null)
      s.close();
  }
}
```

Listing 5.30

In this pattern code, a static attribute and instantiation block are used to create the SessionFactory object, making sure there is only a single object for the application. To obtain a Session object, the application calls the openSession() method. The code tries to determine if a Session object has already been instantiated by calling the session attribute's get() method. Notice that the session attribute is declared as a ThreadLocal variable: This means the JVM will ensure that only one session object is available for all the threads that call the openSession() method. If an object isn't available, a new one is instantiated and returned to the caller.

When using this pattern, Hibernate looks for the hibernate.cfg.xml file and pulls all the necessary database connection information as well as the mapping document references. For example, we might have a hibernate.cfg.xml file that looks like Listing 5.31.

```xml
<?xml version="1.0" encoding="utf-8"?>
<!DOCTYPE hibernate-configuration PUBLIC
"-//Hibernate/Hibernate Configuration DTD//EN"
 "http://hibernate.sourceforge.net/hibernate-configuration-2.0.dtd">

<hibernate-configuration>

 <session-factory>
<property name="connection.driver">com.mysql.jdbc.Driver</property>
<property name="connection.url">jdbc:mysql://localhost/products</property>
<property name="dialect">net.sf.hibernate.dialect.MySQLDialect</property>

<mapping resource="book.hbm.xml"/>
</session-factory>

</hibernate-configuration>
```

Listing 5.31

Summary

Mapping Java classes to permanent database storage is a fundamental issue with any production application. Our goal in this chapter was to provide you with experience in creating the Hibernate mapping document between simple and more complex classes. We've exercised many of the elements found in Chapter 4 in order to create the mappings. In the next chapter, we'll expand our discussion to include collections and components. Collections let you include in your mappings lists, maps, and sets of data; and components give you the ability to support object-oriented composition.

Working with Collections

In Chapter 5, you saw how to persist Java classes that contain attributes consisting of Java basic types as well as serializable classes. What was missing from all our examples were *collections*. When we talk about collections, we're specifically interested in those classes that implement the java.util.Collection interface as well as traditional arrays. Hibernate can persist attributes defined as the following collections interfaces and their corresponding implementation classes:

- ❑ **java.util.Map:** HashMap
- ❑ **java.util.SortedMap:** TreeMap
- ❑ **java.util.Set:** HashSet
- ❑ **java.util.SortedSet:** TreeSet
- ❑ **java.util.List:** ArrayList
- ❑ Any array of basic types or other persisted classes

One of the most important issues with collections and Hibernate is the fact that you can use them just as you've been using them in your applications; with the proper mapping, Hibernate will persist them as easily as it persists an integer value. However, Hibernate doesn't just persist the collections but replaces the standard Map, Set, and List classes with its own versions to support the persisting mechanism. Therefore, the extra semantics of, say, a HashMap are *not* persisted. You'll see examples of this behavior later in the chapter.

Associations

Before we start the process of mapping collection examples, we need to talk about the different associations that can occur between a collection and a class where the collection is defined. A collection can be instantiated to hold values and is associated with a single class. In this type of situation, the collection has a parent that it must be associated with. In addition, you might have a situation where a single collection is referenced by more than one class. You need to be able to handle these associations.

Let's begin with a collection called pictures, which is defined in a class called Album:

```
public class Album {
  private String name;
  private List pictures;
  public void setName(String s) {
    name = s;
  }
  public String getName() {
    return name;
  }
  public void setPictures(List l) {
    pictures = l;
  }
  public List getPictures() {
    return pictures;
  }
}
```

The Album class has two attributes: the name of the album and a List for all the pictures that are part of the album. From Chapter 5, you know there will be a mapping for the Album class that contains an element called <list> to handle the mapping of the pictures attribute. In to keep track of the parent of the pictures collection, Hibernate creates a foreign key based on the parent's identifier. Hibernate calls the foreign key a *collection key*; it's defined using a <key> element. The <key> element contains a single attribute called column. The value of the attribute is the name of the identifier column in the parent class. Hibernate also requires a collection table for the elements of the collection.

Index Elements

If the collection is based on an index, List, array, or Map, you must have a column in the table to hold the index position of each element in the collection. In the case of an array or List, the column type is an integer. The map can use any valid Hibernate type to fully emulate the functionality of the map. There are four <index> elements, to support a variety of situations.

Here's the simple case for an array, List, or Map:

```
<index
  column="column"
  type="type"
  length="length"
/>
```

The <index> element has three attributes: column, type, and length. The column attribute specifies the name of the column in the collection table that will hold the index. The type attribute specifies the type of the column, and the length attribute is the length of the column.

When you're using a map, you'll most commonly use another class as the index to the values in the map. Hibernate supports this using the <index-many-to-many> element:

```
<index-many-to-many
  column="column"
  class="class"
/>
```

It has only two attributes: `column` is the name of the column in the collection table to hold the index values, and `class` is the name of the class for the index.

If you need to use a composite index for your collection, you can specify it using the `<composite-index>` element. This element specifies the class to use for the index and uses the `<key-property>` element to specify the individual pieces of the composite index:

```
<composite-index
class="class">
<key-property name="name" type="type" column="column"/>
>
```

A fourth index is available, which isn't recommended by Hibernate; it allows for a heterogeneous mapping in the collections as far as the index is concerned:

```
<index-many-to-any
  id-type="type"
  meta_type="type">
  <column/>
</index-many-to-any>
```

There are two attributes: `id-type` is an identifier type that needs to be present in a custom type defined by the `meta-type` attribute. The `<index-many-to-any>` element contains `<column>` subelements. The first `<column>` element defines the table of the mapping, and an additional `<column>` element defines the identifier to be used.

Element Elements

All the values of a collection can be basic types or classes except another collection. Hibernate calls the values in the collection *collection element types*. The type is defined using an `<element>` element. There are five different `<element>` elements.

If your collection only contains values, you use the `<element>` element to specify the column to use for the values and the type:

```
<element
  column="column"
  type="type"
/>
```

The column and type are created in the database table, as you'll see shortly.

If your collection contains objects, you use the `<many-to-many>` element to specify those objects:

```
<many-to-many
  column="column"
  class="class"
  outer-join="true | false | auto"
/>
```

The column attribute is the name of the column in the database table to hold the foreign key to the object table that Hibernate uses to store the object. You need a mapping for the objects to be contained in the collection. The `class` attribute is the name of the class to be held in the collection. If you want to let Hibernate use an outer join when pulling collection objects, set the `outer-join` attribute to the appropriate value. The default is `auto`, which lets Hibernate choose for itself.

As you'll see toward the end of the chapter, you can save an entire component in a Java collection by using the `<composite-element>` element:

```
<composite-element class="class">
 <property name=""/>
</composite-element>
```

This element groups together the needed attributes to be saved. The `<property>` subelement is required to determine which of the attributes to pull from the class defined by the `class` attribute.

In most other mappings, you needed a collection table to handle the mapping between the classes in the collections. When you're using a one-to-many relationship, there is no additional table. There is only a single `class` attribute in this element, which is the name of the associated class:

```
<one-to-many
   class="class"
/>
```

When you're using the `<one-to-many>` element in a collection-mapping element like `<set>`, you need to declare a `<key>` element as well so that Hibernate can make the appropriate mappings.

The `index` and `element` elements create considerable variety when you're mapping a collection. You'll see many of these elements in the remainder of this chapter as we do some actual mappings.

Bidirectional Associations

When you're using a collection, you typically have a parent object that contains an attribute of the collection type. For example:

```
public class Parent {
  private List list;
}
```

Here the `list` attribute is a child of the Parent. To access the list, you typically go through the parent. Further, the objects in the list are typically owned by the parent and not shared with other parents. This is a one-to-many relationship. If the objects in the `List` are shared among various parents, it's a many-to-many situation.

If you want to be able to determine the parent of a child, you must establish a bidirectional association for the many-to-many relationship but not for the one-to-many. You do so by putting a `<many-to-many>` element in each of the class or collection elements. You also need to specify the inverse attribute in one end of the association. You'll see an example of using a bidirectional many-to-many association toward the end of the chapter.

Lazy Initialization

Clearly, there can be an issue of performance when considering the loading of a persisted collection. If the collection is very large, there is no reason to bring in the entire collection when you only want to look at a few elements. You can help Hibernate by specifying the proxy attribute in the `<class>` or `<sub-class>` element, defining the class that should be used for lazy initialization. Typically the class is the same as the class being mapped. If you want Hibernate to use lazy initialization in your classes, specify the lazy attribute in the mapping element. For example:

```
<class name="Group" proxy="Group">
<set lazy="true">
  </set>
</class>
```

Mapping Maps/SortedMaps

Java maps are designed to handle key/value pairs, where the key and value can be a primitive type or an object. All maps are defined based on the interface called `java.util.map`, which means you can't instantiate a new map using the code:

```
Map map = new Map();
```

Since `map` is an interface, you need to use an implementation supplied by Java. One of the most popular implementations is the `HashMap`; we'll use it in our example. When Hibernate persists a `HashMap`, you lose the semantics involved in the `HashMap` and provide the functionality from the `Map` interface when the map is pulled from the database. If you're interested in a sorted map, the `SortedMap` interface is supported along with the `TreeMap` class implementation. When you're using objects for the key in a sorted map, it's important to implement both the `equal()` and `hashCode()` methods in the class itself.

As you'll see in an example shortly, we define our own comparator so both Java and Hibernate can accurately insert new key/value pairs into a sorted map. In the `Map` section, we'll show examples that use a map of primitive values, a map using objects, and a sorted map using objects for both the key and value pairs—a ternary example.

Mapping a Values Map

Our first example of persisting a map involves a class called `SupportProperty`, which contains the name of the `support` property, and a `Map` called `properties`. The map will be filled with key/value pairs consisting of a property name for the key using a `String` type. The value is also a `String` type relating to the key. Since the key and values are both `Strings`, we need only a single class for this example. The `SupportProperty` class is defined as shown in Listing 6.1.

```
import java.util.*;

public class SupportProperty {
    private int id;
    private String name;
    private Map properties;
```

```
    public SupportProperty() {
    }

    public void setId(int i) {
      id = i;
    }

    public int getId() {
      return id;
    }

    public void setName(String s) {
      name = s;
    }

    public String getName() {
      return name;
    }

    public void setProperties(Map m) {
      properties = m;
    }

    public Map getProperties() {
      return properties;
    }
}
```

Listing 6.1

It's important to note that we've specified the base map interface as the property type in our example class. Both the accessor and mutator methods also refer to the interface instead of the implementation map. At this point we don't have an implementation map to discuss, but it will be a HashMap.

The SupportProperty class and its Map attribute represent the easiest mapping needed for persistence. Listing 6.2 shows the necessary mapping document.

```
<?xml version="1.0" encoding="UTF-8"?>
<!DOCTYPE hibernate-mapping
PUBLIC "-//Hibernate/Hibernate Mapping DTD//EN"
"http://hibernate.sourceforge.net/hibernate-mapping-2.0.dtd">

<hibernate-mapping>
<class name="SupportProperty"
  table="supportproperty">
  <id name="id">
    <generator class="native"/>
  </id>

<map name="properties">
    <key column="part_id"/>
```

```
            <index column="property_name" type="string"/>
            <element column="property_value" type="string"/>
    </map>
    <property name="name" type="string"/>
    </class>
    </hibernate-mapping>
```

Listing 6.2

The attributes in our SupportProperty class include the identifier, the name of the object, and a map consisting of various key/value pairs. For our mapping document, we've included an <id> element that supports a native generator—this means we'll use the auto increment clause when defining our MySQL database table. We also include a <property> element for the name attribute.

The new element in the mapping document is called <map>; it will be used to map the properties attribute to the database. The <map> element includes three subelements—<key>, <index>, and <element>—and a single name attribute that tells Hibernate the name of the map attribute in the class we're mapping. Hibernate uses a separate database table to hold the map key/value pairs; since we don't supply a table attribute, Hibernate uses the value found in the name attribute.

Next we define the <key> subelement to associate the map with its parent. The attribute column value is the name of a foreign key column where Hibernate puts the primary key of the parent. The <index> subelement specifies the information for the key part of the map, and the <element> subelement is the value part of the map. We've supplied both the column name and the type of the key/value pieces of the map.

From the mapping document, we can derive our database table. There are two tables: one for the parent object and another for the map attribute. The two tables are linked to each other through a primary/foreign key relationship. If your database server requires an explicit foreign key link, you'll need to supply it. The definitions in Listing 6.3 works for MySQL.

```
create table supportproperty (
id int not null auto_increment primary key,
name text);
create table properties (
id int,
property_name text,
property_value text
);
```

Listing 6.3

Notice that we've supplied the auto_increment keyword in the supportproperty table but not in the properties table. The reason is the primary/foreign key association. When Hibernate persists a SupportProperty object, it stores the name of the object and allows MySQL to automatically create a primary key for the supportproperty table. Hibernate obtains the created primary key and inserts it along with the key/values of the properties map into the properties table. When Hibernate needs to load the object from the database, it can pull the row from the supportproperty table and use the primary key to obtain the appropriate key/value pairs from the property table.

The application in Listing 6.4 shows how to use the SupportProperty object and its Hibernate mapping document. This example instantiates a SupportProperty object and populates the name attribute. Next, we create a HashMap object and add two key/value pairs. The map is added to the SupportProperty object; then we save the object to permanent storage. Finally, we pull the object from storage and display the values of the two properties.

```java
import java.io.*;
import java.util.*;

import net. sf.hibernate.*;
import net. sf.hibernate.cfg.*;

public class SupportPropertyTest {

  public static void main(String [] args) {

    try {
      Session session = HibernateSession.currentSession();

      SupportProperty sp = new SupportProperty();

      sp.setName("John Smith");
      HashMap p = new HashMap();
      p.put("color", "blue");
      p.put("lnf", "mac");
      sp.setProperties(p);

      session.save(sp);
      session.flush();

      SupportProperty sp2 = (SupportProperty)session.
          load(SupportProperty.class, new Integer(sp.getId()));

      Map p2 = sp2.getProperties();
      System.out.println(p2.get("color"));
      System.out.println(p2.get("lnf"));

      session.close();
    } catch (Exception e) {
      e.printStackTrace();
    }
  }
}
```

Listing 6.4

The results from the example application are shown below. Hibernate has persisted our SupportProperty, just as we expected. The supportproperty table holds the name attribute and primary key of the object, and the properties table holds the two key/value pairs as well as a foreign key value associating the appropriate object row in supportproperty table with the map rows.

```
mysql> select * from supportproperty;
+----+------------+
| id | name       |
+----+------------+
|  5 | John Smith |
+----+------------+
1 rows in set (0.00 sec)

mysql> select * from properties;
+-----------+---------------+--------------------+
| part_id   | property_name | property_value     |
+-----------+---------------+--------------------+
|         5 | lnf           | mac                |
|         5 | color         | blue               |
+-----------+---------------+--------------------+
2 rows in set (0.00 sec)
```

Mapping an Object Map: <many-to-many> Element

Many times in the development of an application that uses a map, the key is a primitive type like an integer or a string but the value is an object. In this situation, you need to be able to store the object and provide a reference to be used in the map as well as other maps. Since the object can be used in more than one map, it's a many-to-many situation as far as the map element is concerned. This means you use the <many-to-many> element instead of the <element> element to specify the value part of the map's key/value pair.

To illustrate how this works, we'll create an example class called Employee that contains some basic attributes and a Map called benefits. The map uses a key based on a string specifying the name of the benefit and a value using a Benefit class. The two classes needed are shown in Listing 6.5.

```java
import java.util.*;

public class Employee {
   private int id;
   private String name;
   private Map benefits;

   public Employee() {
   }

   public void setId(int i) {
      id = i;
   }

   public int getId() {
      return id;
   }

   public void setName(String s) {
```

```
      name = s;
   }

   public String getName() {
      return name;
   }

   public void setBenefits(Map m) {
      benefits = m;
   }

   public Map getBenefits() {
      return benefits;
   }
}
public class Benefit {
   private int id;
   private int cost;

   public Benefit() {
   }

   public Benefit(int c) {
      cost = c;
   }

   public void setId(int i) {
      id = i;
   }

   public int getId() {
      return id;
   }

   public void setCost(int i) {
      cost = i;
   }

   public int getCost() {
      return cost;
   }
}
```

Listing 6.5

The mapping document required for our Employee class is shown in Listing 6.6. The Employee class includes an identifier using a native generator. In fact, we allow MySQL to generate the identifier for each object added to the employee table. The name attribute of the Employee class is mapped to the database as well as the benefit Map attribute.

All the work takes place in the <map> element. First we define a specific table for the map called employee benefit. This is an association table used to associate rows from the employee table with rows from an as-yet-undefined table called benefit, which will hold specific Benefit objects. The rows in the association table have three columns:

- ❑ **parent id:** Defined using the <key> element. This column holds the identifier from the employee table so Hibernate can persist and load the correct map when handling an Employee object.

- ❑ **benefit name:** Defined using the <index> element, which represents the key parts of the key/value map pair. The key will be stored in the column using a type of string.

- ❑ **benefit id:** Defined using the <many-to-many> element, which represents the value part of the key/value map pair. The class is Benefit.

Notice that there is no type attribute but a class attribute instead. Hibernate notices the difference based on the <many-to-many> element and only persist a foreign key value into the supplied column.

The foreign key value for the association table is obtained from the database mapping the supplied class—in this case, Benefit. The mapping for Benefit is found in the same mapping document as Employee but under a different <class> element. The Benefit class mapping looks like any other class mapping with its attributes mapped to specific columns and an identifier definition using a native generator. So, MySQL automatically generates the identifier values for the Benefit objects as well. The result is an association table that maps many Benefit objects to at least one Employee object. All the work is accomplished in the association table, as you'll see shortly.

```xml
<?xml version="1.0" encoding="UTF-8"?>
<!DOCTYPE hibernate-mapping
PUBLIC "-//Hibernate/Hibernate Mapping DTD//EN"
"http://hibernate.sourceforge.net/hibernate-mapping-2.0.dtd">

<hibernate-mapping>
<class name="Employee"
  table="employee">
  <id name="id" unsaved-value="0">
    <generator class="native"/>
  </id>

<map name="benefits"
        table="employee_benefit" cascade="all">
        <key column="parent_id"/>
        <index column="benefit_name" type="string"/>
        <many-to-many column="benefit_id" class="Benefit"/>
</map>
<property name="name" type="string"/>
</class>
<class name="Benefit"
  table="benefit">
 <id name="id" unsaved-value="0">
        <generator class="native"/>
 </id>
<property name="cost" type="int"/>
</class>
</hibernate-mapping>
```

Listing 6.6

From the mapping document, we find that we need three tables: employee, benefit, and employee benefit. The necessary MySQL SQL to generate the tables is found in Listing 6.7.

```
create table employee (
id int not null auto_increment primary key,
name text
);

create table benefit (
  id int not null auto_increment primary key,
  cost int
  );

create table employee_benefit (
parent_id int,
benefit_name text,
benefit_id int
);
```

Listing 6.7

With the classes, mapping, and database in place, we can discuss an application that shows how Hibernate maps a real object to persistent storage. An example application is shown in Listing 6.8.

```
import java.io.*;
import java.util.*;

import net.sf.hibernate.*;
import net.sf.hibernate.cfg.*;

public class EmployeeTest {

  public static void main(String [] args) {

    try {
      Session session = HibernateSession.currentSession();

      Employee sp = new Employee();
      Employee sp3 = new Employee();

      sp.setName("John Doe");
      HashMap p = new HashMap();
      p.put("health", new Benefit(200));
      p.put("dental", new Benefit(300));
      sp.setBenefits(p);

      sp3.setName("Jim Smith");
      sp3.setBenefits(p);
```

```
        session.save(sp);
        session.save(sp3);
        session.flush();

        Employee sp2 = (Employee)session.load(Employee.class, new
Integer(sp.getId()));

        Map p2 = sp2.getBenefits();
        System.out.println(((Benefit)p2.get("health")).getCost());
        System.out.println(((Benefit)p2.get("dental")).getCost());

        session.close();
    } catch (Exception e) {
        e.printStackTrace();
    }
  }
}
```

Listing 6.8

This code creates two `Employee` objects and assigns them different names. For the benefits, we create two key/value pairs. Notice that the key is a `String` and the value is a `Benefit` object. In this example, we're assuming that both employees have the same benefits, so the `HashMap` created to hold the `Benefit` objects is assigned using the `setBenefits()` method on both `Employee` objects. This example shows how Hibernate can handle shared objects.

Once the example application executes, Hibernate needs to store both `Employee` objects as well as both `Benefit` objects in the database. The result is the tables below. The result includes two rows in the `employee` table, as we expect: one for each object instantiated. The same is true for the two `Benefit` objects. The two tables are associated in the `employee_benefit` table; as you can see, there are two rows for each of the employees, since we associated two benefits with each in their maps.

```
mysql> select * from employee;
+----+-----------+
| id | name      |
+----+-----------+
|  7 | John Doe  |
|  8 | Jim Smith |
+----+-----------+
2 rows in set (0.00 sec)

mysql> select * from benefit;
+----+------+
| id | cost |
+----+------+
|  9 |  300 |
| 10 |  200 |
+----+------+
2 rows in set (0.00 sec)
```

```
mysql> select * from employee_benefit;
+-----------+--------------+------------+
| parent_id | benefit_name | benefit_id |
+-----------+--------------+------------+
|         7 | dental       |          9 |
|         7 | health       |         10 |
|         8 | dental       |          9 |
|         8 | health       |         10 |
+-----------+--------------+------------+
4 rows in set (0.00 sec)
```

Mapping a TreeMap

In the previous two examples, we've handled maps where the key/value pair consisted of primitive types and the value was a persistable object; but what about a situation where both the key and the value are objects? This is called a *ternary association*; we'll cover such an example in this section.

For our ternary example, we're also going to move away from the HashMap and focus on the TreeMap so the key values are sorted based on a comparison algorithm. We'll write a comparator class to handle the comparison of the key value objects. The containing class for this example is called Console, and it represents a gaming console. The Console object contains an identifier, a name, and a SortedMap attribute called games. The games map uses a key value based on a class called Game, which contains a name attribute. The games map uses a value key based on a class called Instructions, which contains an attribute called info. All three class definitions are shown in Listing 6.9.

```java
import java.util.*;

public class Console {
    private int id;
    private String name;
    private Map games;

    public Console() {
    }

    public Console(String name) {
        this.name = name;
    }

    public void setId(int i) {
        id = i;
    }

    public int getId() {
        return id;
    }

    public void setName(String n) {
        name = n;
    }
}
```

```
    public String getName() {
      return name;
    }

    public void setGames(Map m) {
      games = m;
    }

    public Map getGames() {
      return games;
    }
}

public class Game {
  private int id;
  private String name;

  public Game() {
  }

  public Game(String name) {
    this.name = name;
  }

  public void setId(int i) {
    id = i;
  }

  public int getId() {
    return id;
  }

  public void setName(String s) {
    name = s;
  }

  public String getName() {
    return name;
  }

    public boolean equals(Object obj) {
        if (obj == null) return false;
        if (!this.getClass().equals(obj.getClass())) return false;

        Game obj2 = (Game)obj;

        if ((this.id == obj2.getId()) &&
            this.name.equals(obj2.getName())) {
            return true;
        }

  return false;
    }
```

```
      public int hashCode() {
          int tmp = 0;
          tmp = (id + name).hashCode();

          return tmp;
      }
}

public class Instructions {
    private int id;
    private String info;

    public Instructions() {
    }

    public Instructions(String info) {
        this.info = info;
    }

    public void setId(int i) {
        id = i;
    }

    public int getId() {
        return id;
    }

    public void setInfo(String s) {
        info = s;
    }

    public String getInfo() {
        return info;
    }
}
```

Listing 6.9

The mapping document required for the three classes in this example is more complex than the other mapping examples; see Listing 6.10. First, all three classes are defined in the single Console.hbm.xml file, more for convenience than for any other reason. The Console mapping begins with an identifier using a native generator like we've used in the past. There is also the familiar <property> element for the name of the console. Notice that we're using <map> as the element even though the ultimate class will be a TreeMap. In the <map> element, we define the name of the attribute being mapped as well as the association table to be used. We have an association table because we aren't mapping primitive types but instead objects in the map. We also have a sort attribute, since we'll be dealing with a SortedMap class. In our example, we've specified a custom class called GameComparator, which we'll discuss shortly. Finally, we use the cascade attribute to tell Hibernate that it should attempt to persist all objects when the Console object is saved. As you'll see later, this doesn't always do the job.

The subelements in the <map> element include <key>, to hold the primary key from the parent so Hibernate knows which map elements are associated with the parent Console object. Instead of an <index> element, we use the element <index-many-to-many> when the key value for a map is an object and not a primitive type like integer or String. The element includes the column attribute to map the object's primary key to a specific column as well as the class being represented in the column. Just as in the previous example, Hibernate uses the specified column to hold a row identifier for the Game object being used as a key. The same is true for the value object through the <many-to-many> element specified for the Instruction object used in the map pair.

After the <class> element for the Console class are the appropriate <class> elements for the Game and Instructions classes. Both of the classes need an identifier and a generator so Hibernate has a primary key to place in the foreign key columns defined by the <index-many-to-many> and <many-to-many> elements in the <map>.

```xml
<?xml version="1.0" encoding="UTF-8"?>
<!DOCTYPE hibernate-mapping
PUBLIC "-//Hibernate/Hibernate Mapping DTD//EN"
"http://hibernate.sourceforge.net/hibernate-mapping-2.0.dtd">

<hibernate-mapping>
<class name="Console"
  table="console">
  <id name="id" unsaved-value="0">
        <generator class="native"/>
  </id>

  <map name="games"
        table="game_instructions" sort="GameComparator" cascade="all">
        <key column="parent_id"/>
        <index-many-to-many column="game_id" class="Game"/>
        <many-to-many column="instructions_id" class="Instructions"/>
  </map>
  <property name="name" type="string"/>
</class>

<class name="Game"
  table="game">
  <id name="id" unsaved-value="0">
        <generator class="native"/>
  </id>
  <property name="name" type="string"/>
</class>

<class name="Instructions"
  table="instructions">
  <id name="id" unsaved-value="0">
        <generator class="native"/>
  </id>
  <property name="info" type="string"/>
</class>

</hibernate-mapping>
```

Listing 6.10

From the mapping document, we can create the necessary tables for this example. The MySQL SQL needed to create them is found in Listing 6.11.

```
create table console (
id int not null auto_increment primary key,
 name text
 ) ;


create table game (
 id int not null auto_increment primary key,
 name text
 ) ;


 create table instructions (
 id int not null auto_increment primary key,
 info text
 ) ;


 create table game_instructions (
 parent_id int,
 game_id int,
 instructions_id int
 ) ;
```

Listing 6.11

The first three database tables hold the three objects in our example: `console`, `game`, and `instructions`. Each has its own identifier, which is automatically generated by the database server. The `game_instructions` table is used as an association table to create the ternary relationship between the `Console` object and the map object containing the `Game` and `Instructions` objects. Once Hibernate has all the main objects stored in the database, it pulls the identifiers as primary keys and places them in the association table as foreign keys.

As we mentioned earlier, we need to define a `Comparator` class so Java can sort the `Game` objects properly. Listing 6.12 shows the `Comparator` class; it overrides the `compare()` and equals() methods as defined by the `Comparator` interface.

Listing 6.13 shows the code for an example application that uses all of our classes and mappings. The code begins by creating a `Console` object and setting its name attribute. It instantiates a `TreeMap` object using our new `Comparator`, and then creates two `Game` objects and assigns them to the appropriate variables. Next, we add two pairs to the `TreeMap` object, creating the appropriate `Instructions` at the same time.

It may seem strange that we aren't building the `Game` objects as we did the `Instructions` objects, using the `put()` to the map. The reason comes out of the `cascade` attribute found in the `<map>` element. As you might expect, Hibernate should persist both the `Game` and `Instructions` objects when a `Console` object is persisted. Unfortunately, Hibernate only persists the `value` object and not the key objects. We have to manually save the key objects and flush them before saving the `Console` object; otherwise we get an exception.

```java
import java.util.*;

public class GameComparator implements Comparator {
    public int compare(Object o1, Object o2) {
        Game game1 = (Game)o1;
        Game game2 = (Game)o2;

        return game1.getName().compareTo(game2.getName());
    }

    public boolean equals(Object obj) {
        if (obj == null) return false;
        if (!this.getClass().equals(obj.getClass())) return false;

        return true;
    }

}
```

Listing 6.12

```java
import java.io.*;
import java.util.*;

import net.sf.hibernate.*;
import net.sf.hibernate.cfg.*;

public class ConsoleTest {

    public static void main(String [] args) {

        try {
            Session session = HibernateSession.currentSession();

            Console sp = new Console("New Console");

            TreeMap p = new TreeMap(new GameComparator());
            Game g = new Game("Donkey Kong");
            Game g2 = new Game("Asteroids");
            p.put(g, new Instructions("Instructions for Donkey Kong"));
            p.put(g2, new Instructions("Instructions for Asteroids"));
            sp.setGames(p);

            session.save(g);
            session.save(g2);
session.flush();

            session.save(sp);
            session.flush();
```

```
      session.close();
    } catch (Exception e) {
      e.printStackTrace();
    }
  }
}
```

Listing 6.13

When the example application is executed, we obtain the rows found below. Notice that once the Game object is persisted, Hibernate can populate the game_instructions association table with the proper primary keys from both the game and instructions tables.

```
mysql> select * from console;
+----+-------------+
| id | name        |
+----+-------------+
|  5 | New Console |
+----+-------------+
1 row in set (0.00 sec)

mysql> select * from game;
+----+-------------+
| id | name        |
+----+-------------+
|  3 | Donkey Kong |
|  4 | Asteroids   |
+----+-------------+
2 rows in set (0.00 sec)

mysql> select * from instructions;
+----+-----------------------------+
| id | info                        |
+----+-----------------------------+
|  3 | Instructions for Asteroids  |
|  4 | Instructions for Donkey Kong|
+----+-----------------------------+
2 rows in set (0.00 sec)

mysql> select * from game_instructions;
+-----------+---------+-----------------+
| parent_id | game_id | instructions_id |
+-----------+---------+-----------------+
|         5 |       4 |               3 |
|         5 |       3 |               4 |
+-----------+---------+-----------------+
2 rows in set (0.00 sec)
```

Based on the rows in the database shown in the previous example, you can clearly see how Hibernate takes the identifiers from the three object tables and builds the association table.

Mapping Set/SortedSets

The Set and SortedSet are other important collection interfaces and classes available in Java. As you might expect, the Java set interface is based on the mathematical set, where elements are added in a manner such that no two elements are identical. As you might expect, objects to be added to a set must implement both the equals() and hashCode() methods so Java can determine whether any two elements/objects are identical. Since we need to be able to persist Sets just as we did Maps, we'll show an appropriate mapping document for an example.

From a practical sense, we'll use the classes HashSet and TreeSet to implement the example. This example is based on two classes: GameScore and HighScores, as shown in Listing 6.14. The GameScore class holds two attributes: the name of a game and the score achieved. The HighScores class holds a name as well as a Set containing GameScore objects.

```java
public class GameScore {
  private int id;
  private String name;
  private int score;

  public GameScore() {
  }

  public GameScore(String name, int score) {
    this.name = name;
    this.score = score;
  }

  public void setId(int i) {
    id = i;
  }

  public int getId() {
    return id;
  }

  public void setName(String s) {
    name = s;
  }

  public String getName() {
    return name;
  }

  public void setScore(int i) {
    score = i;
  }
```

```java
   public int getScore() {
     return score;
   }

     public boolean equals(Object obj) {
         if (obj == null) return false;
         if (!this.getClass().equals(obj.getClass())) return false;

         GameScore obj2 = (GameScore)obj;

         if ((this.id == obj2.getId()) &&
             (this.name.equals(obj2.getName())) &&
             (this.score == obj2.getScore())
             ) {
             return true;
         }

     return false;
       }

     public int hashCode() {
         int tmp = 0;
         tmp = (id + name + score).hashCode();

         return tmp;
     }
}


import java.util.*;

public class HighScores {
   private int id;
   private String name;
   private Set games;

   public HighScores() {
   }

   public HighScores(String name) {
     this.name = name;
   }

   public void setId(int i) {
     id = i;
   }

   public int getId() {
     return id;
   }

   public void setName(String n) {
     name = n;
   }
```

```
    public String getName() {
      return name;
    }

    public void setGames(Set games) {
      this.games = games;
    }

    public Set getGames() {
      return games;
    }
}
```

Listing 6.14

Based on our two classes and the Set object contained in the `HighScores` object, we create the Hibernate mapping document shown in Listing 6.15. This mapping document looks very similar to the `Map` object documents; the only real change is the `<set>` element. The document includes two `<class>` elements for each of our classes. The `GameScore` `<class>` element defines the attributes from the class that need to be persisted. It's referenced from the `<set>` element in the `HighScores` `<class>` element. For the `<set>` element, we define both a `<key>` element and a `<one-to-many>` element: in our case, `<one-to-many>` to handle the relationship between the two classes. The `<key>` is the column in the `gamescore` table that holds the foreign key to the parent object. We use the `<one-to-many>` element to tell Hibernate the column and class for the objects stored in the Set; it indicates that one `HighScores` object relates to many `GameScore` objects and, as such, the `GameScore` object must have a `HighScores` parent associated with it. The element also means we don't need an association table but only the object tables. We also use the cascade attribute in the `<set>` element to tell Hibernate to persist the `GameScore` objects at the same time as the `HighScore` object.

```xml
<?xml version="1.0" encoding="UTF-8"?>
<!DOCTYPE hibernate-mapping
PUBLIC "-//Hibernate/Hibernate Mapping DTD//EN"
"http://hibernate.sourceforge.net/hibernate-mapping-2.0.dtd">

<hibernate-mapping>
<class name="HighScores"
  table="highscores">
  <id name="id" unsaved-value="0">
        <generator class="native"/>
  </id>

  <set name="games" cascade="all" >
        <key column="parent_id"/>
        <one-to-many class="GameScore"/>
  </set>
  <property name="name" type="string"/>
</class>

<class name="GameScore"
  table="gamescores">
```

```
    <id name="id" unsaved-value="0">
        <generator class="native"/>
    </id>
        <property name="name"/>
        <property name="score"/>
</class>

</hibernate-mapping>
```

Listing 6.15

Of course, we need a couple of database tables for our three classes. There shouldn't be any surprises: We have two tables for each of our objects and a single association table to handle the objects in the Set. Listing 6.16 shows the SQL to build the MySQL tables.

```
create table HighScores (
id int not null auto_increment primary key,
name text
);

create table gamescores (
id int not null primary key auto_increment,
name text,
score int,
parent_id int
);
```

Listing 6.16

Listing 6.17 shown an example application that takes our classes, instantiates the appropriate objects, and persists the entire thing to the database. The key to the application lies in instantiating the HashSet object and populating it with GameScore objects. The HashSet is attached to the HighScore object through the setGames() method, and the HighScores object is saved to the database. Notice that we haven't saved the GameScore objects to the database—only the HighScores object. The cascade attribute in the mapping document tells Hibernate to save the object automatically when the parent object is saved.

```
import java.io.*;
import java.util.*;

import net. sf.hibernate.*;
import net. sf.hibernate.cfg.*;

public class GameScoreTest {

  public static void main(String [] args) {

    try {
      Session session = HibernateSession.currentSession();
```

```
        HighScores sp = new HighScores("James");

        HashSet set = new HashSet();
        set.add(new GameScore("Asteroids", 3784783));
        set.add(new GameScore("PacMan", 20823));
        sp.setGames(set);

        session.save(sp);
        session.flush();

        session.close();
    } catch (Exception e) {
        e.printStackTrace();
    }
  }
}
```

Listing 6.17

The results in the database tables from the example are shown below. There are only two tables because of the one-to-many relationship stipulated in the mapping document. The primary relationship between the tables is the primary key of the `highscores` table and the foreign key column, `parent_id`, of the gamescores table.

```
mysql> select * from highscores;
+----+-------+
| id | name  |
+----+-------+
|  7 | James |
+----+-------+
1 row in set (0.00 sec)

mysql> select * from gamescores;
+----+-----------+---------+-----------+
| id | name      | score   | parent_id |
+----+-----------+---------+-----------+
|  1 | Asteroids | 3784783 |         7 |
|  2 | PacMan    |   20823 |         7 |
+----+-----------+---------+-----------+
2 rows in set (0.00 sec)
```

SortedSet Interface Mapping

If you need to use a `SortedSet` interface through the `TreeSet` implementation class, you handle the situation using the same functionality as found in the `SortedMap` example in the previous section. Only three changes are needed. First, use a `TreeSet` in the example application instead of the `HashSet`. Of course, using a `TreeSet` means you need a `Comparator` class just like the `TreeMap`. Finally, add the sort attribute to the `<set>` element.

Mapping Lists

Some developers use the Map and Set functionality mentioned in the previous two sections, but most use a List collection. The list collection is based on the interface java.util.List, and the typical implementation classes are the ArrayList and the Vector. Because of the popularity of the list functionality, we'll show how Hibernate can handle persisting this Java construct. For this example, we'll use two classes called Group and Story, shown in Listing 6.18. An object instantiated from the Group class contains a list of Story objects. The list can be any length and contain duplicates if necessary. There is no sorting involved—just a list of objects.

```java
import java.util.*;

public class Group {
  private int id;
  private String name;
  private List stories;

  public Group(){
  }

  public Group(String name) {
    this.name = name;
  }

  public void setId(int i) {
    id = i;
  }

  public int getId() {
    return id;
  }

  public void setName(String n) {
    name = n;
  }

  public String getName() {
    return name;
  }

  public void setStories(List l) {
    stories = l;
  }

  public List getStories() {
    return stories;
  }
}

import java.util.*;

public class Story {
  private int id;
```

```
   private String info;

   public Story(){
   }

   public Story(String info) {
     this.info = info;
   }

   public void setId(int i) {
     id = i;
   }

   public int getId() {
     return id;
   }

   public void setInfo(String n) {
     info = n;
   }

   public String getInfo() {
     return info;
   }
 }
```

Listing 6.18

At this point, you might be able to write the mapping document without much help; the current mapping document in shown in Listing 6.19. The only real difference between this mapping document and the previous ones is the use of the `<list>` element instead of `<map>` or `<set>`. The current `<list>` element looks quite a bit like the `<set>` element with `<key>` and `<one-to-many>` elements; but there's also an `<index>` element because lists and vectors are indexed using an integer value. The indexing is basically the order in which the objects were added to the list, so we maintain that functionality in the mapping. The `parent_id` and `idx` columns specified in the `<list>` element are added to the story table because of the one-to-many mapping. If we changed this example to use a many-to-many relationship, we'd need an association table to map between the parent and the child objects.

```
<?xml version="1.0" encoding="UTF-8"?>
<!DOCTYPE hibernate-mapping
PUBLIC "-//Hibernate/Hibernate Mapping DTD//EN"
"http://hibernate.sourceforge.net/hibernate-mapping-2.0.dtd">

<hibernate-mapping>

<class name="Group"
  table="grouptable">
  <id name="id" unsaved-value="0">
        <generator class="native"/>
  </id>

  <list name="stories" cascade="all">
```

```
            <key column="parent_id"/>
            <index column="idx"/>
            <one-to-many class="Story"/>
    </list>
    <property name="name" type="string"/>
</class>
<class name="Story"
    table="story">
    <id name="id" unsaved-value="0">
            <generator class="native"/>
    </id>
        <property name="info"/>
</class>

</hibernate-mapping>
```

Listing 6.19

The databases required for the mappings are shown in Listing 6.20. As we mentioned in the previous section, the columns needed for the `<list>` element are added to the story table because of the one-to-many relationship. Both the tables have independent identifiers with the grouptable identifier used as a foreign key in the story table.

```
create table grouptable (
id int not null primary key auto_increment,
name text
);

create table story (
id int not null primary key auto_increment,
info text,
idx int,
parent_id int
);
```

Listing 6.20

Finally, Listing 6.21 shows an example application to use the `Group` and `Story` objects. We've used the `ArrayList` implementation class to hold all the `Story` objects. Again, we don't need to persist the `Story` objects because of the cascade attribute in the `<list>` element. Hibernate handles all the details for the child objects as well as the parent.

```
import java.io.*;
import java.util.*;

import net.sf.hibernate.*;
import net.sf.hibernate.cfg.*;

public class GroupTest {

  public static void main(String [] args) {
```

```
    try {
        Session session = HibernateSession.currentSession();

        Group sp = new Group("accounting");

        ArrayList list = new ArrayList();
        list.add(new Story("A Story"));
        list.add(new Story("And yet another story"));
        sp.setStories(list);

        session.save(sp);
        session.flush();

        session.close();
    } catch (Exception e) {
        e.printStackTrace();
    }
  }
}
```

Listing 6.21

When we execute the example application, Hibernate produces three rows in our two tables, as shown below. The rows look similar to the ones from the <set> example. Hibernate persists the Story objects to the story table and updates them with the primary key from the grouptable database table.

```
mysql> select * from grouptable;
+----+-----------+
| id | name      |
+----+-----------+
|  3 | accounting|
+----+-----------+
1 row in set (0.00 sec)

mysql> select * from story;
+----+----------------------+------+-----------+
| id | info                 | idx  | parent_id |
+----+----------------------+------+-----------+
|  1 | A Story              |  0   |        3  |
|  2 | And yet another story|  1   |        3  |
+----+----------------------+------+-----------+
2 rows in set (0.00 sec)
```

Bag Mapping

If you don't care about the list's index functionality, you can persist the `ArrayList` or `Vector` as a *bag*. A bag is a random grouping of the objects in the list. Using a bag is a simple matter of changing the `<list>` element to a `<bag>` and removing the `<index>` subelement. The mapping using a `<bag>` element in shown in Listing 6.22.

```xml
<?xml version="1.0" encoding="UTF-8"?>
<!DOCTYPE hibernate-mapping
PUBLIC "-//Hibernate/Hibernate Mapping DTD//EN"
"http://hibernate.sourceforge.net/hibernate-mapping-2.0.dtd">

<hibernate-mapping>

<class name="Group"
  table="grouptable">
  <id name="id" unsaved-value="0">
        <generator class="native"/>
  </id>

  <bag name="stories" cascade="all">
        <key column="parent_id"/>
        <one-to-many class="Story"/>
  </bag>
<property name="name" type="string"/>
</class>
<class name="Story"
  table="story">
  <id name="id" unsaved-value="0">
        <generator class="native"/>
  </id>
      <property name="info"/>
</class>

</hibernate-mapping>
```

Listing 6.22

When the example application from the `<list>` mapping is used with the bag, we obtain the rows in the database tables as shown below.

```
mysql> select * from grouptable;
+----+-----------+
| id | name      |
+----+-----------+
|  4 | accounting|
+----+-----------+
1 row in set (0.00 sec)
```

```
mysql> select * from story;
+----+----------------------+------+-----------+
| id | info                 | idx  | parent_id |
+----+----------------------+------+-----------+
|  3 | A Story              | NULL |         4 |
|  4 | And yet another story| NULL |         4 |
+----+----------------------+------+-----------+
2 rows in set (0.00 sec)
```

Mapping Arrays

Our last collection-mapping example uses a traditional array commonly used before the days of collections. As you might expect, not much change is needed in the mapping document when using an array. Listing 6.23 shows an example of the Group/Story classes being mapped using the <array> element.

```xml
<?xml version="1.0" encoding="UTF-8"?>
<!DOCTYPE hibernate-mapping
PUBLIC "-//Hibernate/Hibernate Mapping DTD//EN"
"http://hibernate.sourceforge.net/hibernate-mapping-2.0.dtd">

<hibernate-mapping>

<class name="Group"
  table="grouptable">
  <id name="id" unsaved-value="0">
        <generator class="native"/>
  </id>

  <array name="stories" cascade="all">
        <key column="parent_id"/>
        <index column="idx"/>
        <one-to-many class="Story"/>
  </array>
  <property name="name" type="string"/>
</class>
<class name="Story"
  table="story">
  <id name="id" unsaved-value="0">
        <generator class="native"/>
  </id>
      <property name="info"/>
</class>
</hibernate-mapping>
```

Listing 6.23

As you can see from the array mapping, we need an index because we're using an array as well as an element. We've used the <one-to-many> element to associate the Story objects with the array. As you'd expect, the outcome of the <array> element is just like that of <list> and <set>, for the most part.

Mapping a Bidirectional Association

Since Hibernate doesn't support the idea of a bidirectional association when using an indexed collection like the list, map, or array, we'll consider an example of establishing the association using a Set. Bidirectional association provides a way to reference the parent through a child object. We already have a way to go from the parent to the child, so we want to add the additional association.

To set the stage, we'll use the Group/Story examples from the previous examples. First we have the Group and Story class, as shown in Listing 6.18. Those classes were designed for a List example, so we change the List definition to Set. The mapping document for the classes is shown in Listing 6.24.

```xml
<?xml version="1.0" encoding="UTF-8"?>
<!DOCTYPE hibernate-mapping
PUBLIC "-//Hibernate/Hibernate Mapping DTD//EN"
"http://hibernate.sourceforge.net/hibernate-mapping-2.0.dtd">

<hibernate-mapping>

<class name="Group"
  table="grouptable">
  <id name="id" unsaved-value="0">
        <generator class="native"/>
  </id>

  <set name="stories" cascade="all">
        <key column="parent_id"/>
        <one-to-many class="Story"/>
  </set>
 <property name="name" type="string"/>
</class>

<class name="Story" table="story">
  <id name="id" unsaved-value="0">
        <generator class="native"/>
  </id>
      <property name="info"/>
</class>

</hibernate-mapping>
```

Listing 6.24

We now use code like the following in a test application, as we've done in the past:

```
Group sp = new Group("accounting");

HashSet set = new HashSet();
set.add(new Story("A Story"));
sp.setStories(set);

session.save(sp);
session.flush();

session.close();
```

From a database perspective, we get three SQL statements: one to save Group sp, one to save a Story object, and an update statement to associate the Story object with the Group object. If we want to obtain the Story object, we can use Hibernate to load it; but we won't know anything about the parent Group object. If we want to load the Group, we have the association to the child because of the Set attribute in the Group object.

We can add the bidirectional association by making a few changes to the Story object and the mapping document. First we add a new attribute and necessary methods to the Story object, as follows:

```
private Group parent;
public void setParent(Group g) {
   parent = g;
}
public Group getParent() {
   return parent;
}
```

Now, for each Story object, Hibernate can associate the Group parent object. In addition, Hibernate can save the objects to the database without using the UPDATE command and using only the two INSERTs. Of course, we also need to change the mapping document. The new mapping document in shown in Listing 6.25.

```
<?xml version="1.0" encoding="UTF-8"?>
<!DOCTYPE hibernate-mapping
PUBLIC "-//Hibernate/Hibernate Mapping DTD//EN"
"http://hibernate.sourceforge.net/hibernate-mapping-2.0.dtd">

<hibernate-mapping>

<class name="Group"
  table="grouptable">
  <id name="id" unsaved-value="0">
        <generator class="native"/>
  </id>

  <set name="stories" cascade="all" inverse="true">
        <key column="parent_id"/>
        <one-to-many class="Story"/>
  </set>
```

```
      <property name="name" type="string"/>
  </class>

  <class name="Story" table="story">
    <id name="id" unsaved-value="0">
          <generator class="native"/>
    </id>
        <property name="info"/>
        <many-to-one name="parent" column="parent_id" not-null="true"/>
  </class>

  </hibernate-mapping>
```

Listing 6.25

We've made two changes to the system. First, we've added a `<many-to-one>` element to the `Story` child class. This element lets Hibernate know that each child object is associated with a parent object and, as such, that we need to supply the parent identifier to each child row. We've provided a column called `parent_id` to hold the identifier of the parent. Second, we've added an inverse attribute to the parent's `<set>` element. When set to `true`, this attribute tells Hibernate that a bidirectional association is set up and the additional UPDATE query command is unnecessary.

Summary

This extensive chapter has shown you how to map one of the most important constructs in the Java language. The `Collections` interfaces and associated classes are used in most Java applications to handle the storage of some amount of data. It would be unfortunate if we had to re-create the collections each time the application was executed. Hibernate provides the ability to persist `Collection` objects using many different mapping techniques.

7

Using Persistent Objects

Now that we've introduced Hibernate and the mapping documents, you should have a good feel for how to set things up to persist your Java objects. You've seen a few examples of storing objects in an underlying database. Now we'll dive into the persistence and loading process and show you some of Hibernate' more advanced features. In this chapter, we'll cover the basics like saving and loading Java objects; we'll also discuss advanced topics like performing queries against the database to find the right objects and validating object attributes.

Persisting Objects

In the previous chapters, we've shown how to build a Java class and a related mapping document so the Hibernate system knows how to persist the object to the underlying database. Of course, creating the Java class and its mapping document doesn't do much for saving the object. You can instantiate Java objects from the class all day long, and the objects will disappear when the application terminates. The mapping document you create for the objects tells Hibernate how to take each of the objects' attributes and store them in the database. To persist the newly instantiated objects, you need to use a specific method associated with the Session. The primary method is called save(); the Session object contains the following signatures for the method:

```
public Object save(Object obj);
public void save(Serializable id);
```

The save() method persists the provided object to the database. Of course, things aren't always that simple. First, the method must make sure the object hasn't already been saved (otherwise you'd get duplicate objects in the database). The method checks the identifier attribute you're required to add to the Java class and makes sure it's a null value. Remember, in the mapping document you supply an attribute called not-saved to the `<id>` element; this value tells Hibernate the value of the Java object's identifier attribute if the object hasn't been saved to the database. Typically, you'll set the not-saved value to be the default value of the attribute type; so if the identifier is an integer, the not-saved value is 0. The save() method checks to be sure you aren't trying to save an object that has already been saved.

After the save check, Hibernate creates a unique identifier using the associated `<generator>` defined in the mapping document. The identifier is set in the Java object; finally, the object is saved to the underlying database using the get methods created in the Java class and referenced in the mapping document.

Let's look at some code. Listing 7.1 shows a class called `User`, and Listing 7.2 is the associated mapping document.

```java
public class User {
   private int id;
   private String username;
   private String password;

   public Group(){
   }

   public Group(String name) {
      this.name = name;
   }

   public void setId(int i) {
      id = i;
   }

   public int getId() {
      return id;
   }

   public void setUsername(String n) {
      username = n;
   }

   public String getUsernme() {
      return username;
   }

   public void setPasswword(String l) {
      password = l;
   }

   public String getPassword() {
      return password;
   }
}
```

Listing 7.1

```xml
<?xml version="1.0" encoding="UTF-8"?>
<!DOCTYPE hibernate-mapping PUBLIC
"-//Hibernate/Hibernate Mapping DTD//EN"
"http://hibernate.sourceforge.net/hibernate-mapping-2.0.dtd">
```

```xml
<hibernate-mapping>
  <class name="User"
         table="user">
    <id name="id">
      <generator class="native"/>
    </id>
<property name="username" type="string"/>
<property name="password" type="string"/>

</class>
</hibernate-mapping>
```

Listing 7.2

The code in Listing 7.3 uses the User object to build and persist an object.

```java
Session session = SessionFactory.openSession();
User user = new User("username", "password");
session.save(user);
```

Listing 7.3

As we've discussed, the code in Listing 7.3 instantiates the necessary `Session` object and the `User` object. In the last line of code, the `User` object is stored in the database using the `save()` method. Notice that you don't need to do anything more than save the object.

We can see the identifier associated with the saved object in a number of ways, as shown here:

```java
session.save(user);
System.out.println(user.getId());
```

or

```java
Long id = (Long)session.save(user);
```

The first section of code takes advantage of the value returned by the `save()` method. Of course, the output received depends on the generator used in the mapping document.

If there is a problem, the `save()` method throws the `HibernateException` exception; as such, your code needs to be wrapped in a try-catch block. If an exception occurs when trying to persist an object, not much can be done directly. Either a database error has occurred (such as a connection failure) or the database server itself has gone down. You must be careful about one case, though.

In later chapters, we'll discuss how to create relationships between your objects: for example, in the case of composition, one object has an attribute relating to another object or a collection of objects. In many cases, you have the option of setting a cascade attribute when building the mapping document. The cascade attribute tells Hibernate that when the parent object is persisted, the associated attribute with the proper cascade value should also be saved. In these cases, Hibernate handles all the saves and relationship housekeeping itself.

However, if you choose to use the not-null value for an attribute, then the order in which you call the save() method is important. Consider an example where object A has an attribute that is the B object. In the mapping document for class A, the B attribute has the not-null attribute set to true. This means that if Hibernate hasn't already stored object B and knows about its identifier, a save() on object A will cause a constraint error based on the not-null attribute. Hibernate will throw an exception if the not-null constraint is violated. Therefore, when using the not-null attribute in your mapping document for an attribute of the class, you must be sure to note the order in which the objects should be saved.

If you look back at the two save() methods available through the Session object, you'll find that one is available that lets us directly specify the identifier for the object. As you might expect, this version of the save() method needs to be used with some caution.

First, the identifier for an object shouldn't be created in a manner that provides a business function. Many organizations build database tables in such a manner that the row identifier is an account number or a combination of fields in a complex identifier string. Both of these cases cause the database row to use an identifier that means something other than a unique row index. So, when using the <id> and <generator> elements in a mapping document, the identifier is created to be unique but otherwise has no value to the object itself. You should follow this same rule when using the save(object, id) method.

Second, the identifier passed to the method must be unique. This requirement can't be overstated. An identifier is a unique integer or string that provides uniqueness for your object in the database. Remember that you can create two identical objects in Java and persist those objects. The saved attributes is the same between the two objects--the only thing that keeps the objects unique is the identifier. Thus, if you provide your own identifier, it must be unique; otherwise a database error will occur, because the server will be unable to add the row.

Loading Data into an Object

Once an object has been persisted to the database, there will come a time when you want to retrieve the object and use it in your application. Hibernate provides many different ways to obtain objects from the database, and you'll see many of them in this chapter; however the easiest way is to use the load() method defined as part of the Session object. The Session object includes three versions of the load() method:

```
public Object load(Class class, Serializable id, LockMode mode);
public Object load(Class class, Serializable id);
public void load(Object object, Serialiable id);
```

As you can see, all three methods return an Object based on the identifier passed as a parameter. Two of the methods return the requested object as a return value; this means the load() method instantiates the object. In the third method, you must create the object and pass it to the method. In all three cases, you must pass in the identifier of the object that should be pulled from the persistent store. This is interesting, because how do you know the identifier? In most cases, you won't know it, which creates a situation that we'll resolve later in the chapter.

For now, let's discuss situations where we know the identifier of the object we need to load. Consider the following code:

```
Session session = SessionFactory.openSession();

User user = (User)session.load(User.class, 0);
```

This code creates a session object and asks Hibernate to pull an object from the database based on the User class and identifier value 0.

We've mentioned how the identifier pulls the appropriate object from the database, but we didn't say which database table is used or how Hibernate knows. The answer is the Class parameter, or the Object parameter in the case where the object is passed to the load() method. When the Class parameter is passed to the load() method, the system can easily determine which table to use because it uses the name of the supplied class. Using the name, Hibernate pulls the mapping document relating to the class and accesses the listed table. Using the information from the mapping document, Hibernate knows the appropriate fields that need to be pulled from the database and populated in the newly created object.

Using Previous Sessions

As we've discussed, using Hibernate is a straightforward process: You load an object, use it, and (potentially) update the object in the database. Of course, all straightforward processes have a wrinkle, and this is the case with Hibernate. Java is a popular language for building Web-based applications. If you follow the typical lifecycle of information in a Web application you'll find that the user enters some information into a Web page, the page is transferred to the Web server where the provided information is used to locate an object in the database. The object is passed back to the client using a JSP page and information is displayed. This is basically the end of a 'transaction' for the application. We still have the Web session but we don't want to keep a connection to the database because we don't know the user will be quick in their response. However, we still want the provided object available in the event the user updates information in the object. We'll need to have the object updated in the database.

However, we no longer have the original Session object used when we accessed the object originally. So what do we do? We must reattach to a new Session and then update the object. Hibernate provides the lock() method to perform the reattachment of the object with a new session. Here's an example:

```
//in first session
Session session = SessionFactory.openSession();
User user = session.load(User.class, 0);
SessionFactory.closeSession();

user.setPassword("NewPassword");
session = SessionFactory.openSession();
session.lock(user, LockMode.NONE);
SessionFactory.closeSession();
```

First this code obtains a session and pulls a User object based on the identifier value of 0. Once the object is loaded, the session is closed. Next, we change an object attribute and open a new Session. We use the lock() method to lock the object and reassociate with the new session. The key part of the lock() method is the LockMode value: This value tells Hibernate how to handle a situation where the current object is different from the object in the database. Since the objects in the database are available to other threads or sessions of our application, there is a chance the object has been changed. The available lock modes are as follows:

- ❏ **LockMode.NONE:** No lock occurs with the row in the database. Thus any thread can make a change to the object.

- ❏ **LockMode.READ:** A read lock occurs on the object.

- ❏ **LockMode.UPGRADE:** A lock occurs on the object row, and the in-memory object is updated with the object information in the database table.

- ❏ **LockMode.UPGRADE_NOWAIT:** An upgrade lock is attempted using a SELECT FOR UPDATE NOWAIT.

- ❏ **LockMode.WRITE:** A write lock is obtained when the object is either inserted (for a new object) or updated.

As you probably know, some locks are more expensive than others, and you should take care when obtaining a lock. Depending on your choice, some threads using the same object may be blocked from updating the database.

Flushing Objects

At any time during the processing of objects, you can call the flush() method on the Session object. During the execution of the flush, all queued SQL statements are executed. As you might have noticed, when you persist or update an object, the work doesn't automatically occur in the database; this is part of Hibernate's caching mechanism. When a flush() method executes, all the SQL statements are executed against the database. As a developer, you can flush the queue at any time. Hibernate executes a flush automatically when a commit() method is called as well as during the find() and iterate() methods.

Deleting Objects

Most of the life cycle of a Java object in the Hibernate arena involves inserting a new object in the database and updating the object. This process occurs over and over during one run of an application. Of course, sometimes an object needs to be deleted. The delete process isn't just the process of releasing the object in memory at the end of a function; instead, it involves deleting the row that represents the object from the database table. Hibernate provides the delete() method to do the job. The format of the command is as follows:

```
public void delete(Object object);
public void delete(String query);
```

Here's an example that deletes a single object using the first version of delete():

```
Session session = SessionFactory.openSession();
User user = (User)session.load(User.class, 0);
session.delete(user);
SessionFactory.closeSession();
```

In this code, we obtain an object from the table and then pass the object to the `delete()` command; the object is permanently removed from the database.

Hibernate generates a SQL query based on the id field of the user table. If you've turned on the showSQL property, you'll see a statement like the following:

```
delete from user where id = 0;
```

A second `load()` method that returns the object via its return statement also accepts a `LockMode` parameter.

Finally, we can also use the version of the `load()` method where we must supply the object. Here's the code using the third method type:

```
User user = new User();
// do anything you want with the object here

Session session = SessionFactory.openSession(); session.load(user, 0);
session.close();
```

In this code, we begin by instantiating a new `User` object. Here we've chosen to use a default constructor, but this doesn't have to be the case. Once the object has been instantiated, you're free to do just about anything you want with the object. When you're ready to populate the object based on values stored in the database, call the `load()` method, passing in the object and the identifier for the desired persisted object. Hibernate determines the class type of the object passed to the `load()` method and uses the appropriate mapping document and setter functions to load the passed object with the database field values.

When you're using the various `load()` methods, you may encounter a compile error at times. This may happen when you have a statement like the following:

```
User user = session.load(User.class, 0);
```

Notice we've forgotten the `(User)` cast before the `session.load()` call. You must always cast the object returned from the `session.load()` method call to the appropriate class; otherwise you'll receive a compile error.

If Hibernate attempts to load a row from the database with the provided identifier and it doesn't exist, an exception will occur and will need to be caught by the application. You could use the `get()` method instead of `load()`--the `get()` method doesn't throw an error if the row doesn't exists but instead returns a null value. The signatures for the `get()` methods are:

```
public Object get(Class class, Serializable id);
public Object get(Class class, Serializable id, LockMode mode);
```

Here's an example:

```
User user = (User)session.get(User.class, 0);
if (user == null) {
// doesn't exist - maybe build a new User object
}
```

In this code, we try to load the User object based on the identifier value of 0. If the object doesn't exist in the database, we may consider creating a new one.

Refreshing Objects

At any time during the execution of your application, you have the option of reloading or refreshing the object from the database. The refresh() command does the job:

```
public void refresh(Object object);
public void refresh(Object object, LockMode mode);
```

You could use the refresh in a multiuser situation where another user of the system might be updating the same object and you aren't part of a transaction. In this type of situation, two threads of an application have objects based on the same row in the database. If one thread updates the object in the database, the other thread is out of sync. The thread can reload the object to be sure it has the lasted information.

Updating Objects

You've persisted an object and loaded it into your application so you can use it. Your application might be such that the object is changed based on an operation. In the case of the User class, the user of the system may change their password; when the password changes, the user expects the new value to be stored, so you need a way to update the persistent store with the new value.

There are four ways to update a persisted object. The methods are update(), saveOrUpdate(), and flush(), and their signatures are as follows:

```
public void saveOrUpdate(Object object);
public void update(Object object);
public void update(Object object, Serializable id);
public void flush();
```

If you load an object and then change part of it, Hibernate can figure this out on its own when the flush() or close() method is executed against the Session object. For example:

```
Session session = SessionFactory.openSession();
User user = (User)session.load(User.class, 0);

user.setPassword("newpassword");
session.flush();
```

In this code, we load an object, change it, and then flush the session. The flush() method looks at all currently loaded persistent objects and automatically issues the appropriate SQL update statement to make sure the database reflects the changes made to the object. (More information about flush() is presented toward the end of the chapter.) For the purpose of updating the object, you just need to know that the flush() method can determine whether a change has been made to the object.

A second mechanism for updating an object uses the `saveOrUpdate()` method. This method determines whether the provided object should be either saved for the first time or updated. The method can make the determination based on the identifier and the not-saved value specified for the identifier in the mapping document. Remember that any object that hasn't been persisted to the database has a default value in its identifier attribute. An integer has a 0 value, and a string is null. When an object is passed to the `saveOrUpdate()` method, the method looks at the identifier value and calls either `save()` or `update()`.

You've already seen the `save()` method.

There are two different signatures for `update()`: The first provides the object to be updated as a parameter, and the second includes a specific identifier. Here's an example:

```
Session session = SessionFactory.openSession();
User user = (User)session.load(User.class, 0);
user.setPassword("newpassword");
session.update(user);
```

Hibernate determines whether the object truly needs to be updated and then issues the appropriate SQL statement to make the changes in the underlying database. If you want to provide the identifier for the object yourself, you can use the second signature of the `update()` method where the identifier is passed to the method code. Note that an exception is thrown if a row with the identifier value doesn't exists. Also, it should be clear that if you provide the wrong identifier, you may corrupt your database.

Finding Objects

All the code to this point has assumed that you know the identifier of the object you wish to pull from the database. In most cases, this won't be a valid assumption. Consider the `User` object as an example. If the user supplies a username/password combination in a Web application, you need to pull the `User` object from the persisted store based on the username value. You don't have the identifier value to use, since the identifier is a unique value and doesn't have any business purpose. You find the object in the database using the `Session` object's `find()` method. The signatures for the various `find()` methods are as follows:

```
public List find(String query);
public List find(String query, Object value, Type type);
public List find(String query, Object[] values, Type[] types);
```

The most basic `find()` method accepts a string. The method passes a query string to the method based on some criteria that need to be satisfied in order to return a particular object from the database. The method's return type is the `List` because there is always the potential for more than one object to be returned. The criteria used to determine whether a particular object is returned are specified as a query string based on the Hibernate Query Language (HQL), which we discuss in detail in Chapter 13.

Let's look at a simple example:

```
Session session = SessionFactory.openSession();
List users = session.find("from User");
session.close();
```

In this example, we execute the find() method using a string that pulls all the objects from the User table. The HQL string looks like SQL, which would read "select * from User". We assume that the entire object should be returned, so the select * part of the string is redundant. The result of this code is a List containing all the previously persisted User objects. We could now look through all the objects and try to find the one that matches the username supplied by our user. Of course, this is too much work; we should let the database server do the work for us.

Consider this code:

```
Session session = SessionFactory.openSession();
List users = session.find("from User where username " + username + "");
session.close();
```

Here we've changed the query string to include the WHERE clause, which causes the database to narrow the results based on supplied criteria. For this example, our criteria is "username = ?". We want to find only those objects (just one, we hope) where the username attribute of a stored object is equal to the Java variable username that contains the string entered by the user. The result is all the objects where the username attribute is equal to the value supplied by the user.

If you've used SQL, you know that using string concatenation as in this example isn't good practice. Instead, we should use placeholders like this:

```
Session session = SessionFactory.openSession();
List users = session.find("from User where username = ?",
                username,
                Hibernate.STRING
);
session.close();
```

In our new code example, we've removed the string concatenation and added a ? placeholder to the query string. In addition, we've used a different version of the find() command that has three parameters instead of one. The second parameter in the new method is either a single object or an array consisting of the values to be substituted in the query string. All the supplied values are substituted in order from left to right; a ? placeholder is needed for each supplied values. The third parameter in the find() method is a single object or an array of types for each of the supplied placeholder values. In this example, we only have a single placeholder, so we provide the value and type.

The result of this find() method is the same as for the string concatenation, but placeholders are better from a coding and style perspective. The following example shows how we might use multiple placeholders.

```
Session session = SessionFactory.openSession();
List users = session.find("from User where username = ? or upper(username)",
                new Object[] { username, username },
                new Type[] { Hibernate.STRING, Hibernate.STRING }
);
session.close();
```

In this example, we want to search on the string itself as well as make a comparison based on an uppercase version to be sure we catch both string formats. We've used internal arrays to build the second and third parameters to the method.

Finding Large Resultsets

In our previous examples, we've assumed that the number of objects returned is small—on the order of hundreds of objects. However, sometimes many more rows could be returned. There will be problems with the system if you try to return and instantiate a million objects that have been previously persisted. In these cases, you need to try to stay away from the find() method and use a query method called iterate(). The signature for iterate() is as follows:

```
public Iterator iterate(String query);
public Iterator iterate(String query, Object value, Type type);
public Iterator iterate(String query, Object[] values, Type[] types);
```

Consider the following example:

```
Session session = SessionFactory.openSession();
try {
Iterator iter = session.iterate("from User user order by user");
while (iter.hasNext()) {
User user = (User)iter.next();
//do something with the user object
if (user.equals ("middleoftheroad")) {
break;
}

} catch(Exception e) { SessionFactory.closeSession0;
```

The iterate() command executes a supplied query string and then lets you iterate over the results one at a time and, if you wish, stop using the result at some point in the resultset. Query strings can be provided in the iterate() method with placeholders and the appropriate values and types, as in the find() methods.

Filtering Collections

Collections are used in most Java applications, and Hibernate offers complete support for them (as discussed in Chapter 6). When you're using persisted objects, sometimes you want to obtain objects from a collection that might be part of another object. You could load the containing object, but you can also use the filter() method of the Session object to obtain object from the collection directly. The signatures for the filter() methods are as follows:

```
public Collection filter(Object collection, String filter);
public Collection filter(Object collection,
   String filter Object value, Type type);
public Collection filter(Object collection,
    String filter Object[] values, Type[] types);
```

Consider the following example (for this example, assume there is a Site object that contains an attribute with the definition List users representing a collection of User objects and an accessor method called getUsers()):

```
Session session = SessionFactory.open Session();
Site site = session.load(Site.class, 0);
Collection users = session.filter(site.getUsers(), "where this.username like
'a%');
SessionFactory.closeSession();
```

The code starts by obtaining a Site object. We assume that we've indicated lazy initialization so nothing is pulled for the Site object until we use it. Next, we use the filter() method to return a Collection object representing all User objects where the username start with the letter a. As you can see, the filter() method is a little different from find(), load(), and iterate(); the key difference is the first parameter, which tells the filter where to obtain the collection to perform the filtering. Hibernate can access the Site object provided and pull only its collection of users. From a table standpoint, you can imagine Hibernate producing the appropriate queries to get the identifier of the specified Site object and using that identifier as a foreign key to the User table. The result is a resultset of only those User objects that are part of the provided Site object's user collection. At this point, Hibernate can filter the list. Of course, most of this is performed using one or two queries based on how well Hibernate can formulate the needed query statements.

Notice the use of the this qualifier in the query string: The this qualifier references the collection we're trying to filter. The collection is always the result of the first parameter to the method.

Like the other query commands associated with the Session object, the filter() method can use placeholders. The values and types of the placeholders are specified like the other methods. Scalar queries can also be used with the filter() method. For example:

```
Session session = SessionFactory.openSession();
Site site = session.load(Site.class, 0);
Collection users = session.filter(site.getUsers(),
                         "select this.password where this.username like
'a%'");

SessionFactory.closeSession();
```

Here we're returning only the password instead of the entire object.

Scalar Queries

In all the examples so far in this chapter, we've relied on the fact that the result of a query is an object or a list of objects. Hibernate lets you return not only a complete object previously stored in the database but also individual attributes or groups of attributes. These queries are called *scalar queries*.

If you use SQL on a regular basis, you're accustomed to writing queries where SELECT * isn't in the query string: Instead you have something like:

```
SELECT name, zipcode, count(zipcode)
```

In this query string, we're pulling the values for the name and zipcode columns; but in addition, an aggregate function pulls the count of each zip code. Here's an example of using scalar queries:

```
Session session = SessionFactory.openSession();
List list = session.find("select site.name, size(site.users) from users");
for (int I=();I<list.size;I++) {

  Object[] row = list.get(i);

  String name = (String)row[0];
  Integer count = (Integer)row[1];
}

SessionFactory.close();
```

Things are a little different when you use a scalar query. Hibernate executes the appropriate query against the specified database and returns a resultset. Since we don't want to just use a resultset, Hibernate assembles the values in the resultset as an array of objects. Each element of the resulting List is an array of the objects from a particular row. As you can see in our example, each row is pulled from the List and assigned to an Object array called row. The actual values are in the row object. We pull each object, cast to the appropriate type, and assign to individual variables.

Of course, we aren't limited to pulling the individual attributes of our object; we can also retrieve the full object as well as the attributes. Here's an example:

```
Session session = SessionFactory.openSession();
List list = session.find("select user, site.name,
   size(site.users) from users");

for (int I=0;1<list.size;I++) {

  Object[] row = list.get(i);

  User user = (String)row[0];
  String name = (String)row[1];
  Integer count = (Integer)row[2];
}

SessionFactory.close();
```

In this example, we pull the object to begin with and then the attributes of the site object.

Queries and Named Queries

You've seen two different ways to query the objects from the database. The first is a straight query using the find() method; in this type of query, you basically get all or nothing from the database. In the second query, you can use the iterate() method, which returns a single object at a time based on your requesting each one.

Hibernate provides another query, using the Query object, which allows more control over the results. The following table shows the methods available on the Query object.

Query Object	Methods
String[ ]	getNamedParameters()
String	getQueryString()
Type[ ]	getReturnTypes()
Iterator	iterate()
List	list()
ScrollableResults	scroll()
Query	setBigDecimal(int position, BigDecimal number)
Query	setBigDecimal(String name, BigDecimal number)
Query	setBinary(int position, byte[] val)
Query	setBinary(String name, byte[] val)
Query	setBoolean(int position, boolean val)
Query	setBoolean(String name, boolean val)
Query	setByte(int position, byte val)
Query	setByte(String name, byte val)
Query	setCacheable(boolean cacheable)
Query	setCacheRegion(String cacheRegion)
Query	setCalendar(int position, Calendar calendar)
Query	setCalendar(String name, Calendar calendar)
Query	setCalendarDate(int position, Calendar calendar)
Query	setCalendarDate(String name, Calendar calendar)
Query	setCharacter(int position, char val)
Query	setCharacter(String name, char val)
Query	setDate(int position, Date date)
Query	setDate(String name, Date date)
Query	setDouble(int position, double val)
Query	setDouble(String name, double val)
Query	setEntity(int position, Object val)
Query	setEntity(String name, Object val)
Query	setEnum(int position, Object val)
Query	setEnum(String name, Object val)
Query	setFirstResult(int firstResult)
Query	setFloat(int position, float val)
Query	setFloat(String name, float val)

Table continued on following page

Query Object	Methods
Query	setInteger(int position, int val)
Query	setInteger(String name, int val)
Query	setLocale(int position, Locale locale)
Query	setLocale(String name, Locale locale)
void	setLockMode(String alias, LockMode lockMode)
Query	setLong(int position, long val)
Query	setLong(String name, long val)
Query	setMaxResults(int maxResults)
Query	setParameter(int position, Object val)
Query	setParameter(int position, Object val, Type type)
Query	setParameter(String name, Object val)
Query	setParameter(String name, Object val, Type type)
Query	setParameterList(String name, Collection vals)
Query	setParameterList(String name, Collection vals, Type type)
Query	setParameterList(String name, Object[] vals)
Query	setParameterList(String name, Object[] vals, Type type)
Query	setProperties(Object bean)
Query	setSerializable(int position, Serializable val)
Query	setSerializable(String name, Serializable val)
Query	setShort(int position, short val)
Query	setShort(String name, short val)
Query	setString(int position, String val)
Query	setString(String name, String val)
Query	setText(int position, String val)
Query	setText(String name, String val)
Query	setTime(int position, Date date)
Query	setTime(String name, Date date)
Query	setTimeout(int timeout)
Query	setTimestamp(int position, Date date)
Query	setTimestamp(String name, Date date)
Object	uniqueResult()

Some of the most important features of the Query object are the ability to fetch a particular set size and specify the starting position in the entire resultset. Using Query also allows the use of named queries defined in the mapping document. This is convenient because you don't need to define query strings in the compiled code—just in the mapping document.

Query Results Control

The first feature of the Query object is the ability to control the resultset returned from the execution of the query. Consider the following code:

```
Session session = SessionFactory.openSession();
Query query = session.createQuery(
"from Users users where users.access > 50");

query.setMaxResults(25);
query.setFirstResult(5);
List users = query.list();

SessionFactory.closeSession();
```

In this example code, we open a session and then instantiate a Query object from the session. As part of the Query construction, we supply the HQL string to be executed against the database. To control the outcome of the query, we use two different methods:

```
setMaxResults(int);
setFirstResults(int);
```

The setMaxResults() method is passed an integer value indicating the maximum number of results that should be returned from the database. The final results include up to the maximum value provided to the method. The setFirstResults() method provides an integer value indicating where in the entire resultset the current results should be returned. For example, we might want 20 results to be returned, starting at position 20. Once the various criteria have been set up, we use the list() command to execute the query and return our desired results as a List object.

If your JDBC driver supports scrollable results, you can also execute and request the results of the query using the scroll() method. The scroll() method returns a ScrollableResults object that can be used to access the objects in the results returned. The methods available in the ScrollableResults object are shown in the following table.

ScrollableResults	Methods
void	afterLast()
void	beforeFirst()
void	close()
boolean	first()
Object[]	get()
Object	get(int i)

Table continued on following page

ScrollableResults	Methods
Object	get(int i, Type type)
BigDecimal	getBigDecimal(int col)
byte[]	getBinary(int col)
Blob	getBlob(int col)
Boolean	getBoolean(int col)
Byte	getByte(int col)
Calendar	getCalendar(int col)
Character	getCharacter(int col)
Clob	getClob(int col)
Date	getDate(int col)
Double	getDouble(int col)
Float	getFloat(int col)
Integer	getInteger(int col)
Locale	getLocale(int col)
Long	getLong(int col)
int	getRowNumber()
Short	getShort(int col)
String	getString(int col)
String	getText(int col)
TimeZone	getTimeZone(int col)
Type	getType(int i)
boolean	isFirst()
boolean	isLast()
boolean	last()
boolean	next()
boolean	previous()
boolean	scroll(int i)
boolean	setRowNumber(int rowNumber)

Notice that you can also set whether Hibernate should cache the results from this query. If you want the results to be cached, use this code:

```
query.setCacheable(true);
```

Single Row

Another interesting method available in the Query object is called uniqueResult(). You can use this method to test the database and whether objects based on a query are available. The method returns a null value if no results are available for a particular query or if a single object is returned. For example:

```
Session session = SessionFactory.open Session();

Query query = session.createQuery(
   "from Users user where user.access > 50");
if (query.uniqueResult()) {
// objects are available
}
SessionFactory.closeSession();
```

In this code, the uniqueResult() method is called and the results are used as a condition for a decision statement. If an object is returned based on the query, additional work can occur; otherwise, the statement is false and is skipped.

Named Queries

Some of the real power of the Query object lies in its ability to use queries that have been previously defined and stored in a mapping document. This ability gives you more flexibility in your applications because HQL query strings aren't hard-coded into the application code; thus the code is easier to change and tweak on the fly.

Let's consider two different queries: one without parameters and one with. For the query without parameters, the first step is to define a query in the mapping document. We do so using the <query> element:

```
<query name="find.users.access.greaterthan.50">
 <! [CDATA[from users user where user > 50]
]>
</query>
```

The <query> element requires two components: the name attribute we'll use to access the query in our application code, and the query string. Notice that we use the CDATA section designator to contain our query string: This is required if your query contains any characters that would be considered XML markup. (This is a common area for bugs to appear.) You might define a simple query without the CDATA designator but later change the string and still not include the designator. You should consider always using CDATA, but that's a matter of style.

Once the query has been named in the mapping document, we need to use it in the application code. This is accomplished as follows:

```
Session session = SessionFactory.open Session();

Query query = session.getNamedQuery(
"find.users.access.greaterthan.50");
```

```
query.setMaxResults(25);
query. setFirstResult(5);
List users = query.list();

SessionFactory.closeSession();
```

The only change in this code snippet is the use of the `getNamedQuery()` method. This method accepts a string that identifies the name of the query that should be pulled from the mapping document and used as part of the instantiated `Query` object. Once the query has been pulled from the mapping document, the `Query` object can be used as normal.

Few queries are this simple--most require the use of parameters. Consider the following query, which is a slight modification of the previous one:

```
<query name="find.users.access.greaterthan"> <! [CDATA
[from users user where user > ?] ] >
</query>
```

Notice that we've removed the explicit value of 50 from the query and replaced it with a placeholder. The code to use the query is

```
Session session = SessionFactory.openSession();

Query query = session.getNamedQuery("find.users.access.greaterthan");
query.setMaxResults(25);
query.setFirstResult(5);
query.setInt(0, 100);
List users = query.list();

SessionFactory.closeSession();
```

In this code, we've changed the name of the named query to pull from the mapping document in order to obtain the right query. An additional line of code has been added:

```
query.setInt(0,100);
```

As shown in a previous table, numerous `set*` methods are used to replace the placeholder with an actual value. In our example, the first placeholder is replaced with a value of 100. (Note that the placeholders start with 0 instead of 1.) Once the placeholder has been populated with a value, the query can be executed.

Named Parameters

You can also replace the placeholders with named parameters. Named parameters are string values starting with a colon character (`:`). For example, here's a named query using the named parameter:

```
<query name="findnusers.access.greaterthan">
<! [CDATA
[from users user where user > :accesses]
] >
</query>
```

Instead of putting in an actual value or using the ? placeholder, we've added the named parameter : accesses to the query. The code to use the query is:

```
Session session = SessionFactory.openSession();
Query query = session.getNamedQuery("find.users.access.greaterthan");
query. setMaxResults(25);
query. setFirstResult(5);
query.setlnt("accesses", 100);
List users = query.list();

SessionFactory.closeSession();
```

Instead of using the setInt(int, int) method, we use the setInt(String, int) method, which accepts a named parameter and the value to replace the parameter. In the end, the result of using the Query object, named queries, and named parameters is the ability to fully object-orient the queries and not rely on hard-coded strings.

Finally, if you have a situation where you need to include a list of parameters, the Query object includes the setParameterList() method. For example, consider the following named query:

```
<query name="find.users"> <! [CDATA
[from users user where username in (userlist)] ]>
</query>
```

Here we've changed our named query to look for users whose username is found in a particular list. The code to use the query is:

```
Session session = SessionFactory.openSession();
Query query = session.getNamedQuery("find.users");

List users = new ArrayList(); users.add("jsmith");

users.add("joem");
query.setParameterList("userlist", users);
List users = query.list();

SessionFactory.closeSession();
```

In this code, we've created a list of names using an ArrayList object. Once all the names of the users we want to query against are added, we call the setParameterList() method with the name of the named parameter in our query and the ArrayList object. Hibernate formulates the appropriate query string and executes it against the database.

Query Timeout

Finally, the Query object lets you control the amount of time that a query is allowed to reside on the database server. Using the setTimeout(int) method, you can give the query object X number of seconds to execute before it's cancelled. When you're working on production systems, it's vital that queries not be allowed to take infinite or unreasonable amounts of time to execute. By using the timeout functionality as well as the methods to limit the number of rows returned by the query, you can provide the user with fast results.

SQL Queries

If you need to use good 'ol native SQL in your queries, Hibernate lets you do so with a little extra work. Consider the following code:

```
Session session = SessionFactory.openSession();

List users = session.createSQLQuery("SELECT * FROM users", users ,
Users.class)
.list();
SessionFactory.closeSession();
```

The SQL query string in this example looks like any other native SQL you might execute against the database server without Hibernate. The result is a List of the values from the selected database table rows.

If you need to use an alias in your SQL query, you must surround the alias with { } characters. Here's an example:

```
Session session = SessionFactory.openSession();
List users = session.createSQLQuery(
"SELECT * FROM users as {user} where {user}.username= 'test"',
"users",
Users.class).list();
SessionFactory.closeSession();
```

Notice the {user} alias. Any time you use native SQL, all of the aliases must be wrapped in order for Hibernate to create the proper query.

Criteria Objects

All our examples so far have used either native SQL or HQL to access the objects in the database. If you don't have experience with SQL or don't want to use it, you can use Hibernate's Criteria object to build queries without SQL.

You need a couple of different classes to use Criteria objects. The first is Criteria; its methods are displayed in the next table. You use the Expression object to build the actual criteria for querying the database; its methods are shown in the subsequent table.

Criteria	Methods
Criteria	add(Criterion criterion)
Criteria	addOrder(Order order)
Criteria	createAlias(String associationPath, String alias)
Criteria	createCriteria(String associationPath)
Criteria	createCriteria(String associationPath, String alias)
Class	getCriteriaClass()
Class	getCriteriaClass(String alias)
List	list()
Criteria	setCacheable(boolean cacheable)
Criteria	setCacheRegion(String cacheRegion)
Criteria	setFetchMode(String associationPath, FetchMode mode)
Criteria	setFirstResult(int firstResult)
Criteria	setLockMode(LockMode lockMode)
Criteria	setLockMode(String alias, LockMode lockMode)
Criteria	setMaxResults(int maxResults)
Criteria	setResultTransformer(ResultTransformer resultTransformer)
Criteria	setTimeout(int timeout)
Object	uniqueResult()

Expression Class	Methods
static Criterion	allEq(Map propertyNameValues)
static Criterion	and(Criterion lhs, Criterion rhs)
static Criterion	between(String propertyName, Object lo, Object hi)
static Conjunction	conjunction()
static Disjunction	disjunction()
static SimpleExpression	eq(String propertyName, Object value)
static Criterion	eqProperty(String propertyName, String otherPropertyName)
static SimpleExpression	ge(String propertyName, Object value)

Table continued on following page

Expression Class	Methods
static SimpleExpression	gt(String propertyName, Object value)
static Criterion	ilike(String propertyName, Object value)
static Criterion	ilike(String propertyName, String value, MatchMode matchMode)
static Criterion	in(String propertyName, Collection values)
static Criterion	in(String propertyName, Object[] values)
static Criterion	isNotNull(String propertyName)
static Criterion	isNull(String propertyName)
static SimpleExpression	le(String propertyName, Object value)
static Criterion	leProperty(String propertyName, String otherPropertyName)
static SimpleExpression	like(String propertyName, Object value)
static SimpleExpression	like(String propertyName, String value, MatchMode matchMode)
static SimpleExpression	lt(String propertyName, Object value)
static Criterion	ltProperty(String propertyName, String otherPropertyName)
static Criterion	not(Criterion expression)
static Criterion	or(Criterion lhs, Criterion rhs)
static Criterion	sql(String sql)
static Criterion	sql(String sql, Object[] values, Type[] types)
static Criterion	sql(String sql, Object value, Type type)

The following is a simple example of how to use the `Criteria` and `Expression` classes to build a query against a database using Hibernate:

```
Session session = SessionFactory.openSession();
Critieria criteria = session.createCriteria(User.class);
criteria.add(Expression.eq("username", "johndoe"));
criteria.setMaxResults(5);
List users = criteria.list();
SessionFactory.closeSession();
```

In this code, we begin by creating a `Criteria` object from the `Session`. The `Criteria` object acts like a container for the SQL to be executed against the database. In order for the `Criteria` object to do anything useful, we need to add expressions to it using the various methods of the `Expression` object. In this example, we want to find all the `User` objects where the `username` has been set to `johndoe`. You can add as many `Expression` objects as needed; many methods are available, as shown in the previous table.

The `Criteria` is executed when the `list()` method is called. When you call this method, Hibernate creates an appropriate SQL query statement and sends it to the database server. The result of the query is appropriate objects returned as a `List` collection object.

Summary

This chapter, combined with Chapter 6, has shown you the true power of Hibernate. Regardless of how objects are persisted to the database, Hibernate gives you the ability to retrieve them in a variety of ways that aren't necessarily related to the way the objects are stored.

Hibernate Query Language

In most of our previous examples, we obtained an object from the database using the object's identifier. Although this approach works well in our examples, it won't be so easy in an actual application. In a typical application, you'll use a username or account number to access an object. With this information, you'll find the necessary objects that have been previously persisted to the database. To find the objects, you must use the Hibernate Query Language (HQL). HQL is a SQL-like language specifically designed to pull objects as well as attributes from objects. In this chapter, we'll provide a comprehensive review of all the HQL clauses and how they work in an example.

Chapter Example

In order to bring HQL to life, we need to work with a real application that incorporates many of the different issues we've discussed in the previous chapters. For our example, we'll incorporate a `Group` class and a single derived class called `NewsGroup`. The `Group` class contains a couple of basic attributes as well as a `List` collection object for `Story` objects. The `Group` class also contains a `Server` object to represent object-oriented composition.

Example Classes

As we mentioned, our example application uses four classes. These are `Group`, in Listing 8.1; `NewsGroup`, in Listing 8.2; `Story`, in Listing 8.3; and `Server`, in Listing 8.4.

```
import java.util.*;

public class Group {
    private int id;
    private String name;
    private boolean active;
    private List stories;
    private Server primaryserver;
```

```java
   public Group(){
   }

   public Group(String name) {
      this.name = name;
   }

   public void setId(int i) {
      id = i;
   }

   public int getId() {
      return id;
   }

   public void setName(String n) {
      name = n;
   }

   public String getName() {
      return name;
   }

   public void setActive(boolean b) {
      active = b;
   }

   public boolean getActive() {
      return active;
   }

   public void setStories(List l) {
      stories = l;
   }

   public List getStories() {
      return stories;
   }

   public void setPrimaryserver(Server s) {
      primaryserver = s;
   }

   public Server getPrimaryserver() {
      return primaryserver;
   }
}
```

Listing 8.1

```java
public class Newsgroup extends Group {
  private int first;
  private int last;

  public Newsgroup() {
  }

  public Newsgroup(String s) {
    super(s);
  }

  public void setFirst(int i) {
    first = i;
  }

  public int getFirst() {
    return first;
  }

  public void setLast(int i) {
    last = i;
  }

  public int getLast() {
    return last;
  }
}
```

Listing 8.2

```java
import java.util.*;

public class Story {
  private int id;
  private String info;

  public Story(){
  }

  public Story(String info) {
    this.info = info;
  }

  public void setId(int i) {
    id = i;
  }

  public int getId() {
    return id;
  }

  public void setInfo(String n) {
    info = n;
```

```
  }

  public String getInfo() {
    return info;
  }
}
```

Listing 8.3

```
public class Server {
  private int id;
  private String servername;
  private String ip;
  private int port;
  private String username;
  private String password;

  public Server() {
  }

public Server(String name, String ip, int port,
    String username, String password) {
    this.servername = name;
    this.ip = ip;
    this.port = port;
    this.username = username;
    this.password = password;
  }

  public void setId(int i) {
    id = i;
  }

  public int getId() {
    return id;
  }

  public void setServername(String s) {
    servername = s;
  }

  public String getServername() {
    return servername;
  }

  public void setIp(String s) {
    ip = s;
  }

  public String getIp() {
    return ip;
  }
```

```
    public void setPort(int i) {
      port = i;
    }

    public int getPort() {
      return port;
    }

    public void setUsername(String s) {
      username = s;
    }

    public String getUsername() {
      return username;
    }

    public void setPassword(String s) {
      password = s;
    }

    public String getPassword() {
      return password;
    }
}
```

Listing 8.4

Example Mapping Document

The four classes all interact with each other. The Group class is the primary container, with a composition Server attribute and a List of Story objects. The NewsGroup class is derived from the Group class and includes two additional attributes for the first and last article numbers. Creating a Hibernate mapping document is key to making all the class work together.

We want the Sever objects to be independent elements of the system; we'll assign one of them to the Group as needed. We may have many different server objects in the application that aren't associated with a Group, so we've included a <many-to-one> element in the Group <class> to handle the association. The final mapping document in shown in Listing 8.5.

```
<?xml version="1.0" encoding="UTF-8"?>
<!DOCTYPE hibernate-mapping

PUBLIC "-//Hibernate/Hibernate Mapping DTD//EN"
"http://hibernate.sourceforge.net/hibernate-mapping-2.0.dtd">

<hibernate-mapping>

<class name="Group"
 table="grouptable"
       discriminator-value="parent">
```

```
    <id name="id" unsaved-value="0">
        <generator class="native"/>
    </id>

        <discriminator column="type"/>

    <list name="stories" cascade="all">
        <key column="parent_id"/>
        <index column="idx"/>
        <one-to-many class="Story"/>
    </list>

  <property name="name" type="string"/>
  <property name="active" type="boolean"/>

  <many-to-one name="primaryserver" class="Server"
    column="server_id" cascade="all"/>

        <subclass name="Newsgroup"
                   discriminator-value="newsgroup">
            <property name="first"/>
            <property name="last"/>
        </subclass>
</class>

<class name="Story"
  table="story">
  <id name="id" unsaved-value="0">
            <generator class="native"/>
  </id>
            <property name="info"/>
</class>

<class name="Server"
        table="servertable">
  <id name="id" unsaved-value="0">
            <generator class="native"/>
  </id>

  <property name="servername"/>
  <property name="ip"/>
  <property name="port"/>
  <property name="username"/>
  <property name="password"/>
</class>

</hibernate-mapping>
```

Listing 8.5

Example Tables

From the Hibernate mapping document in Listing 8.5, we find that we need three tables in the database to persist the four objects. We use a discriminator to handle the `Group` and `NewsGroup` classes in a single table. Listing 8.6 shows the SQL create commands that build the necessary tables in MySQL.

```
create table grouptable (
id int not null primary key auto_increment,
name text,
first int,
last int,
type text,
server_id int,
active int
) ;

create table story (
id int not null primary key auto_increment,
info text,
idx int,
parent_id int
) ;

create table servertable (
id int not null primary key auto_increment,
servername text,
ip text,
port int,
username text,
password text
) ;
```

Listing 8.6

Example Application

Pulling all the classes, mapping document, and table creation SQL together, we can build an application as shown in Listing 8.7. This application creates three groups and associates a `List` of `Story` objects with two of the `Group` objects. We also instantiate three server objects and assign one of them as an attribute to a single `Group` object. Finally, we build a `NewsGroup` object and persist everything to the database.

```
import java.io.*;
import java.util.*;

import net. sf.hibernate.*;
import net. sf.hibernate.cfg.*;

public class GroupTest {
```

```
public static void main(String [] args) {


    try {
      Session session = HibernateSession.currentSession();

      Newsgroup sp = new Newsgroup("misc.hibernate");
      Newsgroup sp2 = new Newsgroup("misc.software");
      Group sp3 = new Group("alt.donothing");

      ArrayList list = new ArrayList();
      list.add(new Story("A Story"));
      list.add(new Story("And yet another story"));
      sp.setStories(list);

      list = new ArrayList();
      list.add(new Story("For the good of men"));
      list.add(new Story("Venus and Mars"));
      list.add(new Story("All The Rest"));
      sp3.setStories(list);

      Server server = new Server(
        "Forte", "news.forteinc.com", 485, "mrfred", "freds");
      sp.setServer(server);
      sp.setActive(true);


      session.save(sp);
      session.save(sp2);
      session.save(sp3);
      session.save(server2);
      session.save(server3);

      session.flush();
      session.close();
    } catch (Exception e) {
      e.printStackTrace();
    }
  }
}
```

Listing 8.7

Example Rows

As a result of the application in Listing 8.7, we get appropriate rows in the three database tables as shown below. As you can see, the mappings have been made between the Group object, the Story objects, and the Server objects.

```
mysql> select * from grouptable;
+----+----------------+-----------+-----------+-------+------+--------+
| id | name           | type      | server_id | first | last | active |
+----+----------------+-----------+-----------+-------+------+--------+
| 16 | misc.hibernate | newsgroup |         9 |     0 |    0 |      1 |
| 17 | misc.software  | newsgroup |      NULL |     0 |    0 |      0 |
| 18 | alt.donothing  | parent    |      NULL |  NULL | NULL |      0 |
+----+----------------+-----------+-----------+-------+------+--------+
3 rows in set (0.00 sec)

mysql> select * from story;
+----+----------------------+-----+-----------+
| id | info                 | idx | parent_id |
+----+----------------------+-----+-----------+
| 36 | A Story              |   0 |        16 |
| 37 | And yet another story|   1 |        16 |
| 38 | For the good of men  |   0 |        18 |
| 39 | Venus and Mars       |   1 |        18 |
| 40 | All The Rest         |   2 |        18 |
+----+----------------------+-----+-----------+
5 rows in set (0.00 sec)

mysql> select * from servertable;
+----+------------+--------------------+------+----------+----------+
| id | servername | ip                 | port | username | password |
+----+------------+--------------------+------+----------+----------+
|  9 | Forte      | news.forteinc.com  |  485 | mrfred   | freds    |
| 10 | comcast    | news.comcast.net   |    0 | mrfred   | freds    |
| 11 | free news  | news.freenews.com  |    0 | mrfred   | freds    |
+----+------------+--------------------+------+----------+----------+
3 rows in set (0.00 sec)
```

Example Use

When someone is writing a book on technology, a "catch-22" scenario often occurs—and we've hit that point. In Chapter 7, we discussed the ways of querying the persisted storage without trying to cover too much of the query language; but in this chapter, we'll need the methods for obtaining the information from the database. As we discuss HQL, we'll access both objects and attributes. In Chapter 7, we discussed methods for pulling results as a single resultset or through an iterator/scrollset, depending on the expected size. For the examples in this chapter, we'll stick to using the find() method to bring back our objects. As mentioned, we'll obtain both objects and scalars from the database, and they will need to be processed in different manners.

When you pull objects from the database, you obtain a List where the entries are the actual objects. So, you can use get() or obtain an iterator to access each of the objects and cast them to the right Java object class. When you use HQL to pull more than one object—maybe a scalar or two, and possibly aggregated values—Hibernate returns a `List` object containing an array of `Object`. For example, we can use the `find()` method in the following fashion:

```
List stuff = session.find(
    "select name, date, sum(records) from table....");
```

The result of this query is a `List` of `Object` arrays. To access each of the values, we might use code like the following:

```
Iterator iter = stuff iterator();
while (iter.hasNext()) {
   Object[] temp = (Object[])iter.next();
   String name = (String)temp[o];
   Date date = (Date)temp[1];
   Integer sum = (Integer)temp[2];
}
```

Select Clause

The `SELECT` clause pulls information from a database table. It works in a variety of ways in HQL including pulling a single object, a group of objects, or an attribute from in an object. In this section, we'll consider the formats of `SELECT` and what is returned based on our example classes and objects.

If we need to pull a group of objects from storage, we can use an abbreviated format of the `SELECT` query to obtain those objects. For example:

```
List groups = session.find("from groups.Group");
```

This query returns a `List` object containing all the objects in the database of type groups: `Group` as well as any derived classes. Using our example objects, the result is a list of three `Group` objects. Note that one of these objects will be of type `Group`, and two will be of type `NewsGroup`.

If we want to limit the objects returned to those of type `NewsGroup`, we use this code:

```
List groups = session.find("from groups.Newsgroup");
```

In both cases, we specify the Java class along with the package where the class has been defined. If your class isn't contained in a package, we can leave off the package string. This is a prime location for errors to occur in an application because the package name was accidentally left off the query string. Be sure to note these locations if the number of objects returned by your application isn't what you expected.

As you begin to build more complex queries, you'll need to reference the object you're trying to obtain. For example, you might want to limit the objects returned based on some value using the `WHERE` clause discussed in the next section. In the `WHERE` clause, you need to reference the object being accessed. You facilitate the reference to the object using an alias. For example:

```
List groups = session.find("from groups.Group as group");
```

In this example, we pull all the Group objects, but we also alias the Group object using the string "group". As you'll see later in the chapter, the alias can be used to reference the object in a clause. The "as" alias clause is optional, so you could also alias the Group object using the following:

```
List groups = session.find("from groups.Group group");
```

The as clause is removed, and the first string after the class name is used as the alias. If you've used SQL, you know that more than one database table can appear with the FROM clause. You can do the same with HQL by referencing more than one class. For example:

```
List groups = session.find("from groups.Group as group, Server as server");
```

The result is a List object containing both Group and Server objects. You need to use the instanceof Java keyword to determine which class each of the individual objects references.

Once you have a List of object, you can use each of the objects in a traditional Java manner by accessing and changing the various attributes of the object. What if you wanted to access and return individual attributes from the objects directly from the database? You can do this using the SELECT clause and HQL. For example:

```
List servers = session.find(
    "select group.server from groups.Group as group");
```

The result of this query is a List object containing all the Server objects that are attributes of a persisted Group object. Notice that we've used and taken advantage of the alias "group" for the attribute we wanted to view. Note that the list of objects returned in our previous find() is different than the following find():

```
List server = session.find("from groups.Server");
```

The previous find() only returns Server objects that have been instantiated and assigned as an attribute to a Group object. This new find() returns all the Server objects in the database. In some cases, a Server object might be instantiated and never used as an attribute value; thus is wouldn't be found through the select group.server clause.

The ability to return an attribute of an object isn't limited to composition objects as in the previous examples; you can return any Java type. Here are a couple of examples:

```
List servers = session.find(
    "select group.name from groups.Group as group");
List servers = session.find(
    "select group.server.port from groups.Group as group");
```

Notice that you can drill into objects as in the case of group.server.port. What if you have an attribute that is a collection? You can obtain just the collection using a function called elements(). For example:

```
List servers = session.find(
    "select elements (group.articles) from groups.Group as group");
```

This example returns a List of all Article objects associated with the group.articles attribute, which happens to be a List type. All our recent HQL examples only use a single value for the SELECT command. We return either a List of String objects or a List of Servers, but no examples return two or more types. For example, we might like to perform the following query:

```
List servers = session.find(
    "select group.server.ip, group.server port from groups.Group as group");
```

You can even build new objects on the fly and return them:

```
List machines = session.find(
    "select new Machine (group.server.ip, group.server.port)
    from groups.Group as group");
```

In this find() method, Hibernate instantiates Machine objects using the ip and port values for each Group object found in the database. Of course, your application must have a Machine class defined with the appropriate constructor.

Narrowing the SELECT Using the WHERE Clause

In the previous HQL examples, all the objects in the database are returned to the application without any kind of restriction. If you want to narrow the specific objects that are returned from storage, you use the WHERE clause. In this section, we'll provide examples that use the WHERE clause in a variety of ways.

Let's look at a simple use of the WHERE clause:

```
List servers = session.find("from Server as server where server.port = 0");
```

This example gives us a way to pull all the Server objects where the port attribute has a value of 0. For our example data, we'll get two objects where the port is 0, however, one of our Server objects has a port value of 485 and it will not be returned. The equality provided in this HQL example handles a comparison of an attribute with a specific value. We can also compare objects during the HQL query as needed. For example, let's say we want to pull all Group objects that use the same Server object:

```
List servers = session.find(

"from Group as group, Group as samegroup where

group.server = samegroup.server");
```

In this HQL query, we join the Group table with itself to compare the Server objects with each other. Those Group objects that have the same Server objects are returned. In our example classes for this chapter, both the Group and Newsgroup classes are available to the application. In fact, our example code uses both classes to instantiate objects.

If we want to return all Newsgroup objects but ignore the Group objects, we can use a special property called class. For example:

```
List groups = session.find(
  "from Group as group where group.class = Newsgroup");
```

This code instructs Hibernate to pull all the Group classes from the database and narrow the results to only those objects that are specifically of the Newsgroup class type. Hibernate can to do this using the discriminator-value provided in our mapping document for both the Group and Newsgroup <class> definitions.

HQL also defines another special property called id, which we can use to pull objects from the database based on the identifier value:

```
List servers = session.find("from Server as server where server.id = 0");
```

At first glance, this HQL query string doesn't seem noteworthy, because we define our identifier column with the string name "id"; but if we'd used the name "ident" or "identifier", we could still use the id special property to access the true identifier of the objects.

Working with Collections in HQL

In our example classes and objects, we've included a collection in the form of a List attribute. We use the attribute to assign individual stories to a group. HQL provides quite a few operations for working directly with collections.

.size, size()

Using the size special property or the size() function, HQL can use the size of a collection as a criteria in a WHERE clause:

```
List groups = session.find(
  "from Group as group where group.stories.size > 3");
List groups = session.find(
  "from Group as group where size(group.stories) > 3");
```

In both of these examples, Hibernate accesses all the group objects currently stored in the database, determines the total number of Story objects in the stories attribute, and returns the Group objects where the count is greater than 3.

Note that the size property requires a subselect and generally appears in a WHERE clause.

.minIndex, minindex(), .maxIndex, maxindex()

If the collection used in an object is indexed, like an array or a List, you can use the minimum and maximum index values in a query as well. If the collection in an object uses Java basic types like integer, float, and other, you can use the minimum and maximum element special properties to select results based on values in the collection. Our example doesn't use one of these, but consider the following class example:

```
public class Test {
  private int[] values;
}
```

We could return `Test` objects from the database based on a comparison against the maximum element in the array with the following query:

```
List tests = session.find(
  "from Test as test where test.values.maxElement > 5000");

List tests = session.find(
  "from Test as test where maxelement(test.values) > 5000");
```

Notice that you can use either the special property notation where the property is added to the end of the attribute being compared or the method notation.

index()

If you're interested in the index value of an element in a collection of values or a one-to-many association, use the `index()` property. For example, we can pull all the stories that have an index value of 2 using the following HQL:

```
List stories = session.find("from Story story where index(story) = 2");
```

Based on our example, we return an object based on the following row:

```
+----+-----------------------+------+-----------+
| id | info                  | idx  | parent_id |
+----+-----------------------+------+-----------+
| 10 | All The Rest          |   2  |        6  |
+----+-----------------------+------+-----------+
```

any(), some(), all(), exists(), in(), elements(), indices()

SQL includes a few predicates that you can use to compare and determine whether a value is part of a set. These predicates are as follows:

- **any/some:** Returns a result when a compared value is true for any value in the subquery.

- **all:** Returns a result when a compared value is true for all values in the subquery.

- **exists:** Returns a result when the row from the query is found in a subquery.

- **in:** Returns results when a value in the database matches a value in a result set.

One use of these predicates in Hibernate calls for two functions: `elements()` and `indices()`. The `elements()` function returns the values of a collection as a set so the predicates listed here can access the values. The `indices()` function returns the key values of a collection such as those found in a map.

Using this information, we can produce a query based on our example application and those objects persisted to the database:

```
List groups = session.find(
  "from Group groups where :reply exists elements(groups.stories)");
```

Note that properties, elements, and indices require a subselect and generally appear in a WHERE clause. The elements() and indices() functions can be used in the SELECT clause even in a database that doesn't support the subselect.

[]

You've seen how to access the minimum and maximum indices as well as the size of a collection, but what if you want to access the value of an indexed collection at cell 5, or a map element? You can use the [ ] operator for this purpose:

```
List stories = session.find(
  "select story from Story story, Group group where group.stories[1] =
story");
```

Note that the [ ] symbols can only be used in a WHERE clause.

Other HQL WHERE Expressions

In this part of the chapter, we'll discuss the other expressions that can appear in a WHERE clause. Many of these expressions will be familiar if you've used SQL. Each expression is categorized based on its functionality.

Logicals

When you're building a query string to narrow the results of a query, you sometimes need more than one criterion to fully achieve the narrowing. This situation calls for the use of a logical operator such as AND, OR, and NOT. For example:

```
List servers = session.find(
  "from Server as server where server.port = 0 and server.password is not
null");
```

Here we'll only return Server objects that have a port of 0 and a password that isn't null. The AND relational requires that both conditions be true in order for the entire condition to be true.

NULL Expression

When you're persisting Java objects to the database, there will undoubtedly be times when an attribute has a null value associated with it instead of a reference to another object. For example, we might instantiate a Group object and not add anything to the stories attribute or the server attribute. In this case, Hibernate persists the Group object and enters null values for the appropriate places in the database table row.

HQL lets you use the null value as a condition to narrow a query. There are two commands to test for null:

❑   is null

❑   is not null

Notice that you don't use the equality symbol to test against null. It's important to always test for null using the is and is not keywords. For example:

```
List groups = session.find(
    "from Groups as group where group.server is null");
```

The result of the HQL query is a list of Group objects that don't have the server attribute set to a Server object. This is a quick way to retrieve objects that need to be repaired or filled with additional information. You can use the is not null command to find objects that have the appropriate attribute filled with an object.

Groupings

In many cases, you'll want to narrow the results of a query based on a set of values or a range. For example, we might want to pull the Server objects that have port values in the range of 0 through 1024. To do this, we can use the between keyword:

```
List servers = session.find(
    "from Server as server where server.port between 0 and 1024");
```

Hibernate checks each stored Server object and retrieves only those that have a port value between 0 and 1024. If by chance you want to narrow your results based on several different values, you can use the in keyword. For example, we might want to pull the objects were the password string is "password" or "test" for a Server object. The HQL would appear as follows

```
List servers = session.find(
    "from Server as server where server.port in ('password', 'test')");
```

We can also perform the negation of both the in and between keywords:

```
List servers = session.find(
    "from Server as server where server.port not between 0 and 1024");
List servers = session.find(
    "from Server as server where server.port not in ('password', 'test')");
```

Scalar Functions

If the underlying database where Hibernate is persisting your objects supports scalar functions, you can use them in your HQL query string as well. Consider the MySQL database server, which includes many scalar functions such as ABS, ASIN, CURRENT_DATE(), and others. Two commonly used functions are upper() and lower(), which change the case of a value found in the database.

For example, we might want to pull objects from the database based on the name of the group. Because a Group object might have a name attribute in both uppercase and lowercase, we need to use one of the functions to make sure we select the right objects. The query might look like the following:

```
List groups = session.find(
   "from Group group where lower(group.name) like 'www.%'");
```

For this query string, the name attribute of the Group object is changed to lowercase and then compared against the "www." String.

Equality

While we're on the subject of checking equality of an attribute against a value, Hibernate supports all the common equality operators found in SQL. These include:

- ❑   =: Equality
- ❑   <=: Less than or equal
- ❑   >=: Greater than or equal
- ❑   <>: Not equal
- ❑   !=: Not equal
- ❑   **like:** Allows for matching a substring using a wildcard—the most common wildcard, %, can appear before, after, or in a string

Named Parameters

Hibernate supports the concept of a named parameter, where a variable can be added to a HQL query string and a method used to set the value of the variable. For example, we might have code like the following:

```
Query q = session.createQuery(
   "from Group group where group.name = :groupname");
q.setString("groupname", "alt.mygroup");
Iterator iter = q.iterate();
```

The power of the named parameter is its ability to dynamically set a value in the query as needed by the application. There is no need to deal with string concatenations or other gimmicks to add dynamic information to a query string.

Booleans

The issue of boolean values in a database is an interesting topic because not all database servers support a specific boolean column type. Typically, a boolean column contains one or two different values—true or false—but for those database servers that don't directly support a true Boolean column, the values 0 and 1 provide the same functionality. Consider the following query:

```
List groups = session. find("from Group group where group.active = true");
```

The query returns all Group objects that currently have the active parameter set to true. But if your database server doesn't support the idea of true/false, the query produces an error. The solution is to use the query substitutions allowed in the Hibernate configuration file. Recall that you can add a query substitution with the `hibernate.query.substitution` property. Using this property, you can tell Hibernate to substitute the appropriate values for true and false when found in a query. The statements would be

```
hibernate.query.substitution true = 1
hibernate.query.substitution false = 0
```

When Hibernate sends this query to the underlying database server, the query string appears as follows:

```
select * from Group group where group.active = 1
```

Subselects

Most modern database servers support the idea of performing a series of selects in order to produce a single result set. This multiple-selection capability is often called a *subselect*. The basic idea is to perform a SELECT query on a database table and then use the results of the first SELECT as the input to a final SELECT that produces the results to be returned to the application. Hibernate supports the idea of a sub-select as long on the underlying database supports the construct.

In the following query, we obtain the average size of the stories attribute in the subselect and then compare the size of each story list with the obtained average:

```
from Group as group where size(group.stories) > (
  select avg(size(storygroup.stories)) from Group storygroup)
```

The result is those Group objects that have a List attribute greater than the average of all lists.

Polymorphism

Since we've created a hierarchy in our example, and Hibernate is designed to be used with Java (an object-oriented language), you might expect we can obtain objects from the database based on the hierarchy and taking advantage of polymorphism. In fact, a query used in Hibernate can include any valid class type. For example, if we execute the following query, we'll obtain all the objects of type Group or based on Group (such as Newsgroup):

```
List groups = session.find("from Group");
```

Now we can obtain the Newsgroup objects based on the following query:

```
List groups = session.find("from Newsgroup");
```

Finally, we can obtain all objects that have been persisted with this query:

```
List allobjects = session.find("from java.lang.Object");
```

Order By Clause

As you've seen throughout this chapter, the result of the find() method is a List of the objects matching the HQL query string. As you might expect, there is no guarantee of the order in which the objects are returned from the database table. If you want Hibernate to return the objects in a specific order, you can use the order by clause.

Looking back at the example application used to instantiate and persist the Group, Story, and Server objects, you can see that the Group objects are instantiated in the following order:

```
misc.hibernate
misc.software
alt.donothing
```

Clearly, this order isn't sorted. You might expect the Group objects to be placed in the database in the same order in which they were instantiated. If you look back at the beginning of the chapter in Listing 8.6, we display the tables for the Group objects, the objects were placed in the database in the same order. Now we won't rely on this fact from an application standpoint: We can use the Order By clause to return the objects in a specific order. For example:

```
List sortedgroups = session.find(
   "from Group as group order by group.name asc");
```

The result of this query is a List of Group objects that are returned based on an ascending sort using natural ordering for a string attribute. The objects are in this order:

```
alt.donothing
misc.hibernate
misc.software
```

If you'd like the sorting performed in descending order, use this example:

```
List sortedgroups = session.find(
   "from Group as group order by group.name asc");
```

Now we can create even more complex object results using multilevel sorting:

```
List sortedgroups = session.find(
   "from Group as group order by group.server.port asc, group.name asc");
```

In this query, the Group objects are returned based first on a sort of the server.port value and then on a sort in ascending order of the Group object name. The sorting of the objects based on the name attribute is seen only when multiple objects have the same server.port value.

Aggregate Functions

HQL includes a few aggregate functions you can use to combine values in the attributes of stored objects. The available functions are as follows:

- **count(*):** Provides a count of the total number of objects persisted to the database; possibly limited by a WHERE clause.

- **count(query):** Provides a count of the total number of objects based on the supplied query.

- **count(distinct attribute):** Provides a count of the objects having distinct attribute values.

- **count(attribute):** Provides a count of all objects in a specific class.

- **avg(attribute):** Provides the average value for the field provided.

- **sum(attribute):** Provides the sum of all values supplied in the attribute.

- **min(attribute):** Provides the minimum value found for all supplied attribute values.

- **max(attribute):** Provides the maximum value found for all supplied attribute values.

Here's an example of using an aggregate function:

```
List group = session.find(
    "select max(size(group.stories)) from Group as group");
```

Here we ask for the value of the maximum List size for all the Group objects. As you'll see shortly, the aggregate functions are used extensively when you're adding a group by clause to the query.

Group By Clause

Sorting through the order by clause is one way to group a series of objects, but an even more powerful option is the group by clause. This clause lets Hibernate pull information from the database and group it based on a value of an attribute and, typically, use the result to include an aggregate value. When you're using the group by clause, the column in the clause must:

- Be from one of the tables in the FROM clause.

- Not be part of an aggregate function.

- Be in the SELECT clause.

Any other column included in the SELECT clause must be either part of the group by or part of an aggregate function. For example:

```
List group = session.find(
"select groups.server.name, count(groups)
from Group groups group by groups.server.name");
```

In this query, we've grouped the Group objects based on the name of the Server and returned the server name as well as the number of groups using the server. Let's say we also wanted the IP address of the server, so we tried the following query:

```
List group = session.find(
  "select groups.server.name, count(groups),
groups.server.ip from Group groups group by groups.server.name");
```

We'll get an error on this query because the SELECT clause contains an attribute, groups.server.ip, that isn't part of an aggregate function or in the group by clause.

HAVING Clause

The HAVING clause is probably one of the most misunderstood SQL clauses. It works in much the same way as WHERE, except the attributes in the HAVING clause are a subset of those used in an accompanying group by clause. Thus, the HAVING clause limits the results of a query and is used in conjunction with the group by clause.

It's possible to have both a WHERE and a HAVING clause in a query. In this type of situation, the WHERE clause narrows the results used in the group by clause using columns that aren't part of any aggregate functions. The HAVING clause then narrow the results even further after the aggregation has occurred using a subset of the columns used in the aggregate functions. Therefore, in order to use the HAVING clause, the query must:

❑   Include a group by clause.

❑   Use one or more columns used in an aggregation function.

Working with HQL Joins

In the final section of this chapter, we'll discuss joins. Our goal is to provide some of the basics about joins and show how they can be used in Hibernate. If you're familiar with SQL, Hibernate joins are no different than those found in SQL. Hibernate supports the following joins:

❑   Left outer join

❑   Right outer join

❑   Inner join

❑   Full join

We'll discuss each of these in detail in the following sections of this chapter.

Left Outer Join

In many situations, you need to obtain information from one or more tables in a single query. The left outer join is designed to join tables that have a common column between them. The result of the join is rows containing values from both tables matched on the common column. Rows in the source table that don't match a row in the joined table are included in the result. The values for the joined table in these unmatched rows have null values. (The "Left" part of the clause says that the table on the left is the source table and all of its rows are included in the result regardless of a match.)

For example, let's say we want to obtain the name of a group as well as a count of all stories in the group based on the story name. Here's what the query looks like:

```
Select group.name, count(items)
From Group as group
Left outer join group.stories as items
Group by group.stories.name
```

Right Outer Join

The right outer join has the same functionality as the left outer join, but the table on the right is the source and all of its rows are included in the result.

Inner Join

The inner join is used in places where you want to join two tables that have a common column. For example, if you have an account table and an address tables, the tables may share an account number. You can join the tables using the account number column. The result of the join is those rows from both tables where the account number is the same for each table.

Full Join

In a full join, the result is a match between all rows in the joined tables. If there are 10 rows in each table, there will be 100 rows in the final result. You must use this join used with caution due to the total number of rows in the result.

Fetch Join

Finally, Hibernate supports the idea of a fetch join. This allows Hibernate to fully initialize an object along with its associated collection. For example, we might do the following query:

```
From Group as group
   Left join fetch group.stories
```

Summary

This chapter has provided an overview of the Hibernate Query Language and shown many examples of how to use the various clauses and constructs. In most cases, you'll write applications where you don't know the identifier of a specific object you wish to pull from persisted storage, so using HQL will be mandatory. If you're new to SQL and HQL, the best way to learn is to start using the language and view the objects returned. In some cases, you won't receive the objects you might expect, so revise your HQL query string and try again.

Hibernate Caching

In a typical application, you instantiate objects, persist those objects, reuse the objects, load objects from the database, change the objects, update the objects, and so forth. This process happens over and over as the application executes. In the vast majority of standalone application, you don't need to worry about object availability and performance beyond keeping the database server operational. However, there are a few situations like large multiuser applications and Web-supported situations where you need to consider what the underlying system does with objects. Caching can mean the difference between a sluggish system and a responsive system, but it requires you to think about what approach you take.

Why Cache? What Does Hibernate Provide?

Caching is so important with Hibernate that there isn't a single caching mechanism; instead, Hibernate utilizes a multilevel caching scheme. The first-level cache is the Session object. In previous chapters, you've seen how the Session object acts in a cache-like manner when you pull objects from the database. It works hard to present you with the basics of an object as fast as possible while doing the real work in the background using lazy initialization. At the other end of the spectrum, the Session object keeps an object under its own power before committing it to the database. If the application needs the object, it's available in memory; Hibernate doesn't need to run to the database to provide the object. If you issue multiple updates to an object, Hibernate tries to delay doing the update as long as possible to reduce the number of update SQL statements issued. If you close the session, all the objects being cached are lost and either persisted or updated in the database. When you open a new session, the objects can be pulled and further cached by the current session.

Why do we need other caches beyond the Session object? The answer comes in two parts. The first is called a *Java Virtual Machine (JVM)* or *SessionFactory-level class*. Hibernate delegates some caching of specific classes and collections to this second-level cache. If you have a second-level cache at the

SessionFactory level, the application objects are cached in a manner where they are available across sessions.

The second cache is called the *query cache*. Using this cache, Hibernate can, obviously, cache queries and their results in the event the application executes the same query again. Of course, the query cache takes memory, and cached queries should have a high likelihood of being executed again.

Caching the Survey Object Example Code

This section presents the complete code for the sample Survey application used in this chapter. You can also download this code at www.wrox.com. Listing 9.1 contains the contents of the Hibernate.cfg.xml file, Listing 9.2 contains the contents of the ehcache.xml configuration file, Listing 9.3 contains the Survey object mapping file, and Listing 9.4 contains the Survey source and unit test.

```xml
<?xml version="1.0" encoding="UTF-8"?>
<!DOCTYPE hibernate-configuration PUBLIC "-//Hibernate/Hibernate
Configuration DTD 2.0//EN" "http://hibernate.sourceforge.net/hibernate-
configuration-2.0.dtd">

<!-- Generated file - Do not edit! -->

<hibernate-configuration>

    <!-- a SessionFactory instance listed as /jndi/name -->
    <session-factory>

        <!-- properties -->
        <property name="dialect">net.sf.hibernate.dialect.
HSQLDialect</property>
        <property name="show_sql">true</property>
        <property name="use_outer_join">false</property>
        <property name="connection.username">sa</property>
        <property name="connection.driver_class">org.hsqldb.
jdbcDriver</property>
        <property name="connection.url">jdbc:hsqldb:
hsql://localhost</property>
        <property name="hibernate.cache.provider_class">net.sf.
ehcache.hibernate.Provider</property>

        <!-- mapping files -->
        <mapping resource="example/survey/Survey.hbm.xml"/>

    </session-factory>

</hibernate-configuration>.
```

Listing 9.1

```
<ehcache>

    <diskStore path="java.io.tmpdir"/>

    <defaultCache
        maxElementsInMemory="1000"
        eternal="false"
        timeToIdleSeconds="120"
        timeToLiveSeconds="120"
        overflowToDisk="true"
        />


    <cache name="example.survey.Survey"
        maxElementsInMemory="1000"
        eternal="false"
        timeToIdleSeconds="3600"
        overflowToDisk="false"
        />

</ehcache>
```

Listing 9.2

```
<?xml version="1.0"?>

<!DOCTYPE hibernate-mapping PUBLIC
    "-//Hibernate/Hibernate Mapping DTD 2.0//EN"
    "http://hibernate.sourceforge.net/hibernate-mapping-2.0.dtd">

<hibernate-mapping>
    <class
        name="example.survey.Survey"
        table="SURVEYS"
        dynamic-update="false"
        dynamic-insert="false"
    >
        <cache usage="read-write"/>
        <id
            name="id"
            column="SURVEY_ID"
            type="java.lang.Long"
        >
            <generator class="native">
            </generator>
        </id>

        <property
            name="name"
            type="java.lang.String"
            update="true"
            insert="true"
            access="property"
```

```
            column="name"
        />
        </class>

</hibernate-mapping>
```

Listing 9.3

```java
package example.survey;

/**
 *
 * @author Eric Pugh
 *
 */
public class Survey {
    private Long id;
    private String name;

    /**
     *
     * @return Returns the id.
     */
    public Long getId() {
        return id;
    }

    /**
     *
     * @param id
     *                The id to set.
     */
    public void setId(Long id) {
        this.id = id;
    }

    /**
     * @return Returns the name.
     */
    public String getName() {
        return name;
    }

    /**
     * @param name
     *                The name to set.
     */
    public void setName(String name) {
        this.name = name;
    }

}
package example.survey;
```

```
import junit.framework.TestCase;
import net.sf.hibernate.Session;

public class SurveyTest extends TestCase {

    public void testCreateSurvey() throws Exception{
        Session session = HibernateHelper.getSessionFactory().openSession();
        Survey survey = new Survey();
        survey.setName("Test Survey Caching");
        assertNull(survey.getId());
        session.save(survey);
        assertNotNull(survey.getId());
        Survey surveyInSessionCache = (Survey)session.
get(Survey.class,survey.getId());
        assertEquals("Two objects shouldn't be equal.",survey,
surveyInSessionCache);

    }
}
package example.survey;

import net.sf.hibernate.HibernateException;
import net.sf.hibernate.SessionFactory;
import net.sf.hibernate.cfg.Configuration;

public class HibernateHelper {
    private static SessionFactory sessionFactory;

    private static Configuration configuration;

    public static SessionFactory getSessionFactory() throws
HibernateException {
        if (sessionFactory == null) {
            sessionFactory = getConfiguration().buildSessionFactory();
        }
        return sessionFactory;
    }

    public static Configuration getConfiguration() throws
HibernateException {
        if (configuration == null) {
            configuration = new Configuration().configure();
        }
        return configuration;
    }
}
```

Listing 9.4

Setting Up a SessionFactory Cache

We'll begin our caching discussion by setting up the `SessionFactory` cache so you can give the `Session` object help with specific classes or collections. The first step is to set up the cache and make it available. The following properties are available in the Hibernate Configuration files to handle cache setup:

❑ **hibernate.cache.provider_class:** Indicates the class name of a custom `CacheProvider`. For example, `classname.of.CacheProvider`.

❑ **hibernate.cache.use_minimal_puts:** Optimizes second-level cache operation to minimize writes, at the cost of more frequent reads (useful for clustered caches). Possible values are `true` and `false`.

❑ **hibernate.cache.use_query_cache:** Enables the query cache. The query cache is disabled by default. Possible values are `true` and `false`.

❑ **hibernate.cache.region_prefix:** Provides a prefix to use for second-level cache region names. For example, prefix.

The two important properties are `hibernate.cache.provider_class` and `hibernate.cache.use_query_cache`. By default, Hibernate is configured to use the `EHCache` class for the second-level cache. If you need or want to change the cache type, specify the `hibernate.cache.provider_class` property for the cache you want.

The following table summarizes the caches and what they provide.

Cache	Provider Class	Type	Cluster Safe	Query Cache Supported
EHCache	net.sf.hibernate.ehcache .hibernate.Provider	Memory, disk	No	Yes
OSCache	net.sf.hibernate.cache .OSCacheProvider	Memory, disk	No	Yes
SwarmCache	net.sf.hibernate.cache .SwarmCacheProvider	Clustered (IP multicast)	Yes (clustered invalidation)	No
TreeCache	net.sf.hibernate .cache. TreeCacheProvider	Clustered (IP multicast), transactional	Yes (replication)	No

As you can see, it's important to choose the right second-level cache class for your application. Your choice is limited if you also want to use a query cache. The only requirement is that the cache provider must implement `net.sf.hibernate.cache.CacheProvider`.

A couple of the providers are designated as clustered. This means more than one machine can be used to cache the object pulled by a session. The idea is to distribute the load over several machines instead of just one. Using clustered caches is a viable option for a large application, but you must take care when mapping out this type of architecture: The clustered caches aren't aware of changes made to a cached object across clustered machines.

If you're just starting out using caching, then EHCache is a good choice (the *EH* stands for Easy Hibernate). It's available from http://ehcache.sourceforge.net/. It was implemented by the Hibernate developers and therefore was designed with Hibernate in mind. We'll walk through the configuration of an EHCache-based second-level cache later in the chapter.

Using the Persistent Object Cache

Once you've configured Hibernate with a second-level cache, you cache your classes and collections using the `<cache>` element available to the `<class>` and various collection-mapping elements. The format of the `<cache>` element is as follows:

```
<cache usage="transactional |
                    read-write |
                    nonstrict-read-write |
                    read-only"
/>
```

Include the element in those classes that you want to be cached. In the included Survey example application, we've marked the object Survey as a read-write cache:

```
<class name="Survey">
<cache usage="read-write"/>
</class>
```

For the Survey class, the second-level cache is used for both read and write situations. If you have a class that is immutable (read-only), you can use read-only:

```
<class name="Question" mutable="false">
  <cache usage="read-only"/>
</class>
```

As mentioned, the cache can be used in collections. For example:

```
<class name="Survey">
  <cache usage="read-write"/>
  <set name="Questions">
    <cache usage = "read-only"/>
  </set>
</class>
```

Now let's look at the different possible values for the usage attribute.

Read-Only Cache Usage

If your application's Session object will be loading various classes and the classes don't and won't change during the execution of the application, you can use the read-only cache usage. As you might expect, the read-only usage is very fast for the cache provider. A typical example is to look up data for an application.

Read-Write Cache Usage

When the objects being cached need to be updated, the read-write usage mechanism is an appropriate option to choose. As you might expect, the time requirements for supporting a read-write cache are more involved than in a read-only situation. Therefore, you should study the requirements for the cache closely.

Unfortunately, you must follow a few rules when you're using a read-write cache. The first rule comes into play when you're using the read-write cache in a JTA environment. In this case, you must specify the property `hibernate.transaction.manager_lookup_class`. This property tells Hibernate how to find the appropriate JTA TransactionManager class.

If the read-write cache is used outside of JTA but still in a transactional environment, it's imperative that the transaction be completed before the session is closed or the connection to the database is disconnected. Otherwise the cache will potentially become corrupted.

Also note that if the database is being updated by other processes external to Hibernate, such as a data import job or other applications, then a read-write cache may not be suitable—the data cached by Hibernate may become inaccurate due to the other processes.

Finally, if you're using a clustered cache, a mechanism must be available to lock the database in order to ensure that the database and cache remain in sync. Further, the system architect needs to determine whether the clustered class will handle situations where one application updates an object in the database and all other clustered caches become invalid. These situations aren't handled by the cache-provider classes listed earlier in the chapter.

Nonstrict Read-Write Cache Usage

The nonstrict read-write cache mechanism works in the same fashion and has the same rules as the read-write cache usage described in the previous section, but you can use it when an application will only occasionally update the application objects. Using this cache usage relaxes the transaction isolation provided in the read-write pattern.

Transactional Cache Usage

Of the built-in provider classes, the JBoss TreeCache is the only one that fully supports a transactional cache strategy. You can only use this provider in a JTA environment. It provides a high level of support for caching objects when used with JTA.

SessionFactory Support Methods

You can manage the `SessionFactory` second-level cache using the following methods:

```
public void evict(Class class);
public void evict(Class class, Serializable id);
public void evictCollection(String name);
public void evictCollection(String name, Serializable id);
```

The primary role of each of these methods is to permanently remove objects from the cache. If the object is currently part of a transaction, it's removed from the cache. No rules block an object from being removed. In the case of the first method, `evict(Class class)`, all objects of the supplied class type are removed from the cache.

The methods work on either classes or collections, depending on the one used. If you supply an identifier, then that specific object is removed. This is the only way to update an object that has been set up to be cached as read-only and nonexpiring.

Using the Query Cache

Objects aren't the only entity that you can cache in Hibernate. You can also cache specific queries and the result returned by those queries in the form of a set of identifiers. To use the query cache, you must first activate it using the `hibernate.cache.use_query_cache="true"` property. By setting this property to `true`, you make Hibernate create the necessary caches in memory to hold the query and identifier sets. Note that in order for a query to be picked from the cache, it must match the exact query string including all supplied parameters. This is no different than query caches provided by many database servers.

To use the query cache, you use the `setCacheable(Boolean)` method of the `Query` class. For example:

```
Session session = SessionFactory.openSession();
Query query = session.createQuery("from Survey");
query.setCacheable(true);
List users = query.list();
SessionFactory.closeSession();
```

In this code, we define a `Query` object and supply a query string. Next, we use the `setCacheable()` method to tell Hibernate two things: that this query is cacheable and should be placed in the query cache once it's executed, and that it should attempt to find the query in the cache before executing the query.

Hibernate also supports very fine-grained cache support through the concept of a *cache region*. A cache region is part of the cache that's given a name. For example, you might have a cache area for user support or an area for sites. You use `setCacheRegion()` to specify the region to be used:

```
Session session = SessionFactory.openSession();
Query query = session.createQuery("from Survey");
query.setCacheable(true);
query.setCacheRegion("surveys");
List users = query.list();
SessionFactory.closeSession();
```

This code uses the method to tell Hibernate to store and look for the query in the surveys area of the cache.

At any point, you can tell the `SessionFactory` to remove all cached queries from the entire cache or a particular cache region with these methods:

```
public void evictQueries();
public void evictQueries(String region);
```

Session Cache Functionality

As we've mentioned, the `Session` object contains its own cache to hold individual objects relative to the current session. The class supports several methods for controlling the objects in the cache. These methods are as follows:

```
public void evict(Object object);
public void clear();
boolean contains(Object object);
Serializable getIdentifier(Object object);
```

Just as in the `SessionFactory`, these methods are designed to both remove and identify objects in the cache. The familiar `evict()` method removes a specific object from the `Session` object's cache. The `clear()` method clears the entire cache. The `contains()` method returns a boolean value depending on whether the specified object exist in the persistent store. The `getIdentifier()` method works in much the same way, except it returns the identifier of the supplied object if it exists in the cache; otherwise an exception is thrown.

Setting Up EHCache

EHCache is by far the easiest production-ready caching provider to set up. It comes with Hibernate, but it's also available at http://ehcache.sourceforge.org; newer versions may also be available. It's a suitable caching engine for any application that requires a generic caching solution.

To explicitly use `EHCache` with Hibernate, set the `hibernate.cache.provider_class` in hibernate .cfg.xml to the EHCache provider:

```
<property name="hibernate.cache.provider_class">net.sf.ehcache.hibernate
.Provider</property>
```

Then add an ehcache.xml file to your classpath. Ehcache.xml defines all the cache settings for the different objects:

```
<ehcache>

    <diskStore path="java.io.tmpdir"/>

    <defaultCache
        maxElementsInMemory="1000"
        eternal="false"
        timeToIdleSeconds="120"
        timeToLiveSeconds="120"
```

```
                overflowToDisk="true"
                />

        <cache name="example.survey.Survey"
                maxElementsInMemory="1000"
                eternal="false"
                timeToIdleSeconds="3600"
                overflowToDisk="true"
                />

        <cache name="example.survey"
                maxElementsInMemory="1000"
                eternal="true"
                overflowToDisk="true"
                />
    </ehcache>
```

The `<diskStore />` attribute specifies where EHCache should spool objects to disk when it runs out of space in memory. In this example, it outputs them to the default temporary file path. You can also use user.home to store in the user home directory, or user.dir to store in their current working directory.

The `<defaultCache>` attribute specifies the values to use for objects without a specific cache defined. In this example, by default only 1000 objects are stored in memory. After that, they're spooled to disk. If a cache is marked as external, then the object never expires. Otherwise `timeToIdleSeconds` specifies how long an object can be idle before it expires. The `timeToLiveSeconds` value specifies the overall length of time that an object can be cached before being expired.

The `example.survey.Survey` objects have been defined as never expiring, and after the first 1000 have been loaded, the remainder are spooled to disk. You can look back at the section "SessionFactory Support Methods" to see how to instruct EHCache to clear all cached `Survey` objects.

The Survey application object model has mapped this Java object to a Hypersonic database. To run the example, start Hypersonic by running either startHsql.bat or startHsql.sh in the /etc directory, depending on your platform. Doing so starts up a preconfigured database called surveydb in the /etc directory.

Then, enter ant test; you should get output that looks similar to this:

```
C:\clients\book\9\survey>ant test
Buildfile: build.xml

init:
     [echo] Build survey-om-chapter9

compile:

compile-tests:

test:
    [junit] Running example.survey.SurveyTest
    [junit] Tests run: 1, Failures: 0, Errors: 0, Time elapsed: 3.435 sec
```

```
    [junit] ------------- Standard Output ---------------
    [junit] 2004-08-02 16:25:48,385 [main] INFO  net.sf.hibernate.cfg
.Environment - Hibernate 2.1.5
    [junit] 2004-08-02 16:25:51,199 [main] DEBUG net.sf.hibernate.impl
.SessionImpl - resolved object in session cache [example.survey.Survey#23]
    [junit] ------------- ---------------- ---------------

BUILD SUCCESSFUL
Total time: 4 seconds
C:\clients\book\9\survey>
```

As you can see from the steps, the Java source has been compiled, the unit tests compiled, and the `SurveyTest` unit test run.

The log4j.properties file has been set to DEBUG level so that you can see all the logging produced by Hibernate. In this example, most of the standard output has been removed. If you look through the logs, you'll see EHCache being checked to see whether a valid `Survey` object is stored in it.

When Not to Use Caching

As we've mentioned, caching takes up resources in your application and requires careful tuning to balance the amount of memory used versus the benefit gained. There are definitely times when caching isn't indicated:

❑   If your database is being modified by multiple applications, then Hibernate won't be able to ensure that the data is valid. You may be able to deal with this issue by specifying a `version` or `timestamp` property for your object and using the `Session.lock()` method to verify that the object hasn't been changed.

❑   Some data is retrieved and then not reused so that the data expires from the cache. In this case, there is no point in caching the information and taking up more memory. Caching only helps when the same data is used multiple times within the expiry time period.

❑   The database provides additional functionality, such as auditing your data retrieval. Some applications have a requirement that all SQL statements are logged in order to track who is using what data. Typically this is done at the database level via triggers. In these situations, the cache may be handing the data to various users but without reissuing the SQL statements. This would bypass the SELECT statements that are required for the database triggers to fire.

❑   The application is preserving the first-level session cache for long periods of time. Often in a thick client application a single session is created when the application is started. This session is held open for the lifetime of the application. In this case, the session provides all the caching required.

❑   You're loading very large numbers of objects. If you're loading and parsing millions of objects, then there may not be enough memory available to cache them. However, remember that you don't have to cache everything. Many applications have large subsets of data that are reused frequently.

Summary

Caching of database objects is often a bandage applied to the design at the end of development when performance problems are discovered. It's often applied as another layer to your application, and it can make the code accessing the database harder to read. But when you're using Hibernate, the integrated cache can revolutionize the speed of an application without changing the data access code. Using caching requires analysis and tuning of parameters, but it can make a barely useable application lightning fast.

Between the integrated caching and the sophisticated minimizing of SQL statements that Hibernate is capable of, Hibernate almost always outperforms any corresponding data-access code written by hand for any but the most trivial application. Regardless of how an object is persisted to the database, Hibernate lets you retrieve those objects in a variety of ways that aren't only related to the way the objects are stored.

10

Hibernate Transactions and Locking

All major applications, both desktop and Internet-based, that use a database rely on the fact that the information within the database will be accurate and correct. This is especially true when the database is used in a multiuser environment. In order to illustrate this point, consider two database tables from Chapter 6 based on two classes called `Group` and `Story`. An object instantiated from the `Group` class has some number of `Story` objects associated within it using a `List Collection` object. Within the mapping document for the `Group` class, we specified that Hibernate should cascade a save or update to all of the `Story` objects when a `Group` object is persisted to the database. By specifying the `cascade` attribute, we ensure that the `Story` objects will be properly stored or updated and the `Group` object will maintain a proper level of integrity.

Consider a situation where an application creates a `Group` object and associates several different `Story` objects to it through the `List` attribute within `Group`. Once the application executes the `save()` method on the session, all of the `Story` objects and the single `Group` object will be saved to the database. If we set the `show_sql` `Hibernate` property to true, you can see the SQL that Hibernate attempts to execute:

```
Hibernate: insert into grouptable (name) values (?)
Hibernate: insert into story (info) values (?)
Hibernate: insert into story (info) values (?)
Hibernate: update story set parent_id=?, idx=? where id=?
```

After the SQL is executed, we have rows in the database tables corresponding to our objects, as shown in Listing 10.1.

```
mysql> select * from grouptable;
+----+-----------+
| id | name      |
+----+-----------+
|  5 | accounting |
+----+-----------+
1 rows in set (0.00 sec)


mysql> select * from story;
+----+------------------------+------+-----------+
| id | info                   | idx  | parent_id |
+----+------------------------+------+-----------+
|  5 | A Story                |  0   |         5 |
|  6 | And yet another story  |  1   |         5 |
+----+------------------------+------+-----------+
2 rows in set (0.02 sec)
```

Listing 10.1

Looking back at the SQL Hibernate used to store the objects, you can see that the sequence is:

1. Store the Group object.
2. Store the Story objects.
3. Update the Story objects based on the identifier, the primary key, for the Group object.

Probably the most important step is number 3, where Hibernate will provide the proper linkage between the Story object rows and the Group object row. So what does any of this have to do with transactions? The answer is plenty, and you need to understand what would happen when an error occurs at any of the steps in the process.

❑ **Case 1:** There is an error on step 1. When Hibernate tries to store the Group object to the database, there could be an error with a column value or maybe the identifier value. Any error will cause the database server to issue an error message and status.

❑ **Case 2:** There is an error on step 2. Hibernate will attempt to store each of the story objects found in the List object of the Group object. Again, there could be an issue with the attribute values for the Story object or the generated identifier for any of the Story objects.

❑ **Case 3:** There is an error on step 3. If an error occurs on either case 1 or case 2, case 3 will fault as well, since the identifier for the Group object won't be available to use in the update of the Story objects or the Story objects won't be available in the table. In fact, if we had to persist five Story objects but one of them failed, the SQL for step 3 would update only four table rows and we would effectively lose an object from our list.

Clearly, if there are any problems with steps 1 through 3, there is an integrity issue within the database. Since the database is our sole copy of the data when the application terminates, we must do everything in our power to preserve the integrity of the data. The solution used in all database servers for data integrity is called the transaction.

What Are Transactions?

A *transaction* is a unit of work that consists of two possible outcomes: failure or success. The outcome relates to the entire unit of work and is triggered by the outcomes of the individual elements of the transaction's unit of work. In relating a transaction to our previous example, the steps to save the Group object, the Story objects, and updating the relationship between the database rows would be considered a single transaction. If any of the steps within the transaction fail, the entire transaction will fail. The application where the transaction takes place will see just a failure of the transaction, but to the database server, all of the changes made to the database up to the failure will need to be reversed.

When an error occurs within the transaction, the database will roll back all changes made. On the other hand, if there are no errors with each individual component that makes up the transaction, the changes will be committed. Since we have such a definitive answer from the transaction, we won't run into the situation described earlier. Of course, the definitive answer comes at a cost. The cost is different from database server to database server, but some table locking must occur and there must be some decision making when it comes time to commit or roll back the transaction.

Configuration

By default, Hibernate doesn't use transactions while persisting data to the database. There are two configuration options that can be used to handle transactions:

```
hibernate.transaction.factory_class jta.userTransaction
hibernate.transaction.manager_lookupclass
```

Of the three, `hibernate.transaction.factory_class` is the most important because it tells Hibernate which of two built-in mechanisms to use for transactions. The mechanisms are

- ❏ JDBC transactions
- ❏ JTA transactions

Differentiating between the two mechanisms is quite easy. If you are working outside an application server environment, use JDBC transactions; otherwise, use JTA transactions. To specify and use JDBC transactions, set the property `hibernate.transaction.factory_class` equal to `net.sf.hibernate.transaction.JDBCTransactionFactory`. With this setting, Hibernate will use the transaction facilities found within the JDBC driver.

If you are working within an application server environment, you will want to utilize the Java Transaction API, or JTA transaction mechanism. To use JTA, set `hibernate.transaction.factory_class` equal to `net.sf.hibernate.transaction.JTATransactionFactory`. The JTA mechanism is designed to work in an environment where transactions within the application will potentially be distributed. The JTA transaction manager will handle all of the details necessary to ensure that a transaction remains a single unit of work. When using the JTA transaction, you will need to specify a strategy based on the application server being used. The following table shows the value used to assign the property `hibernate.transaction.manager_lookup` class based on the application server being used in the application.

Application Server	Factory Class
Jboss	net.sf.hibernate.transaction.JbossTransactionManagerLookup
Weblogic	net.sf.hibernate.transaction.WeblogicTransactionManagerLookup
WebSphere	net.sf.hibernate.transaction.WebSphereTransactionManagerLookup
Orion	net.sf.hibernate.transaction.OrionTransactionManagerLookup
Resin	net.sf.hibernate.transaction.ResinTransactionManagerLookup
JOTM	net.sf. hibernate.transaction.JOTMTransaction ManagerLookup
JOnAS	net.sf.hibernate.transaction.JOnASTransactionManagerLookup
JRun4	net.sf.hibernate.transaction.JRun4TransactionManagerLookup

Database Support

As you might expect, a transaction isn't something that either JDBC or JTA just happens to support. Remember that when the first part of a transaction is executed, the database server will be making actual changes to the database, such as an update. Thus, the application will tell the JDBC driver the SQL to execute, and the JDBC driver with its transaction support will execute the SQL against the database. It might not be until the very last SQL query where an error occurs. The database server will then need to roll back all of the changes previously made to the database tables. This process of updating the database and rolling back changes is fundamentally a process performed by the database server, and therefore the tables being used by the application must support transactions.

In most all of the commercial databases such as Oracle and Microsoft SQL Server that are supported by Hibernate, this really isn't a problem. However, if you are using an open source database, you will need to look carefully at the documentation to determine whether you are using the right database table. A case in point is MySQL. By default, MySQL's ISAM table type doesn't support transactions. You will see an example later in the chapter, where we attempt to perform a transaction on a table that isn't compatible with transactions. In MySQL's case, there are two transaction tables available: InnoDB and BDB.

In addition to the database table type, you also need to be slightly concerned with the issue of the isolation level. As mentioned in Chapter 3, the isolation level can be defined using one of four different level indicators.

Depending on the isolation level, concurrent processes accessing the database during a transaction from another process will see varying results. For example, the isolation levels from the previous table suggest the different accesses that will potentially occur. If you have an application that must be completely free of any conflicts during transactions, the serializable isolation level should be used; however, your application will take quite a performance hit when using this level. Each database server has its own default level. For example, in MySQL, the InnoDB and BDB table types default to the REPEATABLE READ isolation level. The InnoDB table type also supports the other three levels, and BDB also supports READ-UNCOMMITTED.

❑ In Microsoft SQL Server, READ-COMMITTED is the default isolation level.

❑ In Sybase, READ-UNCOMMITTED is the default isolation level.

❑ In Oracle, the READ-COMMITTED level is the default.

The problems inherent with transaction include the following:

❑ **Dirty reads:** In a dirty read, one transaction changes a value in the database, but before the first transaction is committed or even possibly rolled back, another transaction reads the new data. If the first transaction does indeed perform a rollback of the transaction, the second transaction will have a bad value.

❑ **Non-repeatable reads:** In a non-repeatable read, the first transaction performs a read on a row in the database. A second transaction updates the row and commits the transaction. The first transaction performs a re-read on the row and gets modified data and possibly no data if the first transaction deleted the row.

❑ **Phantom insert:** In a phantom insert, the first transaction performs a read on a number of rows with a specific query. Another transaction inserts new rows that happen to match the specific query. If the first transaction performs another read with the specific query, it will receive a different resultset.

All three of these situations can be solved using the isolation levels associated with a database and ANSI SQL. The following table shows the isolation level needed to solve these issues. Note that not all databases support all four isolation levels, and as the level increases, so does the time needed by the database to handle the issues.

Name	Dirty Read	Non-repeatable	Read Phantom Insert
Read Uncommitted	May occur	May occur	May occur
Read Committed	Cannot occur	May occur	May occur
Repeatable Read	Cannot occur	Cannot occur	May occur
Serializable	Cannot occur	Cannot occur	Cannot occur

Using Transactions

So how do you use the transaction ability within Hibernate? It's actually quite simple, and it should be as transparent as possible. Here's an example use of transactions:

```
Session session = sessionFactory.openSession();
Transaction transaction = null;

try {
  transaction = session.beginTransaction();

  session.update(myObject);
```

```
    transaction.commit();
  } catch (Exception e) {
    if (transaction != null) {
      transaction.rollback();
      throw e;
    }
  } finally {
    session.close();
  }
```

The primary work within this code example occurs when we tell Hibernate that we'd like to begin a transaction. The method `beginTransaction()` associated with the `Session` object is the catalyst. When we made the call to `beginTransactionQ`, Hibernate performed any necessary communication with the database server, letting it know that a transaction is starting. This usually means the autocommit variable of the database server will be set to the proper value. At this point, there isn't anything for Hibernate to do until a save or update is performed. In the example code above, we tell Hibernate to update an object to the database called `myObject`. Of course, since we are in a transaction, the change to the object or any of its dependents, such as `List` attribute objects, won't be made permanent to the database just yet.

Once we've performed all of the saves and updates needed for the transaction, we execute the `commit()` method associated with the `Transaction` class. Note, we could have just said `transaction.rollback()` to get rid of the changes to the database table. Instead, we just execute `transaction.commit()` so that the database will make our changes permanent. If there are any problems with the SQL and associated update to the tables, an exception will be thrown. Our code catches the exception and immediately calls the `rollback()` method so that none of the changes will be made to the database. At this point, we can either rethrow the exception to our parent or handle the problem locally. We make use of the `finally` construct so the session will be closed whether or not the transaction is successful.

It is important that transactions used in an application be considered a unit of work and that unit of work be as small as possible. It makes little sense to have a transaction that consists of hundreds or even tens of individual SQL queries. The transaction should perform a simple operation consisting of a handful of operations and then either commit or roll back the changes. There is nothing that says you cannot open another transaction after completing the first one. However, you will never want to open two or more transactions on the same session whether or not you are in a threaded environment. In fact, you should never have more than one session per thread either, as we've mentioned in the past. Just create a transaction, use it, commit it, and open another one if necessary.

The Transaction API

The primary interface for transactions within Hibernate is called `net. sf.hibernate.Transaction`. This interface is implemented by both the `JDBCTransaction` and `JTATransaction` classes. The methods available in the interface are

❑   **void commit():** Instruct Hibernate to perform the necessary operations to finish up the transaction and make permanent all of the changes to the database.

❑   **void rollback():** Force Hibernate to undo all of the changes made to the database.

❑ **boolean wasCommitted():** Return a boolean value indicating whether or not the transaction was committed to the database.

❑ **boolean wasRolledBack():** Return a boolean value indicating whether or not the transaction was rolled back within the database.

If there is an issue with any of the `Transaction` class methods, the `HibernateException` exception will be thrown.

Transaction Example Using MySQL

Now that you have a good basis for transactions within Hibernate, consider the code in Listing 10.2. The code is designed to create a `Group` object and place several `Story` objects within a Java list. The code to persist the `Group` object is wrapped within a transaction using the code we outlined earlier. If the transaction should fail, the code will catch the exception and the rollback operation will be performed. Notice that the code isn't much different from what we've done throughout the book to this point. The only real difference is the addition of the transaction.

```
import java.io.*;
import java.util.*;

import net. sf.hibernate.*;
import net. sf.hibernate.cfg.*;

public class GroupTest {

  public static void main(String [] args) {

    try {
      Session session = HibernateSession.currentSession();

      Group sp = new Group("accounting");

      ArrayList list = new ArrayList();
      list.add(new Story("A Story"));
      list.add(new Story("And yet another story"));
      sp.setStories(list);

Transaction transaction = null;

try {
  transaction = session.beginTransaction();

  session.save(sp);

  transaction.commit();
} catch (Exception e) {
  if (transaction != null) {
    transaction.rollback();
    throw e;
  }
```

```
    } finally {
      session.close();
    }
      } catch (Exception e) {
        e.printStackTrace();
      }
    }
  }
}
```

Listing 10.2

ISAM Table Type

So what happens when we execute the code above using MySQL's ISAM table? The answer is that the code works as expected. The proper rows appear in the group table and story tables just as if we hadn't used transactions. Why? Hibernate and MySQL basically work together, and since we are just using a MyISAM table type, MySQL "downgrades" the transaction request, and the proper rows are placed in the database. This type of functionality will be dependent on the database server you are using for your application.

InnoDB Table Type

If we try to do the right thing and use an appropriate transaction table type in MySQL such as BDB, there are a few steps that must take place. The first is compiling or using a binary distribution of MySQL that includes either BDB or InnoDB support. Typically, this is a Max distribution as found on the MySQL Web site (www.mysql.com). Once the appropriate server is installed, support for transaction table types needs to be turned on in the my.cnf configuration file. Typically, this file in found in /etc on the UNIX side and c:/ under Windows. If you open the file, you will see the BDB and InnoDB configuration options commented out. Just uncomment them and restart the server. In a production setting, you will want to adjust the configuration options appropriately.

Now for a MySQL database server, we would create two InnoDB tables using the following syntax:

```
mysql> create table grouptable (
    -> id int not null auto_increment primary key,
    -> name text
    -> ) type = InnoDB;


mysql> create table story (
    -> id int not null auto_increment primary key,
    -> info text,
    -> idx int,
    -> parent_id int
    -> ) type = InnoDB;
```

There really isn't anything special about the SQL, just the use of the type = InnoDB clause at the end. If we execute the code found in Listing 10.2 again, the proper values will be placed in the database if there is no error. But what if there is an error; how do we know Hibernate, JDBC, and the database server will act properly?

Forced Rollback Example

To see what Hibernate will do when a forced rollback occurs, consider the code in Listing 10.3. In the code, we persist the `Group` object and its Story objects within the `List` attribute. After the save, we immediately force a rollback of the save. Listing 10.3 shows the snippet of code to do the rollback.

```
try {
    transaction = session.beginTransaction();

    session.save(sp);

    transaction.rollback();
} catch (Exception e) {
```

Listing 10.3

In Listing 10.3, we manually call the `rollback()` method of the `Transaction` object. If the tables were empty before the example code was executed, they should be empty after the rollback. If you are using a database table that doesn't support the rollback, you will still have rows in the table. In an example run of the rollback code in Listing 10.3 using a MyISAM table, a non-transaction table type, the `Group` and `Story` object rows were in the table but some of the fields were left with null values in them. Since the table didn't support transactions, Hibernate and MySQL were unable to roll back the rows.

Optimal Session Use

As we've touched on several times throughout the book and this chapter, the `Session` object is designed to be used for a business purpose and the transaction for a unit of work. When the `Session` object is instantiated and some number of objects loaded from the database, there has been a bit of work accomplished. When the `Session` object is closed, the loaded objects are no longer tracked by Hibernate for persistence purposes. We've said that it is good practice to create a session, use it, and then close it as soon as possible. For most applications, this practice will be fairly easy to accomplish, but there will be times when interactions need to take place between the application and a user or some other outside interface. In these cases, keeping the session open means the connection to the database also remains open. In an active database, such as an Internet store, a connection pool could easily become overwhelmed if database connections aren't returned in a timely manner. Why wouldn't the connections be returned? Probably the most common situation would be a web store where a user is trying to pick appropriate merchandise to buy. In this case, we would have opened a session to obtain objects associated with the current use and potentially created a shopping cart and persisted it so it's available in the near future—if the user were to be logged off suddenly, she could get her cart back without having to refill it.

If we create the session when the user logs in and close it when she either times out on a page or makes a purchase, a database connection will be made with the database server and kept for quite a long time. During the entire session, one or many transactions might have occurred with the database server, for example, to pull inventory and place it in the user's cart. Instead of keeping the session open for this period of time, we are going to employ a mechanism called *session disconnect*.

In session disconnect, we are assuming there is a single business function to accomplish, but the time to finish the task is large and there will be periods where the user will be doing offline work. During this time period, we don't want to keep the database connection open, so we will disconnect from the server. However, we need to be sure that all open transactions have been completed. To disconnect from the database server, we execute the code:

```
session.disconnect();
```

At this point, our session object is still valid and will be tracking any changes we make to the objects previously loaded to the application through the Session object; however, the connection associated with the database will be returned to the connection pool. When the application gets control back, it will reconnect to the database using the code:

```
session.reconnect();
```

The application will now have the ability to load new objects or store changes to the objects previously loaded. When Hibernate updates the database, it always assumes the data is dirty, and so the update will overwrite what is currently in the object's row. If you want to have a little more control over the concurrency associated with the database, you can choose to lock the database based on the rows needed for a particular object.

Locking

So what's the purpose of the lock() method? Consider the code in Listing 10.3, which is designed to work with a membership Web site. The site includes a number of HTML pages, including a login page and another to select a time for reserving a conference room. When the user accesses the login page, the code in Listing 10.3 will execute the code within the if (action.equals("Login")) construct. As you can see, we start a session within the application server and also open a Session object and immediately assign the Session object to an application session variable called hibernatesession. We want to keep the Session object we've instantiated private to this user, so we store it in the user's session. Now we also know that when the Session object is instantiated, a connection is made to the database, so once we've stored the object, we need to use it.

The code pulls information needed for this user, stores it, and also obtains a list of all conference rooms and their reservation times. All of this information is stored in the ConferenceRoom object using a Map attribute. The object is stored in the application session so that the conference information can be displayed to the user. Now for the trick. We disconnect the Session object from the database but maintain the information in the Session object--namely the user's information and the ConferenceRoom object. At this point, the code will display the conference room information to the user and wait for the user to respond. Clearly we didn't want to keep a connection to the database during this time; otherwise, we could easily overwhelm the total connections available.

If the user chooses to refresh the conference room information, the code in Listing 10.3 will execute the code within the if (action. equal s("Refresh")) construct. The code will reconnect with the database using the reconnect() method. In order to refresh the information in the ConferenceRoom object, we can just ask for a READ lock on the objects within the Map of the ConferenceRoom object as we build an updated Map object. The new ConferenceRoom object is sent back to the user for display purposes.

When the user selects a specific conference room to reserve, the code in Listing 10.4 will execute the code within the if (action.equals ("Reserve")) construct. The first action within the code block is to reconnect the Session object to the database. Now we don't really know how much time has passed since we obtained the conference room information and the reservation, so there is a good chance that the conference room selected is already reserved. What we need to do is perform a version check on the specific object we are interested in and make sure it hasn't changed. The code pulls a new copy of the room object and then checks the version number associated with it against the room object obtained when the user first logged in to the system. If there is a version problem, the updated information will be displayed to the user. Otherwise, we start a transaction, reserve the room, and commit the change.

```java
package Courts;
import java.io.*;
import java.servlet.*;
import javax.servlet.http.*;

public class Court extends HttpServlet {
public void doGet (HttpServletRequest request,
HttpServletResponse response)
throws ServletException, IOException {

response.setContentType("text/html");
PrintWriter out = response.getWriter();

ServletContext app = getServletContext();
HttpSession appSession = request.getSession(true);

String action = request.getParameter("action");
if (action.equals("Login")) {
Session session = SessionFactory.openSession();

ConferenceRoom cr = session.load(ConferenceRoom.class, new Integer(1));

String username = request.getParameter("username");
String password = request.getParameter("password");

Login login = session.find("from logins I where I.username='" + username + "'
and I.password='" + password + "'");

appSession.setAttribute("login", login);
appSession.setAttribute("rooms", conferenceRooms);
appSession.setAttribute("hibernatesession", session);

RequestDispatcher displatch =
  app.getRequestDispatcher("/loginresponse.jsp");
dispatch.forward(request, response);

} else if (action.equals("Refresh")) {
Session session = (Session)appSession.getAttribute("hibernatesession")
session.reconnect();
```

```
ConferenceRoom cr = (ConferenceRoom) appSession.getAttribute("rooms");

Iterator iter = cr.getRooms().iterator();
HashMap map = new HashMap();

while (iter.hasNext()) {
Room room = (Room) iter.next();
session.lock(room, LockMode.READ);
map.add(room.getNumber(), room);
}
cr.addRooms(map);

appSession.setAttribute("rooms", cr);
appSession.setAttribute("hibernatesession", session);

RequestDispatcher displatch =
  app.getRequestDispatcher("/refreshresponse.jsp");
dispatch.forward(request, response);
} else if (action.equals("Reserve")) {

Session session = (Session)appSession.getAttribute("hibernatesession");
session.reconnect();

ConferenceRoom cr = (ConferenceRoom) appSession.getAttribute("rooms");

Room oldRroom =
cr.getRooms().elementAt(Integer.parseInt(
request.getParameter("roomnumber")));

Room newRoom = session.load(Room.class, oldRoom.getId());
if (oldRoom.getVersion() != newRoom.getVersion()) {
RequestDispatcher displatch =
app.getRequestDispatcher("/updated.jsp");
dispatch.forward(request, response);
} else {
  try {
    Transaction t = session. beginTransaction();

      oldRoom.setReserved();

    t.commit();
          } catch (Exception e) {
            if (t!=null) t.rollback();
            throw e;
          }

          RequestDispatcher displatch =
            app.getRequestDispatcher("/alreadyreserved.jsp");
          dispatch.forward(request, response);
      }
  }

  public void doPost(HttpServletRequest request,
                     HttpServletResponse response)
```

```
                    throws ServletException, IOException {
               doGet (request, response);
      }
  }
```

Listing 10.4

There are five different locks that can be obtained. Note that for the most part, the developer doesn't need to manually lock on an object, but as the previous example shows, there are times when it is needed.

- ❑ **LockMode.WRITE:** Hibernate updates an object or saves a new object.

- ❑ **LockMode.UPGRADE:** Hibernate obtains this lock when using the SELECT <string> FOR UPDATE SQL command.

- ❑ **LockMode.UPGRADE -NO WAIT:** Hibernate obtains this lock when using the SELECT <string> FOR UPDATE SQL command under the Oracle database server.

- ❑ **LockMode.READ:** Hibernate obtains this lock either at the user's request as in our previous example or when needed for reading an object.

- ❑ **LockMode.NONE:** Hibernate obtains this lock when a transaction finishes or during the start of a call to update () or saveOrUpdateQ.

All of the modes can be used with three different methods:

- ❑ **Session.load():** Loads a new object from the database using the specified LockMode.

- ❑ **Session.lock():** Obtains a specific lock on a specified object.

- ❑ **Query.setLockMode():** Sets the specified lock mode for the query.

A subtle point can be found in the lock mode descriptions above, and that is not all database servers support all lock modes. When a server doesn't support a lock mode, Hibernate doesn't throw an exception but instead tries to select another mode that the database server will accept.

There are two additional methods you should be aware of within the Session object that relate to locking:

- ❑ **refresh(Object, LockMode):** Refreshes the specified object using the supplied LockMode. This method will reload the object from the persistence store. Hibernate does not recommend using this method for reloading the object when using disconnected or long sessions. It is better to do a session.lock () as we did in our previous code example.

- ❑ **LockMode getCurrentLockMode(Object):** Returns the current LockMode of the specified object.

Summary

In this chapter, we've taken the opportunity to explore the topic of transactions and locking. Transactions are an important part of any application that uses a database to store information. If your application will be working in a multithread or multiuser environment, it is advisable to use transactions to make sure your data has the highest possible integrity. As you work with web-based applications, the issue of session disconnect will become important, and this chapter has provided the information needed to solve that problem.

11

J2EE and Hibernate

One of the most popular Java technologies is J2EE. One of the goals of J2EE was creating an easy way for developers to build enterprise-level applications using a multitiered architecture. In the minds of many people, J2EE didn't quite live up to the ease-of-use expectation. There are many files to build, rules to follow, and other tedious requirements that make using J2EE more difficult than it should be. We can use Hibernate to remove one of those obstacles: the entity beans. In this chapter, we will show how to use Hibernate along with both stateful and stateless session beans as well as Container Managed Transactions (CMT).

Installing an Application Server

There are many different application servers on the commercial market and in the open source arena. Sun has one, IBM has one, Weblogic has one, and there are also Tomcat and JBoss. For the examples in this chapter, we won't be using any special features of any one application, so you should be able to use the information found in this chapter with your current J2EE applications. We will use Tomcat for these examples because we have a specific chapter for JBoss.

You can download Tomcat for a variety of platforms at http://jakarta.apache.org/site/binindex.cgi. For this chapter, we've specifically downloaded and installed Tomcat 5.0.24.

Configuring Tomcat for Hibernate with JNDI

There are two steps to configuring Tomcat for use with Hibernate:

1. Configure Tomcat for JNDI.
2. Create the necessary Hibernate configuration file.

We will use the Session pattern described in Chapter 5 for the actual connections to the database from within our beans.

Configuring Tomcat for JNDI

The first step in our configuration process is to build a resource declaration for the connection to our database and add it to the Tomcat configuration file found in the directory *<tomcat installation>*/conf/server.xml. Listing 11.1 shows an example resource declaration that is added to the server.xml file.

```xml
<Context path="/hiber" docBase="hiber">
<resource name="jdbc/hiber" scope="Shareable" type="javax.sql.DataSource"/>
    <ResourceParams name="jdbc/hiber">
    </ResourceParams>
    <parameter>
        <name>factory</name>
        <value>org.apache.commons.dbcp.BasicDataSourceFactory</value>
    </parameter>
    <parameter>
        <name>url</name>
        <value>jdbc:mysql://localhost/products</value>
    </parameter>
    <parameter>
        <name>driverClassName</name>
        <value>com.mysql.jdbc.Driver</value>
    </parameter>
    <parameter>
        <name>username</name>
        <value></value>
    </parameter>
    <parameter>
        <name>password</name>
        <value></value>
    </parameter>
</Context>
```

Listing 11.1

As you can see from the configuration, we've assumed that our application will be in the /hiber directory and access will be through the URL http://localhost:8080/hiber.

Creating the Necessary Hibernate Configuration File

Now we need to create a Hibernate configuration file that uses the resource defined previously. The file is shown in Listing 11.2.

```xml
<?xml version="1.0" encoding="utf-8"?>
<!DOCTYPE hibernate-configuration PUBLIC "-//Hibernate/Hibernate
Configuration DTD//EN" "http://hibernate.sourceforge.net/hibernate-
configuration-2.0.dtd">
```

```
<hibernate-configuration>

    <session-factory>
<property name="connection.datasource">java:comp/env/jdbc/hiber</property>
<property name="dialect">net.sf.hibernate.dialect.MySQLDialect</property>

<mapping resource="DemoBean.hbm.xml"/>

</session-factory>

</hibernate-configuration>
```

Listing 11.2

The primary change in our Hibernate configuration file for J2EE is that we are using a connection .datasource property to specify the JNDI resource to use when communicating with our persistent storage.

SessionFactory Singleton Class

As in our previous examples, we need to have a singleton class to handle creating the new Session options. Listing 11.3 shows the singleton class used in our application server examples. The most important part of the class is the ctx.lookp() method call, where we obtain access to our database connection through Tomcat.

```
import net. sf.hibernate.*;
import net. sf.hibernate.cfg.*;
import javax.naming.Context;
import javax.naming.InitialContext;
import javax.naming.NamingException;

public class HibernateSession {
  private static final SessionFactory sessionFactory;

  static {
    try {
      Context ctx = new InitialContext();
      sessionFactory = (SessionFactory)ctx.lookup("jdbc/hiber ");

    } catch (HibernateException e) {
      throw new RuntimeException("SessionFactory Error - " + e.getMessage(),
e);
    }
  }

  public static final ThreadLocal session = new ThreadLocal();

  public static Session currentSession() throws HibernateException {
    Session s = (Session) session.get();
```

```
    if (s == null) {
      s = sessionFactory.openSession();
      session.set(s);
    }

    return s;
  }

  public static void closeSession() throws HibernateException {
    Session s = (Session) session.get();
    session. set(null);
    if (s != null)
      s.close();
  }
}
```

Listing 11.3

Building a Stateless Session Bean

The first example we will cover for Enterprise JavaBeans (EJB) is a stateless session bean. The idea behind the stateless session bean is building a structure that can be used by any business activity without the need to keep track of session details from one interaction to another. For instance, we have a session bean that can be used to install a new user row into a database. Listing 11.4 shows such an example bean.

```
import java.util.*;
import javax.ejb.*;

public class DemoBean implements SessionBean {

public void ejbCreate() throws CreateException {
  }

  public void installUser(String name, String address) {
    Session session = HibernateSession.openSession();
    User user = new User(name, address);

    Session.save(user);

    session.flush();
    session.close();
  }

  public CartBean() { }
  public void ejbRemveO { }
  public void ejbActivate() { }
  public void ejbPassivate() { }
  public void setSessionContext(SessionContext sc) {}
}
```

Listing 11.4

The DemoBean in Listing 11.4 shows how a business method would be created to handle creating the new user, an object called User, and saving the object in the database. Notice that we obtain the necessary Hibernate Session object at the start of the business method and then close the session when we have finished with the method. This is important because a stateless session bean doesn't guarantee any type of state from user to user or even one business method call to another. For this reason and because we don't want to keep the database connection open, we don't want to store the session as an attribute in the bean. For this example, we also need the appropriate remote and home interfaces as well as the deployment descriptor. These entities are shown in Listings 11.5, 11.6, and 11.7.

```java
import java.io.Serializable;
import java.rmi.RemoteException;
import javax.ejb.CreateException;
import javax.ejb.EJBHome;

public interface DemoBean extends EJBHome {
  void create() throws RemoteException, CreateException;
```

Listing 11.5

```java
import javax.ejb.EJBObject;
import java.rmi.RemoteException;

public interface Demo extends EJBObject {
  public void addUser(String name, String address) throws RemoteException;
}
```

Listing 11.6

```xml
<?xml version="1.0"?>
<!DOCTYPE ejb-jar PUBLIC "-//Sun Microsystems Inc.//DTD
Enterprise JavaBeans 1.2//EN'
'http://java.sun.com/j2ee/dtds/ejb-jar_1 2.dtd'>

<ejb-jar>
  <display-name>Cart</display-name>
  <enterprise-beans>
      <session>
              <ejb-name>DemoBean</ejb-name>
              <home>DemoHome</home>
              <remote>Demo</remote>
              <ejb-class>DemoEJB</ejb-class>
              <session-type>Stateless</session-type>
      </session>
  </enterprise-beans>
<ejb-jar>
```

Listing 11.7

Building a Stateful Session Bean

Of course, the power in EJBs can be extruded when a stateful session bean is used. For a stateful session bean, we will have one session bean object for each user of our system. By using one object per user, we have the ability to keep important information from the user between tasks. Probably the best example of a stateful session bean is a shopping cart. When a user logs in to a Web site or signs in to an application, a new session bean can be created along with the internal attributes needed to hold items from the Web site or application. As the user interacts with the site or application, the session bean is kept and used whenever the user needs to interact with the database. Items can be added or removed as needed, and there isn't any chance of one user using the shopping cart of another user because they are separate sessions. Listing 11.8 shows the code for a simple shopping cart, stateful EJB.

```java
import java.util.*;
import javax.ejb.*;

public class CartBean implements SessionBean {
  Cart cart;
  String id;
  String name;
  private Session session;

  public void ejbCreate(String name, String id) throws CreateException {
    if (name == null) {
      throw new CreateException ("null not allowed");
    } else {
      this.name = name;
    }

    this.id = id;

    session = HibemateSession.openSessionQ;
    Query q = new Query("from Cart carts where carts.id = :id");
    q.setName("id",  this.id);

    session.disconnect();
  }

  public void addltem(Item item) {
    session.reconnect();
    cart. addItem(item);
    session.disconnect();
  }

  public void removeltem(Item item) {
    session.reconnect();
    cart.removeItem(item);
    session.disconnect();
  }


  public CartBean() { }
  public void ejbRemve() { }
  public void ejbActivate() { }
```

```
    public void ejbPassivate() { }
    public void setSessionContext(SessionContext sc) {
      session = HibernateSession.openSession();
    }
  }
```

Listing 11.8

The code in Listing 11.8 is designed to be used with the Hibernate Session pattern, and one of the attributes of the bean is used to hold a `Session` variable. Since each of the individual users of the system will have separate session beans, they will also have separate `Session` objects. We handle the creation and store of the `Session` objects within the `setSessionContext()` method, which is guaranteed to be executed when the session bean object is instantiated. Since our EJB is stateful, we have the ability to keep the Hibernate `Session` object available throughout the entire "session" of the user. For each of the operations where the bean needs to access the `Cart` object, the session is reconnected using the `reconnect()` method to create a database connection back to the underlying database server. When all of the work for the method is finished, we make sure to disconnect from the database server because we don't really know how long it will be between the current user's task and the next time he needs to access the database. As you know, a user can browse a site for quite some time before actually adding an item to a shopping cart. Therefore, we need to be sure to always disconnect from the database server.

In addition to the code in Listing 11.8, we need to make sure the descriptor for the bean is accurate. The changes for the stateful EJB are found in Listing 11.9.

```xml
<?xml version="1.0"?>
<!DOCTYPE ejb-jar PUBLIC "-//Sun Microsystems Inc.//DTD
Enterprise JavaBeans 1.2//EN' http://java.sun.com/j2ee/dtds/ejb-jar_1 2.dtd'>
  <ejb-jar>
          <display-name>Cart</display-name>
          <enterprise-beans>
                  <session>
                      <ejb-name>CartBean</ejb-name>
                      <home>CartHome</home>
                      <remote>Cart</remote>
                      <ejb-class>CartEJB</ejb-class>
                      <session-type>Stateful</session-type>
                  </session>
          </enterprise-beans>
  </ejb-jar>
```

Listing 11.9

The `Remote` and `Home` interface code for the `CartBean` class is shown in Listings 11.10 and 11.11. There will need to be an appropriate deployment descriptor file, as shown in Listing 11.12, for our `CartBean` as well.

```
import java.io.Serializable;
import java.rmi.RemoteException;
import javax.ejb.CreateException;
import javax.ejb.EJBHome;

public interface CartHome extends EJBHome {
    Cart create(String name, String id) throws RemoteException,
CreateException;
```

Listing 11.10

```
import javax.ejb.EJBObject;
import java.rmi.RemoteException;

public interface Cart extends EJBObject {
    public void addItem(Item item) throws RemoteException;
    public void removeItem(Item item) throws RemoteException;
}
```

Listing 11.11

```
<?xml version="1.0"?>
<!DOCTYPE ejb-jar PUBLIC "-//Sun Microsystems Inc.//DTD
Enterprise JavaBeans 1.2//EN'
'http://java.sun.com/j2ee/dtds/ejb-jar_1 2.dtd'>

<ejb-jar>
    <display-name>Cart</display-name>
    <enterprise-beans>
        <session>
                <ejb-name>CartBean</ejb-name>
                <home>CartHome</home>
                <remote>Cart</remote>
                <ejb-class>CartEJB</ejb-class>
                <session-type>Stateless</session-type>
        </session>
    </enterprise-beans>
<ejb-jar>
```

Listing 11.12

Using Container Managed Transactions (CMT)

If you've used a variety of Java application servers, you will find that, fundamentally, Tomcat isn't a full-blown application server but is really just a servlet server with some application features thrown in. Specially, Tomcat doesn't include a transaction manager by default. For this reason, we need to provide Tomcat with a transaction manager before we can show how to use Hibernate with Tomcat utilizing the server transactions.

The Java Transaction API (JTA) is the specification designed for providing transactions, and Java Open Transaction Manager (JOTM) is an open-source implementation of JTA. JOTM can be obtained at http://www.objectweb.org/jotm. In order to use JOTM, both Hibernate and Tomcat will need to know about the manager, just as we saw in the Transactions chapter. First, we will set up Tomcat to use the transaction manager. Obtain JOTM from the URL above and copy the following files to the *<tomcat installation directory>*/common/lib directory:

❑ jotm.jar

❑ jotm_jrmp_stubs.jar

❑ jonas_timer.jar

❑ carol.jar

❑ jta-spec1_0_1.jar

❑ jts1_0.jar

❑ objectweb-datasource.jar

❑ xapool.jar

Within the *<tomcat installation directory>*/common/classes directory, create a file called carol.properties and include the following text:

```
carol.protocols=lmi
carol.start.jndi=false
carol.start.ns=false
```

Now, with JOTM set up, let's provide Tomcat with the necessary configuration. Within the *<tomcat installation directory>*/conf/server.xml directory, place the following information within the <Context> element added to Tomcat from Chapter 3:

```
<Resource name="UserTransaction" auth="Container"
  type="javax.transaction.UserTransaction"/>
<ResourceParams name="UserTransaction">
  <parameter>
    <name>factory</name>
    <value>org.objectweb.jotm.UserTransactionFactory</value>
  </parameter>
  <parameter>
    <name>jotm.timeout</name>
    <value>60</value>
  </parameter>
</ResourceParams>
```

This information tells Tomcat about JOTM as well as configures a couple parameters. Now, as we saw in the Transactions chapter, we will need to put the transaction factory class of JOTM within the hibernate .cfg.xml file. Listing 11.13 shows the full hibernate.cfg.xml file for our example.

```
<hibernate-configuration>
<session-factory>
<property name="connection.datasource">
```

```
      java:comp/env/jdbc/cdviewer
</property>

<property name="transaction.factory_class">
org.objectweb.jotm.UserTransactionFactory
</property>

<property name="show_sgl">false</property>

<property name="dialect">
net.sf.hibernate.dialect.MySQLDialect
</property>

<mapping resource="CartBean.hbm.xml"/>
</session-factory>
</hibernate-configuration>
```

Listing 11.13

Finally, we need to change the ejb.xml file for the session bean in the previous chapter. Listing 11.14 shows the new XML file.

```
<?xml version="1.0"?>
<!DOCTYPE ejb jar PUBLIC "-//Sun Microsystems Inc.//DTD
Enterprise JavaBeans 1.2//EN'
http://java.sun.com/j2ee/dtds/ejb-jar_1 2.dtd'>

<ejb-jar>
  <display-name>Cart</display-name>
  <enterprise-beans>
        <session>
                <ejb-name>CartBean</ejb-name>
                <home>CartHome</home>
                <remote>Cart</remote>
                <ejb-class>CartEJB</ejb-class>
                <session-type>Stateful </session-type>
                <transaction-type>container</transaction-type>
        </session>
  </enterprise-beans>
  <assembly-descriptor>
        <container-transaction>
                <method>
                        <ejb-name>CartBean</ejb-bean>
                        <method-intf>Remote</method-intf>
                        <method-name>removeItem</method-name>
                        <method-param>Item</method-param>
                </method>
                <method>
                        <ejb-name>CartBean</ejb-bean>
                        <method-intf>Remote</method-intf>
                        <method-name>addItem</method-name>
                        <method-param>Item</method-param>
                </method>
```

```
                    <trans-attribute>Required</trans-attribute>
           </container-transaction>
    fs</assembly-descriptor>
  </ejb-jar>
```

Listing 11.14

In this new XML file we've added a few things. The first is the `<transaction-type>` element with its container value. This element tells the application server that all transactions are to be managed by the container and not the bean itself. This means we can basically ignore the transaction code discussed in Chapter 10 because the application server itself will do all of the transaction work. Next in the XML file is the `<assembly-descriptor>`, which is designed to tell the application server the methods that will use transactions. We have two `<method>` elements to do the specification of the methods: one for `removeItem` and one for `addItem`. Finally, we have the `<trans-attribute>` element, which is used to configure the application server as to how transactions are to be handled. The possible values are

❑   **Required:** This option will guarantee that all of the statements within the method are part of a transaction.

❑   **RequiresNew:** This option tells the manager to commit the results unconditionally.

❑   **NotSupported:** This option tells the manager to not use a transaction.

❑   **Supports:** This option tells the manager to use a transaction if the caller is part of a transaction.

❑   **Mandatory:** This option tells the manager to always use transactions.

❑   **Never.:**This option tells the manager to never use a transaction.

With all of these new configuration options in place, we needn't do anything to our `CartBean` code for transactions because both Tomcat and Hibernate have been instructed to do the transactions automatically.

Summary

In this chapter, we've shown you how to use Hibernate within J2EE applications in order to reduce the amount of work needed in the development of entity beans. The techniques in this chapter can be applied to new developments as well as in projects that are already using J2EE to provide enterprise-level functionality.

12

Hibernate and DAO Design Pattern

When building a new application, there is always some sort of data access involved. The tricky part of the development comes when we try to support more than one type of data storage. For example, we might want to store our data in a flat file arrangement in one deployment situation or in a relational database in another. The testing group might want to forego the entire data access layer and just use mock objects in order to simulate the accessing of data. In all of these cases, the data is accessed by different means and will require the developer to write different code. The real problem presents itself when we try to write the application code in a manner that will allow all three different access mechanisms to be used without distributing different applications. Thus, we might use a system property to indicate which type of access to support, or we might just use a command-line flag. In either case, the application code will need to use the access indicator in all places where code will be accessing the underlying data. For example, we might have the following code:

```
if (access_flag == MOCK_OBJECTS) {
else if (access_flag == RELATIONAL) {
else if (access_flag == FLAT_FILE) {
}
```

Obviously, if we have this type of code in every place where we access the underlying data, we will have confusion, code blot, and many places for nasty little bugs to appear. Therefore, we need to have a mechanism to handle our data access problem in a clean, design-oriented fashion. The solution is the Data Access Object design pattern.

Data Access Object Design Pattern

The Data Access Object (DAO) design pattern is one of the core J2EE patterns found in the Core J2EE Pattern Catalog at http://java.sun.com. The purpose of the design pattern is to provide a clean design-oriented mechanism for accessing all types of data from your application. The key to the pattern is designing a series of objects where the application doesn't know any of the details of how data is saved or retrieved from the underlying source and, for that matter, doesn't even know what the underlying data source is. A developer just needs to ask for data, and the data will appear regardless of how it is stored.

Let's begin our look at the DAO design pattern by using a class diagram, as shown in Figure 12.1.

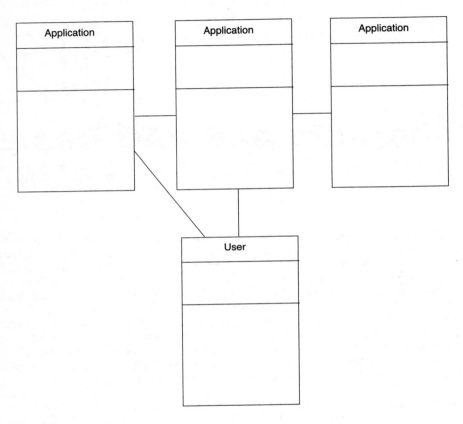

Figure 12.1

In Figure 12.1 we have four different classes, each representing a component within the design pattern. On the left side of the diagram is the Application class, which needs some data represented by the Data class. From the diagram we see that the Application class either accesses the data or mutates it, depending on the business rules within the application. The key aspect of the design pattern rests in the DataAccessObject class and the DataSource class. Instead of allowing the application to access the data on its own, we will provide a wrapper or adapter between the DataSource class and the Application. In Figure 12.1, the DataAccessObject creates a Data class so the application will be able to use it for storing and retrieving data. That's all there really is to the Data Access Object design pattern—just a middleman between the application and the data source.

To put the design pattern in real terms, consider an application that needs to access Account and User objects from the underlying data source. In this situation, we would build two different DataAccessObject classes, like those shown in Figure 12.2.

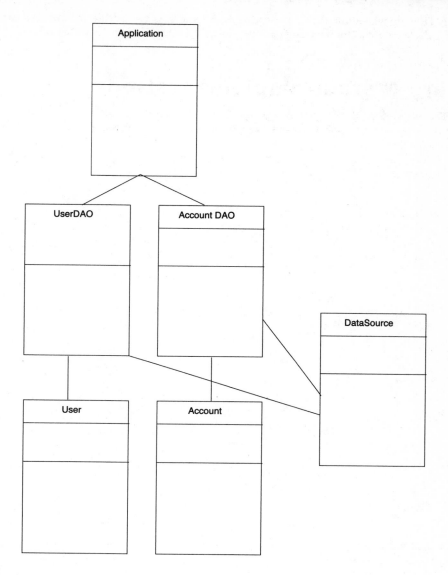

Figure 12.2

When the application object needs to access an Account object, it will instantiate an AccountDAO object and call the methods declared within it to access the Account object. Likewise, accessing a User object will be through the UserDAO class.

If we use this information and look back at our original problem, we see that we've solved the problem of having the application know anything about the data source. But what about the three different data sources? How do we handle those? The answer is by applying two additional design patterns found in the book *Design Patterns* by the Gang of Four: Abstract Factory and Factory Method.

Factory Method Implementation

In the Factory Method design pattern we design an implementation of DAO that uses a `Factory` to build the various adapters or wrappers to the underlying data. For example, consider the classes in Figure 12.3.

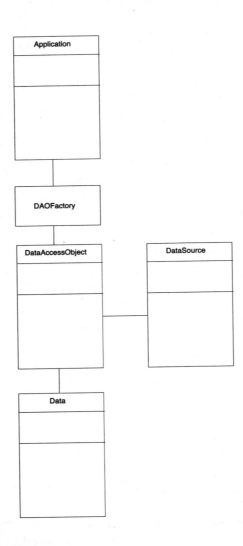

Figure 12.3

In Figure 12.3 we have two different factories. The first is called DAOFactory, and its purpose is to build a specific DAO factory for the underlying data source. The specific DAO factory called SDAOFactory will be responsible for creating DAO objects for each of the different classes represented in the underlying data source. Figure 12.4 shows the Factory Method design pattern applied to the Account/User example we introduced earlier.

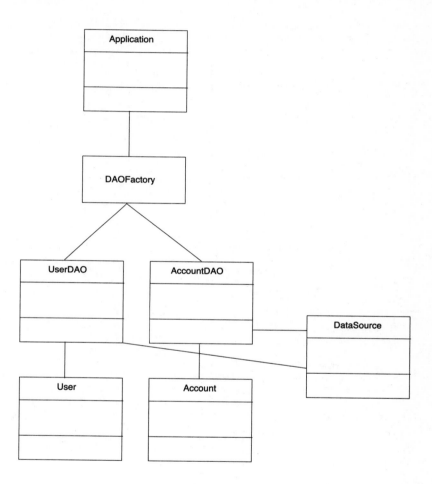

Figure 12.4

As you can see from the example, we've made an assumption that our underlying data source is a MySQL database; thus we've called the specific DAO factory MySQLDAOFactory. Clearly we could change the name depending on the data source. The MySQLDAOFactory will create individual DAO classes for the User and Account objects. All of the code to access the database and build the User and Account objects will be contained in the UserDAO and AccountDAO classes, respectively. Yes, I know we still haven't discussed how we are going to handle multiple data sources, but that is where the Abstract Factory pattern comes into play.

Abstract Factory Implementation

In the Abstract Factory pattern we expand the functionality of the `DAOFactory` class found in Figure 12.3 to build numerous specific DAO factories, depending on the data source. Consider the diagram in Figure 12.5.

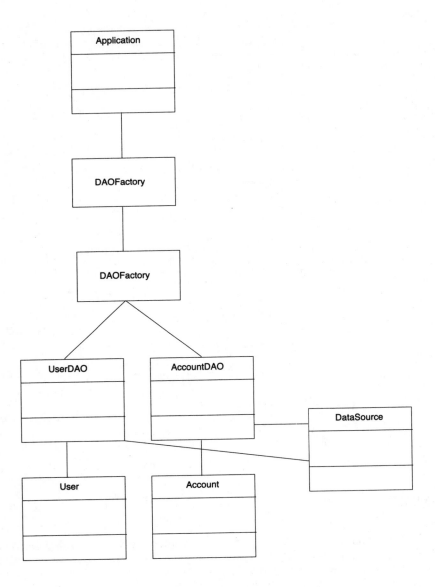

Figure 12.5

In this example, we have allowed the DAOFactory class to instantiate not just a single, specific DAO Factory but three of them—one for each of our possible underlying data sources. Notice how each of the specific DAO factories will produce its own UserDAO and AccountDAO classes. All of the implementation code for accessing the User and Account objects from the specific data sources will be contained in those classes. Clearly the code to pull a User object from a relational database will be different from the code to pull one from a flat file.

As we've introduced the DAO pattern, it should begin to become clear where Hibernate fits into the picture. In the implementation classes, UserDAO and AccountDAO, all of the Hibernate code can be found to ease the persistence of the Java objects. Instead of using JDBC, we just use Hibernate. Let's look at a concrete example so the pattern becomes clear in its interaction with Hibernate.

Concrete DAO Example

In Chapter 10, we used two classes called Story and Group to illustrate how to use transactions within Hibernate. We are going to use the same two classes in this DAO example. Figure 12.6 shows the class diagram we are after in this example. There are two specific data sources: MySQL and a mock source.

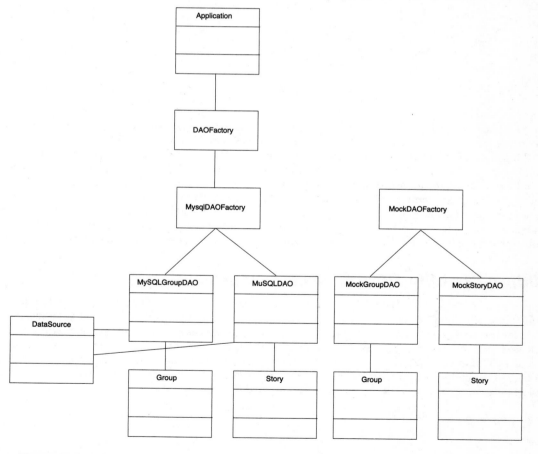

Figure 12.6

Building a DAO Factory

The first step in our example is to build the abstract DAO factory. Remember, this factory will be tasked with instantiating a specific data source DAO factory. The code for the abstract factory can be found in Listing 12.1.

```
public abstract class DAOFactory {

    public static final int MYSQL = 1;
    public static final int MOCK = 2;

    public abstract GroupDAO getGroupDAO();
    public abstract StoryDAO getStoryDAO();

    public static DAOFactory getDAOFactory(int factory) {
      switch(factory) {
        case MYSQL:
          return new MySQLDAOFactory();
        case MOCK:
          return new MockFactory();
        default:
          return null;
      }
    }
}
```

Listing 12.1

As mentioned earlier, the abstract DAO factory is designed to produce a specific factory for one of the supported data sources. Our example includes two sources: a mock source and a MySQL source. Looking at the code in Listing 12.1, we find that the class is defined as abstract but includes a single static method called getDAOFactory(), which returns a new specific factory depending on the integer supplied in the parameter list. At the beginning of the code, we have two defined enums called MYSQL and MOCK, which are compared against the supplied parameter. We've included two abstract method definitions called getGroupDAO() and getStoryDAO(), which will return the specific DAO class for either the Group or Story class. Since the methods are abstract, all specific DAO factory classes must implement these two methods. Of course, we will need to build the specific DAO factories.

Building Specific Data Source Factories

The purpose of the specific DAO factories is to implement the abstract methods defined in the abstract DAO class, which will return the DAO objects for each type we need to persist. Listing 12.2 shows the code for the MySQL DAO factory, and Listing 12.3 shows the code for the Mock DAO factory. As you can see in the code, both of the classes extend the DAOFactory class defined in Listing 12.1 and thus define each of the getGroupDAO and getStoryDAO methods. For our purposes, the only code needed in each of the methods is a return statement. The return statement provides the caller with a new DAO object for each of the class types we need to store or load from persistent storage.

```
public class MySQLDAOFactory extends DAOFactory {

  public GroupDAO getGroupDAO() {
    return new MySQLGroupDAO();
  }

  public StoryDAO getStoryDAO() {
    return new MySQLStoryDAO();
  }
}
```

Listing 12.2

```
public class MockDAOFactory extends DAOFactory {

  public GroupDAO getGroupDAO() {
    return new MockGroupDAO();
  }

  public StoryDAO getStoryDAO() {
    return new MockStoryDAO();
  }
}
```

Listing 12.3

Building the DAO Objects

All of the implementation work for the DAO pattern occurs in the DAO class for each of the types we have persisted. In our case, we have two value classes: Story and Group. Each of the value classes needs specific DAO classes for each of the data sources we've decided to support. Thus, we will need to build four DAO classes: two for Mock and two for MySQL.

We will begin with the classes for the Group value object. Listing 12.4 shows an interface that must be defined by the DAO classes regardless of the data source. In the interface, we provide all of the methods the client will need to interact with the underlying data source. For this example, we include two methods: findGroup and insertGroup. These two methods give us the ability to save and load objects from the underlying data source without worrying about or needing to know about the details. We simply pass in a Group value object or get a Group value object as a return value. If you need additional business methods, you should add them to the interface first so that all DAO classes implement the entire suite and thus allow one data source to be substituted for another when any code changes.

```
public interface GroupDAO {
  public Group findGroup(int id);
  public void insertGroup(Group group);
}
```

Listing 12.4

Listings 12.5 and 12.6 provide the actual code for the `Group` DAO classes. We will concentrate on the MySQL class because it includes our Hibernate code. The code starts with two helper methods called `getSession()` and `closeSession()`. These methods allow the object to obtain a Hibernate session from the `HibernateSession` singleton object. All of the exception handling for obtaining and releasing the `Session` object should occur in these two methods. Next, we have the code for the required `findGroup()` and `insertGroup()` methods.

```
import net.sf.hibernate.*;
import net.sf.hibernate.exception.*;

public class MySQLGroupDAO implements GroupDAO {

  public MySQLGroupDAO() {
  }

  private Session getSession() {
    try {
      Session session = HibernateSession.currentSession();
      return session;
    } catch (Exception e) {
    }

    return null;
  }

  private void closeSession() {
    try {
      HibernateSession.closeSession();
    } catch (Exception e) {
    }
  }

  public Group findGroup(int id) {

    Group group = null;
    try {
      Session session = getSession();

      group = (Group)session.load(Group.class, new Integer(id));
    } catch(Exception e) {

    } finally {
      closeSession();
    }

    return group;
  }

  public void insertGroup(Group group) {

    try {
      Session session = getSession();

      session.save(group);
```

```
        } catch(Throwable e) {

        } finally {
          closeSession();
        }
      }
    }
  }
```

Listing 12.5

```
public class MockGroupDAO implements GroupDAO {
  public MockGroupDAO() {
  }

  public Group findGroup(int id) {
    return new Group("MockGroup");
  }

  public void insertGroup(Group group) {
    // do nothing
  }
}
```

Listing 12.6

The purpose of the findGroup() method is to accept the ID value of a previously stored object and return that specific object from the data source. The method will return a null value if the object is not found. As you can see from the code in Listing 12.5, the method first obtains a Hibernate Session object and then tries to execute the load() method using the Group class type and the ID value passed to the method. If the method is successful, the Group object matching the specified ID will be returned to the caller; otherwise, an exception will occur and a null value will be returned. Notice we don't do anything special when an exception occurs. We've already set the return object, group, to null at the start of the method. If you need to perform some type of additional exception work such as logging, you can do it within the catch clause. Most users of the DAO pattern agree that the best option is to do as little exception handling as possible in the DAO class and instead allow the business object to handle errors. Thus, you might just rethrow any exception that occurs in the DAO class and let the developer worry about it.

Moving to the insertGroup() method, we find the same type of code as in the findGroup() method; however, instead of loading an object, we call the save() method using the Group object passed to the method. This method will save the new object. You might choose to do a saveOrUpdate() method call instead of a save() in the event the developer calls this method on an object that has already been persisted, but that's a design decision.

In Listing 12.6, you will find the code for the MockGroupDAO class implementing the findGroup() and insertGroup() methods. As you can see, the code isn't as complex since we are just mimicking the function of loading or saving an object. What is important to notice is that adding a data source using the DAO pattern is very simple. Just create the appropriate factory and DAO classes.

The same process for implementing the StoryDAO classes is used as for GroupDAO. The appropriate classes are found in Listings 12.7, 12.8, and 12.9. Listing 12.7 is the interface for all StoryDAO classes or derived classes. Again, we just include two methods called findStory() and insertStory().

Listing 12.8 is the actual code for the `MySQLStoryDAO` class, and it matches the `MySQLGroupDAO` class. Listing 12.9 mimics the `MockStoryDAO` class.

```
public interface StoryDAO {
  public Story findStory(int id);
  public void insertStory(Story story);
}
```

Listing 12.7

```java
import net.sf.hibernate.*;

public class MySQLStoryDAO implements StoryDAO {

  public MySQLStoryDAO() {
  }

  private Session getSession() {
    try {
      Session session = HibernateSession.currentSession();
      return session;
    } catch (Exception e) {
    }

    return null;
  }

  private void closeSession() {
    try {
      HibernateSession.closeSession();
    } catch (Exception e) {
    }
  }

  public Story findStory(int id) {
    Story story = null;
    try {
      Session session = getSession();

      story= (Story)session.load(Story.class, new Integer(id));
    } catch(Exception e) {

    } finally {
      closeSession();
    }

    return story;
  }

  public void insertStory(Story story) {
    try {
      Session session = getSession();

      session.save(story);
    } catch(Exception e) {
```

```
      } finally {
        closeSession();
      }
    }
  }
}
```

Listing 12.8

```
public class MockStoryDAO implements StoryDAO{
  public MockStoryDAO() {
  }

  public Story findStory(int id) {
    return new Story("Mock New Story");
  }

  public void insertStory(Story story) {
    // do nothing
  }
}
```

Listing 12.9

Testing It All

Finally, we can pull together all of the different classes in an example application. Listing 12.10 shows how to use the DAO pattern and classes to build and store a Group object.

```
import java.io.*;
import java.util.*;

public class GroupTest {

  public static void main(String [] args) {

    DAOFactory mysqlFactory = DAOFactory.getDAOFactory(DAOFactory.MYSQL);

    GroupDAO groupDAO = mysqlFactory.getGroupDAO();

    Group sp = new Group("accounting");

    ArrayList list = new ArrayList();
    list.add(new Story("A Story"));
    list.add(new Story("And yet another story"));
    sp.setStories(list);

    groupDAO.insertGroup(sp);
  }
}
```

Listing 12.10

The first step to using the DAO classes is to obtain the specific DAO factory we will need to use in storing and loading objects. The code is:

```
DAOFactory mysqlFactory = DAOFactory.getDAOFactory(DAOFactory.MYSQL);
```

Here we use the static `getDAOFactory()` method from the `DAOFactory` class. We are passing in the `MYSQL` constant to indicate that the `DAOFactory` class needs to instantiate and return a `MySQLDAOFactory` class in order for us to access the MySQL data source. After the DAO factory is created, we obtain a `GroupDAO` object from the MySQL factory. Next, we instantiate and populate the `Group` object for our application. Basically, we just do the business work needed and ignore the fact that we have a connection to an underlying data source. After we've created our `Group` object and used it, we can persist it with the code:

```
groupDAO.insertGroup(sp);
```

This code makes a call to the `insertGroup()` method of the `GroupDAO` object, and the Hibernate code within the `insertGroup()` method will store the object in an appropriate manner.

It is important to note the power of the DAO pattern and our example application. Notice that there is no Hibernate code within the application. If we wanted to use the Mock data source, we would just change the `getDAOFactory()` method to:

```
DAOFactory mysqlFactory = DAOFactory.getDAOFactory(DAOFactory.MOCK);
```

No other code needs to change in the application for any of the DAO classes. We might have other DAO classes for other data sources, and we would just make the single code change.

Summary

In this chapter, we've explored the J2EE Core Pattern called Data Access Object. Using DAO and Hibernate allows for complete transparency between an application and the underlying data source. Using Hibernate with DAO gives us the best of both worlds by allowing for clean persistence of Java objects.

Hibernate and XDoclet

Throughout all of the chapters to this point, using Hibernate has required quite a few steps to integrate into an application. The steps have included writing a mapping document and building the appropriate Java object relating to the mapping document. We might have created the files in the reverse order, but we still would have needed to write more than just the classes for the application. If you've done any J2EE work, you know that the same sort of situation exists when writing entity or session beans. You must have the Java object as well as numerous support files.

XDoclet was created in order to help with the development of code that requires multiple support files, thereby reducing the amount of work involved. In this chapter we will look at what XDoclet is and how it can be used with Hibernate to speed up development.

> **The complete code for the Survey application discussed in this chapter can be found in Chapter 9 and on the Web at www.wrox.com.**

The first section of this chapter will give a brief overview of what XDoclet is and why it should be used. The second section will discuss the XDoclet modules for Hibernate. We will use the object model for a Survey application consisting of questions and answers as an example of using XDoclet. The topics this chapter covers include:

- ❑ Why code generation can simplify development
- ❑ How to generate the `hibernate.cfg.xml` file
- ❑ How to generate the Hibernate mapping files
- ❑ How to generate the MBean descriptor files for use when managing Hibernate objects in JBoss
- ❑ Best practices for using XDoclet

The example code was written using Ant, Hibernate 2.1.4, XDoclet 1.2.1, and Hypersonic for a database. An XDoclet2 project is under way.

> *XDoclet grew out of a project to simplify generating Enterprise JavaBeans called EJBGen. EJBGen supported generating EJBs only, but developers saw how useful it was to place tags in their source code and then perform code generation from the data in tagged Java source code. Thus, XDoclet was born.*
>
> *Today, there are many modules for XDoclet, including modules for generating JDO mapping files, servlet web.xml files, and WebWork and Struts action files. As the original XDoclet code was pulled and stretched to support so many varied uses, limitations in the original code base became visible, especially in the support for writing templates. Thus, the XDoclet2 project was born as an attempt to componentize the code base and integrate better template solutions using Velocity. XDoclet2, at the time of this writing, was not yet ready for primetime use. However, some modules have been ported over to XDoclet2, and more progress is being made.*

Introduction to XDoclet

XDoclet is a code-generation tool. Code generation means that it parses source code, reads tags, and outputs new generated code. While there are many purpose-specific code generators available, such as JAXB (Java API for XML Beans), which generates Java classes for translating XML files in Java objects, XDoclet is a general-purpose code generator. XDoclet consists of a basic framework for code generation with multiple pluggable modules. The modules provide the specific templates and logic for parsing the source code and generating the output files. The functionality of XDoclet is exposed to users through a collection of Ant tasks.

XDoclet has found support in a variety of different technologies including:

❑   EJB

❑   Servlets

❑   Hibernate

❑   JDO

❑   JMX

❑   SOAP

❑   MockObjects

❑   Struts

❑   Eclipse

❑   JBoss

❑   WebLogic

Our goal in the remainder of this chapter is to guide you step-by-step through the basics of using XDoclet so that you are ready to apply it. The knowledge you learn using the hibernatedoclet module for XDoclet is applicable to other modules of XDoclet such as jmxdoclet or webdoclet.

What Is Javadoc?

One of the most important issues in software development I try to get across when teaching new computer science students is the need to document the code. There must be some defect in the documentation gene when software engineers are created, because no matter how hard teachers pound this topic, nobody seems to get it right. In an attempt to help with the defective gene, Java architects chose to provide the technology of self-documenting code within the language itself and to provide the tools for building much of the needed documentation. This technology is called Javadoc, and we need to explore it before looking at XDoclet. Of course, no code is self-documenting without the software engineer providing the necessary tags within the code, but that's another story.

Javadoc is a technology in which defined attributes are placed in comment blocks of the code in order to provide a processor application with information about the code itself. Consider this example:

```
/**
 * The JavaHelpMe class has been documented
 * using multiple lines of comments
 */

public class JavaHelpMe {
}
```

Here we have a simple class with a comment block used to describe the class. All of the text between the beginning /* and the closing */ symbols will be ignored by the Java compiler and left for the reader of the code or Javadoc. The comment blocks can be found on many of the language constructs, as we see here:

```
/**
 * The JavaHelpMe class has been documented
 * using multiple lines of comments
 */
public class JavaHelpMe {

  /** a method comment */
  public int returnHelpO {
  }
}
```

Of course, these comment blocks aren't anything new, because we used the same type of construct when we wrote our C code; at least we were suppose to comment that code. The Javadoc technology adds to the comment blocks using tags and tag descriptions. For example:

```
/**
 * The JavaHelpMe class has been documented
 * using multiple lines of comments
 * @see com.my.OtherClass
 */
```

```
public class JavaHelpMe {

   /** a method comment
    *   @return int value
    */
   public int returnHelpO {
   }
}
```

In this example, we've added two Javadoc tags, @see and @return. Javadoc will process each of these tags and take specific actions when they are encountered. In the case of the @see, additional output will be added to the description of the class such as:

```
See Also: class
```

where class is a link to another Javadoc page.

There are countless additional Javadoc tags, which can be found at http://java.sun.com/j2se/javadoc/. The code can basically self-document as long as the developer uses the Javadoc tags and provides comment blocks.

How XDoclet Works

Each module merges a template with attributes in your source code to produce a generated file. An attribute is a Javadoc-like tag that provides information to the XDoclet generator to produce the final output file. For instance, to identify that a Java class should be persisted to the database via Hibernate, we add the following to the top of our source code:

```
/**
 * @author Eric.Pugh
 *
 * @hibernate.class
 *
 */
public class Survey {
}
```

As you can see, we have a normal @author Javadoc tag, as well as an @hibernate.class XDoclet tag. When the Javadocs are generated, the @author tag will be used to provide the author information. The @hibernate.class tag will be ignored. Then, when XDoclet is run over the source code, the @hibernate.class tag will be parsed and will signify that a Survey.hbm.xml file should be generated, and the @author tag will be ignored.

Because XDoclet reads in attributes from the source code versus parsing an XML file or reading the Java code, it is often referred to as Attribute-Oriented Programming. Becoming familiar with using attributes in your source code will help when moving to JDK1.5 with the JSR-175 support for runtime metadata.

Code Generation Templating

XDoclet processes input files and produces some type of output file(s). Of course, XDoclet will need a way to obtain the input files, as you can see in Figure 13.1. Instead of reinventing another preprocessor for XDoclet, the XDoclet team chose to use the power of Ant to trigger the XDoclet process. Via a series of tasks, discussed in more detail later, an Ant build script will trigger XDoclet to process specific source files, generating new code in the form of Java source files, configuration files, and others. To take advantage of all the power of XDoclet, all a developer needs to do is define the Ant task for XDoclet, add specific XDoclet tags within the source code, call the Ant target, and sit back as the code is automatically generated.

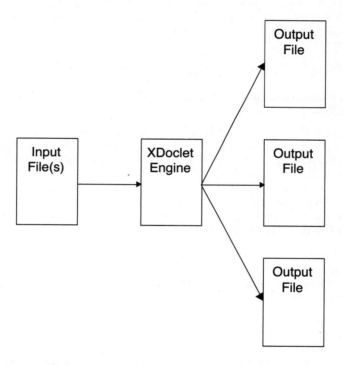

Figure 13.1

Why XDoclet Simplifies Development

XDoclet promises to help tackle one of the biggest challenges for J2EE developers: complexity. For example, in a typical J2EE-based Web application, there are multiple tiers, including a presentation tier, a middle tier, and a database tier. If a developer needs to add an extra field to a form in a Web page, he must edit multiple files, including the HTML template, the validation script, the middle tier data object, and the Hibernate configuration and mapping files, and finally add the column into the database. If the developer forgets to perform any of these steps, then the entire application breaks.

By using XDoclet to generate the Hibernate mapping files and configuration files, a developer can code faster. Adding another database column onto a table involves merely adding another property to the corresponding middle-tier Java data object, tagging it with the appropriate XDoclet tags, and letting XDoclet run. No more worrying whether all the required files are up-to-date. The mapping files and configuration file are generated every time the build is performed.

Installing XDoclet

As mentioned earlier, XDoclet requires Ant in order to do its required work and, of course, Java. For this reason, the first step in installing XDoclet is to install Ant. Once you have Ant in place and have verified it to be working correctly, fire up your browser and surf to http://xdoclet.sourceforge.net. On this page, you can click the Download and Install link on the left navigation bar. This link will bring you to a page where you can download XDoclet. The options include:

- ❑ **xdoclet-lib-1.x:** Includes libs
- ❑ **xdoclet-bin-1.x:** Includes libs, samples, and docs
- ❑ **xdoclet-src-1.x:** Includes all source code

Most developers can just download the binary and uncompress it on your system. Within the uncompressed files, you will find a directory called /lib. You will need to keep track of this directory and set the appropriate variable within your Ant build script. The various XDoclet JARs have also been packaged with the included sample application.

Using XDoclet with Hibernate

XDoclet can generate the Hibernate mapping files, the XML-based configuration file, and MBean descriptor files for managing Hibernate objects in JBoss. Before we look at the variety of Hibernate tags available, let's work through a simple example in order to illustrate the process of using XDoclet and Hibernate.

Simple Example

XDoclet is made up of Ant tasks that are run from a build.xml file. An appropriate <fileset> element has been added to instruct Ant where to find the JAR library files needed for XDoclet. In the example Survey applications in /lib/xdoclet-1.2.1 are the minimum set of JARs required to run the XDoclet task. The lib.dir property is assumed to point to this directory. Follow these steps:

1. Specify the classpath that includes the XDoclet jars:

   ```
   <path id="xdoclet.class.path">
       <fileset dir="${lib.dir}/xdoclet-1.2.1">
           <include name="*.jar"/>
       </fileset>
   </path>
   ```

2. Then define the `hibernatedoclet` task with a reference to the already defined classpath for XDoclet:

```
<taskdef
    name="hibernatedoclet"
    classname="xdoclet.modules.hibernate.HibernateDocletTask"
    classpathref="xdoclet.class.path"
/>
```

3. After the task definition has been created, you need to configure the actual task. The attributes for the task include the destination directory where all of the resulting mapping document files should be placed, whether the generation of the mapping documents should be forced or not regardless of whether the source files have been updated or not, the merge directory, and finally how much information should be generated to the console during execution of the task. Next, you define the location of the source directory for all of the Java source code to be parsed by the task and, finally, indicate that you are dealing with version 2.0 of Hibernate:

```
<target name="hibernate " description="Generate hibernate documents">
    <hibernatedoclet
        destdir="${classes.dir}"
        force="true"
        mergedir="${classes.dir}"
        verbose="false">

        <fileset dir="${src.dir}">
        <include name="**/*.java"/>
        </fileset>

        <hibernate version="2.0"/>

    </hibernatedoclet>
</target>
```

This is a very barebones example of generating the mapping files, but it demonstrates how XDoclet works. The `<hibernatedoclet>` task takes a `fileset` of Java source files and outputs the generated code in the ${classes.dir} directory. Supplying the specific subtask:

```
<hibernate version="2.0"/>
```

instructs the `<hibernatedoclet>` to generate mapping files for version 2.0 of Hibernate. In the source code for Chapter 13 is a build1.xml file. Verify that everything works by running the Hibernate target in the build1.xml file by entering `ant -f build1.xml hibernate`. You should receive the following output from Ant on the console:

```
C:\clients\book\13\survey>ant -f build1.xml hibernate
Buildfile: build.xml

init:
     [echo] Build survey-om-chapter13

hibernate-hbm:
[hibernatedoclet] 0 [main] INFO XDocletMain.start  - Running <hibernate/>

BUILD SUCCESSFUL
Total time: 1 second
```

If you get an error like "Buildfile: build.xml does not exist!" then check that you passed the -f
build1.xml switch.

Now that you have verified that Ant is properly set up, you are ready to start generating your Hibernate
support files!

Generating Hibernate.cfg.xml

By generating the hibernate.cfg.xml file using XDoclet, you don't have to remember to add a reference to
each individual .hbm.xml file. Instead, let XDoclet take care of the plumbing!

The <hibernatecfg> subtask instructs <hibernatedoclet> to generate the hibernate.cfg.xml file.
The easiest way to start up Hibernate is to put the hibernate.cfg.xml file in the root of the class path. This
will allow Hibernate to configure itself automatically.

The <hibernatecfg> subtask requires a number of attributes to be passed into the subtask. This is
data that isn't available as @ tags in the source code and is therefore passed in. Below is a minimal set of
attributes that the <hibernatecfg> subtask requires:

```
    <target name="hibernate" depends="init" description="Generate hibernate
documents">
        <hibernatedoclet
            destdir="${classes.dir}"
            verbose="false"

            force="true">


            <fileset dir="${src.dir}">
            <include name="**/*.java"/>
            </fileset>


            <hibernatecfg
                jdbcUrl="jdbc:hsqldb:hsql://localhost"
                driver="org.hsqldb.jdbcDriver"
                dialect="net.sf.hibernate.dialect.HSQLDialect"
                userName="sa"
                password=""
            />


            <hibernate version="2.0"/>

        </hibernatedoclet>
    </target>
```

Notice that we have added force="true" to the <hibernatedoclet> attributes. Normally, XDoclet
will regenerate a file only if the source code has a timestamp greater than the generated code. This will
force XDoclet to always generate the file.

The `<hibernatecfg>` subtask takes in quite a few attributes. Because we are planning on running Hibernate against a Hypersonic database running out of a process database, we have configured it to connect to a database using the URL jdbc:hsqldb:hsql://localhost. The default username and password combination for Hypersonic databases is being used.

`<hibernatecfg>` needs to know which Java classes are Hibernated classes. As you saw in the introduction to the chapter, `@hibernate.class` is all that needs to be added to distinguish regular classes from Hibernated classes:

```
/**
 *
 * @author Eric Pugh
 *
 * @hibernate.class
 */

public class Survey {

}
```

`<hibernatecfg>` will parse through all the source files, and any classes it finds with a `@hibernate`.class attribute will be added as a `<mapping>` to the hibernate.cfg.xml file.

Now run the supplied build2.xml's Hibernate task to generate the `hibernate.cfg.xml` file by entering `ant -f build2.xml hibernate`, and Ant should generate output similar to this:

```
C:\clients\book\13\survey>ant -f build2.xml hibernate
Buildfile: build2.xml

init:
     [echo] Build survey-om-chapter13

hibernate:
[hibernatedoclet] 0 [main] INFO XDocletMain.start   - Running <hibernatecfg/>
[hibernatedoclet] Generating hibernate.cfg.xml file
[hibernatedoclet] 150 [main] INFO XDocletMain.start   - Running <hibernate/>
[hibernatedoclet] Generating mapping file for example.survey.Survey.
[hibernatedoclet]     example.survey.Survey

BUILD SUCCESSFUL
Total time: 1 second
```

In the /build/classes/ directory will be the generated hibernate.cfg.xml:

```
<?xml version="1.0" encoding="UTF-8"?>
<!DOCTYPE hibernate-configuration PUBLIC "-//Hibernate/Hibernate
Configuration DTD 2.0//EN" "http://hibernate.sourceforge.net/hibernate-
configuration-2.0.dtd">

<!-- Generated file - Do not edit! -->

<hibernate-configuration>
```

```
        <!-- a SessionFactory instance listed as /jndi/name -->
        <session-factory>

            <!-- properties -->
            <property
name="dialect">net.sf.hibernate.dialect.HSQLDialect</property>
            <property name="show_sql">false</property>
            <property name="use_outer_join">false</property>
                <property name="connection.username">sa</property>
                <property
name="connection.driver_class">org.hsqldb.jdbcDriver</property>
            <property name="connection.url">jdbc:hsqldb:hsql:survey</property>

            <!-- mapping files -->
            <mapping resource="example/survey/Survey.hbm.xml"/>
        </session-factory>

</hibernate-configuration>
```

XDoclet has inserted a `Generated file - Do not edit!` comment into the file to remind developers not to directly edit the file. In addition, all the attributes passed in via the Ant subtask have been used to provide the information required to create the JDBC connection that Hibernate will need. Lastly, the Survey Java class that was tagged with `@hibernate.class` has had its corresponding mapping file added as a mapping. As other files are tagged with `@hibernate.class` they will be added to `hibernate.cfg.xml` as well.

Generating an MBean Descriptor File for JBoss

JBoss is an open source application server designed around the Java Management Extensions (JMX) API. JMX is a standard API for providing a management interface to Java applications and components. For more information on JBoss visit http://www.jboss.org.

JBoss can manage your Hibernate database connection information by reading a special MBean descriptor file. While you can generate this XML file by hand, it requires a lot of data that you already have; therefore, it is an obvious candidate for code generation. While a detailed example of using Hibernate with JBoss is beyond this chapter, we will look at how XDoclet can help by using the `<jbossservice>` Ant task.

The `<jbossservice>` task is very similar to the `<hibernatecfg>` task:

```
        <hibernatecfg
            jdbcUrl="jdbc:hsqldb:hsql:survey"
            driver="org.hsqldb.jdbcDriver"
            dialect="net.sf.hibernate.dialect.HSQLDialect"
            userName="sa"
            password=""
        />

        <hibernate version="2.0" />
```

```
<jbossservice
    destdir="${build.dir}"
    jndiname="java:/hibernate/Survey"
    servicename="HibernateSurvey"
    dialect="net.sf.hibernate.dialect.HSQLDialect"
    datasource="java:/DefaultDS"
    username="sa"
    password=""/>
```

We provided some of the same parameters used in `<hibernatecfg>` such as `dialect`, `username`, and `password`. We also provided some additional information, including the data source name to use to create the `SessionFactory` and the JNDI name under which to store the `SessionFactory`.

Look at the resulting \build\jboss-service.xml file:

```
<?xml version="1.0" encoding="UTF-8"?>
<!DOCTYPE server>

<!-- Generated file - Do not edit! -->

<server>
    <mbean code="net.sf.hibernate.jmx.HibernateService"
name="jboss.jca:service=HibernateSurvey">
        <depends>jboss.jca:service=RARDeployer</depends>
        <attribute name="MapResources">
          example/survey/SurveyTaker.hbm.xml,
          example/survey/Survey.hbm.xml,
          example/survey/Answer.hbm.xml,
          example/survey/Question.hbm.xml
        </attribute>
        <attribute name="JndiName">java:/hibernate/Survey</attribute>
        <attribute name="Datasource">java:/DefaultDS</attribute>
        <attribute
name="Dialect">net.sf.hibernate.dialect.HSQLDialect</attribute>
        <attribute name="UserName">sa</attribute>
        <attribute name="UseOuterJoin">false</attribute>
        <attribute name="ShowSql">false</attribute>
    </mbean>

</server>
```

This file contains everything that JBoss needs to manage the Hibernated classes. The power of XDoclet code generation really becomes apparent when you look at the list of mapping files to be included:

```
<attribute name="MapResources">
    example/survey/SurveyTaker.hbm.xml,
   example/survey/Survey.hbm.xml,
   example/survey/Answer.hbm.xml,
   example/survey/Question.hbm.xml
</attribute>
```

In the example we have only three classes and already the single line is wrapping. In a real application, this could easily be 50 classes stretching across many lines. Maintaining that list would be very tedious and error prone.

Tagging Source Files with Mapping Attributes

Without using XDoclet, we would just create a normal mapping document for the User class by hand, but whenever we change the class, we would need to remember to also change the mapping document. With XDoclet, we can put the information right in the source code!

Tagging the source files involves setting attributes at the class level and method level. This section will walk through tagging the included example Survey application's Java classes, leading up to more complex relationships. For a refresher on the types of mappings available with Hibernate, refer back to Chapter 5, "Creating Persistent Classes," and Chapter 6, "Working With Collections."

Tagging Properties

We'll start out by tagging a very simple class Question, which consists at this point of two properties: id and question. The questions will be stored in the Question table of the database and the id will be the primary key. We are letting the database provide the primary key, so we will specify that the generator for the primary key will be native. We have also specified that we want to cache Question objects using a read-write cache. For more information on caching, refer back to Chapter 9, "Hibernate Caching."

```
package example.survey;

/**
 *
 * @author Eric Pugh
 *

 * @hibernate.class
 *   table="QUESTIONS"
 * @hibernate.cache
 *   usage="read-write"

 */
public class Question {
    private Integer id;
    private String question;

    /**

     * @hibernate.id generator-class="native" column="QUESTION_ID"

     *
     * @return Returns the id.
     */
    public Integer getId() {
        return id;
    }
    /**
     * @param id The id to set.
     */
    public void setId(Integer id) {
        this.id = id;
    }
```

```
        /**

         * @hibernate.property column="QUESTION_AS_STRING"

         *
         * @return Returns the question.
         */
        public String getQuestion() {
            return question;
        }
        /**
         * @param question The question to set.
         */
        public void setQuestion(String question) {
            this.question = question;
        }
    }
```

The class-level attribute @hibernate.class indicates that this file should produce a mapping file called /example/survey/Question.hbm.xml. The objects will be mapped to a table named QUESTIONS. The other class-level attribute @hibernate.cache specifies that the second-level cache read-write is to be used with Question objects.

Because most databases use numbers as a primary key, the Question class has the property id mapped as an Integer object. The method-level attribute @hibernate.id specifies which method has the primary key associated with this row in the database.

XDoclet passes parameters into an attribute by following the attribute with a space-delimited list of parameter name=value pairs. Because Hibernate has multiple methods of generating a primary key, the @hibernate.id attribute has an extra parameter, generator-class. In the previous example, working with the Hypersonic database, the identity generator can be used. To port to another database such as Oracle that doesn't support identities, but instead uses sequences, the attribute would be:

```
        /**

         * @hibernate.id generator-class="sequences" column="QUESTION_ID"
         * @hibernate.generator-param

         *  name="sequence"
         *  value="sequences"
         *
         * @return Returns the id.
         */
        public Integer getId() {
            return id;
        }
```

The question property is a basic String data type, so it is tagged with @hibernate.property but with the actual database column called QUESTION_AS_STRING.

The resulting /example/survey/Question.hbm.xml file looks pretty typical, with many defaults provided. XDoclet produces a very readable XML format with plenty of whitespace.

```
<?xml version="1.0"?>

<!DOCTYPE hibernate-mapping PUBLIC
    "-//Hibernate/Hibernate Mapping DTD 2.0//EN"
    "http://hibernate.sourceforge.net/hibernate-mapping-2.0.dtd">

<hibernate-mapping>
    <class
        name="example.survey.Question"
        dynamic-update="false"
        dynamic-insert="false"
    >
        <cache usage="read-write" />

        <id
            name="id"
            column="QUESTION_ID"
            type="java.lang.Integer"
        >
            <generator class="native">
            </generator>
        </id>

        <property
            name="question"
            type="java.lang.String"
            update="true"
            insert="true"
            access="property"
            column="QUESTION_AS_STRING"
        />

    </class>

</hibernate-mapping>
```

In the next section we'll look at tagging more complex relationships.

Tagging Object References

Tagging basic data type properties via the @hibernate.property is relatively simple. Slightly more complex is tagging references to other objects. For instance, in our application every survey is made up of questions with answers. Therefore, each Answer object needs a reference to the Question it belongs to, as well as to the person taking the survey, called the SurveyTaker. Here is the Answer class with just the class-level tags:

```
/**
 *
 * @author Eric Pugh
 *
 * @hibernate.class
 *   table="ANSWERS"
 */
public class Answer {
```

```java
private Integer id;
private String answer;
private Question question;
private SurveyTaker surveyTaker;

/**
 * @return Returns the id.
 */
public Integer getId() {
    return id;
}

/**
 * @param id The id to set.
 */
public void setId(Integer id) {
    this.id = id;
}

/**
 * @return Returns the answer.
 */
public String getAnswer() {
    return answer;
}

/**
 * @param answer The answer to set.
 */
public void setAnswer(String answer) {
    this.answer = answer;
}

/**
 * @return Returns the question.
 */
public Question getQuestion() {
    return question;
}

/**
 * @param question The question to set.
 */
public void setQuestion(Question question) {
    this.question = question;
}

/**
 * @return Returns the surveyTaker.
 */
public SurveyTaker getSurveyTaker() {
    return surveyTaker;
}
```

```
    /**
     * @param surveyTaker The surveyTaker to set.
     */
    public void setSurveyTaker(SurveyTaker surveyTaker) {
        this.surveyTaker = surveyTaker;
    }
}
```

The first step is to tag the id and answer properties. This is very similar to the tags in the Question class:

```
    /**
     * @hibernate.id generator-class="native" column="ANSWER_ID"
     *
     * @return Returns the id.
     */
    public Integer getId() {
        return id;
    }
    /**
     * @hibernate.property column="ANSWER"
     *
     * @return Returns the answer.
     */
    public String getAnswer() {
        return answer;
    }
```

Then proceed to tag the references to Question and SurveyTaker:

```
    /**
     * @hibernate.many-to-one
     *   column="QUESTION_ID"
     *   not-null="true"

     * @return Returns the question.
     */
    public Question getQuestion() {
        return question;
    }
    /**
     * @hibernate.many-to-one
     *   column="SURVEYTAKER_ID"
     *   not-null="true"

     * @return Returns the surveyTaker.
     */
```

```
        public SurveyTaker getSurveyTaker() {
            return surveyTaker;
        }
```

As you can see, both of the many-to-one references follow the same pattern. Both mappings are set to be not null. This ensures that an `Answer` isn't saved into the database without a `Question` and a `SurveyTaker` associated with it. The column property of the `@hibernate.many-to-one` attribute specifies the name of the foreign key column in the `ANSWERS` table. The SQL that would be generated would look something like this:

```
create table ANSWERS (
    ANSWER_ID BIGINT NOT NULL IDENTITY,
    ANSWER VARCHAR(255),
    QUESTION_ID BIGINT not null,
    SURVEYTAKER_ID BIGINT not null
)
create table SURVEYTAKER (
    SURVEYTAKER_ID BIGINT NOT NULL IDENTITY
)
create table QUESTIONS (
    QUESTION_ID BIGINT NOT NULL IDENTITY,
    SURVEY_ID BIGINT not null,
    IDX INTEGER,
    QUESTION_AS_STRING VARCHAR(255) not null
)
create table SURVEYS (
    SURVEY_ID BIGINT NOT NULL IDENTITY
)
alter table ANSWERS add constraint FKF8494455B9CDF014 foreign key
(QUESTION_ID)
references QUESTIONS
alter table ANSWERS add constraint FKF84944555400E689 foreign key
(SURVEYTAKER_I
D) references SURVEYTAKER
alter table QUESTIONS add constraint FK3BDD512D1869DC20 foreign key
(SURVEY_ID)
references SURVEYS
```

The SQL produced generates the four tables and provides all the referential integrity specified by the XDoclet mapping files. The `not-null="true"` properties of the `@hibernate.many-to-one` tags for the `Answer` class are translated into `NOT NULL` references and foreign key constraints on `QUESTION_ID` and `SURVEYTAKER_ID`. If an `Answer` object is mistakenly saved to the database without either a `Question` or `SurveyTaker` associated with it, then the foreign key constraint will kick in and a `HibernateException` will be thrown.

Tagging a Collection

A survey is made up of questions. Properly tagging the `Question` and `Survey` classes to work together can be the most difficult part of using the XDoclet tags for Hibernate, because it requires you to work with two separate source files and use fairly complex tags. We'll begin by adding to a `Survey` a set of `Questions`, and then we'll modify the code so that instead of an unordered `Set`, a `List` will be used so that the questions are presented in a specific order.

> If you don't recall how Collections work, you may want to refer back to
> Chapter 6, "Working with Collections."

Here is the Set of questions related to a Survey:

```
public class Survey {
    private Integer id;
    private String name;
    private Set questions;

    /**
     * @return Returns the questions.
     */
    public Set getQuestions() {
        return questions;
    }

    /**
     * @param question A question to add to the Survey
     */
    public void addQuestion(Question question) {
        question.setSurvey(this);
        getQuestions().add(question);
    }
}
```

Note the addQuestion() helper method that facilitates setting up the bidirectional link. This method will be called by Hibernate if it exists and ensures that all Questions have a reference to the survey they belong to.

Now add the tags:

```
public class Survey {
    private Integer id;
    private String name;
    private Set questions;

    /**

     * @hibernate.set
     *   inverse="true"
     *   cascade="all"
     * @hibernate.collection-key
     *   column="SURVEY_ID"
     * @hibernate.collection-one-to-many
     *   class="example.survey.Question"


     *
```

```
 * @return Returns the questions.
 */
public Set getQuestions() {
    return questions;
}

/**
 * @param question A question to add to the Survey
 */
public void addQuestion(Question question) {
    question.setSurvey(this);
    getQuestions().add(question);
}
```

The attribute `@hibernate.set` specifies that this is a Set mapping. The `@hibernate.collection-one-to-many` attribute specifies what type of reference this is. Possible values could have been `@hibernate.collection-one-to-one` or `@hibernate.collection-many-to-many`, depending on the type of reference desired.

`@hibernate.collection-key` specifies that the SURVEY_ID column in the QUESTIONS table indicates which questions belong to a specific survey.

Because the link between the `Survey` object and its `Questions` is bidirectional, the parameter `inverse=true` is added to the `@hibernate.set` attribute. If a `Question` object didn't have a reference to the `Survey` it was part of, then the mapping would be

```
 * @hibernate.set
 *    inverse="false"
 *    cascade="all"
```

To simplify the task of saving changes to `Question` objects, the `cascade="all"` parameter is included to ensure that whenever a `Survey` object is saved, any changes to its dependent questions are also changed. This allows you to add or remove `Question` objects but save only their parent `Survey` object:

```
Session session = HibernateHelper.getSessionFactory().openSession();
Survey survey = new Survey();
survey.setName("Hibernate Survey");
Question firstQuestion = new Question();
firstQuestion.setQuestion("What is the best thing about Hibernate?");
Question secondQuestion = new Question();
secondQuestion.setQuestion("What is the hardest thing about
Hibernate?");
survey.addQuestion(firstQuestion);
survey.addQuestion(secondQuestion);
session.save(survey);
session.flush();
```

However, at this point, the order of the questions in the survey isn't defined. Contrary to many set implementations, Hibernate's `Set` implementation really follows the semantics of a `Set`. In the previous example, just because `secondQuestion` was saved into the database after `firstQuestion` doesn't mean that when it is retrieved it will be in the same order! Specifying the order of the questions in a survey requires mapping using a Hibernate `List` and specifying a column in the database to establish order.

To start out you must add an index property to the `Question` object to explicitly preserve the order of the questions in a `Survey`:

```java
public class Question {
    private Integer id;
    private String question;

    private int index;


    /**
     * @return Returns the index.
     */
    public int getIndex() {
        return index;
    }
    /**
     * @param index The index to set.
     */
    public void setIndex(int index) {
        this.index = index;
    }
}
```

The index property of a `Question` is an `int` data type stored in a column in the database called `IDX`. Tag this using the `@hibernate.property`:

```java
    /**
     * @hibernate.property column="IDX"
     *
     * @return Returns the index.
     */
    public int getIndex() {
        return index;
    }
```

Now that you have added the index property, you can tag the `Survey` class to have an ordered list of `Questions`:

```java
public class Survey {
    private Integer id;
    private String name;
    private Set questions;

    /**
     * @hibernate.list
     *    inverse="true"
     *    cascade="all"
     * @hibernate.collection-key
     *    column="SURVEY_ID"
     * @hibernate.collection-index
     *    column="IDX"
     * @hibernate.collection-one-to-many
     *    class="example.survey.Question"
```

```
 *
 * @return Returns the questions.
 */
public List getQuestions() {
    return questions;
}

/**
 * @param question A question to add to the Survey
 */
public void addQuestion(Question question) {
    question.setSurvey(this);
    getQuestions().add(question);
}
```

The change from @hibernate.set to @hibernate.list required passing in some extra collection information. Hibernate needs to know which column provides the ORDER BY information. Tagging with @hibernate.collection-index specifies that the IDX column will provide the order of questions.

Fully Specifying a Property

Often, someone else such as a DBA has already defined the database schema. This person may have used column names that don't cleanly map to the Java object's method names. Or the SchemaExport task is being used, and more information is needed to generate the SQL for the database. Hibernate allows you to add extra attributes to your Javadocs to specify this extra information.

In the following example, the text of the question to be asked is stored in a 256-character column called questionAsStr. We want every question to be unique, and they can't be blank. The extra properties required are appended to the end of the @hibernate.property tag:

```
/**
 * @hibernate.property column="questionAsStr"
 * length="512"
 * not-null="true"
 * unique="true"
 *
 * @return Returns the question.
 */
```

They will also produce extra information in the mapping file:

```
<property
    name="question"
    type="java.lang.String"
    update="true"
    insert="true"
    access="property"
    column="questionAsStr"
    length="512"
    not-null="true"
    unique="true"
/>
```

Tagging Getters versus Setters

Many attributes can be applied to either getters or setters. @hibernate.property can be tagged to either a getter or a setter. But be careful, because if both a getter and setter for the same property receive the @hibernate.property, then the resulting .hbm file will contain two properties with the same name.

Some attributes have specific meanings based on being tagged to a getter or a setter. The attribute @hibernate.id is assigned to a setter when it is part of a composite primary key field. For normal single-property primary keys, the @hibernate.id must be assigned to the getter field only.

Hibernate XDoclet Tags and Description

In the previous example, we showed how to use a couple of the Hibernate XDoclet tags to document our User class. There are many more tags available than just those shown above. In this section, we list all of the Hibernate tags and provide a description of each tag.

@hibernate.class

This is a class-level tag and is used to specify a class within the mapping document. If the tag is part of a Java source file, there should be only one of them. The attributes and possible values are shown in the following table.

Attribute	Description	Required	Values
table	Database table.	N	Table name string
discriminator-value	Subclass string.	N	String to distinguish different subclasses
mutable	Specifies whether or not a class is read-only.	N	True, false
dynamic-update	If true, only changed fields will be updated.	N	True, false (default)
dynamic-insert	If true, null columns are not included in an insert.	N	True, false (default)
polymorphism	Enables "explicit" polymorphism.	N	Implicit, explicit
schema	Schema name for this class.	N	Schema name
proxy	Supports a proxy for this class.	N	Proxy name

@hibernate.cache

This is a class-level tag and is used to determine whether or not a particular class should be part of the second-level cache. The attributes and possible values are as follows:

Attribute	Description	Required	Values
usage	How the class should be cached	N	Read-write, nonstrict-read-write, read-only, transactional

@hibernate.discriminator

This is a class-level tag and is used to specify that this class is part of a hierarchy and the column to use for the discriminator value specified in this tag. The attributes and possible values are listed here:

Parameter	Description	Required	Values
column	Database column to be used	Y	Database column name
type	Type	N	Hibernate type
length	Length	N	Length of column

@hibernate.joined-subclass

This is a class-level tag and is used to specify that this class is a join subclass. The attributes and possible values are as follows:

Parameter	Description	Required	Values
proxy	The class to use as a proxy.	N	Class name
dynamic-update	If true, only changed fields will be updated.	N	True, false (default)
dynamic-insert	If true, only set fields will be inserted.	N	True, false (default)
schema	The schema to use for this class.	N	Schema name

@hibernate.joined-subclass-key

This is a class-level tag and specifies the key column to be used for a joined-subclass.

Parameter	Description	Required	Values
column	The column name to be used for the key	Y	Database table column name

@hibernate.query

This is a class-level tag and specifies the name of a query and the query SQL string.

Parameter	Description	Required	Values
name	Query name	Y	Query name
query	SQL query	Y	Query string

@hibernate.subclass

This is a class-level tag and specifies that the current class is a subclass.

Parameter	Description	Required	Values
discriminator-value	The discriminator value for the subclass	N	Discriminator value
proxy	The proxy class	N	Proxy class name
dynamic-update	If true, only changed fields will be updated.	N	True, false (default)
dynamic-insert	If true, only changed fields will be inserted.	N	True, false (default)

@hibernate.array

This is a method-level tag and defines an array for a particular class.

Attribute	Description	Required	Values
table	The collection table name	N	Table to be used to store the collection
schema	Schema name for this collection	N	Schema name
cascade	Determines whether or not operations on the parent are cascaded to the child	N	All, none, save-update, delete
where	A WHERE clause for this collection	N	SQL string for a WHERE clause

@hibernate.bag (0..1)

This is a method-level tag and defines a bag for a particular class.

Attribute	Description	Required	Values
inverse	Specifies if the collection is inverse or not	N	True, false (default)
table	The collection table	N	Table name
schema	Table schema for this collection	N	Scheme name
lazy	Specifies this class should be lazy initialized	N	True, false (default)
cascade	Determines whether or not operations on the parent are cascaded to the child	N	All, none, save-update, delete
order-by	The order in which the results should be returned	N	Column names
where	A WHERE clause	N	WHERE clause string

@hibernate.collection-cache

This is a method-level tag and determines how a collection is specified in the second-level cache.

Attribute	Description	Required	Values
usage	How the collection is cached: read-write nonstrict-read-write read-only transactional	Y	Read-write, nonstrict-read-write, read-only, transactional

@hibernate.collection-composite-element

This is a method-level tag and specifies a composite collection element.

Attribute	Description	Required	Values
class	The element class for the element	Y	Class name

@hibernate.collection-element

This is a method-level tag and specifies a collection element.

Attribute	Description	Required	Values
column	Database table column	Y	Column name
type	Type	Y	The type for the field
length	Length	N	Length of the field
not-null	If true, the column can be null	N	True, false
unique	If true, the column must be unique	N	True, false

@hibernate.collection-index

This is a method-level tag and defines a collection index.

Attribute	Description	Required	Values
column	Database table column	Y	Column name
type	Type	N	Column type
length	Length	N	Length of the column

@hibernate.collection-key

This is a method tag and defines a key for a specific collection.

Attribute	Description	Required	Values
column	Database table column	Y	Column name

@hibernate.collection-key-column (0..*)

This is a method-level tag and defines the column to use for a collection key.

Attribute	Description	Required	Values
name	Column to use for the key.	Y	Column name
length	Length of column.	N	Length
unique	If true, the column is unique.	N	True, false
not-null	If true, the column cannot hold a null value.	N	True, false
index	Index to use.	N	Index name
unique-key	Unique constraint name.	N	Constraint name
sql-type	Actual SQL type.	N	SQL type

@hibernate.collection-many-to-many

This is a method tag and defines a many-to-many relationship between a class and a collection.

Attribute	Description	Required	Values
column	Mapped database table column	Y	Table column
class	Class name	N	Fully qualified class name
outer-join	Specifies if outer-join fetching should be used	N	Auto (default), true, false

@hibernate.collection-one-to-many

This is a method tag and defines a one-to-many relationship

Attribute	Description	Required	Value
class name	The associated class	N	Fully qualified class

@hibernate.column

This is a method tag and is used to fully customize a column mapping.

Attribute	Description	Required	Values
name	The column name.	Y	Column name
length	The column length.	N	Length
unique	If true, the column is unique.	N	True, false
not-null	If true, the column cannot contain a null value.	N	True, false
index	The name of the index.	N	Index name
unique-key	The name of a unique constraint.	N	Constraint name
sql-type	Actual SQL column type.	N	SQL type

@hibernate.component

This is a method tag and defines a component.

Attribute	Description	Required	Values
class	A class name.	N	Fully qualified class name
prefix	If column types are the same, this prefix will be added.	N	Prefix name

@hibernate.generator-param

This is a method tag and defines an ID generator value.

Attribute	Description	Required	Values
name	The name of the parameter	Y	Parameter name
value	The parameter value	Y	Parameter value

@hibernate.id

This is a method tag and defines an identifier property.

Attribute	Description	Required	Values
column	The mapped database table column	N	Column name
type	Type	N	The type
length	Length	N	length
unsaved-value	Value that determines if an object has been persisted	N	Null (default), value
generator-class	The key generator class; specifying native will require either identity or sequence strategies depending on what the underlying database supports	Y	uuid.hex uuid.string increment assigned native identity sequence hilo seqhilo foreign

@hibernate.index-many-to-many

This is a method tag and defines a many-to-many collection index.

Attribute	Description	Required	Values
column	The mapped database table column	Y	Column name
class	The key for the mapping	Y	Class name
foreign-key	The foreign key constraint	N	Constraint name

@hibernate.list

This is a method-level tag and defines a list.

Attribute	Description	Required	Values
table	The collection table name	N	Table name
schema	Table schema to use	N	Schema name
lazy	Lazy initialization	N	True, false
cascade	Specifies how operations on the parent should be cascaded to the child	N	All, none, save-update, delete
where	A WHERE clause	N	WHERE clause string

@hibernate.many-to-one

This is a method-level tag and defines a many-to-one association.

Attribute	Description	Required	Values
column	The mapped database table column	N	Column name
class	The associated class	N	Class name
cascade	Specifies how operations on the parent should be cascaded to the child	N	All, none, save-update, delete
not-null	If true, the column cannot contain a null value	N	True, false
unique	If true, the column is unique	N	True, false
outer-join	Determines if an outer-join should be used	N	True, false, auto
insert	If true, column will appear in the insert command	N	True, false
update	If true, column will appear in the update command	N	True, false
property-ref	The foreign key table name to the associated class	N	Table name
foreign-key	Name of the foreign key for the association	N	Foreign key column name

@hibernate.map

This is a method-level tag and defines a map.

Attribute	Description	Required	Values
table	Collection table name	N	Table name
schema	Schema to use for map	N	Schema name
lazy	Activates lazy initialization	N	True, false
cascade	Determines if an operation on the parent is cascaded to the child	N	All, none, save-update, delete
sort	Determines the sorting	N	Sort class
order-by	The order of the collection	N	Column names for order
where	A WHERE condition	N	SQL WHERE string

@hibernate.one-to-one

This is a method-level tag and defines a one-to-one association.

Attribute	Description	Required	Values
class	Associated class	N	Class name
property-ref	Table name to a bidirectional association	N	Table name
constrained	If true, there is a foreign key constraint	N	True, false
cascade	Determines if an operation on the parent is cascaded to the child	N	All, none, save-update, delete
outer-join	Determines if an outer-join should be used	N	True, false, auto
foreign-key	Name of a foreign key constraint	N	Constraint column name

@hibernate.primitive-array

This is a method-level tag and defines a primitive-array.

Attribute	Description	Required	Values
table	Collection table name	N	Table name
schema	Table schema to use	N	Schema name
cascade	Determines if an operation on the parent is cascaded to the child	N	All, none, save-updated, delete
where	A WHERE condition	N	WHERE clause

@hibernate.property

This is a method-level tag and defines a property.

Parameter	Description	Required	Values
column	The mapped database table column	N	Column name
type	The type	N	Class name
length	The length	N	Length
not-null	If true, the column cannot contain a null value	N	True, false
unique	If true, the column is unique	N	True, false
insert	If true, column will appear in the insert command	N	True, false
update	If true, column will appear in the update command	N	True, false

@hibernate.set

This is a method-level tag and defines a set.

Attribute	Description	Required	Values
inverse	Determines if it is an inverse collection	N	True, false
table	The collection table name	N	Table name
schema	Table schema to use	N	Schema name
lazy	If true, lazy initialization is used	N	True, false
cascade	Determines how operations on the parent are cascaded to the child	N	All, none, save-updated, delete
sort	How the collection is sorted	N	Sort class name
order-by	The iteration order for the collection	N	Column names for the order
where	A WHERE clause	N	WHERE clause

@hibernate.timestamp

This is a method-level tag and defines a timestamp property.

Attribute	Description	Required	Values
column	The timestamp column	N	Column name

@hibernate.version

This is a method-level tag and defines a version property.

Attribute	Description	Required	Values
column	The version number column	N	
type	The type for the version property	N	integer short long timestamp calendar
access	How Hibernate accesses the value	N	Field, property, class name
unsaved-value	The value for an unsaved object	N	Null, negative, undefined

Full-Circle Process

The full circle during development is writing your Java classes, tagging them with attributes, generating the mapping files from the Java source, compiling the source, running the unit tests, and then repeating this cycle. Using the included sample Survey application, enter `ant -f build4.xml test` to see the full process.

The final code for the XDoclet version of the Survey application appears in the next listings. Listing 13.1 is a complete listing of the build.xml file (this file is available as a download from www.wrox.com and is called build4.xml); it is a good example when writing your own build.xml file. Listing 13.2 contains the Java source files, and Listing 13.3 contains the Java JUnit test files.

```xml
<project name="Survey OM (Chapter 13)" default="test" basedir=".">

  <!-- Give user a chance to override without editing this file or typing -D -->
  <property file="build.properties"/>
  <property file="${user.home}/.ant.properties"/>

  <!-- Name of project and version, used to create filenames -->
  <property name="name" value="survey-om"/>
  <property name="version" value="chapter13"/>

  <!-- set global properties for this build -->
  <property name="src.dir" value="src/java"/>
  <property name="test.src.dir" value="src/test"/>
  <property name="etc.dir" value="etc"/>
  <property name="lib.dir" value="lib"/>
  <property name="build.dir" value="build"/>
  <property name="classes.dir" value="${build.dir}/classes"/>

  <path id="xdoclet.class.path">
    <fileset dir="${lib.dir}/xdoclet-1.2.1">
     <include name="*.jar"/>
    </fileset>
  </path>

  <taskdef
    name="hibernatedoclet"
    classname="xdoclet.modules.hibernate.HibernateDocletTask"
    classpathref="xdoclet.class.path"
    />

  <path id="lib.class.path">
    <fileset dir="${lib.dir}">
      <include name="**/*.jar"/>
    </fileset>
  </path>

  <patternset id="jar.files">
    <include name="**/*.dtd"/>
    <include name="**/*.xml"/>
    <include name="**/*.xslt"/>
  </patternset>
```

```xml
<!-- Targets Available -->

<target name="clean" description="Cleans up directories">
  <delete dir="${build.dir}"/>
</target>

<target name="init"  description="Initialize the build">

  <echo message="Build ${name}-${version}"/>

  <mkdir dir="${classes.dir}"/>
  <copy todir="${classes.dir}">
    <fileset dir="${src.dir}">
      <patternset refid="jar.files"/>
    </fileset>
  </copy>

</target>

<target name="compile" depends="init" description="Compile the Java source
code">
  <javac
    srcdir="${src.dir}"
    destdir="${classes.dir}"
    classpathref="lib.class.path"
    debug="${javac.debug}"
    optimize="${javac.optimize}"
    nowarn="on">
  </javac>
</target>

<target name="hibernate" depends="compile" description="Generate hibernate
documents">
  <hibernatedoclet
      destdir="${classes.dir}"
      verbose="false"
      force="true">

      <fileset dir="${src.dir}">
      <include name="**/*.java"/>
      </fileset>

      <hibernatecfg
          jdbcUrl="jdbc:hsqldb:hsql://localhost"
          driver="org.hsqldb.jdbcDriver"
          dialect="net.sf.hibernate.dialect.HSQLDialect"
          userName="sa"
          password=""
      />

      <hibernate version="2.0" />

      <jbossservice
```

```
            destdir="${build.dir}"
            jndiname="java:/hibernate/Survey"
            servicename="HibernateSurvey"
            dialect="net.sf.hibernate.dialect.HSQLDialect"
            datasource="java:/DefaultDS"
            username="sa"
            password=""/>

   </hibernatedoclet>
  </target>

  <target name="compile-tests" depends="init,compile,hibernate"
description="Compile the Java test code">
    <javac
      srcdir="${test.src.dir}"
      destdir="${classes.dir}"
      classpathref="lib.class.path"
      debug="${javac.debug}"
      optimize="${javac.optimize}"
      nowarn="on">
    </javac>
  </target>

  <target name="test" depends="compile-tests" description="Run unit tests">

    <mkdir dir="${build.dir}/test-reports"/>

    <junit
      printSummary="true"
      fork="false">
        <formatter type="xml"/>
        <formatter type="brief" usefile="false"/>
        <classpath>
          <pathelement location="${classes.dir}"/>
          <path refid="lib.class.path"/>
        </classpath>

        <batchtest todir="${build.dir}/test-reports">
          <fileset dir="${classes.dir}">
              <include name="**/*Test*"/>
          </fileset>
        </batchtest>
    </junit>
  </target>

</project>
```

Listing 13.1

```
package example.survey;

import java.util.List;
```

```
/**
 *
 * @author Eric Pugh
 *
 * @hibernate.class
 *  table="SURVEYS"
 */
public class Survey {
    private Integer id;
    private String name;
    private List questions;

    /**
     * @hibernate.id generator-class="native" column="SURVEY_ID"
     *
     * @return Returns the id.
     */
    public Integer getId() {
        return id;
    }

    /**
     *
     * @param id
     *              The id to set.
     */
    public void setId(Integer id) {
        this.id = id;
    }

    /**
     * @return Returns the name.
     */
    public String getName() {
        return name;
    }

    /**
     * @param name
     *              The name to set.
     */
    public void setName(String name) {
        this.name = name;
    }

    /**
     * @hibernate.list
     *  lazy="true"
     *  inverse="true"
     *  cascade="all"
     * @hibernate.collection-key
     *  column="SURVEY_ID"
     * @hibernate.collection-index
```

```
     *    column="IDX"
     * @hibernate.collection-one-to-many
     *   class="example.survey.Question"
     *
     * @return Returns the questions.
     */
    public List getQuestions() {
        return questions;
    }

    /**
     * @param question A question to add to the Survey
     */
    public void addQuestion(Question question) {
        question.setSurvey(this);
        getQuestions().add(question);
    }

    /**
     * @param questions
     *              The questions to set.
     */
    public void setQuestions(List questions) {
        this.questions = questions;
    }
}

package example.survey;

import java.util.List;

/**
 *
 * @author Eric Pugh
 *
 * @hibernate.class
 *   table="SURVEYTAKER"
 */

public class SurveyTaker {
    private Integer id;
    private String name;
    private Survey survey;
    private List answers;

    /**
     * @hibernate.id generator-class="native" column="SURVEYTAKER_ID"
     *
     * @return Returns the id.
     */
    public Integer getId() {
        return id;
    }
```

```
    /**
     * @param id The id to set.
     */
    public void setId(Integer id) {
        this.id = id;
    }

    /**
     * @return Returns the answers.
     */
    public List getAnswers() {
        return answers;
    }

    /**
     * @param answers The answers to set.
     */
    public void setAnswers(List answers) {
        this.answers = answers;
    }

    /**
     * @return Returns the name.
     */
    public String getName() {
        return name;
    }

    /**
     * @param name The name to set.
     */
    public void setName(String name) {
        this.name = name;
    }

    /**
     * @return Returns the survey.
     */
    public Survey getSurvey() {
        return survey;
    }

    /**
     * @param survey The survey to set.
     */
    public void setSurvey(Survey survey) {
        this.survey = survey;
    }


}

package example.survey;
```

```java
/**
 *
 * @author Eric Pugh
 *
 * @hibernate.class
 *   table="QUESTIONS"
 * @hibernate.cache
 *   usage="read-write"
 */
public class Question {
    private Integer id;
    private String question;
    private int index;
    private Survey survey;

    /**
     * @hibernate.id generator-class="native" column="QUESTION_ID"
     *
     * @return Returns the id.
     */
    public Integer getId() {
        return id;
    }

    /**
     * @param id The id to set.
     */
    public void setId(Integer id) {
        this.id = id;
    }

    /**
     * @hibernate.many-to-one
     *   outer-join="true"
     *   cascade="save-update"
     *   column="SURVEY_ID"
     *   not-null="true"
     *
     * @return Returns the survey.
     */
    public Survey getSurvey() {
        return survey;
    }

    /**
     * @param survey The survey to set.
     */
    public void setSurvey(Survey survey) {
        this.survey = survey;
    }

    /**
     * @hibernate.property column="IDX"
     *
```

```
     * @return Returns the index.
     */
    public int getIndex() {
        return index;
    }

    /**
     * @param index The index to set.
     */
    public void setIndex(int index) {
        this.index = index;
    }

    /**
     * @hibernate.property column="QUESTION_AS_STRING"
     * length="256"
     * not-null="true"
     * unique="true"
     * sql-type="CHAR(255)"
     *
     * @return Returns the question.
     */
    public String getQuestion() {
        return question;
    }

    /**
     * @param question The question to set.
     */
    public void setQuestion(String question) {
        this.question = question;
    }
}

package example.survey;

/**
 *
 * @author Eric Pugh
 *
 * @hibernate.class
 *   table="ANSWERS"
 */
public class Answer {
    private Integer id;
    private String answer;
    private Question question;
    private SurveyTaker surveyTaker;

    /**
     * @hibernate.id generator-class="native" column="ANSWER_ID"
     *
     * @return Returns the id.
     */
```

```java
public Integer getId() {
    return id;
}

/**
 * @param id
 *              The id to set.
 */
public void setId(Integer id) {
    this.id = id;
}

/**
 * @hibernate.property column="ANSWER"
 *
 * @return Returns the answer.
 */
public String getAnswer() {
    return answer;
}

/**
 * @param answer
 *              The answer to set.
 */
public void setAnswer(String answer) {
    this.answer = answer;
}

/**
 * @hibernate.many-to-one
 *   column="QUESTION_ID"
 *   not-null="true"
 * @return Returns the question.
 */
public Question getQuestion() {
    return question;
}

/**
 * @param question
 *              The question to set.
 */
public void setQuestion(Question question) {
    this.question = question;
}

/**
 * @hibernate.many-to-one
 *   column="SURVEYTAKER_ID"
 *   not-null="true"
 * @return Returns the surveyTaker.
 */
public SurveyTaker getSurveyTaker() {
```

```
            return surveyTaker;
    }

    /**
     * @param surveyTaker
     *              The surveyTaker to set.
     */
    public void setSurveyTaker(SurveyTaker surveyTaker) {
        this.surveyTaker = surveyTaker;
    }
}
```

Listing 13.2

```
package example.survey;

import org.apache.commons.logging.Log;
import org.apache.commons.logging.LogFactory;

import net.sf.hibernate.Session;
import junit.framework.TestCase;

public class SurveyTest extends TestCase {

    public void testCreateSurvey() throws Exception{
        Session session = HibernateHelper.getSessionFactory().openSession();
        Survey survey = new Survey();
        survey.setName("New Survey");
        assertNull(survey.getId());
        session.save(survey);
        assertNotNull(survey.getId());



    }

}
package example.survey;

import net.sf.hibernate.HibernateException;
import net.sf.hibernate.SessionFactory;
import net.sf.hibernate.cfg.Configuration;

public class HibernateHelper {
    private static SessionFactory sessionFactory;

    private static Configuration configuration;

    public static SessionFactory getSessionFactory() throws
HibernateException {
        if (sessionFactory == null) {
            sessionFactory = getConfiguration().buildSessionFactory();
        }
```

```
        return sessionFactory;
    }

    public static Configuration getConfiguration() throws HibernateException {
        if (configuration == null) {
            configuration = new Configuration().configure();
        }
        return configuration;
    }
}
```

Listing 13.3

Tips on Using XDoclet

Adding XDoclet to the mix of technologies you use, while simplifying the ongoing development process, does make your build process more complex. A common complaint is that developers don't want to run an Ant task just to update the mapping files. Another concern for some developers is not being comfortable leaving the crafting of the mapping files to XDoclet.

To alleviate the first complaint, most modern Java IDEs such as Eclipse and IntelliJ support calling Ant tasks from inside the IDE. This helps reduce the flow of thought that a developer may incur when having to switch from her favorite IDE to running an Ant task just to update the mapping files. Also, to make generating the files faster, make sure that the force attribute of <hibernatedoclet> is set to false. This ensures that only the mapping files for changed Java classes are regenerated.

To address the second complaint of leaving the generation of the mapping files up to XDoclet, having comprehensive unit tests is critical. The standard for unit testing is JUnit (http://www.junit.org), and it is very simple to set up your build so that a database is generated from the Hibernate mapping files. As developers add to the object model, they should be writing their unit tests in parallel with their development. That way, there are unit tests verifying that the objects interact with each other *and* with Hibernate properly. It is very easy to make a change to an XDoclet tag that has unintended consequences—especially when using the cascade or lazy loading functionality provided by Hibernate.

It also helps to *not* check in the mapping files. Generated code is typically treated as a build artifact, not as source code. If you don't check the JAR file produced by a build into CVS, then you shouldn't check in the .hbm files either.

Lastly, having a solid continuous integration plan is key. Using a tool such as CruiseControl (http://cruisecontrol.sf.net) to build the code constantly throughout the day verifies that no one checks in something that XDoclet can't parse (see *Professional Java Tools for Extreme Programming* by Rick Hightower, et al., for more information about using XDoclet, CruiseControl, and other tools together). Your continuous integration tool should perform *all* the steps of the build automatically. This ensures that a developer who checks out the code will immediately be able to perform a successful build.

Summary

The goal of using Hibernate and XDoclet is to reduce the amount of time needed to build and maintain the mapping documents for all of the classes in your application. Incorporating XDoclet into your Ant build script will reduce the number of files to manage by hand and ensure that all changes to the source code will produce the right mapping documents.

Hibernate and Maven

Time and time again we see the open source community pull together tools that just make their life easier in the area of software development. One of the latest tools is called Maven, and it has the following stated goals:

- Making the build process easy
- Providing a uniform build system
- Providing quality project information
- Providing clear development process guidelines
- Providing guidelines for thoroughly testing practices
- Providing coherent visualization of project information
- Allowing transparent migration to new features

Maven, as found at http://maven.apache.org, is a tool designed to provide a clear view and development of your project through the Project Object Model (POM). The idea is that a project should be defined in a manner such that performing a build should be simple and not require lots of custom scripting.

With these goals in mind, we can see that Hibernate fits in well—not from the standpoint of the tools itself but by automatically incorporating the creation of the Hibernate mapping documents while Maven does its magic.

The first section of this chapter will give a brief overview of what Maven is and will demonstrate some simple functionality. The second section will discuss the Hibernate plug-in for Maven. We will use the database-driven Survey application that we tagged in Chapter 13, "Hibernate and XDoclet," as a starting point. The rest of the chapter will cover best practices with regard to Maven. In this chapter we will also cover

- ❑ What Maven is and how to use it
- ❑ How to run XDoclet tasks directly to generate code
- ❑ How to use the XDoclet plug-in for Maven to generate code
- ❑ How to use the Hibernate plug-in for Maven to export a schema
- ❑ How to weave Hibernate code generation and schema export steps into a build

The example code was written using Maven 1.0, Hibernate 2.1.6, XDoclet 1.2.1, and Hypersonic for a database.

Installing Maven

The first step toward using Maven and Hibernate is to download and install Maven, which can be found at http://maven.apache.org/start/download.html. You will find various downloads for different platforms, so just pick the one most appropriate for your platform. After you've downloaded the tool, you will need to install it. Uncompress the file using the appropriate tool, and a full directory structure will be created based on the current version of Maven. Within the home directory you will find the familiar /bin and /lib directories along with a /plugins directory. This directory will be important, as you will see shortly.

Next, you need to create an environment variable called MAVEN_HOME and point it to the Maven install directory. Do this using your .cshrc file or the My Computer/Properties control. If you have used the Windows installer, the variable will be automatically created for you. You might also want to change your PATH environment variable to point to the /bin directory of the installation as well. In order to verify that everything is installed and working correctly, type maven -v at the command prompt, and you should see version information for Maven. If you get a message about MAVEN_HOME being set, you will need to reset the environment variable.

> Maven installs with two working directories: repository is where it stores the downloaded artifacts, and cache is where the plug-ins are expanded. By default, these directories will be in a .maven folder in the temporary documents folder. To keep everything together, define the environment variable MAVEN_HOME_LOCAL and point that to your *MAVEN_HOME*. Then cache, and the repository will be placed in ${*MAVEN_HOME*}/cache and ${*MAVEN_HOME*}/repository, respectively.

Using Maven

Maven instills order into a chaotic build environment. Instead of having you starting from scratch on every project, setting up an Ant script to compile, test, and package the code, Maven provides goals that perform these steps. This ensures that every project built with Maven works the same and that once you are familiar with the Maven setup, you'll be able to build any Maven-enabled project. Maven handles all the interdependencies between goals so that when you run a Maven test, the Java code is compiled for you. There's no need to script basic steps for every new project.

The Project Object Model

To power this functionality, Maven establishes a Project Object Model that describes all the attributes needed to build the project. For instance, the POM lists the specific dependencies required to compile the Java code. The POM also provides a structure for storing meta information about a project, such as who the developers are, the current version of the project, how to access source repositories, and which reports to run, such as Javadoc, CheckStyle, or PMD.

The POM is saved in a file called `project.xml` and lives at the root of your project. It is a very simple human-readable XML document and is the core of Maven.

```xml
<project default="">
  <pomVersion>3</pomVersion>
  <id>survey</id>
  <name>Object Model for Simple Survey</name>
  <currentVersion>chapter-15</currentVersion>
  <inceptionYear>2004</inceptionYear>
  <package>example.survey</package>
  <description>
    Object Model for a system to administer simple
    surveys made up of a list of questions and answers.
  </description>
  <shortDescription>Object Model for Survey System</shortDescription>
  <developers>
    <developer>
      <name>Eric Pugh</name>
      <id>epugh</id>
      <email>epugh@opensourceconnections.com</email>
    </developer>
  </developers>
  <dependencies>
    <dependency>
      <groupId>hibernate</groupId>
      <artifactId>hibernate</artifactId>
      <version>2.1.4</version>
    </dependency>
    <!--
Dependencies Trimmed to Save Space
    -->
  </dependencies>
  <build>
    <sourceDirectory>src/java</sourceDirectory>
    <unitTestSourceDirectory>src/test</unitTestSourceDirectory>
    <unitTest>
      <includes>
        <include>**/*Test*.java</include>
      </includes>
    </unitTest>
  </build>
  <reports>
    <report>maven-javadoc-plugin</report>
  </reports>
</project>
```

As you can see, there are quite a few elements in a Maven project descriptor. In this chapter we aren't going to go over all the elements. You can find a complete description of what is contained in a Maven project descriptor at http://maven.apache.org/reference/project-descriptor.html. However, the core of the POM is contained in the <dependencies> elements, which you will learn about below.

Maven uses the list of dependencies to construct the classpath used to perform various goals, such as compiling and testing the code.

```
<dependency>
   <groupId>hibernate</groupId>
   <artifactId>hibernate</artifactId>
   <version>2.1.6</version>
</dependency>
```

The <groupId> and <artifactId> are used to name the dependency to be downloaded. The <version> tag specifies the exact version of a JAR required. Using explicit versions means no more XML parser hell, because you dropped another version of an XML parser into your /lib directory. The POM forces explicit versioning of each JAR used.

While avoiding XML parser hell is great, the other really nice benefit of going through the tedious process of adding all the dependencies to the POM is that it allows Maven to download all the dependencies from Maven repositories online. A repository in this case is an online Web site set up with a specific directory structure from which Maven can download JAR files. The biggest Maven repository is hosted at http://www.ibiblio.org/maven. Ibiblio is an organization that functions as a digital library. And since a repository functions as a library of JARs, Ibiblio has been set up as the default Maven repository. Maven will parse a dependency like this:

```
<dependency>
   <groupId>hibernate</groupId>
   <artifactId>hibernate</artifactId>
   <version>2.1.6</version>
</dependency>
```

It will then attempt to download a JAR file named hibernate-2.1.6.jar and install it in your local repository from the URL:

```
http://www.ibiblio.org/maven/hibernate/jars/hibernate-2.1.6.jar
```

Of course, you can also provide Maven with your own list of repositories to attempt to download from. Typically, this would include the main Ibiblio repository followed by an internal corporate repository. Maven would first check the Ibiblio repository, and if it doesn't find the dependency, then it would check your internal corporate repository.

Five-Minute Tutorial to Using Maven

Using the sample Survey code, we'll walk through the basic steps of compiling the Java code, creating a JAR file, and generating the site documentation. With Maven, everything is done through goals. Goals are akin to Ant's targets but come as prebuilt functionality.

Compiling Java Code

Compiling Java code is quite simple. Enter `maven java:compile`, and Maven builds the classpath from the dependencies in the POM, finds the Java classes by looking up the `<sourceDirectory>`, and compiles the code into a default location, /target/classes. You should receive output similar to this:

```
C:\clients\book\15\survey>maven java:compile

|  ¯\/¯ |__ _Apache__ ___
|  |\/| / _` \ v / -_) ' \    ~ intelligent projects ~
|_|  |_\__,_|\_/\___|_||_|   v. 1.1-SNAPSHOT

build:start:

java:prepare-filesystem:

java:compile:
    [echo] Compiling to C:\clients\book\15\survey/target/classes
BUILD SUCCESSFUL
Total time: 2 seconds
Finished at: Tue Jun 29 17:46:02 CEST 2004
```

With Maven, any generated artifacts such as .class files will always be generated into the /target directory. This allows you to remove everything by just deleting the /target directory. Or you can run the `maven clean` goal to remove the /target directory.

Producing a JAR

Maven really begins to shine when performing actions, such as producing a JAR file, that build on other goals. Enter `maven jar` and a series of steps will be performed:

1. Java code identified in `<sourceDirectory>` is compiled.

2. Unit tests identified in `<unitTestSourceDirectory>` are compiled and executed. If any of the unit tests fail, then the build fails.

3. A versioned JAR file is produced in the /target directory based on the `<id>` and `<currentVersion>` information in the POM.

Generating the Site Docs

The structure of the POM makes it easy for Maven to generate a fairly well-fleshed-out Web site that includes Javadocs, cross-referenced source code, developer information, and results of unit tests. Enter `maven site` and Maven runs a series of reports that pull information from the POM. The `<reports>` section of the POM allows you to add or remove reports. Adding such reports as PMD, Findbugs, StatCVS, JDepend, and Simian provides powerful tools for gaining visibility into your project.

Goals and Plug-ins and Properties, Oh My!

Providing the various goals in Maven are a set of standardized plug-ins. Plug-ins can be thought of as similar to the tasks in Ant, but they are tightly integrated into Maven's build process. When you run `maven site`, you are executing the default goal of the site plug-in, which is to generate the site documentation. However, you can also write your own goals by creating a top-level maven.xml file to hold custom scripts. To write a goal that uses the Ant Echo task to spill out the eponymous "Hello World" message, you would add the following code to maven.xml:

```
<project xmlns:ant="jelly:ant">
    <goal name="survey:helloworld" description="Emit Hello World">
        <ant:echo message="Hello World"/>
    </goal>
</project>
```

While our goal that emits the text "Hello World" is nice, you might want to be able to change the message without editing the script. In that case, you can set up properties in a project.properties file that functions similarly to the common practice in Ant of including a build.properties file. Just change the <ant:echo> to:

```
<project xmlns:ant="jelly:ant">
    <goal name="survey:helloworld" description="Emit Hello World">
        <ant:echo message="${survey.helloworld}"/>
    </goal>
</project>
```

Then add to a new top-level `project.properties` file the message to emit:

```
# message to display when invoking survey:helloworld
survey.helloworld=It's a beautiful world out there.
```

I always like to prefix all my goal and property names with the name of the project to prevent any chance of running into a conflict with another goal or property set within Maven.

You can also instruct Maven to run your goal before or after another goal. To echo "Hello World" before compiling the Java code, you would use a `preGoal` that then calls your goal via `attainGoal`:

```
<project xmlns:ant="jelly:ant">
    <preGoal name="java:compile">
        <attainGoal name="survey:helloworld"/>
    </preGoal>
</project>
```

The ability to have `preGoals` and `postGoals` weave customizations around the standard Maven goals allows you to integrate the various XDoclet code-generation steps needed to generate Hibernate files seamlessly into the standard Maven build.

Generating Hibernate Files with Maven

There are two approaches to generating the Hibernate files from within Maven. You can either script calling the <hibernatedoclet> task yourself or use the XDoclet plug-in for Maven. The XDoclet plug-in for Maven is typically the simpler method to start with; however, in some environments it may not support everything you need to do. First, we'll walk through using the XDoclet plug-in to generate the Hibernate files, and then we'll follow up by scripting the XDoclet steps ourselves. To see how to integrate the XDoclet steps into the Maven build process, jump to the end of this chapter.

Running the XDoclet Plug-in for Maven

One of the nice things that Maven brings to the table is the ability to download and install plug-ins from online repositories. Just run the following line to download and install the 1.2.1 version of the XDoclet plug-in:

```
maven plugin:download -DgroupId=xdoclet
-DartifactId=maven-xdoclet-plugin -Dversion=1.2.1
-Dmaven.repo.remote=http://xdoclet.sourceforge.net/repository
```

If you are running offline, then the XDoclet plug-in is also available in the /lib/ directory of the XDoclet distribution. Look for a file similar to maven-xdoclet-plugin-1.2.1.jar and copy it to the /plugin directory of your Maven installation.

To verify the installation, enter maven -P xdoclet, and you should receive something like this:

```
Goals in xdoclet
================

[xdoclet]                              ( NO DEFAULT GOAL )
  documentdoclet   ................ documentdoclet
  ejbdoclet   ..................... ejbdoclet
  hibernatedoclet   .............. hibernatedoclet
  jdodoclet   ..................... jdodoclet
  jmxdoclet   ..................... jmxdoclet
  mockobjectdoclet   .............. mockobjectdoclet
  portletdoclet   ................. portletdoclet
  springdoclet   .................. springdoclet
  webdoclet   ..................... webdoclet
  xdoclet   ....................... xdoclet
```

We will be discussing only the hibernatedoclet goal; however, all the XDoclet goals are configured and run in a similar fashion.

Generate Mapping Files

To generate the mapping files, XDoclet needs various information, such as where the source files are located. This information is stored in the project.properties file. Our project.properties file offers this simple example:

```
maven.xdoclet.hibernatedoclet.fileset.0=true
maven.xdoclet.hibernatedoclet.fileset.0.include=**/*.java
maven.xdoclet.hibernatedoclet.hibernate.0.Version=2.0
```

Enter maven xdoclet:hibernatedoclet and the mapping files will be generated into the /target/xdoclet/hibernatedoclet directory. You can override this directory by providing a different value for maven.xdoclet.hibernatedoclet.destDir in the project.properties file.

The structure of the properties for the XDoclet plug-in for Maven is a little different from the properties for most Maven plug-ins in that if you need to provide multiple directories, instead of using a comma-delimited list, you use an indexed list:

```
maven.xdoclet.hibernatedoclet.fileset.0=true
maven.xdoclet.hibernatedoclet.fileset.0.include=**/om/*.java
maven.xdoclet.hibernatedoclet.fileset.1=true
maven.xdoclet.hibernatedoclet.fileset.1.include=**/otherom/*.java
```

You can also disable generation of a fileset by setting the `fileset` index value to `false`:

```
maven.xdoclet.hibernatedoclet.fileset.1=false
```

Generate the Hibernate.cfg.xml File

The `xdoclet:hibernatedoclet` goal also needs some basic data to generate the hibernate.cfg.xml file. You provide this data in a similar fashion to the fileset data used in generating the mapping files:

```
maven.xdoclet.hibernatedoclet.hibernatecfg.0=true
maven.xdoclet.hibernatedoclet.hibernatecfg.0.jdbcUrl=jdbc:hsqldb:hsql:survey
maven.xdoclet.hibernatedoclet.hibernatecfg.0.driver=org.hsqldb.jdbcDriver
maven.xdoclet.hibernatedoclet.hibernatecfg.0.dialect=net.sf.hibernate.dialect
.HSQLDialect
maven.xdoclet.hibernatedoclet.hibernatecfg.0.userName=sa
maven.xdoclet.hibernatedoclet.hibernatecfg.0.password=
```

You also need to supply in the POM a dependency on the specific XDoclet modules that implement the various XDoclet templates. In our case, we need to add `xdoclet-hibernate-module`:

```
<dependency>
    <groupId>xdoclet</groupId>
    <artifactId>xdoclet-hibernate-module</artifactId>
    <version>1.2.1</version>
</dependency>
```

Everything is now configured. Running `maven xdoclet:hibernatedoclet` will download the `xdoclet-hibernate-module` and generate the configuration and .hbm files into the /target/xdoclet/hibernatedoclet directory.

Scripting Directly in Maven.xml

At various times you may discover that an Ant task exists for something you need to have done, but either there is no Maven plug-in or the Maven plug-in doesn't suit your needs. In these cases you will build on your Ant skills by adding your own goal to maven.xml. For more information on calling XDoclet tasks using Ant, refer back to Chapter 13. We'll walk through the process of calling the `xdoclet:hibernatedoclet` task from our own Maven goal.

Set Up Dependencies

First, we'll need to add the various dependencies for the `hibernatedoclet` module to the POM. One of the advantages of using a plug-in is that it downloads its own list of dependencies behind the scenes. But since we aren't using the XDoclet plug-in, we need to add them directly to our POM:

```
<!-- Begin XDoclet Dependencies -->
<dependency>
```

```
      <groupId>xdoclet</groupId>
      <artifactId>xdoclet</artifactId>
      <version>1.2.1</version>
  </dependency>
  <dependency>
      <groupId>xdoclet</groupId>
      <artifactId>xdoclet-hibernate-module</artifactId>
      <version>1.2.1</version>
  </dependency>
  <dependency>
      <groupId>xdoclet</groupId>
      <artifactId>xdoclet-xdoclet-module</artifactId>
      <version>1.2.1</version>
  </dependency>
  <dependency>
      <groupId>xdoclet</groupId>
      <artifactId>xjavadoc</artifactId>
      <version>1.0.3</version>
  </dependency>
```

Then we need to define the new goal in the `maven.xml` file:

```
<goal name="survey:hibernate" description="Generate Hibernate files with
Xdoclet">
    </goal>
```

Just like using any nonstandard Ant task in an Ant build.xml, we need to provide a task definition. As part of this, we'll define the classpath to use as well by just using all the dependencies in the POM:

```
<goal name="survey:hibernate" description="Generate Hibernate files with
Xdoclet">
    <ant:taskdef name="hibernatedoclet"
classname="xdoclet.modules.hibernate.HibernateDocletTask">
        <ant:classpath>
            <ant:path refid="maven.dependency.classpath"/>
        </ant:classpath>
    </ant:taskdef>
</goal>
```

Notice that all of the Ant XML tags are prefixed with `ant:`. Maven handles multiple namespaces in the XML documents by declaring as part of the project definition all the XML namespaces:

```
<project xmlns:ant="jelly:ant">
```

However, because the Maven developers wanted to make it simple for people with an Ant background to port their scripts, by default the Ant namespace is imported. So prefixing the Ant XML elements with `ant:` isn't required.

Generate Mapping Files

And now we're ready to use the `<hibernatedoclet>` task combined with the `<hibernate>` subtask to generate the mapping files:

```
        <goal name="survey:hibernate" description="Generate Hibernate files with
Xdoclet">
            <ant:taskdef name="hibernatedoclet"
classname="xdoclet.modules.hibernate.HibernateDocletTask">
                <ant:classpath>
                    <ant:path refid="maven.dependency.classpath"/>
                </ant:classpath>
            </ant:taskdef>


            <ant:hibernatedoclet destDir="${maven.build.dir}/generated-sources"
                force="true" verbose="true">
                <ant:hibernate version="2.0"/>
                <ant:fileset dir="${maven.src.dir}/java"
                    includes="**/*.java"/>
            </ant:hibernatedoclet>
        </goal>
```

Notice that we're using the Maven-supplied property `maven.build.dir` to build a relative path to our generated source. Maven will translate `${maven.build.dir}/generated-sources` into target/ generated-sources. A strong principle with Maven is that anything generated should go into /target, and anything else should be checked into source control. And since XDoclet is doing the work of generating the Hibernate mapping files, there is no reason to check the generated code into source control.

Generate Hibernate.cfg.xml with Maven

You can imagine how simple it is to generate the Hibernate.cfg.xml file. If you guessed that you would add something as simple as this, then you'd be right!

```
            <ant:hibernatedoclet destDir="${maven.build.dir}/generated-sources"
                force="true" verbose="true">
                <ant:hibernate version="2.0"/>
                <ant:fileset dir="${maven.src.dir}/java"
                    includes="**/*.java"/>
                <ant:hibernatecfg
                    jdbcUrl="jdbc:hsqldb:hsql:survey"
                    driver="org.hsqldb.jdbcDriver"
                    dialect="net.sf.hibernate.dialect.HSQLDialect"
                    userName="sa"
                    password=""
                />
            </ant:hibernatedoclet>
```

To make the project more flexible and less tied to HSQL, you should change all the values being passed into `<ant:hibernatecfg>` into properties that are set in the accompanying project.properties file:

```
            <ant:hibernatecfg
                jdbcUrl="${survey.jdbcurl}"
                driver="${survey.driver}"
                dialect="${survey.dialect}"
                userName="${survey.username}"
                password="${survey.password}"
            />
```

And in `project.properties` add the various properties defining the database connection:

```
# database connection properties
survey.jdbcurl=jdbc:hsqldb:hsql:survey
survey.driver=org.hsqldb.jdbcDriver
survey.dialect=net.sf.hibernate.dialect.HSQLDialect
survey.username=sa
survey.password=
```

Using the Hibernate Plug-in for Maven

At the time of this writing, the functionality that the Hibernate plug-in for Maven provides is an easy interface to the SchemaExport tool and a tool to aggregate multiple .hbm.xml files into a single file.

To view all the goals available for the Hibernate plug-in, enter `maven -P hibernate`:

```
Goals in hibernate
==================

[hibernate]                        ( NO DEFAULT GOAL )
  aggregate-mappings  ............ Aggregate multiple .hbm.xml files into
one
                                   file
  schema-export  ................. Export Hibernate schema
```

hibernate:aggregate-mappings

Keeping the hibernate.cfg.xml file up-to-date can be a challenge if you aren't using XDoclet to generate this file. It's very easy for a developer to forget to add another `<mapping/>` reference when adding new classes. One approach is to aggregate all the .hbm files into a single file and then reference this file in the hibernate.cfg.xml. By default, this file will be output as /target/schema/aggregated-mappings.hbm.xml.

Enter `maven hibernate:aggregate-mappings`, and a resulting aggregated-mappings.hbm.xml file will be produced. Change the hibernate.cfg.xml to use this file by having just a single <mapping > reference:

```
<mapping resource="aggregated-mappings.hbm.xml"/>
```

hibernate:schema-export

The SchemaExport tool, as you may recall, generates your database schema from the various .hbm mapping files. You can instruct it to just generate the schema or to generate and insert the schema into the database. The `<hibernate:schema-export>` goal wraps the SchemaExport tool and integrates it cleanly into Maven. For more information about the SchemaExport tool, jump ahead to Chapter 15, "Hibernate Extensions."

The only required property for this goal is `maven.hibernate.properties`, which should reference a hibernate.properties file. The hibernate.properties file is a standard Java properties file with all the database configuration information required for Hibernate to create a Configuration object from:

```
maven.hibernate.properties=bin/hibernate.properties
```

The other properties duplicate the SchemaExport properties that you will learn about in Chapter 15, "Hibernate Extensions."

An up-to-date list of all the properties and goals is available from the plug-in home page: http://maven.apache.org/reference/plugins/hibernate.

Just generating the SQL statements doesn't require a database connection as long as you set the property `maven.hibernate.text=true`. The SQL is generated according to the `hibernate.dialect` property:

```
hibernate.dialect=net.sf.hibernate.dialect.HSQLDialect
```

But if you wish to insert the schema into a database, then you will need to add to the POM another dependency with the JDBC driver classes to be used. In the Survey example, we added the HSQL database driver to the list of dependencies:

```
<dependency>
  <groupId>hsqldb</groupId>
  <artifactId>hsqldb</artifactId>
  <version>1.7.1</version>
</dependency>
```

To demonstrate exporting the schema, you must first have an HSQL database running. In survey/bin are two files, startHsql.bat and startHsql.sh. Pick the one appropriate for your platform and start up HSQL. Then run `maven hibernate:schema-export` and you will see the SQL statements listed on the console as they are executed. The following table explains the properties for the Hibernate plug-in for Maven.

Attribute	Description	Required	Values
maven.hibernate.properties	The location of the Hibernate properties file with all the information for configuring Hibernate at runtime	Y	Hibernate.properties
maven.hibernate.quiet	How verbose the plug-in should be; set to true to help with debugging	N	True (default), false
maven.hibernate.text	Instructs Hibernate whether to insert the schema into the database; setting to true will write the SQL to the file system only	N	True, false (default)
maven.hibernate.drop	Specify whether to generate just the drop table SQL statements	N	True, false (default)

Table continued on following page

Attribute	Description	Required	Values
maven.hibernate.delimiter	String used to separate SQL commands	N	
maven.hibernate.output.dir	The location to output generated files	N	${maven.build.dir}/ schema
maven.hibernate.output.file	The name of the file created by the schema-export goal	N	${maven.final. name}- schema.sql
maven.hibernate.input.dir	Comma-separated list of base directories indicating where mapping files are located	N	${maven.build. dest}
maven.hibernate. input.includes	Comma-separated list of patterns of Hibernate mapping files to be included in aggregating mappings	N	**/*.hbm.xml
maven.hibernate. input.excludes	Comma-separated list of patterns of Hibernate mapping files to be excluded in aggregating mappings	N	**/*.hbm.xml2 maven.hibernate. aggregate
.output.file	File containing the aggregated mappings	N	aggregated mappings.hbm.xml

Putting It All Together

At this point, you know how to run the various goals needed to perform all the Hibernate-related tasks, either through custom goals in maven.xml or via the various plug-ins. Now in most cases, we want the Hibernate/XDoclet plug-ins to seamlessly weave the various generation steps into the standard Maven process versus adding extra manual steps to the build process.

Generating Files

To generate the mapping files, we'll add to the maven.xml a new `<preGoal>` to run after the `java:compile` step and to call either the `xdoclet:hibernatedoclet` goal or the customized `survey:hibernate` goal, depending on which approach you want to take:

```
<preGoal name="java:compile">
    <attainGoal name="xdoclet:hibernatedoclet"/>
</preGoal>
```

Now, if you run `maven java:compile`, you'll see both the Hibernate mapping files and the hibernate.cfg.xml file generated into the `target/xdoclet` directory. However, this doesn't do you much good, since if you run a goal such as `maven jar`, the generated files will be ignored since they are not in `target/classes` and therefore aren't included. Therefore, you need to declare the generated files as `<resources>` to be included:

```
<build>
  <sourceDirectory>src/java</sourceDirectory>
  <unitTestSourceDirectory>src/test</unitTestSourceDirectory>
  <unitTest>
    <includes>
      <include>**/*Test*.java</include>
    </includes>
  </unitTest>
  <resources>
    <resource>
      <directory>${maven.build.dir}/xdoclet/hibernatedoclet</directory>
      <targetPath>/</targetPath>
      <includes>
        <include>hibernate.cfg.xml</include>
        <include>**/*.hbm.xml</include>
      </includes>
    </resource>
  </resources>
</build>
```

We added information about the generated files to the `<build>` section of the POM. The `<directory>` tag specifies the directory into which the files are generated. The `<targetPath>/</targetPath>` specifies the `target/classes` directory. And the `<includes>` provide pattern matchers to pick up the hibernate.cfg.xml and all the various Hibernate mapping files and copy them into the `target/classes` directory. Run `maven jar` and you will see in /target a survey-chapter-15.jar file. Open it and you will see included in the JAR the XDoclet-generated files!

Configuring a Database Prior to Running Unit Tests

Unit testing has become an accepted part of Java development. Indeed, now the question isn't whether to have unit tests but whether to do test-driven development! Unit testing Java classes mapped to a database using Hibernate provides many benefits, including:

❑   Verifying that the code functions as expected.

❑   XDoclet tags in the Javadocs are generating valid mapping files.

❑   Hibernate has all the required data to start up.

❑   HQL queries use the correct object names and properties.

The easiest way to do this is to have a live database that you can test against. However, testing against a live database presents its own challenges. Developers need to make sure that as they change the object model, the schema is updated as well. While changing the object model is as simple as changing the Java code and updating the XDoclet tags, keeping the schema up-to-date can be a very formidable task.

Fortunately, by using the SchemaExport tool to generate the SQL statements needed to create the schema, it is easy to have an up-to-date database. It is simple to weave the `hibernate:schema-export` goal to run before the unit tests are run, providing a clean, empty database before every unit test is run.

```
<preGoal name="test:test-resources">
    <attainGoal name="hibernate:schema-export"/>
</preGoal>
```

Attaching the `preGoal` to `test:test-resources` ensures that the schema is refreshed regardless of whether you run the `test`, `test:single`, or `test:match` target.

To verify that the mapping file is generated properly, and that `Survey` objects can be saved to and read from a Hypersonic database, we have written a simple `SurveyTest` unit test. `SurveyTest` opens a connection to the database, creates a new `Survey`, saves it, and verifies that a `Survey ID` was assigned as the primary key in the database:

```java
package example.survey;

import net.sf.hibernate.Session;
import junit.framework.TestCase;

public class SurveyTest extends TestCase {

    public void testCreateSurvey() throws Exception{
        Session session = HibernateHelper.getSessionFactory().openSession();
        Survey survey = new Survey();
        survey.setName("Test Survey");
        assertNull(survey.getId());
        session.save(survey);
        assertNotNull(survey.getId());
    }

}
```

Notice the use of the `HibernateHelper` class:

```java
Session session = HibernateHelper.getSessionFactory().openSession();
```

`HibernateHelper` wraps all the logic needed to start up Hibernate and return a Hibernate `SessionFactory`. This simplifies writing multiple unit tests.

```java
package example.survey;

import net.sf.hibernate.HibernateException;
import net.sf.hibernate.SessionFactory;
import net.sf.hibernate.cfg.Configuration;

public class HibernateHelper {
    private static SessionFactory sessionFactory;

    private static Configuration configuration;
```

```
        public static SessionFactory getSessionFactory() throws
HibernateException {
            if (sessionFactory == null) {
                sessionFactory = getConfiguration().buildSessionFactory();
            }
            return sessionFactory;
        }

        public static Configuration getConfiguration() throws HibernateException {
            if (configuration == null) {
                configuration = new Configuration().configure();
            }
            return configuration;
        }
    }
}
```

Because we want to update the schema and run the unit test from two separate threads, we need to manually start Hypersonic. In the /bin directory are two scripts, startHsql.bat and startHsql.sh. Execute the one appropriate for your platform.

After starting up Hypersonic, enter maven test and the SurveyTest will be run. The Java code will be compiled, the mapping files and hibernate.cfg.xml generated, the schema exported, and finally the unit tests run. The logging level is set to DEBUG, so you can see the details of what Hibernate is doing as it runs.

If you wish, enter maven site and the Web site will be generated. This step will take the data generated by the unit tests and provide a nice HTML report that you can view. Again, you need Hypersonic running in its own thread so the unit test will run. If you don't want to run the unit tests, then add the switch –Dmaven.test.skip to the maven site command.

Our Survey Example

This section contains the complete code for a Maven version of the Survey application that we started in Chapter 9. Listing 14.1 contains the project.xml POM, Listing 14.2 contains the project.properties file, and Listing 14.3 contains the maven.xml file. These file are all available for download at www.wrox.com.

```xml
<?xml version="1.0" encoding="UTF-8"?>
<project default="">
  <pomVersion>3</pomVersion>
  <id>survey</id>
  <name>Object Model for Simple Survey</name>
  <currentVersion>chapter-15</currentVersion>
  <inceptionYear>2004</inceptionYear>
  <package>example.survey</package>
  <description>
    Object Model for a system to administer simple
    surveys made up of a list of questions and answers.
  </description>
  <shortDescription>Object Model for Survey System</shortDescription>
  <developers>
    <developer>
```

```
          <name>Eric Pugh</name>
          <id>epugh</id>
          <email>epugh@opensourceconnections.com</email>
        </developer>
    </developers>
    <dependencies>
      <dependency>
        <groupId>cglib</groupId>
        <artifactId>cglib-full</artifactId>
        <version>2.0.1</version>
      </dependency>
      <dependency>
        <groupId>commons-collections</groupId>
        <artifactId>commons-collections</artifactId>
        <version>2.1</version>
      </dependency>
      <dependency>
        <groupId>commons-dbcp</groupId>
        <artifactId>commons-dbcp</artifactId>
        <version>1.1</version>
      </dependency>
      <dependency>
        <groupId>commons-lang</groupId>
        <artifactId>commons-lang</artifactId>
        <version>1.0.1</version>
      </dependency>
      <dependency>
        <groupId>commons-logging</groupId>
        <artifactId>commons-logging</artifactId>
        <version>1.0.3</version>
      </dependency>
      <dependency>
        <groupId>commons-pool</groupId>
        <artifactId>commons-pool</artifactId>
        <version>1.1</version>
      </dependency>
      <dependency>
        <groupId>dom4j</groupId>
        <artifactId>dom4j</artifactId>
        <version>1.4</version>
      </dependency>
      <dependency>
        <groupId>ehcache</groupId>
        <artifactId>ehcache</artifactId>
        <version>0.7</version>
      </dependency>
      <dependency>
        <groupId>log4j</groupId>
        <artifactId>log4j</artifactId>
        <version>1.2.8</version>
      </dependency>
      <dependency>
        <groupId>hibernate</groupId>
        <artifactId>hibernate</artifactId>
```

```xml
      <version>2.1.4</version>
</dependency>
<dependency>
   <groupId>jdbc2_0</groupId>
   <artifactId>jdbc2_0</artifactId>
   <version>stdext</version>
</dependency>
<dependency>
   <groupId>jta</groupId>
   <artifactId>jta</artifactId>
   <version>unknown</version>
   <jar>jta.jar</jar>
</dependency>
<dependency>
   <groupId>odmg</groupId>
   <artifactId>odmg</artifactId>
   <version>3.0</version>
</dependency>
<dependency>
   <groupId>xalan</groupId>
   <artifactId>xalan</artifactId>
   <version>2.4.1</version>
</dependency>
<dependency>
   <groupId>xerces</groupId>
   <artifactId>xerces</artifactId>
   <version>2.4.0</version>
</dependency>
<dependency>
   <groupId>xml-apis</groupId>
   <artifactId>xml-apis</artifactId>
   <version>2.0.2</version>
</dependency>

<!-- Begin XDoclet Dependencies -->
<dependency>
   <groupId>xdoclet</groupId>
   <artifactId>xdoclet</artifactId>
   <version>1.2.1</version>
</dependency>
<dependency>
   <groupId>xdoclet</groupId>
   <artifactId>xdoclet-hibernate-module</artifactId>
   <version>1.2.1</version>
</dependency>
<dependency>
   <groupId>xdoclet</groupId>
   <artifactId>xdoclet-xdoclet-module</artifactId>
   <version>1.2.1</version>
</dependency>
<dependency>
   <groupId>xdoclet</groupId>
   <artifactId>xjavadoc</artifactId>
   <version>1.0.3</version>
```

```
        </dependency>

        <!-- Database to be used in testing -->
        <dependency>
          <groupId>hsqldb</groupId>
          <artifactId>hsqldb</artifactId>
          <version>1.7.1</version>
        </dependency>
      </dependencies>
      <build>
        <sourceDirectory>src/java</sourceDirectory>
        <unitTestSourceDirectory>src/test</unitTestSourceDirectory>
        <unitTest>
          <includes>
            <include>**/*Test*.java</include>
          </includes>
        </unitTest>
        <resources>
          <resource>
            <directory>${maven.build.dir}/generated-sources/xdoclet</directory>
            <targetPath>/</targetPath>
            <includes>
              <include>hibernate.cfg.xml</include>
              <include>**/*.hbm.xml</include>
            </includes>
          </resource>
        </resources>
      </build>
      <reports>
        <report>maven-license-plugin</report>
        <report>maven-linkcheck-plugin</report>
        <report>maven-jdepend-plugin</report>
        <report>maven-junit-report-plugin</report>
        <report>maven-pmd-plugin</report>
        <report>maven-simian-plugin</report>
        <report>maven-javadoc-plugin</report>
        <report>maven-jxr-plugin</report>
        <report>maven-tasklist-plugin</report>
      </reports>
    </project>
```

Listing 14.1

```
# -------------------------------------------------------------------
#  Survey Project settings
# -------------------------------------------------------------------
survey.helloworld=It's a beautiful world out there.

survey.jdbcurl=jdbc:hsqldb:hsql://localhost
survey.driver=org.hsqldb.jdbcDriver
survey.dialect=net.sf.hibernate.dialect.HSQLDialect
survey.username=sa
survey.password
```

```
# ------------------------------------------------------------------
#  XDoclet Plugin for Maven settings
# ------------------------------------------------------------------
maven.xdoclet.hibernatedoclet.fileset.0=true
maven.xdoclet.hibernatedoclet.fileset.0.include=**/*.java
maven.xdoclet.hibernatedoclet.hibernate.0.Version=2.0

maven.xdoclet.hibernatedoclet.hibernatecfg.0=true
maven.xdoclet.hibernatedoclet.hibernatecfg.0.jdbcUrl=jdbc:hsqldb:hsql://local
host
maven.xdoclet.hibernatedoclet.hibernatecfg.0.driver=org.hsqldb.jdbcDriver
maven.xdoclet.hibernatedoclet.hibernatecfg.0.dialect=net.sf.hibernate.dialect
.HSQLDialect
maven.xdoclet.hibernatedoclet.hibernatecfg.0.userName=sa
maven.xdoclet.hibernatedoclet.hibernatecfg.0.password=

maven.xdoclet.hibernatedoclet.destDir=${maven.build.dir}/generated-
sources/xdoclet


# ------------------------------------------------------------------
#  Hibernate Plugin for Maven settings
# ------------------------------------------------------------------
maven.hibernate.properties=bin/hibernate.properties
maven.hibernate.quiet=false
maven.hibernate.output.dir=${maven.build.dir}/generated-sources/schema
```

Listing 14.2

```
<project xmlns:ant="jelly:ant">
    <goal name="survey:helloworld" description="Emit Hello World">
        <ant:echo message="${survey.helloworld}"/>
    </goal>

    <goal name="survey:hibernate" description="Generate Hibernate files with
Xdoclet">
        <ant:taskdef name="hibernatedoclet"
classname="xdoclet.modules.hibernate.HibernateDocletTask">
            <ant:classpath>
                <ant:path refid="maven.dependency.classpath"/>
            </ant:classpath>
        </ant:taskdef>

        <ant:hibernatedoclet destDir="${maven.build.dir}/generated-sources"
            force="true" verbose="true">
            <ant:hibernate version="2.0"/>
            <ant:fileset dir="${maven.src.dir}/java"
                includes="**/*.java"/>
            <ant:hibernatecfg
                jdbcUrl="${survey.jdbcurl}"
                driver="${survey.driver}"
                dialect="${survey.dialect}"
                userName="${survey.username}"
```

```
                    password="${survey.password}"
        />
    </ant:hibernatedoclet>
</goal>

<preGoal name="java:compile">
    <attainGoal name="xdoclet:hibernatedoclet"/>
    <!--
    Alternatively call survey:hibernate:
    <attainGoal name="survey:hibernate"/>
    -->

</preGoal>

<preGoal name="test:test-resources">
    <attainGoal name="hibernate:schema-export"/>
</preGoal>

</project>
```

Listing 14.3

Advantages over Ant

Maven has advantages over Ant, including the ability to insert your own steps between already existing steps via pre- and post-goal processing. This was used to weave the generation of the mapping files and schema export steps into the standard compile/test cycle.

Integrating additional functionality such as PMD reports is as simple as registering the plug-in to use. A developer doesn't have to become an expert on the inner workings of a new tool to leverage it. The plug-ins hide the complexity of the underlying tool.

All Mavenized projects are laid out in similar ways and function identically. To run unit tests, you always type maven test. To build a JAR, you always type maven jar. To generate the site documentation, you use maven site. When getting started with a new Mavenized project, a developer already knows how to execute the basic functionality.

And finally, Maven builds on your existing Ant skills. All Ant tasks function the same way in Maven!

Things to Be Aware Of

Maven's POM is based on the idea that you will produce one artifact per project. So, if you have a project where you have two Ant tasks—one that produces a JAR file containing just your Hibernate code and another one that produces a JAR file of your entire project—then you will find this setup hard to reproduce in Maven. Maven would push you to have two projects—one whose sole output is a JAR with your Hibernate object model and another project that depends on the first JAR.

Initial setup can be tedious as well. Hibernate has quite a few dependencies! You will need to add all of them to your project.xml. And, when a new version of Hibernate is released, you'll need to carefully verify that you have updated all the version numbers and removed or added any changed dependencies. This is more work than just grabbing a bunch of JAR files and dragging them into your /lib directory, but the increased control and certainty over what you are building pays off in the long run.

Maven also has expectations about how projects are organized. For example, if your unit tests live in a /src/java/.../test directory that is in the same file system as your regular .java class files, then Maven will want you to move them into a /src/test directory tree instead.

When using Eclipse as your IDE, you will be presented with some additional integration steps. The Eclipse plug-in for Maven makes it easy to generate the .classpath and .project files needed to create an Eclipse project. The challenge arises when Eclipse performs a clean compile. The various mapping files in the /target/classes directory will all be removed. Unless you have the XDoclet steps as part of the Eclipse build, you will be missing all the generated code when Eclipse finishes compiling the code. Fortunately, the Eclipse plug-in takes this into account. When working with Eclipse, all generated code should be compiled into /target/generated-sources. In the survey example, we would add the following properties:

```
maven.xdoclet.hibernatedoclet.destDir=${maven.build.dir}/generated-
sources/xdoclet
maven.hibernate.output.dir=${maven.build.dir}/generated-sources/schema
```

These properties will generate the code into /target/generated-sources/xdoclet and /target/generated-sources/schema. Run maven eclipse and these two directories will be treated as separate source directories in Eclipse. If you import the survey project into Eclipse, you will see source directories set up. This will allow Eclipse to copy the generated code over as source code into the target classpath whenever the IDE performs a clean compile.

Summary

That's all there is to using Maven with Hibernate. With Maven, you take yet another step toward a fully automated development process. It would be wise to keep up with the XDoclet and Maven products as they mature along with Hibernate.

15

Hibernate Extensions

Throughout this book, we've gone through the exercise of creating Java classes, mapping documents and database table schemas for our examples. In the examples, we have generally created the Java class needed for an application first, then determined the mapping necessary to persist the class, and finally used the mapping document to determine how the resulting database table should appear. Of course, when using a new technology, we need to do things by hand over and over in order to build our confidence in how the technology works. Now that we've used Hibernate for quite some time, we have the opportunity to take advantage of numerous tools available through Hibernate and third-party vendors that will automate a majority of the work in using Hibernate. When using the automation tools described in this chapter, we will still need to be aware of what the tools are generating, since the promise of code generation and automation isn't a perfect art.

Tools

So just what is available to the developer using Hibernate in the way of automation? In this chapter we will cover the following tools:

- ❑ SchemaExport/SchemaUpdate
- ❑ Hibernate Extensions—Code Generator/Map Generator
- ❑ AndroMDA
- ❑ MiddleGen

SchemaExport/SchemaUpdate

One of the developer tools provided in the main Hibernate package is called SchemaExport, or hbm2ddl. This tool is designed to allow the developer to automatically generate a database schema using the information found only within a Hibernate mapping document, along with a few additional attributes to support the tool itself. The tool can be used in a command-line standalone situation, within an application, or even as part of an Ant task.

This tool is really made up to two different classes and applications called `SchemaExport` and `SchemaUpdate`. The `SchemaExport` part is designed to create an initial database schema based on the supplied mapping document. When changes are made to the mapping document, the database table might need to be updated as well. The `SchemaUpdate` application is used for this purpose by creating an appropriate DDL for the deltas between the original and current mapping document. Both of these applications can be found in the *<hibernate installation directory>*/bin directory. There you will find two batch files or scripts called `SchemaExport` and `SchemaUpdate`, as you might expect. From a class standpoint, the classes that implement the functions are:

```
net.sf.hibernate.tool.hbm2ddl.SchemaExport
net.sf.hibernate.tool.hbm2ddl.SchemaUpdate
```

Listing 15.1 shows an example of the Windows SchemaExport.bat file. Notice the JDBC_DRIVER variable.

```
@echo off

rem -----------------------------------------------------------------
rem Execute SchemaExport tool
rem -----------------------------------------------------------------

set JDBC_DRIVER=C:\jars\mysql310.jar
set HIBERNATE_HOME=..
set LIB=%HIBERNATE_HOME%\lib
set PROPS=%HIBERNATE_HOME%\src
***AU: Please indicate where to wrap this line of code. LSR***set
CP=%JDBC_DRIVER%;%PROPS%;%HIBERNATE_HOME%\hibernate2.jar;%LIB%\
commons-logging-
1.0.3.jar;%LIB%\commons-collections-2.1.jar;%LIB%\commons-
lang-1.0.1.jar;%LIB%\cglib-2.0-rc2.jar;%LIB%\dom4j-1.4.jar;%LIB%\
odmg-3.0.jar;%LIB%\xml-
apis.jar;%LIB%\xerces-2.4.0.jar;%LIB%\xalan-2.4.0.jar

java -cp %CP% net.sf.hibernate.tool.hbm2ddl.SchemaExport %*
```

Listing 15.1

There are two areas in this script that you need to change for your application. The first is the JDBC_DRIVER variable, which needs to be set to the JDBC driver you will be using for your database server. The second is the PROPS variable, which needs to point to the directory where your Hibernate property files are located.

Building the Mapping Document and Database Table

The work we want to accomplish with the SchemaExport tool is the automatic generation of a database schema given an appropriate mapping document. As you can tell from our examples throughout this book, the database schema is fairly easy to produce, given just the normal information we provide in each element of the document. We'll look at a simple example and then expand it to include some of the more unique attributes designed specifically for the SchemaExport tool. Consider the mapping document in Listing 15.2.

```xml
<?xml version="1.0" encoding="UTF-8"?>
<!DOCTYPE hibernate-mapping
    PUBLIC "-//Hibernate/Hibernate Mapping DTD//EN"
    "http://hibernate.sourceforge.net/hibernate-mapping-2.0.dtd">

<hibernate-mapping>

<class name="Notes"
       table="notes">
    <id name="id" unsaved-value="0">
        <generator class="sequence"/>
    </id>

  <property name="owner" type="Sstring"/>
  <property name="info" type="string"/>
  <property name="count" type="integer"/>
</class>

</hibernate-mapping>
```

Listing 15.2

The mapping document in Listing 15.2 is designed for a Java class with a couple of attributes and an appropriate identifier. To generate the schema for an appropriate database, we'll need to use the SchemaExport script found in the /bin directory using the mapping document saved in the file Notes.hbm.xml. Here's an example command line:

```
SchemaExport Notes.hbm.xml
```

In order for the tool to work properly, it needs to be able to find the appropriate configuration file with connection information to our database. If we use the script with the above command line, we will be presented with an appropriate database schema on the console, as shown in Listing 15.3. The tool will connect to your database, drop the current tables if they exist, and create the necessary tables based on the mapping document. As you can read, there is a key point in the previous sentence. The tables that the SchemaExport tool will create will be dropped if they already exist. Thus, if you have tables in your database with the names of the classes within the supplied mapping document, they will be deleted.

```
C:\data\books\hibernate-2.1\bin>schemaexport --text Notes.hbm.xml
May 20, 2004 3:16:36 PM net.sf.hibernate.cfg.Environment <clinit>
INFO: Hibernate 2.1.2
May 20, 2004 3:16:36 PM net.sf.hibernate.cfg.Environment <clinit>
INFO: loaded properties from resource hibernate.properties:
{hibernate.connection.username=, hibernate.connection.password=,
hibernate.cglib.use_reflection_opti
mizer=false, hibernate.dialect=net.sf.hibernate.dialect.MySQLDialect,
hibernate.show_sql=true,
hibernate.connection.url=jdbc:mysql://localhost/products,
hibernate.connection.driver_class=com.mysql.jdbc.Driver}
May 20, 2004 3:16:36 PM net.sf.hibernate.cfg.Configuration addFile
```

```
INFO: Mapping file: Notes.hbm.xml
May 20, 2004 3:16:36 PM net.sf.hibernate.cfg.Binder bindRootClass
INFO: Mapping class: Notes -> notes
May 20, 2004 3:16:36 PM net.sf.hibernate.dialect.Dialect <init>
INFO: Using dialect: net.sf.hibernate.dialect.MySQLDialect
May 20, 2004 3:16:36 PM net.sf.hibernate.cfg.Configuration secondPassCompile
INFO: processing one-to-many association mappings
May 20, 2004 3:16:36 PM net.sf.hibernate.cfg.Configuration secondPassCompile
INFO: processing one-to-one association property references
May 20, 2004 3:16:36 PM net.sf.hibernate.cfg.Configuration secondPassCompile
INFO: processing foreign key constraints
May 20, 2004 3:16:36 PM net.sf.hibernate.cfg.Configuration secondPassCompile
INFO: processing one-to-many association mappings
May 20, 2004 3:16:36 PM net.sf.hibernate.cfg.Configuration secondPassCompile
INFO: processing one-to-one association property references
May 20, 2004 3:16:36 PM net.sf.hibernate.cfg.Configuration secondPassCompile
INFO: processing foreign key constraints
May 20, 2004 3:16:36 PM net.sf.hibernate.tool.hbm2ddl.SchemaExport execute
INFO: Running hbm2ddl schema export
drop table if exists notes
create table notes (id INTEGER NOT NULL AUTO_INCREMENT, owner VARCHAR(255),
info
VARCHAR(255), count INTEGER, primary key (id))
May 20, 2004 3:16:36 PM net.sf.hibernate.tool.hbm2ddl.SchemaExport execute
INFO: schema export complete
```

Listing 15.3

Now having the output of the tool displayed on the console is nice for viewing purposes, but you might not always want this done. To facilitate this situation as well as others, the SchemaExport tool allows several command-line options. These options are shown in the following table.

Command-Line Option	Purpose
--quiet	Suppress console output
--drop	Drop the tables upon execution but don't create new ones
--text	Only display the SQL to generate the new tables but don't actually connect to the database
--output=my_schema.ddl	Produce the required SQL for creating the database tables to the specified file
--config=hibernate.cfg.xml	Look for the Hibernate configuration file using the specific filename provided in the option
--properties=hibernate.properties	Look for the Hibernate properties in the provided file
--format	Pretty-print the SQL for the table creation
--delimiter=x	Define a specific end-of-line delimiter for the output

As you can see, there are quite a few options available for the SchemaExport tool. Probably the most important ones are –quiet, --drop, --text, and --output.

When you execute the script, quite a bit of output can be displayed to the console as the script does its work. If you aren't interested in the output or just want to use the script in an automated situation, you can suppress the output using the --quiet command-line option. Related to the console output, if you just want to see the SQL that the SchemaExport script would generate but not actually make any changes to the database, use the --text option. The result will be the SQL needed to build the necessary database tables, but no changes will be made to the database server. The --drop option can be used when you just want the script to drop any tables in the database but not actually create the new tables. Finally, if you are interested in having the SQL generated from the script output to a file, use the --output option such as

```
SchemaExport Notes.hbm.xml --output=schema.sql
```

As mentioned previously, the SchemaExport tool requires the use of a Hibernate configuration file in order to access the database server and generate the necessary tables from the supplied mapping document. The following table shows the fields that must be included in the configuration file. It is very important that the dialect property be accurate because Hibernate will use this property to determine the right SQL to generate. Not all of the databases that Hibernate supports include the default ability to handle foreign keys automatically. The MyIsam table used as the default table type in MySQL is one such example.

Property Name	Description
hibernate.connection.driver_class	The JDBC driver class for the database server
hibernate.connection.url	The URL for connecting to the database server
hibernate.connection.username	The database user to log in to the database server
hibernate.connection.password	The password for the supplied username
hibernate.dialect	The database dialect to use when creating the SQL for the DDL

Advanced Mapping Document Options

The majority of the information needed by the SchemaExport script to build the database tables comes from the elements of the mapping document. As you might expect, the elements need to include enough information to give the script everything needed to build the correct table columns. This means you will need to have elements with more information than <property name="address"/>. This example element doesn't tell the script much about how to create the "address" table column. Clearly, adding a type attribute to the element will give the script enough information to build the column. For example, we might use the element <property name="address" type=" string"/>. Since many database servers don't include a SQL type of string, the result will be a table column such as varchar or text.

If you want to exert more control over how the script generates the table columns, you can use the attributes found in the following table. Some of the attributes can be added directly to a <property> or <element> element; however, some of them need to use a <column> subelement, as indicated in the table. The <column> subelement can be used within any of the elements that detail a database column, such as <property>. Let's look at examples using each of the attributes and the results from the script. We will assume that the Hibernate configuration file for these examples specifies a MySQL database.

Attribute	Values	Interpretation
length	Value	Limits the length of a database column to the specified value
sql-type	Type	The type to use for a particular column overriding the one specified by a type attribute or found during reflection
foreign-key	Name	The name of the foreign key constraint
not-null	True/false	Determines whether or not a column is nullible; the default is false
unique	True/false	Determines whether or not a column has a unique constraint
index	Name	The name of a multicolumn index
unique-key	Name	The name of a multicolumn unique constraint
check	SQL	SQL check constraint

length

When the attribute being mapped from a class to an appropriate database has a limit on its length, usually a string attribute, the developer can specify the maximum size using the length attribute. You can see the difference in the table column created using a mapping document with the following two <property> elements:

```
<property name="owner" type="string" length="32"/>
<property name="info" type="string"/>
```

The script will produce a table with the following description:

```
mysql> describe notes;
+--------+--------------+------+-----+---------+----------------+
| Field  | Type         | Null | Key | Default | Extra          |
+--------+--------------+------+-----+---------+----------------+
| id     | int(11)      |      | PRI | NULL    | auto_increment |
| owner  | varchar(32)  | YES  |     | NULL    |                |
| info   | varchar(255) | YES  |     | NULL    |                |
| count  | int(11)      | YES  |     | NULL    |                |
+--------+--------------+------+-----+---------+----------------+
4 rows in set (0.00 sec)
```

Sql-type

Of course, in most of our examples, we've relied on the script choosing the correct table column type. For example, we supply the attribute "type="string"" and the script produces the MySQL column type of varchar(255) What if we wanted to have a type of text instead? The sql-type attribute gives us the ability to change the type, thus overriding the type defined in the parent element. The `sql-type` attribute requires the use of the `<column>` subelement. For example:

```
<property name="owner" type="string" length="32"/>
<property name="info" type="string">
  <column name="info" sql-type="text"/>
</property>
```

When the SchemaExport script is executed against the elements shown above, we obtain the database schema we are after, as shown here:

```
mysql> describe notes;
+-------+-------------+------+-----+---------+----------------+
| Field | Type        | Null | Key | Default | Extra          |
+-------+-------------+------+-----+---------+----------------+
| id    | int(11)     |      | PRI | NULL    | auto_increment |
| owner | varchar(32) | YES  |     | NULL    |                |
| info  | text        | YES  |     | NULL    |                |
| count | int(11)     | YES  |     | NULL    |                |
+-------+-------------+------+-----+---------+----------------+
4 rows in set (0.01 sec)
```

not-null

If you have a database column that needs to be constrained from the standpoint of not allowing null values, the not-null attribute needs to be set to true. If the not-null attribute is not part of either the primary element such as property or the `<column>` element, a null value can be associated with the object's attribute and stored in the database. An example of the not-null attribute is:

```
<property
          name="count"
          type="integer"
          not-null="true"
/>
```

This mapping will produce the following table schema:

```
mysql> describe notes;
+-------+-------------+------+-----+---------+----------------+
| Field | Type        | Null | Key | Default | Extra          |
+-------+-------------+------+-----+---------+----------------+
| id    | int(11)     |      | PRI | NULL    | auto_increment |
| owner | varchar(32) | YES  |     | NULL    |                |
| info  | text        | YES  |     | NULL    |                |
| count | int(11)     |      |     | 0       |                |
+-------+-------------+------+-----+---------+----------------+
4 rows in set (0.00 sec)
```

Notice that the Null column in the output has a blank for the count field. This indicates that a null value is not allowed when a row is inserted or updated in the table.

foreign-key

When you create a relationship between two different objects, there must be a related link between the tables of the objects. Consider an example of a `Notes` class with a many-to-one relationship with an `Owner` class. Within the mapping document, we will have a `<many-to-one>` element for the `<class name="Notes">` element, as shown here:

```
<class name="Notes"
        table="notes">
   <id name="id" unsaved-value="0">
         <generator class="native"/>
   </id>

   <many-to-one name="owner" class="Owner" foreign-key="fk_foo_bar" not-
null="true"/>
   <property name="info" type="string">
     <column name="info" sql-type="text"/>
   </property>
   <property name="count" type="integer" not-null="true"/>

</class>

<class name="Owner"
        table="owner">
   <id name="id" unsaved-value="0">
         <generator class="native"/>
   </id>

   <property name="fullname" type="string"/>
</class>
```

Notice that we have the name and class attributes within the relationship element, but we've also included a `foreign-key` attribute to indicate the column to be added to the `Notes` table for the relationship between the `Notes` and `Owner` tables. Hibernate will use the column to create the necessary relationship. If your database server supports foreign keys, then the SQL generated by SchemaExport will create the constraint automatically. Here's the SQL generated for both tables and the constraint:

```
create table owner (id INTEGER NOT NULL AUTO_INCREMENT, fullname
VARCHAR(255),
primary key (id))

create table notes (id INTEGER NOT NULL AUTO_INCREMENT, owner INTEGER not
null,
info text, count INTEGER not null, primary key (id))

alter table notes add index (owner), add constraint fk_foo_bar foreign key
(owner)
references owner (id)
```

Notice that the `alter table` command executed after the tables were added to the server. The constraint was created between the two tables.

index

If you would like the script to create an index for a column within the database server, use the index attribute to specify the name of the index. For example:

```
<property name="zipcode" type="string" length="10">
  <column name="zipcode" index="zipidx"/>
</property>
```

When the script encounters the attribute, the SQL generated is:

```
drop table if exists notes

create table notes (id INTEGER NOT NULL AUTO_INCREMENT, info VARCHAR(255),
count INTEGER not null, zipcode VARCHAR(255), primary key (id))

create index zipidx on notes (zipcode)
```

unique

If you have a column within your attribute that must be unique, and you want to extend the constraint to the database, use the unique attribute. Setting the attribute to true will impose the UNIQUE keyword on the column within the SQL string sent to the database server. The default value, where the unique attribute is not used, is false, and thus duplicate values can exist for the column. An example of using the unique attribute is:

```
<property name="socialsecuritynumber" type="string" length="9" >
  <column name="socialsecuritynumber" unique="true"/>
    </property>
```

The resulting SQL from the SchemaExport script is

```
drop table if exists notes

create table notes (id INTEGER NOT NULL AUTO_INCREMENT, info VARCHAR(255),
count INTEGER not null, socialsecuritynumber VARCHAR(255) unique, primary key
(id))
```

For the unique attribute, the script adds the unique clause to our socialsecuritynumber column.

check

A constraint can be associated with a column or table using the check attribute. For example, we could set up a constraint to make sure that the length of the socialsecuritynumber column is equal to 9. Here's what the element would look like:

```
<property name="socialsecuritynumber" type="string" length="9" >
  <column name="socialsecuritynumber" check="len(socialsecuritynumber) = 9"
/>
</property>
```

The result of using the check attribute is shown in the following SQL:

```
drop table if exists notes

create table notes (id INTEGER NOT NULL AUTO_INCREMENT, info VARCHAR(255),
count
INTEGER not null, socialsecuritynumber VARCHAR(255)
check(len(socialsecuritynumber)
= 9), primary key (id))
```

The check attribute adds an appropriate check clause to the SQL command. The database server you are using must support the check command in order for this attribute to work. The MySQL database server does not support this command.

unique-key

If you are interested in creating a multicolumn key for your object and table, then you can use the unique-key attribute to create it. For example:

```
<property name="bigkey" type="string" >
  <column name="bigkey" unique-key="info"/>
  <column name="bigkey" unique-key="count"/>
</property>
```

The result of the above elements is the SQL:

```
create table notes (id INTEGER NOT NULL AUTO_INCREMENT, info VARCHAR(255),
count
INTEGER not null, bigkey VARCHAR(255), primary key (id),  unique (bigkey),
unique
(bigkey))
```

For MySQL, the description of the table shows the MUL value for the Key column, indicating that the column is made from a combination of column values:

```
mysql> describe notes;
+---------+--------------+------+-----+---------+----------------+
| Field   | Type         | Null | Key | Default | Extra          |
+---------+--------------+------+-----+---------+----------------+
| id      | int(11)      |      | PRI | NULL    | auto_increment |
| info    | varchar(255) | YES  |     | NULL    |                |
| count   | int(11)      |      |     | 0       |                |
| bigkey  | varchar(255) | YES  | MUL | NULL    |                |
+---------+--------------+------+-----+---------+----------------+
4 rows in set (0.00 sec)
```

Updating the Database Table

Clearly, we don't always want to drop the current table associated with a mapping document just because a simple change is made to the Java class or the mapping document itself. In these cases, we can switch from the SchemaExport script to SchemaUpdate, which is designed to analyze the currently supplied mapping document and the database table already incorporated on the database server. Let's consider a table based on the mapping document in Listing 15.4.

```xml
<?xml version="1.0" encoding="UTF-8"?>
<!DOCTYPE hibernate-mapping
  PUBLIC "-//Hibernate/Hibernate Mapping DTD//EN"
  "http://hibernate.sourceforge.net/hibernate-mapping-2.0.dtd">

<hibernate-mapping>

<class name="Notes"
       table="notes">
  <id name="id" unsaved-value="0">
      <generator class="native"/>
  </id>

  <property name="info" type="string"/>
  <property name="count" type="integer" not-null="true"/>
</class>

</hibernate-mapping>
```

Listing 15.4

The table would appear as shown here:

```
+-------+-------------+------+-----+---------+---------------+
| Field | Type        | Null | Key | Default | Extra         |
+-------+-------------+------+-----+---------+---------------+
| id    | int(11)     |      | PRI | NULL    | auto_increment|
| info  | varchar(255)| YES  |     | NULL    |               |
| count | int(11)     |      |     | 0       |               |
+-------+-------------+------+-----+---------+---------------+
```

We will change the mapping document as shown in Listing 15.5, where some of the attributes are changed and a couple of new columns are added.

```xml
<?xml version="1.0" encoding="UTF-8"?>
<!DOCTYPE hibernate-mapping
  PUBLIC "-//Hibernate/Hibernate Mapping DTD//EN"
  "http://hibernate.sourceforge.net/hibernate-mapping-2.0.dtd">

<hibernate-mapping>

<class name="Notes"
       table="notes">
  <id name="id" unsaved-value="0">
      <generator class="native"/>
  </id>

  <property name="info" type="string"/>
  <property name="count" type="integer" not-null="true"/>
  <property name="zipcode" type="string"/>
  <property name="fullname" type="string"/>
</class>

</hibernate-mapping>
```

Listing 15.5

Now we can execute the SchemaUpdate script using the command:

```
schemaupdate Notes.hbm.xml
```

The result of the script is the following SQL:

```
alter table notes add column zipcode VARCHAR(255)
alter table notes add column fullname VARCHAR(255)
```

As you can see, the majority of the SQL commands at the end of the processing involve the `alter table` command as expected. Note that updating the schema using the SchemaUpdate functionality must use metadata generated by the JDBC driver, and only well-developed drivers will be able to support the necessary information. Check your driver's documentation for an explanation of how well it implements the JDBC Metadata API. The SchemaUpdate script allows two command-line options, as shown in the following table.

Command-Line Option	Description
--quiet	No output is exposed to the console
--properties=hibernate.properties	Location of the properties file

Application Support

Whether you are building a development tool or some application that will be dynamically changing the mapping documents and database schema, you can execute both the SchemaExport and SchemaUpdate tools from within Java code. The class defined for SchemaExport is called `net.sf.hibernate.tool.hbm2ddl.SchemaExecute` and for SchemaUpdate is called `net.sf.hibernate.tool.hbm2ddl.SchemaUpdate`. Executing from within Java is basically the same process for each class, but the methods available are a bit different. The next table shows the methods and constructors for SchemaExport, and the subsequent table is for SchemaUpdate.

The process to use the classes is shown in the following code snippet:

```
Configuration config = new Configuration();
SchemaExport export = new SchemaExport(config);
export.create(false, false);
```

The same code can be used for the `SchemaUpdate` class as well the `execute()` method, as shown in the following tables.

Method	Description
void create(boolean script, boolean export)	Execute the SchemaExport script to create the new table.
	Export: If true then the SQL will be provided to the database server.
	Script: If true the script information will be displayed to the console.

Table continued on following page

Method	Description
void drop(boolean script, boolean export)	Execute the SchemaExport script to drop the tables in the script.

Export: If true then the SQL will be provided to the database server.

Script: If true the script information will be displayed to the console. |
| SchemaExport setDelimiter(String delimiter) | Set the delimiter to be used between the generated SQL statements. |
| SchemaExport setOutputFile(String filename) | Set the name of the file to output the script. |

Method	Description
void execute(boolean script, boolean doUpdate)	Execute the SchemaUpdate script.

Export: If true then the SQL will be provided to the database server.

Script: If true the script information will be displayed to the console. |

Ant Support

Finally, we need to consider how to incorporate both of these schema scripts into Ant since Ant is the primary build mechanism for Java, and it is a perfect match for the functionality provided within both the SchemaUpdate and SchemaExport scripts. Adding an Ant target for SchemaExport is shown in Listing 15.6.

```
<target name="schemaexport">
    <taskdef name="schemaexport"
        classname="net.sf.hibernate.tool.hbm2ddl.SchemaExportTask"
        classpathref="classpath"/>

    <schemaexport
        properties="hibernate.properties"
        quiet="no"
        delimiter=";">
        <fileset dir="src">
            <include name="**/*.hbm.xml"/>
        </fileset>
    </schemaexport>
</target>
```

Listing 15.6

One of the key points to the script in Listing 15.6 is the classname of `SchemaExportTask` to handle the execution of the export. Any of the needed command-line options can be provided in the Ant task using the `<schemaexport>` element. The `<fileset>` element is used to indicate the various mapping documents that should be used by the SchemaExport task. For completeness, we provide the SchemaUpdate Ant task in Listing 15.7.

```
<target name="schemaupdate">
    <taskdef name="schemaupdate"
        classname="net.sf.hibernate.tool.hbm2ddl.SchemaUpdateTask"
        classpathref="classpath"/>

    <schemaupdate
        properties="hibernate.properties">
        <fileset dir="src">
            <include name="**/*.hbm.xml"/>
        </fileset>
    </schemaupdate>
</target>
```

Listing 15.7

Hibernate Extensions

Several of the tools available to developers are produced by the same folks who created Hibernate. In a separate package called Hibernate Extensions, there are three different tools to help make a developer's job just a little easier:

❑ **hbm2java:** Code generator

❑ **class2hbm:** Map generator

❑ **hibern8IDE:** Interactive tool for browsing and executing HQL queries

Once you've downloaded and installed the Hibernate Extensions from the Hibernate home page, you will find the /tools and /hibern8ide directories. These directories include /bin subdirectories, from which the various tools can be executed.

Code Generator

If you choose to build your application's persistence with the mapping documents first, the Java classes can be built automatically using the Code Generator. The Code Generator is designed to take mapping documents and produce a skeletal Java class that handles the basic parts of the mapping. You can execute the Code Generator either by using the batch file in the /bin directory of the tools installation or through the class itself. If you are using the batch file, be sure to check the setenv.bat file to set all needed environment variables. The execution commands are:

```
hbm2java <mapping document>

java -cp <classpath> net.sf.hibernate.tool.hbm2java.CodeGenerator <options>
<mapping document>
```

The result of the Code Generator will be a Java class with the appropriate constructor and setter/getter methods. The mapping document shown in Listing 15.8 produces the Java class in Listing 15.9.

```xml
<?xml version="1.0" encoding="UTF-8"?>
<!DOCTYPE hibernate-mapping
  PUBLIC "-//Hibernate/Hibernate Mapping DTD//EN"
  "http://hibernate.sourceforge.net/hibernate-mapping-2.0.dtd">

<hibernate-mapping>
<class name="Account">

  <id type="integer">
    <generator class="native"/>
  </id>


  <property name="name" type="string" />
  <property name="acctnum" type="string" />
  <property name="zipcode" type="integer" />
</class>
</hibernate-mapping>
```

Listing 15.8

```java
// default package

import java.io.Serializable;
import org.apache.commons.lang.builder.ToStringBuilder;


/** @author Hibernate CodeGenerator */
public class Account implements Serializable {

    /** nullable persistent field */
    private String name;

    /** nullable persistent field */
    private String acctnum;

    /** nullable persistent field */
    private int zipcode;

    /** full constructor */
    public Account(String name, String acctnum, int zipcode) {
        this.name = name;
        this.acctnum = acctnum;
        this.zipcode = zipcode;
    }

    /** default constructor */
    public Account() {
    }
```

```
    public String getName() {
        return this.name;
    }

    public void setName(String name) {
        this.name = name;
    }

    public String getAcctnum() {
        return this.acctnum;
    }

    public void setAcctnum(String acctnum) {
        this.acctnum = acctnum;
    }

    public int getZipcode() {
        return this.zipcode;
    }

    public void setZipcode(int zipcode) {
        this.zipcode = zipcode;
    }

    public String toString() {
        return new ToStringBuilder(this)
            .toString();
    }
}
```

Listing 15.9

There are a few different options that can be used with the generator, as shown in the following table.

Option	Description
--output=rootDirectory	The root directory where the output should be added
--config=config	The configuration file to use with the generator

The --config indicates that a configuration file may be used with the generator. The purpose of the configuration file is to specify how the code generator creates the underlying code from the mapping document files as well as provide a mechanism for supplying global-level options. The format of the configuration file is:

```
<codegen>
  <meta>
  <generate>
</codegen>
```

The `<generate>` tag defines the renderer to be used within the `CodeGenerator` class for generating the Java classes. Hibernate currently supplies two different code renderers: a default renderer for generating the Java classes, called `BasicRenderer`, and a second renderer for creating EJB finders for specific Hibernate properties.

The `<meta>` tags are used within the mapping document for annotation of the final Java code and are read by the Code Generator as well as added to the configuration file for global use. For example, we might use the `<meta>` tag within a `<class>` tag to insert Javadoc tags or any of the functionality shown in the following table.

Attribute	Description
class-description	Javadoc tags for a class description
field-description	Javadoc tags for a field description
interface	Set to true to generate an interface
implements	Adds an implements clause and class
extends	Adds an extend clause and class for inheritance unless the class is a <subclass> within the mapping document
generated-class	The class name to use when generating the class; probably different than the class="" value in the mapping document
scope-class	Declares the scope for the class
scope-set	Declares the scope for the setter method
scope-get	Declare the scope for getter method
scope-field	Declare the scope for the field
use-in-tostring	Specifies the property to use in a toString();
bound	Adds propertyChangeListener support for a property
constrained	Adds vetoChangeListener support for a property
gen-property	Set to false to not generate a property in the mapping document
property-type	Overrides the default type of the property
finder-method	Supplies the name of a finder method
session-method	Allows the Session object to be obtained within the finder; uses the code SessionTable.getSessionTable().getSession();

Let's look at a simple example of annotating the mapping document files with the `<meta>` tags. Consider the following mapping document:

```
<?xml version="1.0" encoding="UTF-8"?>
<!DOCTYPE hibernate-mapping
  PUBLIC "-//Hibernate/Hibernate Mapping DTD//EN"
  "http://hibernate.sourceforge.net/hibernate-mapping-2.0.dtd">
```

```
<hibernate-mapping>
<class name="Account">
  <meta attribute="extends">
    Loggable
  </meta>

  <id type="integer">
    <generator class="native"/>
  </id>

  <property name="name" type="string">
  <meta attribute="field-description">
    The name of the account - should be full name
    @see StudentName
  </meta>
  </property>

  <property name="acctnum" type="string">
  <meta attribute="field-description">
    The account number of the account
</meta>
  </property>


  <property name="zipcode" type="integer">
   <meta attribute="field-description">
    The zipcode of the account
    @see FullZipcode
  </meta>
  </property>

</class>
</hibernate-mapping>
```

Here we've add a couple of different <meta> tags. The first uses the attribute type of field-descriptor for the various attributes. We want the Code Generator to add the specified Javadoc for each of the properties. We also added a <meta> tag to make sure the generated class also extends the Loggable interface. Once the Code Generator processes the mapping document, the following output will be generated:

```
// default package

import java.io.Serializable;
import org.apache.commons.lang.builder.ToStringBuilder;


/** @author Hibernate CodeGenerator */
public class Account extends
    Loggable
   implements Serializable {

    /** nullable persistent field */
    private String name;
```

```java
/** nullable persistent field */
private String acctnum;

/** nullable persistent field */
private int zipcode;

/** full constructor */
public Account(String name, String acctnum, int zipcode) {
    this.name = name;
    this.acctnum = acctnum;
    this.zipcode = zipcode;
}

/** default constructor */
public Account() {
}

/**
 *      The name of the account - should be full name
 *      @see StudentName
 *
 */
public String getName() {
    return this.name;
}

public void setName(String name) {
    this.name = name;
}

/**
 *       The account number of the account
 */
public String getAcctnum() {
    return this.acctnum;
}

public void setAcctnum(String acctnum) {
    this.acctnum = acctnum;
}

/**
 *      The zipcode of the account
 *      @see FullZipcode
 *
 */
public int getZipcode() {
    return this.zipcode;
}

public void setZipcode(int zipcode) {
    this.zipcode = zipcode;
}
```

```
        public String toString() {
            return new ToStringBuilder(this)
                .toString();
        }
}
```

The command to generate the output is:

```
java -cp <classpath> net.sf.hibernate.tool.hbm2java.CodeGenerator <options>
<mappingFiles>
```

Specifically, we used:

```
java net.sf.hibernate.tool.hbm2java.CodeGenerator Account.hbm.xml
```

As you can see, the generated class extends `Loggable`, and the attributes are properly commented with Javadoc tags. Without the `<meta>` tag, we would not be able to provide this extra level of annotation to the generated Java code. Remember, you can use the `<meta>` tag within the configuration file for global changes to the generated code.

CodeGenerator Finder

When you use Hibernate and EJBs, you still need to use finders for some of the properties of your mapping document. Using the `CodeGenerator` class to create the finders is a two-step process. The first step is to build the appropriate configuration file with the `<generate>` tags to specify the finder renderer. For example, here's a possible configuration file called `codegen.xml`:

```
<codegen>
  <generate renderer="net.sf.hibernate.tool.hbm2java.BasicRenderer"/>
<generate suffix="Genfinder"
          renderer="net.sf.hibernate.tool.jbm2java.FinderRenderer"/>
  </codegen>
```

Here we've just created a new renderer using the `FinderRenderer` class and specified the suffix attribute. The suffix attribute is used to change the output file generated based on the `<class name="<classname>">` tag within the mapping document. If the class name is `Account`, the generated Java file will be `AccountGenfinder.java` where the suffix string is appended to the class name. We could also specify the package for the finders as well if we included the `"package="<string>""` attribute within the `<generate>` element. If you use the package attribute in the configuration file, it will override the package specified in the mapping document file.

After the configuration file is created, we need to annotate the mapping document with the appropriate `<meta>` tags. For example:

```
<property name="zipcode" type="integer">
  <meta attribute="field-description">
   The zipcode of the account
   @see FullZipcode
  </meta>
  <meta attribute="finder-method">findByZipcode</meta>
  </property>
```

Here we've added a `<meta>` element to the `Zipcode` property. The attribute is defined as `"finder-method"` and the value of the element is `findByZipcode`. The code produced for the `finder` method is shown here:

```
// default package

import java.io.Serializable;
import java.util.List;
import java.sql.SQLException;

import net.sf.hibernate.*;
import net.sf.hibernate.type.Type;

/** Automatically generated Finder class for AccountGenfinder.
 * @author Hibernate FinderGenerator  **/
public class AccountGenfinder implements Serializable {

    public static List findByZipcode(Session session, int zipcode) throws
SQLException, HibernateException {
        List finds = session.find("from Account as account where
account.zipcode=?", new Integer( zipcode ), Hibernate.INTEGER);
        return finds;
    }

    public static List findAll(Session session) throws SQLException,
HibernateException {
        List finds = session.find("from Account in class null.Account");
        return finds;
    }
}
```

Map Generator

Many of the tools discussed so far are very helpful when you develop a new application, but there will be many times when you want to use Hibernate to persist Java classes that have already been created and possibly even used in a heritage application. Hibernate includes the `class2hbm` class to automatically create a mapping document from a compiled Java class.

Of course, we should always be concerned when we are talking about using a computer application to analyze another language construct to produce yet another application construct. As you might expect, the Map Generator will use reflection to pull the attributes from the Java class and pretty much guess the type to be used for the mapping. The tool will attempt to map inheritance trees as much as it can. Thus, you as the developer should expect to spend some time looking through the resulting mapping document to fine-tune how the objects will be mapped.

Before we look at the tool itself, let's consider some of the rules that the Map Generator will adhere to when trying to analyze the Java class. The rules include:

❑   The Java class must include a default constructor.

❑   The class cannot be nested, an interface, an array, or a primitive type.

❑   Attributes of the class must have setter/getter functions.

❑   Setter methods must start with set.

❑   Getter methods must start with get or is.

To use the Map Generator tool, execute the following command:

```
java -cp <classpath> net.sf.hibernate.tool.class2hbm.MapGenerator options
classnames
```

You can also execute the tool from the /bin directory using a script called class2hbm.bat. The batch file executes another batch file called setenv.bat. Be sure to open this batch file and set the proper environment values for your specific setup. The options for the Map Generator are shown in the following table.

Option	Description
--interact	Starts interactive mode, allowing responses to the tool
--quiet	Doesn't allow output to appear on the console
--setUID=uid	Sets the list of candidate UIDs to the singleton uid
--addUID=uid	Places the specified uid to the front of the list of candidate UIDs
--select=mode	Selects the mode for subsequently added classes
--depth=<small-int>	Reduces the depth of component data recursion for subsequently added classes
--output=my_mapping.xml	Sends the O-R Mapping output to a file
full.class.Name	Adds the specified class to the mapping
--abstract=full.class.Name	Tells the tool to ignore specified superclasses

Once you've executed the Map Generator on a Java class, you will need to open the mapping document and make any necessary changes.

If you attempt to execute the Map Generator against a class that doesn't have a default constructor, you will receive the following message:

```
<?xml version="1.0"?>
<!DOCTYPE hibernate-mapping PUBLIC
        "-//Hibernate/Hibernate Mapping DTD 2.0//EN"
        "http://hibernate.sourceforge.net/hibernate-mapping-2.0.dtd">
<!-- Class com.gradecki.URLObject has no 0-arg constructor! -->
<hibernate-mapping>
</hibernate-mapping>
```

Hibern8IDE

A very good tool provided with the extensions package is called Hibern8IDE. Although not a true IDE, this application allows you to browse your persisted store using supplied mapping documents as well as perform manual HQL queries. The tool is provided in the /hibern8ide directory and consists of a single JAR and several support JARs within the /lib directory. Make sure all of the JARs are in your classpath, and execute the following command:

```
java net.sf.hibern8ide.Hibern8IDE
```

Or you can use the Ant build.xml file and execute it with the command ant run , as shown in Listing 15.10.

```xml
<project name="Hibern8IDE" default="dist" basedir=".">

    <!-- Name of project and version, used to create filenames -->
    <property name="Name" value="Hibern8IDE"/>
    <property name="name" value="hibern8ide"/>
    <property name="version" value="1.0"/>

    <!-- set global properties for this build -->
    <property name="lib.dir" value="lib"/>
    <property name="jar.name" value="${name}"/>

    <!-- set Hibernate core related properties -->
    <property name="hibernate-core.home" value="../../hibernate-2.1"/>
    <property name="hibernate-core.jar" value="${hibernate-
core.home}/hibernate2.jar"/>
    <property name="hibernate-core.lib.dir" value="${hibernate-
core.home}/lib"/>
    <property name="hibernate-core.doc.api" value="${hibernate-
core.home}/doc/api"/>

    <path id="lib.class.path">
        <path location="${hibernate-core.jar}"></path>
        <fileset dir="${hibernate-core.lib.dir}">
            <include name="**/*.jar"/>
        </fileset>
        <fileset dir="${lib.dir}">
            <include name="**/*.jar"/>
        </fileset>
    </path>


    <!-- Tasks -->

    <target name="run" >
        <java classname="net.sf.hibern8ide.Hibern8IDE"
classpathref="lib.class.path" fork="true">
            <classpath>
                <path location="${src.dir}"/>
            </classpath>
        </java>
    </target>
</project>
```

Listing 15.10

Within the Ant script, you will need to add additional JAR lib directories to the lib.class.path id. specifically to those places where your JDBC drivers are located. Further, you should add an entry to the src.dir variable to point to where your source classes and mapping documents are located. The result of the command is a graphical application, as shown in Figure 15.1.

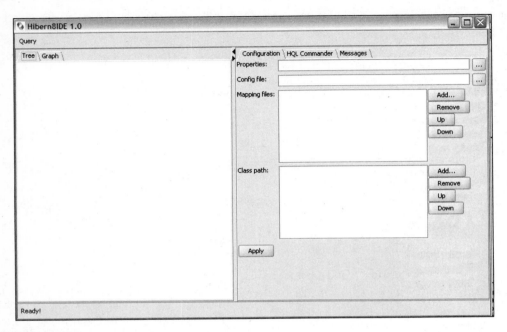

Figure 15.1

There are still a few different tasks we need to do before we can start using the IDE. The first is to load the Hibernate.properties and/or hibernate configuration file. To do this, click the ellipse button next to the Properties and Config File: edit lines. Browse to where the appropriate file(s) are located and click on them. In order for Hibern8IDE to work properly, there must be a <mapping> element within the hibernate.cfg.xml file; otherwise, you would see quite a few errors in the console window where you started the IDE. When you've added the correct properties and/or configuration files, click the Apply button. One of two actions will occur. The first is an error with the supplied files. In this case, the rightmost part of the window will automatically change to the Messages tab, and an error will be displayed. Along with the error there might be some additional stack trace dumps on the console window. Fix the errors and click the Apply button again. You will have a successful Apply when see a GUI like the one shown in Figure 15.2.

On the left -most part of the GUI, you will find a listing of the mapped classes based on the provided mapping documents. If you need to add additional documents, use the Mapping Files: control on the right side of the GUI. Make sure that you load parent mappings before child ones. Once the proper classes have been mapped, you have a few different options available.

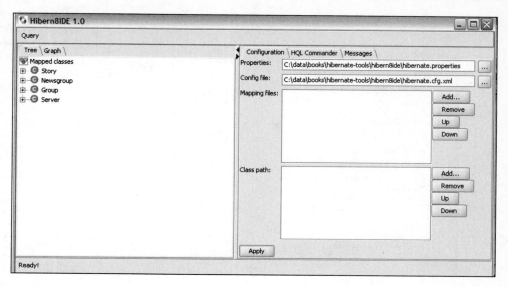

Figure 15.2

Browsing Objects

The first task we can do with the IDE is browse the mapped classes by clicking on the expansion plus signs for each class. In Figure 15.3, we show how the IDE is able to display all of the mapped attributes along with their types. In the case of the Newsgroup class, one of the attributes is a List, and thus the IDE is able to accurately show which class (Story) is stored in the List and its appropriate attributes. Although it's a little hard to see in Figure 15.3, the IDE displays a tiny ID label next to the ID of each mapped class as well as 1-N and N-1 labels to show relationships.

We can also get a pictorial view of the currently displayed mapped classes. Figure 15.4 shows an example of the type of graph that can be displayed just by clicking the Graph tab at the top of the left-most window of the IDE.

Querying Objects

The real power of the IDE comes from the ability to execute HQL queries in an interactive fashion. Figure 15.5 shows an example where we've entered a query in the text area of the HQLCommander tab. The results of the query are displayed in the lower right window of the application.

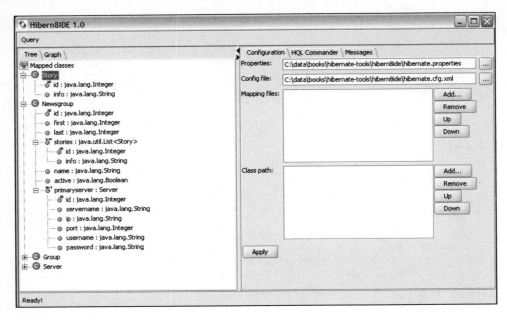

Figure 15.3

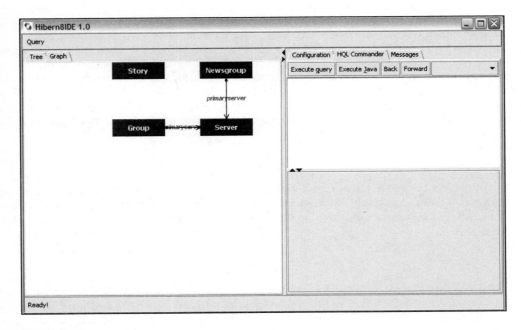

Figure 15.4

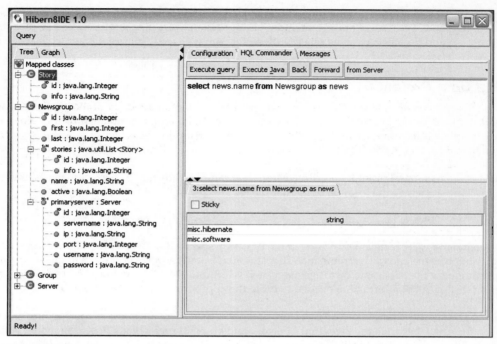

Figure 15.5

AndroMDA

It is considered good practice today to develop new applications using a modeling tool such as UML. From the model, we have the ability to build our classes, mapping document and database tables. What if we had the ability to generate the classes and mapping documents automatically from the UML diagram components? This ability creates a fantastic write-once opportunity and vastly saves production time, so the engineer can work on testing and other tasks that are typically condensed because of schedule issues.

There is one such application available called AndroMDA. AndroMDA is an open source framework that allows an application to be constructed using a UML model. The framework generates the necessary class and components needed to execute an application in a J2EE environment or just a standalone application. So what does this have to do with Hibernate? The answer is that AndroMDA supports the concept of a cartridge, which expands the usefulness of AndroMDA to other technologies such as Hibernate. In fact, there already exists a cartridge for Hibernate, so we can automatically gain the ability to use AndroMDA in our persistent application.

To obtain AndroMDA, browse to http://www.andromda.org and click Installation and then click the link to the download area. Click on the latest version of the application and download it to your machine. Unzip the downloaded application into an appropriate directory. In order to use AndroMDA, you will need a few additional tools. The first is Ant, and the second is some sort of UML editor. We will use Poseidon as our tool. You can download a copy at http://www.gentleware.com/. From this site, you can download and install a community edition of the UML editor, and then you can begin using AndroMDA and Hibernate. For the remainder of this section, we will assume you've downloaded AndroMDA and Poseidon or some other UML editor. You will need Ant installed on your machine as well.

Setting Up a Project

The first step in using AndroMDA is to change into the installation directory of the application and open the samples directory. Within this directory you will find a hibernate-template directory along with other template directories. In addition, there is a wizard.xml build file as well as a wizard.properties file. Open the wizard.properties file and set the appropriate paths for AndroMDA and JBoss.

Now open a command prompt and change into the /samples directory and execute the following command. You can change the location of the sample we are creating:

```
ant -f wizard.xml -Dproject.home=c:/temp/example hibernate
```

This command will create a new project at the directory specified in the command line. Note the hibernate option at the end of the command. This option tells the AndroMDA wizard to generate a project appropriate for the Hibernate cartridge associated with AndroMDA. Cartridges are like plug-ins and give AndroMDA the information needed to build the appropriate files from a UML model.

Now change to the example project directory and notice that there are a few properties files and build scripts for Ant. Change to the /src/uml directory and you will find a blank Poseidon model waiting to be built into your favorite application. Start Poseidon and open the blank model. You should get a GUI, as shown in Figure 15.6.

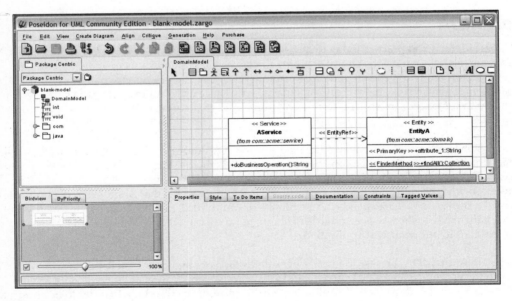

Figure 15.6

You can actually just use the example model provided by AndroMDA because it includes a couple of classes. Now, go back to your command prompt and execute Ant by entering the command ant. After a few moments, the script will stop on a compile error (if you don't have XDoclet installed), but it will still show the information that is output by the Hibernate cartridge.

The result of the Hibernate cartridge for AndroMDA can be found in the /generated directory under the specific directories for the package of the example classes. If you open the EntityA Java class, you will find that Hibernate XDoclet tags have been added and are ready to be processed. Listing 15.11 shows an example of the output.

```
/**
 * Attention: Generated source! Do not modify by hand!
 */
package com.acme.domain;

/**
 *
 * @hibernate.class
 *     table="HIB_ENTITY_A"
 *
 * @hibernate.discriminator
 *     column="class"
 *
 *
 * element.uuid     -64--88-1-100-137008a:f3c983c88d:-7fda
 *
 */
public abstract class EntityA {

    // --------------- attributes ---------------------

    private java.lang.String attribute_1;

    /**
     *
     * @hibernate.id
     *     generator-class="uuid.hex"
     *     column="ATTRIBUTE_1"
     *
     * @hibernate.column
     *     name="ATTRIBUTE_1"
     *     sql-type="VARCHAR(255)"
     *
     */
    public java.lang.String getAttribute_1()
    {
        return this.attribute_1;
    }

    public void setAttribute_1(java.lang.String newValue)
    {
        this.attribute_1 = newValue;
    }
```

```
    // ------------ relations -----------------


    // --------------- business methods -----------------------

}
```

Listing 15.11

Notice how clean the generated code appears and the use of XDoclet. This is important because AndroMDA can generate J2EE -based code using XDoclet as well.

MiddleGen

Our last tool to be covered is called MiddleGen, and it can be found at http://boss.bekk.no/boss/ middlegen. Fundamentally, MiddleGen is a database-driven tool that will automatically create code for you, such as EJBs and Hibernate mapping documents. MiddleGen takes advantage of the XDoclet tags to do most of the work, so you should be somewhat familiar with the XDoclet tags from Chapter 13. For MiddleGen, you will need to download and install several different components. First of all, you will need Ant and XDoclet, and then you will need to download MiddleGen from the site listed above. Finally, there is a demo application available at Hibernate's SourceForge site, http://prdownloads .sourceforge.net/hibernate/. The name of the file is Middlegen-Hibernate-r4.zip.

Once you've downloaded both MiddleGen and the demo application, you have the tools needed to use MiddleGen. Uncompress each of the files. Once the files have been downloaded and uncompressed, change into the Middlegen-Hibernate-r4 directory and type the command ant. The result of the command will be a GUI like that shown in Figure 15.7.

So what is MiddleGen doing, and what do we see in the GUI? MiddleGen is designed to work with a database, its tables, and schemas. The tool will read all of the table information found within the database specified by the following element in the build.xml file:

```
<!DOCTYPE project [
    <!ENTITY database SYSTEM "file:./config/database/hsqldb.xml">
]>
```

The database configuration file looks like the following:

```
<!-- ====================================================================== -->
<!-- ant properties/targets for hsqldb                                       -->
<!-- note: this is not a proper xml file (there is no root element)          -->
<!--       it is intended to be imported from a *real* xml file              -->
<!-- ====================================================================== -->

    <property name="database.script.file"
value="${src.dir}/sql/${name}-hsqldb.sql"/>
```

```
    <property name="database.driver.file"              value="${lib.dir}/hsqldb-
1.7.1.jar"/>
    <property name="database.driver.classpath"
value="${database.driver.file}"/>
    <property name="database.driver"
value="org.hsqldb.jdbcDriver"/>
    <property name="database.url"
value="jdbc:hsqldb:${build.dir}/hsqldb/airline"/>
    <property name="database.userid"              value="sa"/>
    <property name="database.password"            value=""/>
    <property name="database.schema"              value=""/>
    <property name="database.catalog"             value=""/>

    <!-- This isonly for the hsqldb-gui target -->
    <property name="database.urlparams"           value=""/>

    <property name="jboss.datasource.mapping"     value="Hypersonic SQL"/>
```

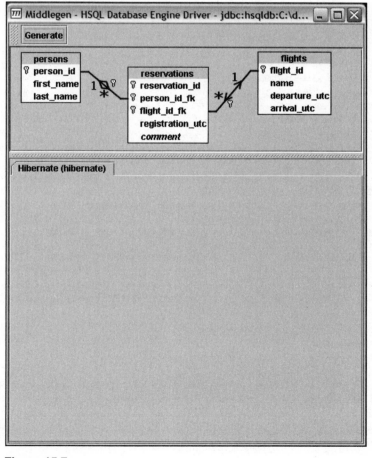

Figure 15.7

Notice that all of the important properties are included, such as the location of the database and the URL string to use for accessing the server and selecting a specific table.

For the demonstration, we use the Hypersonic SQL database, which has already been populated with various tables. The MiddleGen GUI can be used to tweak the schema. Clicking on one of the fields of a visible table will show information about the field as well as other information at the bottom of the GUI, including the description of the field, the scope, and property information. All of this is shown in Figure 15.8.

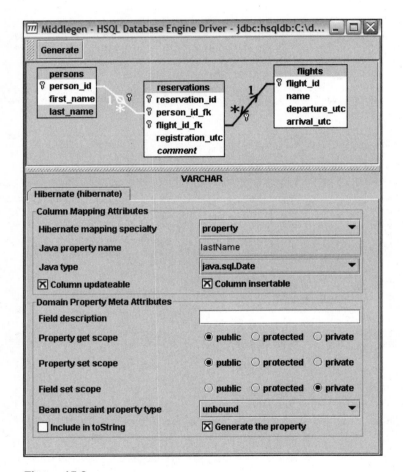

Figure 15.8

Once you've finished the basic tweaking of the fields of the table, you can click the Generate button. The result will be various mapping documents found in the build/gen-src/airline/hibernate directory. For the demo, there are three mapping documents, one for each table. Clearly, you could create an application Ant build script to execute MiddleGen and then the `CodeGenerator` class to build most of your Hibernate functionality.

So how do we use MiddleGen to handle our own database and table? It certainly looks like the application just connects to the database and displays all of the tables. If we have a database that has more than one set of tables, it will display all of them. The answer is the build.xml file. If you open the build.xml file within the demo directory, you will find a paragraph and element like the following:

```
We can specify what tables we want Data generated for.
If none are specified, Data will be generated for all tables.
Comment out the <table> elements if you want to generate for all
    tables.
Also note that table names are CASE SENSITIVE for certain databases,
so on e.g. Oracle you should specify table names in upper case.
-->
<!--table generate="true" name="flights" pktable="flights_pk"/>
<table name="reservations"/-->
```

As you can see, the element is commented out, and thus all of the tables will be processed. If you want to use specific tables, just include them using the `<table>` element.

Summary

As with many new technologies, it's best to learn automation tools through many hands-on examples. Once you've mastered the technology, you can use automation tools with the most efficiency possible. In this chapter we've explored some of the Hibernate and third-party scripts and tools that make generating mapping documents, Java classes, and database schemas much easier and far less time-consuming than by hand.

Hibernate and Eclipse

As many developers will attest, when you start using open source products such as Hibernate, their attraction becomes so overwhelming that you tend to find such products for the other development tools needed during a project. One of those tools that has literally taken the community by storm is Eclipse. Eclipse is an open source IDE designed for the open source community, and it provides for the use of a variety of plug-ins. The plug-ins give Eclipse additional features that the developers didn't initially put into the tool. As you might expect, some of the plug-ins provide features well beyond those typically found in an IDE.

The plug-ins in this chapter are designed to make a connection between Eclipse and Hibernate so that using Hibernate in your project becomes easier than it already is. We'll cover three different plug-ins:

- ❑ Hibernator
- ❑ HiberClipse
- ❑ Hibernate Synchronizer

Of course the plug-ins will need a host, and so you will need to install Eclipse if you don't already use it. You can find Eclipse at the following Web site: http://www.eclipse.org. Download and install the version needed for your platform.

Hibernator

The Hibernator plug-in can be found at http://hiberator.sourceforge.net. There are two available downloads, one that includes all of the necessary libraries from Hibernate and one that doesn't include the libraries. If you choose to install the version without the Hibernator libraries, you will need to include the following libraries from your Hibernate installation into the *<eclipse install directory>*/plugins/hibernator_0.9.6/libs directory:

```
- xml-apis.jar
  - xerces.jar
  - commons-beanutils.jar
  - commons-collections.jar
  - commons-lang.jar
  - commons-logging.jar
  - dom4j.jar
  - hibernate2.jar
  - odmg.jar
  - cglib-asm.jar
  - log4j.jar
```

Of course, if the Hibernator version has changed since 0.9.6, you must change the directory to the version of the new download. If you download the version of Hibernator with the libraries included, just unzip it in the *<eclipse installation directory>* directory. Once it is installed, start Eclipse or restart it if it's already running. You are now ready to use the features available in Hibernator.

Database Connection

You can obtain a connection to a database that is necessary for many of the Hibernator functions to follow by choosing Windows > Open Perspective > Other and double-clicking the Hibernator entry, as shown in Figure 16.1.

Figure 16.1

The result of clicking the Hibernator option will be a new window titled Connection View in the Eclipse browser on the left side of the window. Right-click in the Connection View window and choose Add. The available Eclipse projects will be shown in the resulting dialog of a Connection Wizard, as shown in Figure 16.2. If you haven't created the Eclipse project for your application, you might want to do that first before creating the connection to the database.

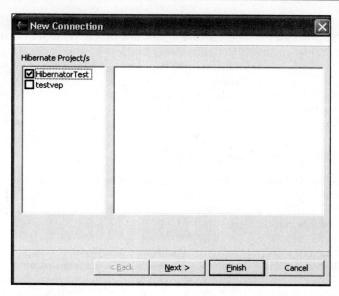

Figure 16.2

Once you've checked the appropriate project to associate a connection, click the Next button of the Connection Wizard. The resulting dialog will provide areas for adding information about the connection. Fill in the areas in a way resembling that found in Figure 16.3.

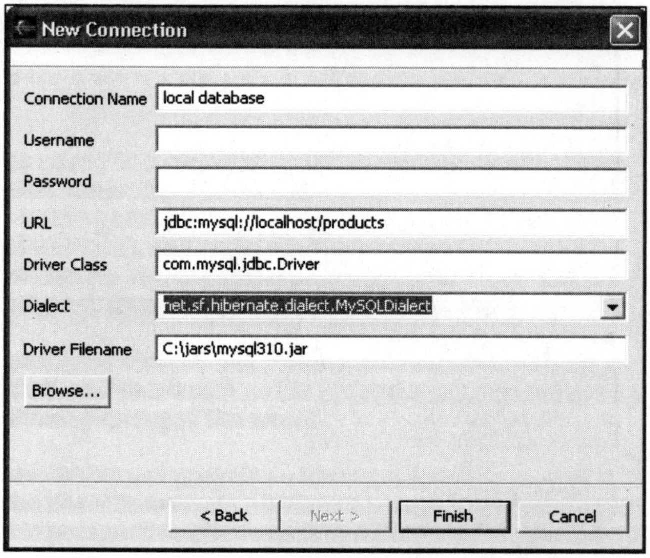

Figure 16.3

After you've filled in the areas in the Connection dialog, click the Finish button. The name you provided in the dialog will appear in the Connection View window. To connect to the database, right-click the name within the window and select Connect. Notice that you have other options available as well when you right-click, including Delete, Add, and Edit.

After you click the Connect! option, a progress dialog will appear. If the connection is successful, you will see additional windows on the right side of the Eclipse window. The dialogs are Query View and Results View. At the bottom of the Results View dialog is a tab for Log View as well.

Creating a Mapping Document

In order to do much with Hibernator, you will need a mapping document, and to create a mapping document, you will need a Java class. In your project, create a new class and add the appropriate attribute and methods as you would for any class that you want Hibernate to persist. At this point, you should still be in the Java Perspective.

Now, you need to open a view relating to the Hibernator plug-in by choosing Window > Show View > Other, selecting Hibernator, and clicking OK. The result will be a window at the bottom-right side of the Java Perspective. To see the mapping document for a Java class, double-click on the class to open it and view the information in the Hibernator window, as shown in Figure 16.4.

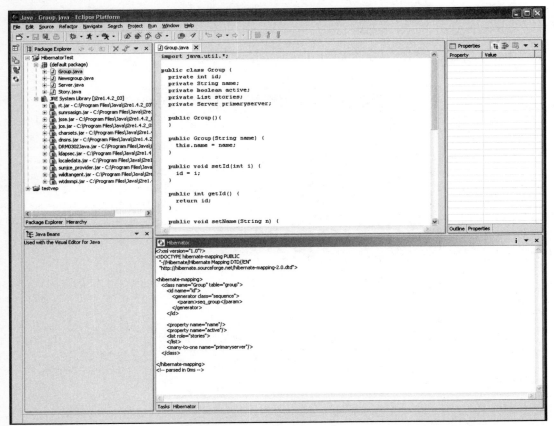

Figure 16.4

To save the contents of the Hibernate window as a mapping document, just right-click in the window and choose Save. The appropriate mapping document will appear in the Package Explorer for the project.

Querying the Database

With a connection to the database provided, you can create a query based on the Hibernate Query Language using the Query View window, which opened when you connected to the database. To perform a query, click in the Query View window and type in your query, as shown in Figure 16.5.

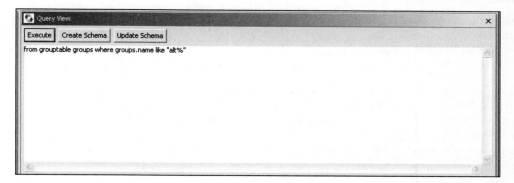

Figure 16.5

To execute the query, click the Execute button. The result of the query will be shown in the Results View. Any errors will be displayed in a dialog and also in the Log View window.

Creating a Schema

If you have just created a class and its resultant mapping document using Hibernator, you can have the tool build the database table by clicking the Create Schema button found in the Query View window. Note that if you click this button, Hibernator will first attempt to drop any table with the name specified in the mapping document.

Updating the Schema

Of course, if you make any changes to your Java class and then generate a new mapping document, you can click the Update Schema button found in the Query View window to update the database table accordingly.

As you might expect, the Hibernator plug-in is a work-in-progress, and errors may occur. A forum is available for the users of Hibernate at http://sourceforge.net/forum/, where you can find some solutions to problems. This is also a good place to look to determine whether you've found a bug or just need help.

HiberClipse

The second plug-in covered here is called HiberClipse, and it can be found at http://hiberclipse
.sourceforge.net/. By far the easiest way to install HiberClipse is to use Eclipse's Update Manager. To do
this, start Eclipse and choose Window > Open > Other and click Install/Update. On the bottom left of
the displayed perspective is a window called Feature Updates. Right-click in this window and select
New > Site Bookmark.

In the dialog that appears, enter the value HiberClipse in the Name field and http://hiberclipse
.sourceforge.net/siteupdate in the URL field, as shown in Figure 16.6.

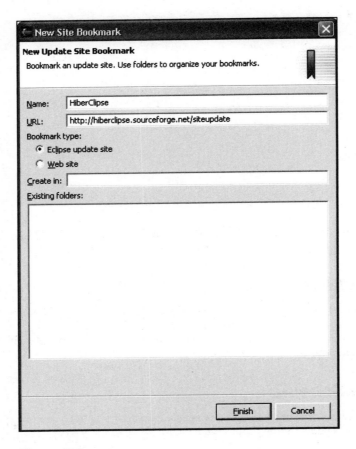

Figure 16.6

Now click Finish. The HiberClipse update icon will appear in the Feature Updates window tree. Expand
the HiberClipse entry twice, and click the entry called net.sourceforge.hiberclipse.feature
<version number>. On the page that appears in the right-most window, click the Install Now button,
as shown in Figure 16.7.

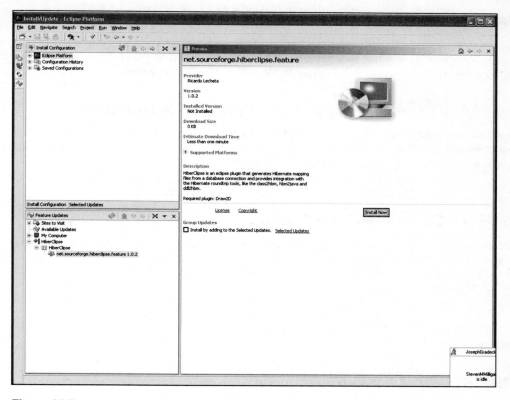

Figure 16.7

When the Update Manager asks if you want to restart the workbench, you will need to click Yes to activate HiberClipse. Finally, you will need to have the Hibernate Tools Extension JAR in a classpath where Eclipse will be able to find it, because this is how HiberClipse performs most of its work.

Configuring a JDBC Connection

The first step in using HiberClipse is to set up the connection to the database used by a Hibernate project. Therefore, you need to create a project first. Once the project is created, right-click on the project and select Properties. In the Properties dialog that appears, click HiberClipse. Next, fill in the JDBC driver and mapping files. For HiberClipse to connect to the database for the project, the `hibernate`
`.properties` or `hibernate.cfg.xml` file must in the root directory of your project.

Creating a Mapping Document

Now let's say you've created a new Java class and added it to your project. To generate the mapping document for the new class, right-click on the class entry in the Package Explorer, locate HiberClipse at the bottom of the page, and choose the MapGenerator menu option. This option will execute the MapGenerator found in the Hibernate Tools Extension. The result will be a mapping document created as part of the project.

Creating Java Code from a Mapping Document

You can also use HiberClipse to go the other direction, from a mapping document to a Java class. To do this, right-click on a mapping document, select HiberClipse, and then select CodeGenerator. The result will be a new Java class matching the description of the mapping document.

Creating a Schema Export or Updating a Schema

You can execute the SchemaExport tool by right-clicking on a mapping document, selecting HiberClipse, and then selecting SchemaExport. Likewise, the SchemaUpdate tool can be executed by selecting the appropriate option on the pop-up menu.

Hibernate Synchronizer

Our final plug-in is called Hibernate Synchronizer, and it can be found at: http://www.binamics .com/hibernatesynch. This plug-in can be installed in Eclipse using the Update Manager as described in the previous section. The URL for the update site is also http://www.binamics.com/hibernatesynch. Note that you must be using Eclipse 3 for this option to work properly. Otherwise, if you're using Eclipse 2.1, you can download the plug-in at http://www.binamics.com/hibernatesynch/releases.

Once the plug-in is installed, you can use it to handle many of the features we discussed for the other plug-ins.

Configuration File Wizard

You can use Hibernate Synchronizer to create a new Hibernate configuration file for a project by selecting File > New > Other > Hibernate > Configuration File from within Eclipse. You will see the dialog shown in Figure 16.8, which has the values filled out as an example.

When you click the Finish button, the plug-in will produce an appropriate configuration file for the project.

Mapping Document Wizard

In the same menu, File > New > Other > Hibernate, there is an option to produce a Mapping Document. Choosing this option will produce the dialog shown in Figure 16.9.

Once you fill in the appropriate fields, an appropriate mapping document will be created Most of the work for Hibernate Synchronizer is performed by allowing the plug-in to automatically make changes to the mapping document based on changes made to a class. You can force the synchronization by right-clicking on a mapping document file listed in the Package Explorer of your project, clicking the Hibernate Synchronizer menu item, and then choosing the Synchronize Files option.

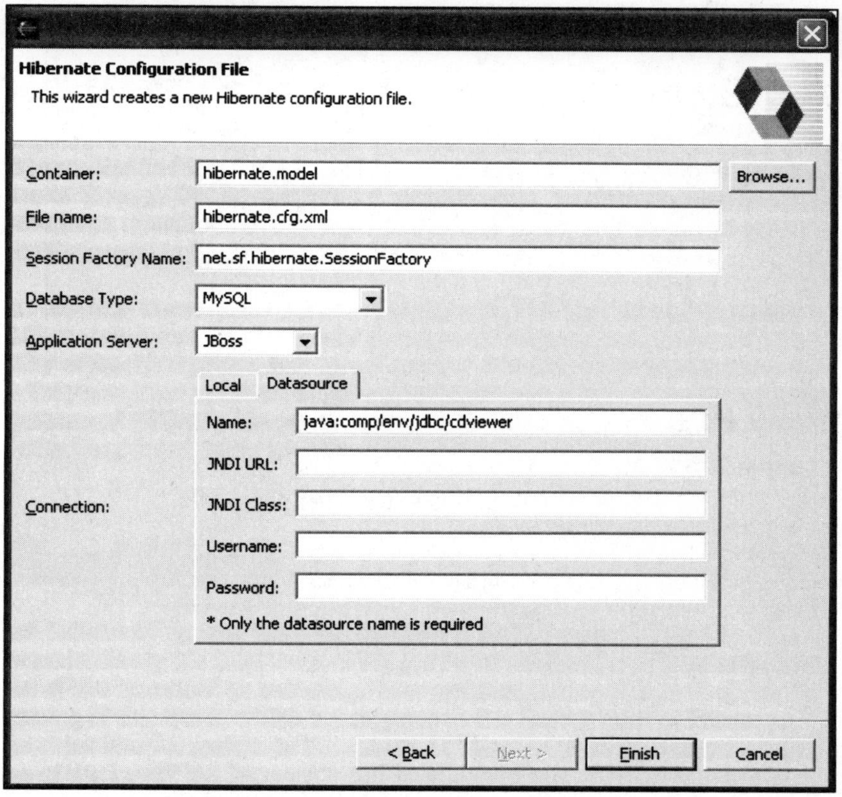

Hibernate Configuration File
This wizard creates a new Hibernate configuration file.

Container:	hibernate.model	Browse...
File name:	hibernate.cfg.xml
Session Factory Name:	net.sf.hibernate.SessionFactory
Database Type:	MySQL
Application Server:	JBoss

Local | Datasource

Connection:

Name: java:comp/env/jdbc/cdviewer

JNDI URL:

JNDI Class:

Username:

Password:

* Only the datasource name is required

< Back   Next >   Finish   Cancel

Figure 16.8

371

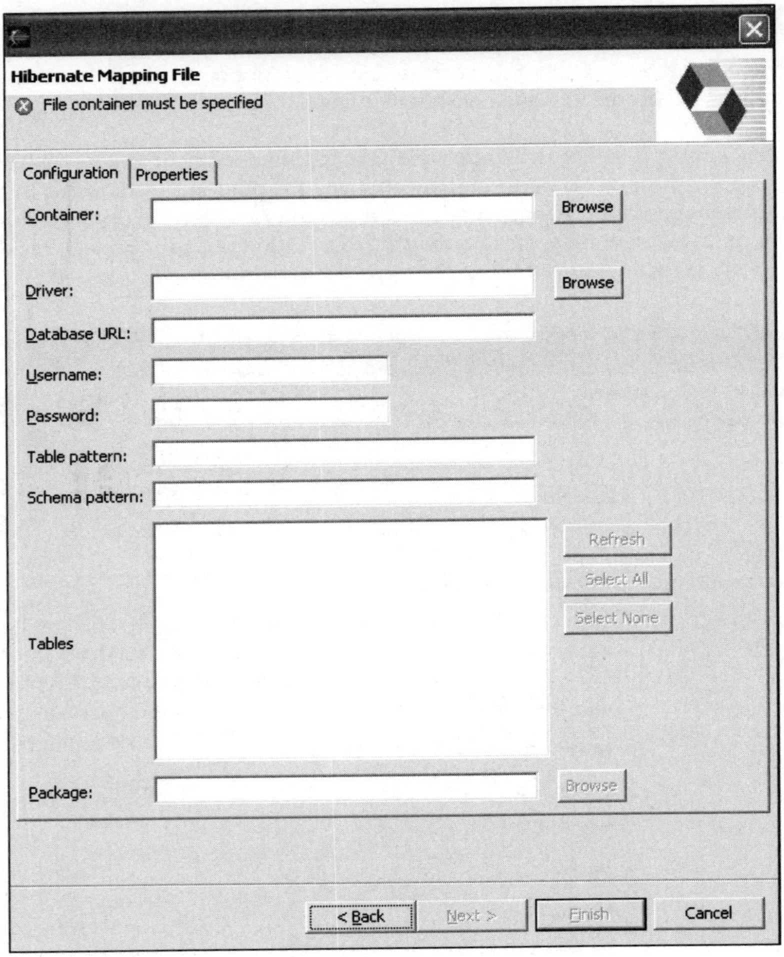

Figure 16.9

Summary

In this chapter we've taken a look at some of the plug-ins available for the Eclipse IDE tool. The three plug-ins in this chapter provide helpful tasks that would otherwise be tedious and time-consuming. As you use Eclipse and Hibernate, be sure to track the state of these plug-ins to make certain you have the most recent version.

17

Using Velocity, Struts, and Hibernate

This chapter introduces three popular technologies and explains how they can be configured to work together. The technologies are Struts, Velocity, and Hibernate. Struts, produced under Apache Jakarta, is probably the most well-known of the Web frameworks available today. In fact, entire books have been written on using Struts. Our goal is to present an introduction to Struts and show how Hibernate can be used to access the database. The primary instruction will occur via an example registration system.

Brief Introduction to Struts

As mentioned above, there are entire books written on the topic of Struts, so this section will be a short introduction to the major components of the system. Figure 17.1 shows a flow diagram of what occurs within the Struts framework.

Struts Flow Diagram

As you can see from the diagram in Figure 17.1, the entire process starts with a home page of sorts that presents the user with links or HTML forms to be filled out. In our example later in the book, we will be presenting the user with a form to register with a Web application. When the user clicks on the link or clicks the Submit button, the Struts ActionServlet will be invoked. This servlet is designed to take the URL specified in the action attribute of the HTML form or the link URL and determine an action to perform. The action is defined in a configuration file along with the action class, the action JavaBean, and the response HTML pages.

The action class is defined around the `Action` base class, and the form data is defined around `ActionForm`. The HTML response pages can be written in JSP or Velocity, as in this chapter. In the remainder of the chapter, we will discuss the prerequisites necessary for Struts and provide an example using both Struts and Velocity.

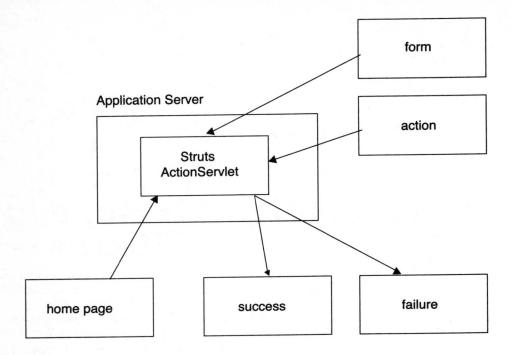

Figure 17.1

Installing Struts

Struts is a framework, and as such it relies on a few friends to accomplish its tasks. Those friends include:

- ❑ An application server such as Tomcat or Resin. We use Tomcat in this chapter.

- ❑ Ant, which is required to compile the source code for Struts or examples but not for the example in this chapter.

- ❑ The JDK, of course.

- ❑ Velocity: You will need the Velocity JAR, Struts library, Struts view, and associated dependencies. To make the download easy, we've included all of the necessary libraries in the source code download for this chapter on the Web site at http://www.wrox.com.

A Sample Application

In order to see how simple it is to use Struts with a Velocity templating solution and Hibernate, we will build a Web application that allows a user to register using a username and password. The system will present a registration page with a form to gather a username, the password, and a copy of the password, which will be used to make sure the user typed in the right combination of characters.

For the registration system, we will look at six steps in the process. All of the steps relate to the Struts process outlined above. These steps are:

1. Create an ActionForm.
2. Build the action.
3. Modify the struts-config.xml file.
4. Create an appropriate web.xml file.
5. Create Success and Failure pages.
6. Create the Register page.

Building the ActionForm

As you might expect, we will use an HTML form to gather the username, password, and second password. There will need to be a way of getting the data entered by the user into the system so it can be processed. In the "old" way, we would obtain the `HttpServletRequest` object and use the `getParameter()` method to get the values. Under Struts, we will use a JavaBean for the transport object. As you learned earlier, when a user clicks a Submit button in a form, the action attribute of the `<form>` tag will specify a Struts action defined in the struts-config.xml file. Associated with the Struts action is an `ActionForm`. For our registration example, we will use the class defined in Listing 17.1.

```java
import org.apache.struts.action.*;

public class RegisterForm extends ActionForm {
  protected String username;
  protected String password;
  protected String password2;

  public String getUsername() { return this.username; }
  public String getPassword() { return this.password; }
  public String getPassword2() { return this.password2; }

  public void setUsername(String username) { this.username = username; };
  public void setPassword(String password) { this.password = password; };
  public void setPassword2(String password) { this.password2 = password; };

}
```

Listing 17.1

The `User` class holds the username and password for each of the users in the system. The code for the class is shown in Listing 17.2.

```
import java.util.*;

public class User{
  private int id;
  private String username;
  private String password;

  public Group(){
  }

  public Group(String name) {
    this.name = name;
  }

  public void setId(int i) {
    id = i;
  }

  public int getId() {
    return id;
  }

  public void setUsername(String n) {
    username = n;
  }

  public String getUsernme() {
    return username;
  }

  public void setPasswword(String l) {
    password = l;
  }

  public String getPassword() {
    return password;
  }
}
```

Listing 17.2

RegisterForm Code

The RegisterForm class is designed to handle all of the data that will be sent from our form. The class must inherit from ActionForm, which is a Struts base class. As you can see, the code in the class is what you would expect from a JavaBean. There are protected attributes and getter/setter methods for each of them. Both the system and the developer will use this Form class. The developer will access it from the Velocity Templates as well as in the action discussed next.

Creating an Action

The action is where all of business work occurs, usually as a result of a user clicking a link or a Submit button of a form. Based on the Struts configuration file, an Action object will be put into play. Listing 17.3 shows the code for the `RegisterAction` class.

```
import org.apache.struts.action.*;
import javax.servlet.http.*;
import java.io.*;
import net.sf.hibernate.*;
import net.sf.hibernate.cfg.*;

public class RegisterAction extends Action {
  public ActionForward perform(ActionMapping mapping, ActionForm form,
HttpServletRequest request, HttpServletResponse response) {
    RegisterForm rf = (RegisterForm) form;

    String username = rf.getUsername();
    String password = rf.getPassword();
    String password2 = rf.getPassword2();
    if (password.equals(password2)) {
      Context ctx = new InitialContext();
      SessionFactory sf =
(SessionFactory)ctx.lookup("emp:/hibernate/SessionFactory");
      Session session = sf.openSession();

      User user = new User();
      user.setUsername(username);
      user.setPassword(password);

      session.save(user);

    }
    return mapping.findForward("failure");
  }
}
```

Listing 17.3

RegisterAction Code

As you might expect, the `RegisterAction` class extends the Struts `Action` base class. The Struts system will call the `perform()` method, providing a `Form` object if appropriate, the `HttpServletRequest`, and `Response` objects. In our case, we immediately cast the `Form` class into `RegisterForm` and pull the values for the username, password, and second password.

The code will check to see if the two passwords match each other. If they do, we tell Struts to return a value of success, which is matched against the configuration file and the `success.vm` template. Otherwise, a value of failure is returned for the `failure.vm` template.

Chapter 17

Configuring Struts

Most of the structure for a Struts Web application is found in the configuration file called struts-conf.xml, as shown in Listing 17.4.

```
<?xml version="1.0" encoding="ISO-8859-1" ?>

<!DOCTYPE struts-config PUBLIC
        "-//Apache Software Foundation//DTD Struts Configuration 1.0//EN"
        "http://jakarta.apache.org/struts/dtds/struts-config_1_0.dtd">

<struts-config>

  <form-beans>
    <form-bean name="registerForm" type="RegisterForm"/>
  </form-beans>

  <action-mappings>
    <action     path="/struts"
                type="RegisterAction"
                name="registerForm">
      <forward name="success" path="/success.vm"/>
      <forward name="failure" path="/failure.vm"/>
    </action>
  </action-mappings>

<plug-in className="edu.arbor.util.pluin.HibernatePlugIn">
  <set-property property="configFilePath" value="/
  <set-property property="storeInServletContext" value="true"/>
</plug-in>
</struts-config>
```

Listing 17.4

The important part of the configuration file for Hibernate is the `<plug-in>` element, which is designed to bring into Struts a plug-in to initialize Hibernate when our Struts application is first accessed. Of course, that means we will also need a plug-in to handle the initialization. The plug-in code is found in Listing 17.5. The plug-in was designed by Bradley M. Handy and was posted to the Hibernate community Web site.

```
package edu.arbor.util.plugin;

import java.net.URL;
import javax.servlet.ServletContext;
import javax.servlet.ServletException;
import net.sf.hibernate.SessionFactory;
import net.sf.hibernate.cfg.Configuration;
import org.apache.commons.logging.Log;
import org.apache.commons.logging.LogFactory;
import org.apache.struts.action.ActionServlet;
import org.apache.struts.action.PlugIn;
import org.apache.struts.config.ModuleConfig;
```

378

```
/**
 * Implements the <code>PlugIn</code> interface to configure the Hibernate
 * data persistence library.  A configured
 * <code>net.sf.hibernate.SessionFactory</code> is stored in the
 * <code>ServletContext</code> of the web application unless the property
 * <code>storedInServletContext</code> is set to <code>false</code>.
 *
 * <p>
 * &lt;plugin
class=&quot;net.sf.hibernate.plugins.struts.HibernatePlugIn&quot;&gt;
 *    &lt;set-property name=&quot;configFilePath&quot"
 *                  value=&quot;path-to-config-file&quot;/&gt;
 *    &lt;set-property name=&quot;storedInServletContext&quot"
 *                  value=&quot;true-or-false&quot;/&gt;
 * &lt;/plugin&gt;
 *
 * @author  <a href="mailto:bhandy@users.sf.net">Bradley M. Handy</a>
 * @version 1.0
 */
public class HibernatePlugIn implements PlugIn {

    /**
     * the key under which the <code>SessionFactory</code> instance is stored
     * in the <code>ServletContext</code>.
     */
    public static final String SESSION_FACTORY_KEY
            = SessionFactory.class.getName();

    private static Log _log = LogFactory.getLog(HibernatePlugIn.class);

    /**
     * indicates whether the <code>SessionFactory</code> instance will be
stored
     * in the <code>ServletContext</code>, or not.
     */
    private boolean _storedInServletContext = true;

    /**
     * the path to the xml configuration file.  the path should start with a
     * '/' character and be relative to the root of the class path.
     * (DEFAULT:  "/hibernate.cfg.xml")
     */
    private String _configFilePath = "/hibernate.cfg.xml";

    private ActionServlet _servlet = null;
    private ModuleConfig _config = null;
    private SessionFactory _factory = null;

    /**
     * Destroys the <code>SessionFactory</code> instance.
     */
    public void destroy() {
        _servlet = null;
```

```
        _config = null;

        try {
            _log.debug("Destroying SessionFactory...");

            _factory.close();

            _log.debug("SessionFactory destroyed...");
        } catch (Exception e) {
            _log.error("Unable to destroy SessionFactory...(exception
ignored)",
                    e);
        }
    }

    /**
     * Initializes the <code>SessionFactory</code>.
     * @param servlet the <code>ActionServlet</code> instance under which the
     *        plugin will run.
     * @param config the <code>ModuleConfig</code> for the module under which
     *        the plugin will run.
     */
    public void init(ActionServlet servlet, ModuleConfig config)
    throws ServletException {
        _servlet = servlet;
        _config = config;

        initHibernate();
    }

    /**
     * Initializes Hibernate with the config file found at
     * <code>configFilePath</code>.
     */
    private void initHibernate() throws ServletException {
        Configuration configuration = null;
        URL configFileURL = null;
        ServletContext context = null;

        try {
            configFileURL =
HibernatePlugIn.class.getResource(_configFilePath);

            context = _servlet.getServletContext();

            if (_log.isDebugEnabled()) {
                _log.debug("Initializing Hibernate from "
                        + _configFilePath + "...");
            }

            configuration = (new Configuration()).configure(configFileURL);
            _factory = configuration.buildSessionFactory();

            if (_storedInServletContext) {
```

```
                    _log.debug("Storing SessionFactory in ServletContext...");

                    context.setAttribute(SESSION_FACTORY_KEY, _factory);
            }

        } catch (Throwable t) {
            _log.error("Exception while initializing Hibernate.");
            _log.error("Rethrowing exception...", t);

            throw (new ServletException(t));
        }
    }

    /**
     * Setter for property configFilePath.
     * @param configFilePath New value of property configFilePath.
     */
    public void setConfigFilePath(String configFilePath) {
        if ((configFilePath == null) || (configFilePath.trim().length() ==
0)) {
            throw new IllegalArgumentException(
                    "configFilePath cannot be blank or null.");
        }

        if (_log.isDebugEnabled()) {
            _log.debug("Setting 'configFilePath' to '"
                    + configFilePath + "'...");
        }

        _configFilePath = configFilePath;
    }

    /**
     * Setter for property storedInServletContext.
     * @param storedInServletContext New value of property
storedInServletContext.
     */
    public void setStoredInServletContext(String storedInServletContext) {
        if ((storedInServletContext == null)
                || (storedInServletContext.trim().length() == 0)) {
            storedInServletContext = "false";
        }

        if (_log.isDebugEnabled()) {
            _log.debug("Setting 'storedInServletContext' to '"
                    + storedInServletContext + "'...");
        }

        _storedInServletContext
                = new Boolean(storedInServletContext).booleanValue();
    }

}
```

Listing 17.5

If you take the time to look through the plug-in, most of the code should be self explanatory. The vast majority of the work is finding the Hibernate configuration file and then initializing the Session object. It is important that the Hibernate configuration file be located relative to the root and start with a / character. The Hibernate configuration file for this example is shown here:

```
<?xml version="1.0" encoding="utf-8"?>
<!DOCTYPE hibernate-configuration PUBLIC
"-//Hibernate/Hibernate Configuration DTD//EN"
"http://hibernate.sourceforge.net/hibernate-configuration-2.0.dtd"> ***AU:
Please indicate where to wrap this line of code. LSR***

<hibernate-configuration>

    <session-factory name="emp:/hibernate/SessionFactory">
<property name="connection.driver">com.mysql.jdbc.Driver</property>
<property name="connection.url">jdbc:mysql://localhost/products</property>
<property name="dialect">net.sf.hibernate.dialect.MySQLDialect</property>

<property name="username">sa</property>
<property name="password">sa</property>

<mapping resource="User.hbm.xml"/>

</session-factory>

</hibernate-configuration>
```

An important part of the configuration is the designator for the JNDI name of the session factory. We will use this name within our Struts application to access the Session object.

Struts Configuration File

In the configuration file, we define the Form JavaBeans, including their name, which is a reference for the `<action>` element and the class name. Next, we define all of the actions that can occur in the application. We have only one, which we have called "struts." When the struts action is called from a `<form>` or link, the framework will activate the `RegisterAction` action and use the `RegisterForm` form to pull the data from the `<form>` data. Also defined in the `<action>` element are the forwards, which represent the pages where results will be provided to the user.

Web.xml File

In addition to the Struts configuration file, we also need to include a web.xml file so the application server knows how to handle requests from the user. Listing 17.6 shows the file.

```
<?xml version="1.0" encoding="ISO-8859-1"?>

<!DOCTYPE web-app
   PUBLIC "-//Sun Microsystems, Inc.//DTD Web Application 2.2//EN"
   "http://java.sun.com/j2ee/dtds/web-app_2_2.dtd">

<web-app>
```

```xml
<!-- Action Servlet Configuration -->
<servlet>
 <servlet-name>action</servlet-name>
  <servlet-class>org.apache.struts.action.ActionServlet</servlet-class>
  <init-param>
    <param-name>config</param-name>
    <param-value>/WEB-INF/struts-config.xml</param-value>
  </init-param>
  <init-param>
    <param-name>debug</param-name>
    <param-value>2</param-value>
  </init-param>
  <init-param>
    <param-name>detail</param-name>
    <param-value>2</param-value>
  </init-param>
  <init-param>
    <param-name>validate</param-name>
    <param-value>true</param-value>
  </init-param>
  <load-on-startup>2</load-on-startup>
</servlet>

<servlet>
  <servlet-name>velocity</servlet-name>
  <servlet-class>org.apache.velocity.tools.view.servlet.VelocityViewServlet</servlet-class>
  <init-param>
   <param-name>toolbox</param-name>
   <param-value>/WEB-INF/toolbox.xml</param-value>
  </init-param>
  <load-on-startup>10</load-on-startup>
</servlet>

<!-- Action Servlet Mapping -->

<servlet-mapping>
  <servlet-name>velocity</servlet-name>
  <url-pattern>*.vm</url-pattern>
</servlet-mapping>

<servlet-mapping>
  <servlet-name>action</servlet-name>
  <url-pattern>*.do</url-pattern>
</servlet-mapping>

<!-- Struts Tag Library Descriptors -->
<taglib>
  <taglib-uri>/WEB-INF/struts-bean.tld</taglib-uri>
  <taglib-location>/WEB-INF/struts-bean.tld</taglib-location>
</taglib>
```

```
    <taglib>
        <taglib-uri>/WEB-INF/struts-html.tld</taglib-uri>
        <taglib-location>/WEB-INF/struts-html.tld</taglib-location>
    </taglib>

    <taglib>
        <taglib-uri>/WEB-INF/struts-logic.tld</taglib-uri>
        <taglib-location>/WEB-INF/struts-logic.tld</taglib-location>
    </taglib>
</web-app>
```

Listing 17.6

The web.xml file consists of two important parts. The first is a definition of the `<servlet-mapping>` and `<servlet>` elements for Struts. The configuration says that any URL with an ending of `*.do` will be redirected to the `ActionServlet` servlet provided with Struts. We also include a configuration section for Velocity. All `*.vm` URLs will be directed to the `VelocityViewServlet`. Notice that there is a parameter to the Velocity `<servlet>` for a toolbox.xml file. This file is found in Listing 17.7.

```
<?xml version="1.0"?>

<toolbox>
    <tool>
        <key>toolLoader</key>
        <class>org.apache.velocity.tools.tools.ToolLoader</class>
    </tool>

<tool>
    <key>link</key>
    <class>org.apache.velocity.tools.struts.LinkTool</class>
</tool>

<tool>
    <key>msg</key>
    <class>org.apache.velocity.tools.struts.MessageTool</class>
</tool>

<tool>
    <key>errors</key>
    <class>org.apache.velocity.tools.struts.ErrorsTool</class>
</tool>

<tool>
    <key>form</key>
    <class>org.apache.velocity.tools.struts.FormTool</class>
</tool>
</toolbox>
```

Listing 17.7

Toolbox.xml File

The toolbox.xml file defines several classes that the Struts `ActionServlet` can use to provide a bridge between Struts, its `Form` JavaBeans, and Velocity Templates. All of the code is found in the Velocity Struts plug-in that we already discussed.

Success Page

When a user provides a username and two passwords that match, the `RegisterAction` class will instruct the Struts `ActionServlet` to use the success forward. The success forward, defined in the Struts configuration file, tells the system to use the `success.vm` Velocity template to display output to the user. The code for the template is found in Listing 17.8.

```
<HTML>
<HEAD>
  <TITLE>Success</TITLE>
</HEAD>
<BODY>
  Registration Success!
  Thanks for logging in $!registerForm.username
  <P><A href="register.vm">Try Another?</A></P>
</BODY>
</HTML>
```

Listing 17.8

Success.vm Template

The template is fairly basic, but you will get the idea. If the user is successful in providing accurate information, we pull the username from the RegisterForm object created when Struts executed the `RegisterAction` action. Notice the use of the `$!` directive. This directive tells Velocity to search all available context objects for the `registerForm` object and the `username()` method.

Success under Struts and Velocity

The Failure page looks like the Success Velocity template but tells the user to try again.

Register Page

Throughout this discussion we have referenced the page where the user can provide information and submit it to the server. Listing 17.9 shows the Register Velocity template that provides this capability.

```
<html>
<head>
<title>Register</title>
<meta http-equiv="Content-Type" content="text/html; charset=iso-8859-1">
</head>
```

```
<body bgcolor="#CCCCCC" text="#006699" link="#006699" vlink="#006699"
alink="#006699">
<table width="80%" border="1" cellspacing="0" cellpadding="0"
bgcolor="#999999"
bordercolor="#000000" align="center">
  <tr>
    <td>
      <table width="100%" border="0" cellspacing="0" cellpadding="0">
        <tr>
          <td>
            <div align="center"><font face="Verdana, Arial, Helvetica, sans-
serif" size="-1"><a href="http://localhost:8080/register.vm">Home</a>
</font></div>
          </td>
        </tr>
      </table>
    </td>
  </tr>
</table>
<table width="80%" border="1" cellspacing="0" cellpadding="0"
bordercolor="#000000"
align="center">
  <tr>
    <td width="22%" align="right"><img src="header2.gif" width="200"
height="75"></td>
  </tr>
</table>
<table width="80%" border="1" cellspacing="0" cellpadding="0"
bordercolor="#000000"
align="center">
  <tr>
    <td align="left" valign="top" height="423">
      <table width="100%" border="0" cellspacing="0" cellpadding="0">
        <tr>
          <td width="20%" height="9"><font face="Verdana, Arial, Helvetica,
sans-serif" size="-2" color="#000000">$date</font></td>
          <td width="43%" height="9"> </td>
          <td width="37%" height="9" bgcolor="#000000">
            <table width="100%" border="0" cellspacing="0" cellpadding="0">
              <tr bgcolor="#000000">

              </tr>
            </table>
          </td>
        </tr>
      </table>
      <table width="69%" border="0" cellspacing="0" cellpadding="0"
align="center">
        <tr>
          <td width="71%" height="246" align="left" valign="top">
            <p> </p>

<form action="struts.do" method="post">
```

```
    username: <input type="text" name="username"/><BR>
    password: <input type="text" name="password"/><BR>
    again    : <input type="text" name="password2"/><BR>
<input type="submit" name="submit" value="Register"/>
</form>

        </td>
      </tr>
    </table>
  </td>
</tr>
</table>
<p> </p>
<p> </p><p> </p>
<p> </p>
</body>
</html>
```

Listing 17.9

Register.VM Template

A large part of the template is formatting information, except at the end. An HTML form is created with an action attribute set equal to "struts.do." Remember that the name of our action in the Struts configuration file is struts. When the struts.do URL is provided to the server, the ".do" will be stripped and the "struts" string matched against the <action> elements in the configuration.

Compile

To compile the Action and Form classes, use the following command:

```
javac "../lib/struts_1_0_2.jar;./;" *.java
```

Once the Java source files have been compiled, you can restart the application server.

Run

You can execute the application by browsing to the following URL:

```
http://localhost:8080/struts/register.vm
```

When you click on the dialog, the Struts action will be triggered. The code will check the passwords provided and build an appropriate User object and store it in the database.

Summary

In this chapter, we've gone through the details of using Velocity, Struts, and Hibernate to provide a comprehensive MVC solution to developing dynamic Web pages and applications. With just a few simple classes, you can combine Hibernate with some of the best-known open source tools.

18

Hibernate and AspectJ

In their book *Mastering AspectJ*, Joseph D. Gradecki and Nicholas Lesiecki discuss how we've all become accustomed to breaking the encapsulation concept when using an object-oriented language to build an application. They provide a clear example using the logging capability found in most production systems. When building objects for a system, we typically want to have the ability to log information from the object to a console window or a file. In Java, we might use the native features founding version 1.4, or we might rely on the open source project log4J found at http://jakarta.apache.org. In either case, the logging functionality is initialized at the start of the application and log methods or other mechanisms are used to put information into the logging system.

The problem with the logging is that it breaks the encapsulation of the objects where the logging statements are placed. An Account class shouldn't know anything about logging since that isn't its contract with the system. An Account class contains attribute and methods that are a specific part of a real-world account. Since we don't have any other clear way of providing the logging functionality needed within the account, we add it anyway. The requirement to log is called a *crosscutting concern* because it is a requirement of the system that will affect more than a single class. In this chapter, we will show how to marry the technology of Aspect-Oriented Programming through AspectJ with Hibernate.

What Is Aspect-Oriented Programming

Developers are still having difficulty fully expressing a problem into a completely modular and encapsulated model. Although breaking a problem into objects makes sense, some pieces of functionality must be made available across objects. Aspect-Oriented Programming (AOP) is one of the most promising solutions to the problem of creating clean, well-encapsulated objects without extraneous functionality. In this chapter, we will explore what object-oriented programming (OOP) did right for computer science, problems that arise from objects, and how AOP can fill in the blanks.

Where OOP Has Brought Us

Object-oriented analysis, design, and programming (OOADP) is no longer the new kid on the block; it has been proven successful in both small and large projects. As a technology, it has gone through its childhood and is moving into a mature adult stage. Research by educational establishments as well as audits by companies have shown that using OOP instead of functional-decomposition techniques has dramatically enhanced the state of software. The benefits of using object-oriented technologies in all phases of the software development process are varied:

- Reusability of components
- Modularity
- Less complex implementation
- Reduced cost of maintenance

Each of these benefits (and others you can think of) will have varied importance to developers. One of them, modularity, is a universal advancement over structured programming that leads to cleaner and more understandable software.

What OOADP Did for Computer Science

The object-oriented methodology—including analysis, design, and programming—brought to computer science the ability to model or design software more along the lines of how you envision a system in the real world. The primary tool used for this modeling is the object. An *object* is a representation of some primary component of the problem domain. The object has attributes representing the state of the object and behaviors that act on the object to change its state. For example, if you were tasked with designing a system to handle selling DVD products, an OO design might include objects such as a product, a DVD, and a Boxset, as well as many others.

The objects must be filled out with attributes and behaviors specific to their roles. A product might have a context defined as follows:

- Attributes
    - Price
    - Title
    - Suppliers
- Behaviors
    - Assign price
    - Assign title
    - Get suppliers

Of course, a production system would include many more attributes and behaviors, but those added to the product object here will suit our purpose. In defining the product, we create or acknowledge a relationship between the product and a supplier object. After further decomposition of the problem, DVD objects are created as well as Boxset objects, as shown in Figure 18.1.

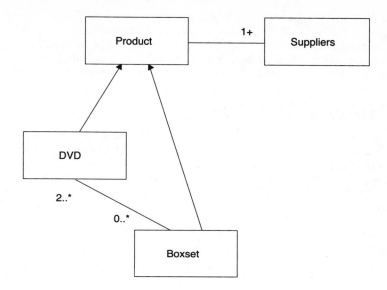

Figure 18.1

One of the goals in object design is encapsulating all the data and methods necessary for manipulating that data fully within the object. There shouldn't be any outside functions that can directly change the product object, nor should the product object make changes to any other object. Instead, a supplier object might send a message to a product object asking it to change its state by adding the supplier object to a list of suppliers in the product object. When a message is sent from one object to another, the receiving object is fully in control of its state. All the attributes of the object are encapsulated in a single entity, which can be changed only through an exposed interface. The exposed interface consists of the methods of the object having a public access type. The object could have internal private methods, but those methods aren't exposed to other objects. The encapsulation of the object is achieved by exposing an interface to other objects in the system. The interface defines the methods that can be used to change the object's state. The functionality behind the exposed interface is kept private.

Designing an object-oriented system in this manner aids in the functioning of the system, debugging if problems arise, and the extension of the system. All the objects in the system know their roles and perform them without worrying about malicious changes being made to their state. From a simplistic view, the system is just a group of objects that execute and send messages to each other, requesting information and changes in the other objects.

As the state of object-oriented technology has evolved, the vocabulary has evolved as well. As you know, an *object* is an instantiation of a class. The class is an abstract datatype used to model the objects in a system. A class is built based on a requirement extracted through an analysis phase (assuming there is an analysis phase). The class might be built on the fly during coding of a solution, with the requirements written in the comments of the class. These requirements and classes can be linked by a concern.

A *concern* is some functionality or requirement necessary in a system, which has been implemented in a code structure. This definition allows a concern to not be limited to object-oriented systems—a structured system can also have concerns. In a typical system, a large number of concerns need to be addressed in order for the system to accomplish its goals. A system designer is faced with building a system that uses the concerns but doesn't violate the rules of the methodologies being used. When all the concerns have been implemented with system code as well as related functional tests, the system is complete.

Problems Resulting from OOP

If you read books and articles about object orientation, they commonly say that OOP allows for the encapsulation of data and methods specific to the goal of a specific object. In other words, an object should be a self-contained unit with no understanding of its environment, and its environment should be aware of nothing about the object other than what the object reveals. A class is the cookie cutter for objects in a system, and it implements a concern for the system. The goal of the class is to fully encapsulate the code needed for the concern. Unfortunately, this isn't always possible. Consider the following two concerns:

❑   **Concern 1:** The system will keep a price relating to the wholesale value of all products.

❑   **Concern 2:** Any changes to the price will be recorded for historical purposes.

The first concern dictates that all products in the system must have a wholesale price. In the object-oriented world, a `Product` class can be created as an abstract class to handle common functionality of all products in the system:

```
public abstract class Product {
   private real price;

   Product() {
      price = 0.0;
   }

   public void putPrice(real p) {
      price = p;
   }

   public int getPrice() {
      return price;
   }
}
```

The `Product` class as defined here satisfies the requirement in concern 1. The principles of OO have been maintained, because the class encapsulates the code necessary to keep track of the price of a product. The same functionality could easily be created in a structured environment using a global array.

Now let's consider concern 2, which requires that all operations involved in changing the price be logged. In itself, this concern does not conflict with the first concern and is easy to implement. The following class defines a logging mechanism:

```
public class Logger {
    private OutputStream ostream;
   Logger() {
```

```
      //open log file
   }
   void writeLog(String value) {
      //write value to log file
   }
}
```

A logger object is instantiated from the `Logger` class by the application's constructor or other initialization function, or individual logger objects are created within those objects needing to log information. Again, the fundamental object-oriented concepts remain in the `Logger` class.

To use the logger, you add the `writeLog()` method to code where the product price might be changed. Because you have only one other class, `Product`, its methods should be considered for logging inclusion. As a result of the class analysis, a new `Product` class emerges:

```
public abstract class Product {
   private real price;
   Logger loggerObject;

   Product() {
      price = 0.0;
      loggerObject = new Logger();
   }

   public void putPrice(real p) {
      loggerObject.writeLog("Changed Price from" + price + " to " + p);
      price = p;
   }

   public int getPrice() {
      return price;
   }
}
```

The change made to the `Product` class is the inclusion of the logging method calls in the `setPrice()` method. When the price is changed using this method, a call is made to the logger object, and the old/new prices are recorded. All objects instantiated from the `Product` class have a local logger object to handle all logging functionality.

Let's look at the idea of encapsulation and modularity within object-oriented methodologies. By adding code to the `Product` class to handle a second concern in the system, it would appear that we've broken the idea of encapsulation. The class no longer handles only its concern, but also must fulfill the requirements of another concern. The class has been crosscut by concerns in the system.

Crosscutting represents the situation when a requirement for the system is met by placing code into objects through the system—but the code doesn't directly relate to the functionality defined for those objects. (Crosscutting is discussed in more detail in the next section.) A class such as `Product`, which is defined to represent a specific entity within the application domain, should not be required to host code used to fulfill other system requirements.

Consider what would happen to the `Product` class if you added timing information, authentication, and long-term data persistence. Are all these concerns supposed to be designed into the `Product` object? Structured and object-oriented languages leave you no other choice when addressing crosscutting concerns. The additional concerns are forced to be part of another concern, thus breaking many of the rules of our favorite methodology.

This mixing of concerns leads to a condition called *code scattering* or *tangling*. With code scattering, the code necessary to fulfill one concern is spread over the classes needed to fulfill another concern. Code tangling involves using a single method or class to implement multiple concerns. Both of these problems break the fundamentals of OO and cause headaches for designers (for more information, see the following section). Consider the following `Product` class, where the two concerns mentioned earlier have been added in pseudocode form. This additional functionality is necessary, but it shouldn't be part of the `Product` class:

```
public abstract class Product {
   private real price;
   Logger loggerObject;

   Product() {
     price = 0.0;
     loggerObject = new Logger();
   }

   public void putPrice(real p) {
    //start timing
    //Check user authentication
     loggerObject.writeLog("Changed Price from" + price + " to " + p);
     price = p;
    // log if problem with authentication
    //end timing
    //log timing
   }

   public int getPrice() {
     //check user authentication
     return price;
   }

   public void persistIt() {
     //start timing
     //save this object
     //end timing
     //log timing
   }

}
```

Once the `Product` class has been created, a DVD concrete class is formulated. The class inherits all the functionality found in the `Product` class and adds a few more attributes. The DVD class includes an attribute and associated methods for the number of copies currently available. This is important information that should be included in all logging activities:

```
public class DVD extends Product {

    private String title;
    private int count;
    private String location;

    public DVD(String inTitle) {
        super();
        title = inTitle;
    }

    private void setCount(int inCount) {
        //start timing
        //check user authentication
        count = inCount;
        //end timing
        //log timing
    }

    private int getCount() {
        return count;
    }

    private void setLocation(String inLocation, int two) {
        //start timing
        //check user authentication
        location = inLocation;
        //end timing
        //log timing
    }

    private String getLocation() {
        return location;
    }

    public void setStats(String inLocation, int inCount) {
        //start timing
        //check user authentication
        setLocation(inLocation, 0);
        setCount(inCount);
        //end timing
        //log timing
    }
}
```

Do you notice any problems with the code? The logging hasn't been included in the methods that change the count information. Unfortunately, the developer missed this concern when creating the new class.

Results of Tangled Code

A developer doesn't have to be in the industry long to find out the effects of tangled and scattered code. Some of the effects are as follows:

❑   Classes that are difficult to change

❑   Code that can't be reused

❑   Code that's impossible to trace

Engineers and managers who need to refactor code commonly encounter one example of dealing with tangled code. If the code is written in clear components using well-defined objects, a relatively obvious cost-benefit ratio can be created. If the time and money can be justified, the components of the system can be refactored. However, in most cases, the code for the components is intertwined, and factoring becomes too cost prohibitive under traditional means. However, AOP allows the refactoring to be performed on a different level and in a manner that helps to eliminate some of the tangled code.

In one of the original AspectJ Tutorial presentations (http://aspectj.org/documentation/papersAndSlides/ OOPSLA2002-demo.ppt), you could analyze the Jakarta Tomcat project to determine where code that performed logging was located in the source code. The result of the project showed that the logging code wasn't in just one place in the code, and not even in a couple of small places—it's spread throughout the source code.

As the Tomcat analysis project showed, code tangling is a major problem. Just think about the nightmare if the code for logging needed to change. The tangled code clearly accomplishes some defined functionality, like logging. The code is tangled because it needs to be spread throughout the application. When a requirement results in tangled code, we say that it crosscuts the system. The crosscutting isn't always a primary requirement of the system, just as logging isn't required for the application software to function properly; but sometimes it is required in the case of user authentication.

How AOP Solves OOP Problems

Aspect-Oriented Programming is a paradigm created to solve the problems discussed so far without the difficulties and complexities encountered with subject-oriented programming (SOP) and multidimensional separation of concerns (MDSOC). AOP isn't necessarily a new idea; its roots lie in the separation of concerns movement, but it has moved into the forefront through work by Gregor Kiczales and his colleagues at Xerox's PARC (www.parc.com/groups/csl/projects/aspectj/).

AOP doesn't require the user to learn a host of new techniques, but instead relies on the features of its host language to solve crosscutting of concerns. Depending on the implementation of AOP, you need to learn only a handful of new keywords. At the same time, AOP supports reuse and modularity of code, to eliminate code tangling and scattering. With the advent of Java and the AspectJ support language, AOP is on the verge of becoming the next big thing in computer science since the adoption of OOP.

What Is AOP?

Aspect-oriented programming is a paradigm that supports two fundamental goals:

❑ Allow for the separation of concerns as appropriate for a host language.

❑ Provide a mechanism for the description of concerns that crosscut other components.

AOP isn't meant to replace OOP or other object-based methodologies. Instead, it supports the separation of components, typically using classes, and provides a way to separate aspects from the components. In our example, AOP is designed to support the separation of the example concerns and to allow both a Logger and a Product class; it also handles the crosscutting that occurs when logging is required in the components supporting another concern.

Development Process with AOP

To get an idea of how AOP helps with crosscutting, let's revisit the example concerns:

❑ **Concern 1:** The system will keep a price relating to the wholesale value of all products.

❑ **Concern 2:** Any changes to the price will be recorded for historical purposes.

The two classes built to implement these concerns separated their functionality, as would seem appropriate. However, when concern 2 is fully implemented, it becomes clear that calls from the Product class will need to be made to the Logger class. Suddenly the Product class isn't completely modular, because it needs to incorporate within its own code calls to functionality that isn't part of a product.

AOP provides several tools that can help with this problem. The first is the language used to code the requirements or concerns into units of code (either objects or functions). The AOP literature commonly calls this the *component language*. The secondary or support requirements (aspects) are coded as well, using an *aspect language*. Nothing in the paradigm states that either language needs to be object-oriented in nature, nor do the two languages need to be the same. The result of the component and aspect languages is a program that handles the execution of the components and the aspects. At some point, the respective programs must be integrated. This integration is called *weaving*, and it can occur at compile, link, run-, or load time.

Using this information, let's look at how AOP handles the issue of putting logging code directly into the Product class. AOP is designed to respect the idea that some requirements can be modularly coded and others will crosscut the previously modular classes. In our example, concern 1 can be implemented in the Product class without violating the modularity of the class. Concern 2 cannot be implemented in a modular fashion within the Product class because it needs to be implemented in different spots throughout the Product class and other classes in the software system.

If we step back from the implementation details behind both concerns, we find that concern 2 doesn't necessarily need to be coded directly in the Product class (and the DVD class, the Boxset class, and so on). Instead, it would be ideal if the logging code could be called when the system calls any log-worthy methods.

For this to occur, an aspect must be created specifying that when the system encounters a call to the method setPrice(), it should first execute code defined in the aspect language. Here's an example of what the aspect might look like in a (fictional) object-oriented aspect language:

```
define aspect Logging{
  Logger loggingObject = new Logger();
  when calling set*(taking one parameter) {
    loggingObject.writeLog("Called set method");
  }
}
```

This aspect is compiled along with the component Product class using a compiler provided by the AOP system. The compiler weaves the aspect code into the component code to create a functioning system. Figure 18.2 shows graphically how the weave looks.

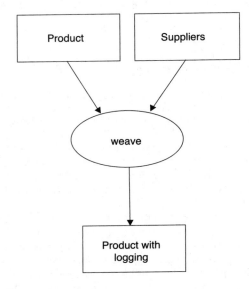

Figure 18.2

The weave occurs based on the information provided in line 3, where the aspect is defined to act when a call is made to any method having a name starting with set and taking a single parameter. Once the system begins to execute, a call is made to the setPrice() method of the DVD object. Just before control is given to the setPrice() method of a target object, the code in line 4 executes and produces the statement "Called set method" in the system log. As a result of using AOP, any call matching the aspect criteria produces an entry in the log—you don't have to scatter code throughout the entire program to support the concern.

Introduction to AspectJ

The primary goal of an AOP language is the separation of concerns. An application is written in a language that best satisfies the needs of the application and the developers. This language could be Java, C++, C#, Visual Basic, or even Cobol; in all these languages, a compiler converts the written language syntax into a format the machine can execute. In the case of Java or .NET, the language syntax is converted to byte code, which in turn is executed by a runtime environment.

During the development of the application, all the requirements are satisfied to produce the final system. The requirements include those necessary to meet the true needs of the application as well as conveniences such as logging and timing. Unfortunately, in most cases, this type of development (whether object-oriented or not) produces tangled code. When you use AOP, the development process isn't the same: The primary concerns are implemented using a language deemed appropriate for the application, and the crosscutting concerns are implemented in an aspect-oriented language.

It doesn't matter what language type is used for the implementation as long as the code written for the crosscuts can be combined with the primary application to produce a fully executable system. Any language that expects to implement concerns must have a specification and implementation.

AOP Language Specification

In the previous section, we briefly touched on the major components of an AOP system. In this section, we will lay out the pieces any AOP language must be able to represent in order to allow the development of code for crosscuts. The major components of an AOP language are as follows:

❑   Join points

❑   A type of language to match join points

❑   Advice

❑   An encapsulating component, such as a class

Join Points

A *join point* is a well-defined location within the primary code where a concern will crosscut the application. Join points can be method calls, constructor invocations, exception handlers, or other points in the execution of a program.

Suppose the specification document for a new system created by an AOP-aware team includes a concern stating that all SQL executions to the database should be logged. To facilitate the development of the primary system, a transaction component class is created to handle all database communication from business-level components. Within the transaction component, a method called updateTables() handles all database updates. To fully implement the crosscut concern, you need to add code to the method to register a timestamp when the method is first called. You must also include code at the end of the method to register a timestamp and add a success flag to the log. Thus, the join point to the implementation is the name of the method along with (possibly) the class name. For example, the following statement describes a join point:

```
public String DBTrans.updateTables(String);
```

The exact syntax will vary from language to language, but the goal of the join point is to match well-defined execution points.

Pointcuts

Given that the join point is a well-defined execution point in an application, you need a construct that tells the aspect-oriented language when it should match the join point. For example, you may want the aspect language to match the join point only when it is used in a call from one object to another or possibly a call from within the same object. To handle this situation, you can define a designator named `call()` that takes a join point as a parameter:

```
call(public String DBTrans.updateTables(String))
```

The designator tells the aspect language that the public `String DBTrans.updateTables(String)` join point should be matched only when it's part of a method call.

In some cases, you may use multiple designators to narrow the join point match or create groupings. Regardless, another construct called a *pointcut* is typically used to group the designators. A pointcut can be named or unnamed, just as a class can be named or anonymous. For example, in the following example the pointcut is called `updateTable()`. It contains a single designator for all calls to the defined join point:

```
Pointcut updateTable() :
   call(public String DBTrans.updateTables(String))
```

The pointcut is used in advice structures, described next.

Advice

In most AOP specifications, advice code can execute at three different places when a join point is matched: before, around, and after. In each case, a pointcut must be triggered before any of the advice code will be executed. Here's an example of using the *before* advice:

```
before(String s) : updateTables(s) {
   System.out.println("Passed parameter - " + s);
}
```

Once a pointcut has triggered, the appropriate advice code executes. In the case of the previous example, the advice code executes before the join point is executed. The `String` argument is passed to the code so it can be used if needed. In most AOP systems, you have access to the object associated with the join point as well as other information specific to the join point itself.

Aspects

A system that has 10 crosscutting concerns might include 20 or so join points and a dozen or more pointcuts with associated advice. By using AOP, you can reduce code tangling and disorganization rather than create more. With this in mind, the aspect syntax was developed to handle encapsulation of join points, pointcuts, and advice.

Aspects are created in much the same manner as classes and allow for complete encapsulation of code related to a particular concern. Here's an example aspect:

```
public aspect TableAspect {
   pointcut updateTable(String s) :
```

```
        call(public String DBTrans.updateTables(String) &&
        args(s);
    before(String s) : updateTable(s) {
        System.out.println("Passed parameter - " + s);
    }
}
```

The TableAspect aspect is an object that implements a concern related to the UpdateTables() method. All the functionality required for this concern is neatly encapsulated in its own structure.

AOP Language Implementation

The examples presented so far are written in the AspectJ AOP language and follow the Java specification because, as you will see shortly, AspectJ is designed to be used with applications written in Java. Once a concern has been written in an AOP language, a good deal of work must still be done to get the primary and AOP applications to run as a complete system. This task of integrating the crosscutting concern code and the primary application is called *weaving*. The following table lists the different types of weaving.

Type	Description	Tool Used
Compile-time	The source code from the primary and aspect languages is weaved before being put through the phases of the compiler where byte code is produced. AspectJ 1.0.x uses this form of weaving.	Compiler
Link-time	The weaving occurs after the primary and aspect language code has been compiled into byte code. AspectJ 1.1.x uses this form of weaving.	Linker
Load-time	The weaving occurs when classes are loaded by the classloader. Ultimately, the weaving is at the byte-code level.	Classloader under Java
Run-time	The virtual machine is responsible for detecting join points and loading and execution aspects.	Virtual machine

Using Java as an example, at some point in development a number of classes and possibly aspects will represent all the concerns defined for a particular application. The primary application can be compiled into Java byte code using the Javac compiler. Once compiled, the application byte code can be executed within the Java Runtime Environment. Unfortunately, a number of aspects also need to execute. Because the aspects are Java code as well, it isn't unreasonable to think that a compiler can be used to convert the aspect code into pure Java code; the aspects are converted to classes, and pointcuts, join points, and designators are turned into other Java constructs. If this step is performed, the standard Java compiler can also be used to produce byte code from the aspects.

Assume that a compiler is available that will convert both the Java and aspect code into Java byte code during the compilation process. You need a way to incorporate the aspect code into the Java code. In compile-time weaving, the aspect code is analyzed, converted to the primary language if needed, and inserted directly into the primary application code. So, using the previous example, you know that a join point has been defined on the updateTables() method and that a pointcut defined to execute before the updateTables() method actually executes. The compile-time weaver finds the updateTables() method and weaves the advice code into the method. If the aspect is converted to a class, the call within the updateTables() method can reference a method of the new aspect object.

Here's a simple example of what the code might look like after the compile-time weaver pulls together the primary Java code and the aspect defined earlier:

```
public String updateTables(String SQL) {
   //start code inserted for aspect
   TableAspect.updateTable(SQL);
   //end code inserted for aspect
   initializeDB();
   sendSQL(SQL);
}
```

In this example, a call is inserted to the updateTable() method of the tablesAspectClass class created from the TableAspect aspect code defined earlier. A preprocessor handles this work before any traditional compilation takes place. Once the aspect has been woven into the primary application code, the resulting intermediate files are sent to the Java compiler. The resulting system code implements both the primary and crosscutting concerns.

One of the downfalls of a compile-time weaving system is its inability to dynamically change the aspect used against the primary code. For example, suppose an aspect handles the way the updateTables() method connects to the database. A simple connection pool can consist of the details within the aspect. It would be interesting if the aspect could be swapped with another aspect during execution of the primary application based on predefined rules. A compile-time weaver cannot do this type of dynamic swapping, although code can be written in an aspect to mimic the swapping. In addition, compile-time weaving suggests that you need to have the source code available for all aspects, and convenience features such as JAR files cannot be used.

A link-time or runtime weaver doesn't weave the aspect code into the primary application during the compile but waits until runtime to handle the weave. A processor is still used to place hooks in the methods/constructor of the primary language as well as other strategic places. When the hooks are executed, a modified runtime system determines whether any aspects need to execute. As you might expect, dynamic weaving is more complicated because of the need to change the system where the application is executing. In a byte-code system where a runtime environment is available, the process isn't as involved as a system like C++, where a compiler produces machine-level code.

AspectJ

This chapter covers the use of a byte-code weaving AOP language called AspectJ. The AspectJ language comes from research work performed at the Xerox Palo Alto Research Center by a team of researchers including Gregor Kiczales (project leader), Ron Bodkin, Bill Griswold, Erik Hilsdale, Jim Hugunin, Wes Isberg, and Mik Kersten. The stated goal of AspectJ is to make the methodology of AOP available to a large number of developers. In order to accomplish this goal, AspectJ is built on top of the Java language and works to provide a seamless integration of primary and crosscutting concerns.

Example Aspect

This example class and related aspect will give you an idea of what writing in AspectJ is all about. Listing 18.1 shows the code for a very simple Java class and `main()` method. The `Simple` class has a single attribute and method. A `main()` method is used to instantiate an object of the class and makes a call to the `getName()` method.

```
public class Simple {
  private String name;

  public String getName() {
    return name;
  }
  public static void main(String args[]) {
    Simple simple = new Simple();
    System.out.println(simple.getName());
  }
}
```

Listing 18.1

Listing 18.2 shows an AspectJ aspect complete with a join point related to the `getName()` method in the primary code, and a pointcut defining the conditions necessary for triggering advice code found in the `before()` statement. The purpose of the aspect is to execute code when a call is made to the `getName()` method of a Simple object.

```
public aspect SimpleAspect {
  pointcut namePC() : call (public String getName());
  before() : MatchAllgetName() {
    System.out.println(thisJoinPoint.getSignature());
  }
}
```

Listing 18.2

If the standard Java compiler is used to compile the `Simple` class and the `SimpleAspect` aspect files, the compiler will produce a few errors related to the `SimpleAspect` aspect. The compiler won't be able to recognize the aspect, pointcut, before, and other statements used in the code. The AspectJ system includes a compiler called ajc that compiles both the aspect code and the primary code. The ajc compiler is built on top of IBM's Eclipse project compiler, which allows a strict compliance to the Java language and resulting byte code. The ajc compiler adds the ability to compile the AspectJ-specific keyword into byte code and facilitates the weaving of the byte codes into class files. The aspect code is converted from an aspect construct into a class, and the other AspectJ-specific constructs are converted to standard Java. The AspectJ compiler weaves the aspect byte code into the byte code of the primary application byte code and produces appropriate Java class files that can be executed by the Java Runtime Environment. AspectJ can be found at http://eclipse.org/aspectj/. Download the most recent version, install it, and we'll begin using it.

Using AspectJ with Hibernate

Probably the easiest aspect to write for Hibernate is explicitly closing the Session after it has been used in a method. If you take a good look at the HibernateSession code, you will see that the closeSession() method call checks to be sure the local Session object isn't null before calling the close() method on the session. This means we don't have to worry about calling closeSession() if the session has already been closed. Therefore, we will write an aspect that will call closeSession() on all methods having a get string in their name and that are part of a class with DAO in the name. The aspect looks like the following:

```
public aspect HibernateCloseSessionAspect {
   pointcut getDAOCall() : call (public void GROUP.set*() )
   void after(): getDAOCall()
   {
     try {
       HibernateSession.closeSession();
     } catch (Exception e) {
     // log exception
     }
   }
}
```

In this aspect, we define a pointcut called getDAOCall, which is used to match all methods having the string "set" in the name. When such a method is called, the pointcut will be matched and the after advice will be executed so we make sure the method is able to perform its work before we close the session.

What about using AspectJ to automatically save an object any time an attribute is changed? AspectJ includes the ability to use an attribute as a join point. So we could have an aspect that looks like the following:

```
public aspect HibernateSaveAllAspect {

   pointcut objectSet(Group group) : set(private * *) && this(group);

   void after(Group group) : objectSet(group) { try {
     Session session = HibernateSession.openSession();
     session.saveOrUpdate(group);
     HibernateSession.closeSession();
   } catch (Exception e) {
     // log exception
   }
}
```

In this aspect, we build a pointcut based on all attributes of the Group class. The set designator tells AspectJ to match when the attributes of the provided call are set to new values.

Summary

In this chapter, we've taken a brief look at the Aspect-Oriented Programming methodology. Using the information gain, Hibernate can be directly incorporated into aspects that have requirements spanning multiple classes within an application.

Hibernate Interceptors

As you might have noticed throughout this book, the objects created and persisted with Hibernate go through a lifecycle. An object will be created and persisted. Once the object has been changed, it becomes dirty and must be saved to the database again using an update operation. This process continues until the next time the object is needed, and it will be loaded from the persistent store. Finally, in some situations, the object will be deleted from the store permanently. As you saw in Chapter 5, an object can choose to implement the `Lifecycle` interface and implement four methods:

- ❑ onSave
- ❑ onUpdate
- ❑ onDelete
- ❑ onLoad

These four methods allow the object some control over itself when Hibernate performs various operations on it. We can also provide an application some control over how the `Session` operates using the `Interceptor` interface. The `Interceptor` interface is designed to work at the `Session` level and affects all of the persisted objects being managed by Hibernate.

Interceptor Interface

The following list shows all of the methods available within the `Interceptor` interface.

- ❑ int[] findDirty(Object obj, Serializable serial, Object[] currentState, Object[] previousState, String[] properties, Type[] types)
- ❑ Object instantiate(Class class, Serializable serial)
- ❑ Boolean isUnsaved(Object obj)

❑ void onDelete(Object obj, Serializable id, Object[] state, String[] properties, Type[] types)

❑ boolean onFlushDirty(Object obj, Serializable id, Object[] currentState, Object[] previousState, String[] properties, Type[] types)

❑ boolean onLoad(Object obj, Serializable serial, Object[] state, String[] propertyNames, Type[] types)

❑ boolean onSave(Object obj, Serializable serial, Object[] state, String[] properties, Type[] types)

❑ void postFlush(Iterator entities)

❑ void preFlush(Iterator entities)

Each method listed in the previous table is designed to be called by the `Session` object when a specific task is executed. The times when the methods are called are as follows:

❑ **findDirty:** Called when the `flush()` method is called on a `Session` object. If null is returned, Hibernate will use its own implementation to determine if a flush should occur. If the return is an empty array, then the object will not be saved. If the return is an array of indices, the object will be saved.

❑ **instantiate:** Called when a persisted class is instantiated. Returns null to allow Hibernate to handle the instantiation or a new object of the class type.

❑ **isUnsaved:** Called when an object is passed to the `saveOrUpdate()` method. If the return value is true, `save()` is called; if false, then `update()` is called. If null, then Hibernate will check the identifier value to determine what should occur.

❑ **onDelete:** Called before an object is deleted.

❑ **onFlushDirty:** Called when Hibernate detects that an object is dirty during a flush operation. If the `currentState` parameter is changed, returns true.

❑ **onLoad:** Called before an object is initialized. The state parameter can be changed as needed, and the return value should be true if the state parameter is changed.

❑ **onSave:** Called before an object is saved. Returns a true value if the state parameter is changed.

❑ **postFlush:** Called after a flush has occurred and an object has been updated in memory.

❑ **preFlush:** Called before a flush.

Now the question remains, just how do we use the `Interceptor` interface?

Building an Interceptor

What good is the `Interceptor` interface? The answer is that it gives us total control over how an object will look to both the application and the database. The first step in using the `Interceptor` interface is to build a traditional interface that a particular class in the application can implement in order to indicate that the class should be visible to the `Interceptor` class.

The class we will build is called `Inquire`, and it will have the following methods defined to work on the object, depending on what the `Session` object is doing at a given time.

- **flushDirty():** We will call this method when the `Session` object thinks an object should be saved.

- **beforeSave():** We will call this method when the object is just about to be saved. The code will update a timestamp attribute within the object itself.

- **justUpdated():** We will call this method when the object in memory has been updated.

The actual code for the `Inquire` class is shown in Listing 19.1.

```
public interface Inquire {
  public void flushDirty();
  public void beforeSave();
  public void justUpdated();
}
```

Listing 19.1

Now the code in Listing 19.1 will be used with all of our objects that should be processed by the `Interceptor`. So, let's look at a class called `User`, which will implement the Inquire interface. The `User` class is shown in Listing 19.2.

```
import java.util.*;

public class User Implements Inquire {
  private int id;
  private String username;
  private String password;

  public Group(){
  }

  public Group(String name) {
    this.name = name;
  }

  public void setId(int i) {
    id = i;
  }

  public int getId() {
    return id;
  }

  public void setUsername(String n) {
    username = n;
  }

  public String getUsernme() {
```

```
      return username;
   }

   public void setPasswword(String l) {
      password = l;
   }

   public String getPassword() {
      return password;
   }

   public void flushDirty() {
      System.out.println("Call to flushDirty");
   }

   public void beforeSave() {
      System.out.println("Call to beforeSave");
   }

   public void justUpdated() {
      System.out.println("Call to justUpdated");
   }
}
```

Listing 19.2

For the User class, we must implement the Inquire interface and provide code for the flushDirty, beforeSave, and justUpdated methods. For our example, we just provide a little indicator to show that the method is called. Now we are getting closer to using the Interceptor interface. The final step is to build the Interceptor class itself. Listing 19.3 shows the code.

```
import java.io.Serializable;

import java.util.Iterator;

import net.sf.hibernate.Interceptor;

public class InquireInterceptor implements Interceptor, Serializable {

    public void onDelete(Object obj,
                         Serializable serial,
                         Object[] state,
                         String[] properties,
                         Type[] types) {

    }

    public boolean onFlushDirty(Object obj,
                                Serializable serial,
                                Object[] currentState,
                                Object[] previousState,
                                String[] properties,
```

```
                              Type[] types) {

      if ( entity instanceof Inquire) {
          obj.flushDirty();
          return true;
      }
      return false;
   }

   public boolean onLoad(Object obj,
                        Serializable serial,
                        Object[] state,
                        String[] properties,
                        Type[] types) {
      return false;
   }

   public boolean onSave(Object obj,
                        Serializable serial,
                        Object[] state,
                        String[] properties,
                        Type[] types) {

      if ( entity instanceof Inquire) {
          obj.beforeSave();
          return true;
      }
      return false;
   }

   public void postFlush(Iterator entities) {
   }

   public void preFlush(Iterator entities) {

   }

   public boolean isUnsaved(Object obj) {
      // need to check each object attributes to determine if this should be
saved
or not
      return null;
   }

   public Object instantiate(Class class,
                        Serializable serial) {
      return null;
   }

   public int[] findDirty(Object obj,
                        Serializable serial,
                        Object[] currentState,
                        Object[] previousState,
                        String[] properties,
```

```
                          Type[] types) {
        // Here we need to compare currentState with PreviousState and return
array of ints
        // for each object that is different
        return null;
    }
}
```

Listing 19.3

The `Interceptor` in Listing 19.3 is fairly basic in that it just calls a method of the passed object or returns a null value to allow Hibernate to use its own default behavior for the requested operation.

Using the `InterceptorSo` how do we use the `Interceptor`? The answer is using a variant of the `openSession()` method of the `Session Factory` class. An example is:

```
Session session    - SessionFactory.openSession(new InquireInterceptor);
```

Or, we could build the `Interceptor` at the `Configuration` level as well with the code:

```
Configuration.setInterceptor(new InquireInterceptor);
```

That's all there is to using Hibernate and its `Interceptor` interface. When the application is executed, all calls to the Interceptor will be routed to a method within the working object.

Summary

In this chapter, we talked about how to extend the functionality of the application as it uses Hibernate to store Java objects. By using the Interceptor interface, we have complete control over how an object is pulled from the database or stored, either for the first time or potentially numerous times.

Hibernate Database Connectivity

In an effort to make Hibernate as easy to use as possible, we've added this appendix to provide you with all of the information you should need to initially get Hibernate working with all of the databases it currently supports. Each database section below will give you the information you need to obtain a specific database, as well as the properties needed for Hibernate to use it.

DB2

DB2 is IBM's primary database product, and it is available in several different versions. For personal use, you can download a copy of the system at http://www14.software.ibm.com/webapp/ download/. There are versions available for Linux for 64-bit and 32-bit as well as Windows 32-bit. Note that the files range from 0.5GB to 1.5GB in size.

The server already has the JDBC driver with it. If you need the client-side tools that come with the JDBC driver, you can download them from here: http://www-3.ibm.com/cgi-bin/db2www/ data/db2/udb/winos2unix/support/index.d2w/report. From this page, click the DB2 Client link appropriate for your database version. The next page that appears provides links for many different products for many different platforms. You need to click the Application Development Client link for the platform where you will be executing your application. Unfortunately, you will get much more than just the JDBC client, so just delete what you don't want to use.

The Hibernate properties for DB2 might look like the following, based on your application and architecture.

```
hibernate.dialect net.sf.hibernate.dialect.DB2Dialect
hibernate.connection.driver_class COM.ibm.db2.jdbc.app.DB2Driver
hibernate.connection.url jdbc:db2:test
hibernate.connection.username name
hibernate.connection.password password
```

DB2/400

If you need to install IBM's DB2 on an iSeries machine, you can visit the following URL to find the necessary product information: http://www-1.ibm.com/servers/eserver/iseries/db2/. The JDBC driver for DB2/400 can be obtained from the JTOPen IBM Toolbox for Java Web site at http://www-124.ibm.com/developerworks/oss/jt400/index.html. The jtopen_4_2.zip file contains the driver named jt400.jar.

```
hibernate.dialect net.sf.hibernate.dialect.DB2400Dialect
hibernate.connection.username user
hibernate.connection.password password
hibernate.connection.driver_class COM.ibm.db2.jdbc.app.DB2Driver
hibernate.connection.url jdbc:db2://localhost
```

HypersonicSQL

From the HypersonicSQL project site, http://sourceforge.net/projects/hsqldb/, "HSQLDB is a relational database engine written in Java, with a JDBC driver, supporting a subset of ANSI-92 SQL. It offers a small (about 100k), fast database engine which offers both in-memory and disk-based tables. This product includes Hypersonic SQL." The Hibernate properties are:

```
hibernate.dialect net.sf.hibernate.dialect.HSQLDialect
hibernate.connection.driver_class org.hsqldb.jdbcDriver
hibernate.connection.username sa
hibernate.connection.password sa
hibernate.connection.url jdbc:hsqldb:hsql://localhost
```

Interbase

Interbase is a Borland database server available at http://www.borland.com/interbase/. Various database types are included, but they aren't open source. A trial download is available along with the InterClient JDBC driver.

```
hibernate.dialect net.sf.hibernate.dialect.InterbaseDialect
hibernate.connection.username sa
hibernate.connection.password sa
hibernate.connection.driver_class interbase.interclient.Driver
hibernate.connection.url jdbc:interbase://localhost
```

McKoi SQL

The McKoi database is open source and is written in Java. It is available at http://mckoi.com/
database/. The download includes both the server and the JDBC driver. The Hibernate properties
are as follows:

```
hibernate.dialect net.sf.hibernate.dialect.MckoiDialect
hibernate.connection.driver_class com.mckoi.JDBCDriver
hibernate.connection.url jdbc:mckoi://localhost/
hibernate.connection.username sa
hibernate.connection.password sa
```

Microsoft SQL Server

Probably the most popular Windows database engine is Microsoft's SQL Server. Although very popular,
Microsoft SQL Server is quite pricey and is usually found only in medium to large corporations.
However, if you are interested in getting your feet wet with this database engine, you can download a
120-day trial at http://www.microsoft.com/sql/evaluation/trial/default.asp. Installing the engine is
just a matter of clicking through a few wizard dialogs.

The trials and tribulations of the relationship between Microsoft and Sun are quite well known, and so
Java support for Microsoft products isn't always the best. There are currently 47 different JDBC drivers
available for Microsoft SQL Server, according to Sun's JDBC driver page. Some of the drivers are certi-
fied for various SDKs, some of them are commercial, and others have a variety of options. Here are a
couple of choices:

The Microsoft driver (although Hibernate does not recommend using this driver):

```
hibernate.dialect net.sf.hibernate.dialect.SQLServerDialect
hibernate.connection.username sa
hibernate.connection.password sa
hibernate.connection.driver_class
com.microsoft.jdbc.sqlserver.SQLServerDriver
hibernate.connection.url
jdbc:microsoft:sqlserver://localhost;DatabaseName=test
```

Weblogic has a driver available at http://e-docs.bea.com/wls/docs81/jdrivers.html. The JDBC is an
evaluation driver available for 30 days. The properties for the driver are as follows:

```
hibernate.dialect net.sf.hibernate.dialect.SQLServerDialect
hibernate.connection.username sa
hibernate.connection.password sa
hibernate.connection.driver_class weblogic.jdbc.mssqlserver4.Driver
hibernate.connection.url jdbc:weblogic:mssqlserver4:localhost:1433
```

MySQL

In Chapter 3, we went through the process of obtaining and installing both MySQL and the JConnector JDBC driver. Refer to that chapter for obtaining those products. The configuration for MySQL is given below:

```
hibernate.dialect net.sf.hibernate.dialect.MySQLDialect
hibernate.connection.driver_class com.mysql.jdbc.Driver
hibernate.connection.url jdbc:mysql://<server>/test
hibernate.connection.username root
hibernate.connection.password root
```

Oracle

When people talk about databases, Oracle always enters the conversation. Oracle has always been considered the primary powerhouse of database servers in the market. You can find versions 8*i*, 9*i*, and 10*g* at http://otn.oracle.com/software/products/database/oracle10g/index.html. There are downloads for all major platforms.

Oracle's JDBC driver can be found at http://otn.oracle.com/software/tech/java/sqlj_jdbc/index.html.

A great deal of information on using Oracle and Oracle's JDBC can be found at the following link: http://download-west.oracle.com/docs/cd/B10501_01/java.920/a96654/preface.htm. The Hibernate configuration options are shown here:

```
hibernate.dialect net.sf.hibernate.dialect.Oracle9Dialect
```

or

```
hibernate.dialect net.sf.hibernate.dialect.OracleDialect
hibernate.connection.driver_class oracle.jdbc.driver.OracleDriver
hibernate.connection.username oracle
hibernate.connection.password oracle
hibernate.connection.url jdbc:oracle:thin:@localhost:1521:test
```

PointBase

Another commercial database that can be used with Hibernate is PointBase. Information on the database can be found at http://www.pointbase.com/products/core_technology.aspx. There are several different product types, including PointBase Embedded, PointBase Server, and PointBase Micro. Currently, an evaluation download is available for PointBase Micro. Everything you need is included with the download. The Hibernate configuration information is shown here:

```
hibernate.dialect net.sf.hibernate.dialect.PointbaseDialect
hibernate.connection.driver_class com.pointbase.jdbc.jdbcUniversalDriver
hibernate.connection.url jdbc:pointbase:micro:test
hibernate.connection.username test
hibernate.connection.password test
```

PostgreSQL

Another very popular open source database is PostgreSQL. This database has many of the same features as commercial servers and has been proven to perform with the best of them. The database is available for a variety of platforms, and you can download it from the following link: http://www.postgresql.org/mirrors-ftp.html. Once you've obtained the server and installed it, you can obtain the JDBC driver at http://jdbc.postgresql.org/.

The Hibernate properties for PostgreSQL are as follows:

```
hibernate.dialect net.sf.hibernate.dialect.PostgreSQLDialect
hibernate.connection.driver_class org.postgresql.Driver
hibernate.connection.url jdbc:postgresql://localhost/template1
hibernate.connection.username pg
hibernate.connection.password pg
hibernate.query.substitutions yes 'Y', no 'N'
```

SAP DB

SAP DB is an open source database that has been rebranded as MaxDB and placed under the MySQL umbrella. SAP DB is a high-powered database that includes views, stored procedures, triggers, automatic failover, as well as a host of other features not currently found in the MySQL database server. You can download MaxDB from http://www.mysql.com/products/maxdb/. Click the Download Binaries and Sources link on the lower-right menu.

At the top of the download page you will find the database server installation files and toward the bottom of the page, the JDBC driver.

```
hibernate.dialect net.sf.hibernate.dialect.SAPDBDialect
hibernate.connection.driver_class com.sap.dbtech.jdbc.DriverSapDB
hibernate.connection.url jdbc:sapdb://localhost/test
hibernate.connection.username TEST
hibernate.connection.password TEST
hibernate.query.substitutions yes 'Y', no 'N'
```

Sybase

There are currently two different databases from Sybase:

❑   Sybase Adaptive Server Enterprise

❑   SQL Anywhere Studio

You are currently able to download an evaluation version of SQL Anywhere Studio for both Linux and Windows. The link to the downloads can be found at http://www.sybase.com/developer under the Developer Downloads menu on the left navigation menu.

The JDBC driver can be found at http://www.sybase.com/products/middleware/jconnectforjdbc. Click the Downloads link on the left navigation menu.

```
hibernate.dialect net.sf.hibernate.dialect.SybaseDialect
hibernate.connection.driver_class com.sybase.jdbc2.jdbc.SybDriver
hibernate.connection.username sa
hibernate.connection.password sasasa
hibernate.connection.rl jdbc:sybase:Tds:co3061835-a:5000/tempdb
```

Getting Involved with Hibernate

So you've read the book from cover to cover. And now you want to become more involved with the Hibernate community? One of the wonderful things about an open source project is that the more you put into it, the better the community becomes, and the more you can get out of it. There are a number of ways you can contribute to the community, including helping answer user questions on the forums, adding material to the Hibernate wiki, and finally, actually working on the further development of Hibernate.

Hibernate Forums

The Hibernate project handles supporting users through online forums available at http://forum.hibernate.org/. There are a number of specialized forums, starting from "Hibernate Beginners" for people who haven't read this book, to intellectually challenging discussions about architecting applications and integrating Hibernate in frameworks in the "Application Architecture" and "System Integration" forums. Plus, because Hibernate is under the JBoss framework, there is a "JBoss and JBossCache" specific forum. Lastly, as the tools for Hibernate progress, you can find support for them in the Tools forum.

In an attempt to keep a high signal-to-noise ratio in the forums, the Hibernate team has posted a "How to Ask for Help" page available here: www.hibernate.org/160.html. This is mainly a list of commonsense steps to perform when you get into trouble, such as: "write a unit test to isolate your problem," "read the Frequently Asked Questions," and, of course, the most basic "search the forum." Chances are that the someone else has had the problem you're experiencing and has already posted the problem and recieved the answer you need. If these approaches don't get you an answer to your problem, then you're ready for the next level of suggestions, such as providing as much information as possible about your problem and writing a professional request for help. The various rules of thumb on how to ask for help are well worth taking to heart when trying to solve a problem you may be experience with any piece of software, not just Hibernate.

The Hibernate forums aren't just a great way to request support—they are also a great way to learn about advanced techniques with Hibernate that you may not yet have had a chance to apply in your own projects. Reading posts and answering them can really build your knowledge of Hibernate.

Hibernate Wiki

One of the strengths of the Hibernate project is its excellent documentation. However, users often come up with ideas for how to use Hibernate that aren't covered in the documentation and want to share these ideas. That is where the wiki comes into play.

> **Taken from wikipedia.org: "A *wiki* (pronounced "wicky" or "weeky") is a website (or other hypertext document collection) that gives users the ability to add content, as on an Internet forum, but also allows that content to be edited by other users."**

People contribute back to the Hibernate community by being able to add new content to the wiki. So, if you discover an interesting technique for using Hibernate, then by adding a new page to the wiki, you are increasing the total sum of knowledge about Hibernate. An example of the type of content available on the wiki is a description of how to write an appender for the Log4j logging tool from the Apache Software Foundation that persists logging events via Hibernate. Another example is how to use Hibernate with PicoContainer, an open source Inversion of Control container available from http://picocontainer.codehaus.org/.

The wiki also encourages a dialog by allowing users to add comments and version their content. Again, if you are trying to solve a problem, searching the wiki is often a good first step to see if anyone else has run up against the same issue.

Contributing to the Further Development of Hibernate

Once you feel like you are a hibernate wiz, you may want to dig into the source code and start contributing to the further development of Hibernate. To get started, you'll want to check out the source code and join the development mailing list. For ideas on what to do, take a look at the outstanding issues list for Hibernate.

Checking Out the Source and Building It

Because Hibernate is an open source project, the source code is freely available. The source is hosted by SourceForge.net, a popular site devoted to providing tools like CVS to support open source development.

To check out the source code you'll need a CVS client. The easiest way is to use the CVS client that is probably already embedded in your favorite IDE. I happen to like the one in Eclipse 3.0. In Eclipse, you would switch to the *Repository View*. Right click and add a new repository using the following settings:

- ❑ **host:** cvs.sourceforge.net
- ❑ **repository path:** /cvsroot/hibernate
- ❑ **user:** anonymous
- ❑ **password:** Leave the password field blank; as an anonymous user you don't need to fill anything in
- ❑ **connection type:** pserver

Once you're connected you will see a couple modules listed under CVS HEAD, including Hibernate2, Hibernate3, and HibernateExt. If you are interested in looking at the current released code for Hibernate, then check out Hibernate2. At the time of writing this is the current production ready code, and releases of this are used in this book. HibernateExt contains various extensions to Hibernate, including the Hibern8ide and tools projects. The next major version, Hibernate 3, is available in the Hibernate3 module. This is the latest and greatest version of Hibernate, but isn't released yet.

Hibernate is built using Ant. Once you have checked out the Hibernate module you would like, just execute ant to build Hibernate. To see all the various targets available, run `ant -projecthelp` to receive a list.

Development Mailing List

To keep abreast of what is happening with the development of Hibernate, you should join the various mailing lists available here: http://sourceforge.net/mail/. Note that the the development list is *not* a place to ask for help. If you are having problems with Hibernate, or trying to use Hibernate in a new manner, then you should post your questions in the forums. The development mailing list focuses solely on the development of the core Hibernate product.

The hibernate commits mailing list allows you to receive notification of each commit to the Hibernate code base. This allows you to keep up with what changes are being applied. Similarly, the hibernate-issues mailing list notifies you of changes filed with the JIRA issue tracker for Hibernate.

Issue Tracking

Hibernate uses the JIRA issue tracker hosted by Atlassian at http://opensource.atlassian.com/projects/hibernate/. You can anonymously browse the various issues, and if you register, you can attach comments as well. The Hibernate team uses JIRA to track bugs and feature requests related to Hibernate. If you have a contribution to make to Hibernate, then you should open a new issue in JIRA if one doesn't already exist. Then attach your new code as a patch file to the issue. When you save your changes to the issue, an email will be generated to the hibernate issues mailing list, notifying the committers that an issue has been updated. A committer will review your code change, and assuming it meets their standards, will take the patch file you supplied and apply it to the code base.

More Information on Open Source

For more information on how open source projects like Hibernate work, visit the following Web sites:

❑ **Open Source Initiative:** www.opensource.org/

❑ **Apache Software Foundation:** www.apache.org/

❑ **The classic article** *The Cathedral and Bazaar:* http://www.catb.org/~esr/writings/ cathedral-bazaar/cathedral-bazaar/

Index

Symbols

A

B

C

Hibernate